STANLEY JOHNSTON'S
BLUNDER

STANLEY JOHNSTON'S
BLUNDER

The Reporter Who Spilled the Secret behind the U.S. Navy's Victory at Midway

ELLIOT CARLSON

Naval Institute Press
Annapolis, Maryland

This book has been brought to publication with the generous assistance of Edward S. and Joyce I. Miller.

Naval Institute Press
291 Wood Road
Annapolis, MD 21402

Library of Congress Cataloging-in-Publication Data
Names: Carlson, Elliot, date, author.
Title: Stanley Johnston's blunder : the reporter who spilled the secret behind the U.S. victory at Midway / Elliot Carlson.
Other titles: Reporter who spilled the secret behind the U.S. victory at Midway
Description: Annapolis, Maryland : Naval Institute Press, [2017] | Includes bibliographical references and index.
Identifiers: LCCN 2017024861 (print) | LCCN 2017037958 (ebook) | ISBN 9781682472743 (ePDF) | ISBN 9781682472743 (epub) | ISBN 9781682472743 (mobi) | ISBN 9781591146797 (hardcover : alk. paper) | ISBN 9781682472743 (ebook)
Subjects: LCSH: Johnston, Stanley. | Midway, Battle of, 1942. | War correspondents—United States—Biography. | Leaks (Disclosure of information)—United States—History—20th century. | Johnston, Stanley—Trials, litigation, etc. | Chicago Tribune (Firm)—Trials, litigation, etc. | World War, 1939–1945—Journalists. | World War, 1939–1945—Cryptography. | World War, 1939–1945—Press coverage. | World War 1939–1945—Censorship.
Classification: LCC D774.M5 (ebook) | LCC D774.M5 C284 2017 (print) | DDC 940.54/26699—dc23
LC record available at https://lccn.loc.gov/2017024861

For Norma

Contents

Author's Note

On 16 December 2016, I received an email letter from Robert Reed, the National Archives' special access archivist, informing me that the seventy-four-year-old grand jury testimony in the Stanley Johnston espionage case was mine to look at, even possibly duplicate and take home, as it now was for other members of the public interested in those fabled documents.

Seemingly routine, the letter was of enormous importance. On the simplest level, it was the happy culmination of a campaign I had launched on my own behalf more than three years earlier. But it was also the outcome of a hard-fought legal battle waged by the organization that later joined me in this campaign: The Reporter's Committee for the Freedom of the Press. In bringing about this result, the Reporter's Committee, or RCFP, made a major contribution to legal history.

Going back in time, this effort stemmed from my resolve to tell the story behind one of the most bizarre, and long forgotten, media episodes of World War II: the Roosevelt administration's decision to charge *Chicago Tribune* war correspondent Stanley Johnston and other members of the *Tribune* staff for violating the Espionage Act. The government contended that an article concerning the 4 June 1942 Battle of Midway, prepared by Johnston and carried on the front page of the 7 June 1942 Sunday *Tribune*, exposed Top Secret U.S. Navy information. This was no minor press relations dustup. The grand jury probe that followed marked the only time in U.S. history that the Department of Justice had sought to prosecute a major newspaper for violating the Espionage Act for printing leaked classified information. When a grand jury convened to hear the case refused to issue indictments, people wanted to know why. They wondered what had happened during the proceedings. No one knew because grand jury testimony is generally considered sacrosanct, off limits to the public. The mystery simmered for decades.

As a biographer with an interest in naval intelligence, I wanted to explore the issues raised by the Johnston case. It seemed to me that the case was more than a fascinating slice of U.S. Navy history: it was also a window into some of the politics boiling in the Roosevelt administration in the early war years as well as a source of insight into some of the personalities who were stirring the pot. I also firmly believed I could not properly tell the story of Stanley Johnston without seeing that elusive and forbidden grand jury testimony.

On 9 August 2013, acting without legal advice, I rather quixotically filed a petition with Chief Judge Ruben Castillo of the United States District Court for the Northern District of Illinois, seeking the testimony by arguing that this material would be of considerable historical interest. When many months passed without receiving any word back from the court, it became obvious that if I was to obtain these documents, I would need outside aid. In what turned out to be a brilliant stroke, I turned for help to the Reporter's Committee, a nonprofit organization based in Washington that has been assisting journalists and defending press freedom since 1970. After meeting with me in the summer of 2014, RCFP's executive director, Bruce D. Brown, and its litigation director, Katie Townsend, generously agreed to represent me in this undertaking. They quickly created a formidable legal team that included an RCFP fellow, Tom Isler, and one other important person: Chicago lawyer Brendan Healey, who represented me as well as the RCFP, handling matters in Chicago that could only be done in Chicago.

Late in 2014, RCFP lawyers, headed by Townsend, petitioned Judge Castillo for release of the testimony in the Johnston case. They argued, among many other things, that "historical interest" was valid grounds for unsealing grand jury testimony. While the effort proceeded with me as lead petitioner, the case was joined by the Reporter's Committee and a coalition of six other interested organizations with a stake in the outcome of the matter: the American Historical Association, the National Security Archive, the Naval Historical Foundation, the Naval Institute Press, the Organization of American Historians, and the Society for Military History. The presence of these groups added heft to our case, but this move did not prevent the Department of Justice from vigorously opposing the petition.

Judge Castillo ruled in our favor in June 2015. He ordered that the grand jury transcripts be released to me, concluding that disclosure "will not only result in a more complete public record of this historic event, but will 'in the long run build confidence in our government by affirming that it is open, in all respects, to scrutiny by the people.'" The government appealed that decision to the U.S. Court of Appeals for the Seventh Circuit. Early in 2016, Townsend argued the case before a three-judge panel of the Seventh Circuit. In September 2016, in a majority opinion by Chief Judge Diane Wood, the

Seventh Circuit affirmed Judge Castillo's order, rejecting the government's argument that the District Court lacked any authority to order that the testimony be made public. Describing the story behind the case as "a thrilling one, involving espionage, World War II, and legal wrangling," the Court of Appeals further concluded that the District Court had not abused its discretion in ordering that the 1942 *Tribune* grand jury transcripts be released. The Court of Appeals also rejected the argument that petitioners lacked standing to seek access to the grand jury transcripts, holding that the fact that this petitioner "is a member of the public is sufficient for him to assert his 'general right to inspect and copy . . . judicial records[,]'" which include grand jury records.

Still, the case was not over. The Justice Department had ninety days to seek further review of the decision. Had they done so, the matter would possibly have reached the U.S. Supreme Court. Only when the government's 14 December deadline passed uneventfully did I, and the RCFP team, know that, finally, we had unequivocally prevailed. Thus, on Monday, 19 December 2016, I went over to the National Archives in College Park, MD (NARAII), to review the 1942 grand jury testimony, a little more than three years after I filed my initial petition. As I think the reader will agree after reading Chapter 12 of this volume ("The Grand Jury Decides"), the documents turned out to be worth the effort. I found waiting for me at NARAII approximately one thousand pages of material, of which four hundred were pages of the actual testimony. The pages reflected the questioning of Special Prosecutor William Mitchell of twelve witnesses—seven Navy officers and five journalists, one of whom happened to be the controversial Stanley Johnston. The essence of these pages is distilled in Chapter 12.

Needless to say, I will always be grateful to Bruce Brown, Brendan Healey, and of course the indefatigable Katie Townsend: Katie and her team distinguished themselves for the legal scholarship and originality of thought they put into this case, not to mention pluck and unrelenting doggedness. I would not have obtained these documents without them; I would have been the poorer, and so would American historiography. One other person needs recognition in this regard: the aforementioned Robert Reed. The whereabouts of this 1942 grand jury testimony had long been unknown; key people at the District Court and Justice Department did not know if these documents still existed, let alone where they might be. Before I submitted my problem to the RCFP, Reed and his staff, in the spring of 2014, had tracked them down in a remote cranny of the archives; they apparently had become separated from related materials in Record Group 60.

～

Gaining access to the grand jury testimony in the Stanley Johnston case may have been the most dramatic—and legally momentous—aspect of this author's project. But the interesting stories told by the witnesses constitute only one part of the Johnston saga. Those accounts would have been unintelligible without crucial facts found in other records. The testimony was just the top of a pyramid of evidence amassed by FBI and Navy investigators during the early summer months of 1942. The great bulk of that material, most of it declassified since 1990, resides in two Record Groups housed at the National Archives in College Park. I was able to pinpoint the location of those documents in the fall of 2012 with the assistance of NARAII archivist Christina Jones, to whom I now pass on my thanks. After requesting the documents through the Freedom of Information Act (FOIA), I finally obtained them in the late summer of 2013, the final step facilitated by the ubiquitous Robert Reed, archivist, special access and FOIA staff.

But the Johnston tale isn't just a collection of government records. It is also a human story, and it is a story of competing newspapers. I would not have gotten this side of the story without help from the many generous people who offered materials that revealed critical aspects of Johnston and his newspaper world. Key among these individuals is Eric Gillespie, director of the Col. McCormick Research Center, First Division Museum at Cantigny Park, Wheaton, Illinois. Receiving my request by email, he had waiting for me and my wife, Norma, when we arrived at the center in the summer of 2012, some sixty boxes of memoranda, oral histories, and internal material from the *Tribune* and McCormick files. Gillespie and his staff ended up copying for us no fewer than two thousand pages of documents related to the Johnston case. We will always remember the courtesy and helpfulness with which Gillespie and his staff fielded our requests.

I am greatly indebted to Pacific War historian John Lundstrom for providing some extraordinary resources that helped me fill in gaps in the Johnston story. Particularly interesting were pages from the long lost papers of Vice Admiral Frederick C. Sherman. John received surviving excerpts of these papers from Navy historian Jeffrey Barlow, who had come across a block of them in Sherman's bio file at the Operational Archives, Naval

History and Heritage Command. John was kind enough to pass on to me a portion of those papers. Even more valuable was John's success recruiting Canberra-based historian Joseph Straczek to look into Johnston's World War I records at the National Archives of Australia in Sydney. The documents he unearthed confirmed, among other things, Johnston's enlistment in the Royal Australian Naval Reserves—a discovery that corrected other versions of the correspondent's early military career. I'm most appreciative to both Lundstrom and Straczek for their efforts on my behalf.

I am especially grateful to four reviewers who read the final draft. Two of them are respected naval historians and discerning editors: Paul Stillwell and Ronald W. Russell. They brought to bear their immense knowledge of the Pacific Fleet during World War II to refine my thinking on many issues and correct technical and historical miscues on my part. Robert J. Hanyok, former senior historian at the Center for Cryptologic History, National Security Agency, provided guidance related to codebreaking and naval communications. Finally, the aforementioned Lundstrom shared insights gained over many years writing histories and biographies covering two epic naval engagements that figure in my story: the Battle of the Coral Sea and the Battle of Midway.

Other historians and writers made valuable contributions to this book. China and Pacific War historian Rich Frank supplied the author with a fascinating memo Admiral King wrote to his Atlantic Fleet and Pacific Fleet commanders shortly after Stanley Johnston's article appeared in the *Chicago Tribune*. King informed them of steps they should take to avoid leaks of U.S. Navy codebreaking efforts. Jon Parshall let me know via email how weak was the U.S. Navy's grasp of Japanese ship names during the early days of the Pacific War. Cryptographic historian Ralph Erskine shared documents from his personal file showing how the Johnston case distressed top officials in British intelligence, leading them to urge their American counterparts to plug leaks in the U.S. Navy's security system.

Librarians and archivists at a number of institutions around the country guided me to key documents. Lee C. Grady, reference archivist at the Wisconsin Historical Society (WHS), in Madison, steered me to a particularly rich trove housed at WHS's library: the papers of the journalist who ran the civilian-controlled Office of Censorship during World War II, Byron Price. At the Library for the Performing Arts, Billy Rose Theatre Division, Lincoln Center, in New York City, librarian John Calhoun helped me track down the 1942 radio transcripts of gossip maestro Walter Winchell. Robert Clark, supervisory archivist at the Franklin D. Roosevelt Library, Hyde Park, New York, pointed my way through that institution's bewildering thicket of papers and documents.

A number of other individuals provided different kinds of help. In the fall of 2012, I acquired an invaluable hands-on feel for what it's like to live in an aircraft carrier when Cecil Johnson, the official historian of *Lexington* (CV 16), spent most of a day escorting me up and down and around every layer of this magnificent ship, now permanently anchored at Corpus Christi, Texas. The ship, commissioned in 1943, was named to commemorate *Lexington* (CV 2), lost during the Battle of the Coral Sea. At the Naval Historical Foundation, Navy Yard, Washington, D.C., Frank Arre aided me in my search for Pacific War photos by tapping into the abundant picture file of the Naval History and Heritage Command. My quest for vivid shots of Stanley Johnston bore fruit, thanks to Robert G. Summers, a San Diego filmmaker and media consultant with a long interest in the Pacific War; he dug into his private file and emailed me several evocative shots of the *Chicago Tribune* war correspondent. In Silver Spring, Maryland, graphic artist Stuart Armstrong retouched and enhanced old archival images that appear in this volume's appendixes, making them acceptable for submission to the Naval Institute Press.

At the Naval Institute Press, I am indebted to its director, Rick Russell, who recognized the historical significance of a book on Stanley Johnston and encouraged me to write it. I also want to thank members of Rick's staff who helped transform my text into a book: Susan Brook, Meagan Szekely, Taylor Skord, and Emily Bakely. I also appreciate the work done by my editor, Michael Levine; Michael's thoughtful and meticulous reading of my manuscript led to many constructive changes for which I am very grateful.

As she did a decade ago when I was writing a book on Joe Rochefort, my wife, Norma, joined me as a co-researcher on many trips I took around the country gathering material for this book. She reviewed each of several drafts of the Stanley Johnston manuscript and, once again, made many important criticisms and observations. Equally important was the enormous encouragement she gave me, without which I could not have completed this project.

—*Elliot Carlson*
Silver Spring, Maryland
April 2017

INTRODUCTION

Mystery in Washington

The story was published in the *Tribune* of June 7;
and so began a chain of events which were to culminate in
one of the most fantastic fiascos of the war.
—*Byron Price*

Admiral Ernest J. King had expected to relax on Sunday, 7 June 1942. The volatile, fiery-tempered commander in chief of the U.S. Fleet had every reason to feel pleased. He had just gotten confirmation that three days earlier, on 4 June, carrier-based warplanes of his Pacific Fleet, commanded by Admiral Chester W. Nimitz, had destroyed four Japanese fleet carriers in the distant waters of the central Pacific, near Midway Atoll. U.S. naval forces had crushed the core elements of an Imperial Japanese Navy (IJN) striking force in what soon would be regarded as one of the epochal campaigns of the Pacific War—the Battle of Midway.[1]

COMINCH (for commander in chief), as King liked to be called, had another reason to feel relieved. Three weeks earlier, he had nearly veered off in the wrong direction; for a time, he resisted Nimitz's forecast that the Imperial Navy intended to invade, and occupy, Midway. King thought the IJN had other targets in mind, probably in the South Pacific, or maybe Hawaii itself. He soon changed his mind when he saw the quality of Nimitz's intelligence. It consisted of intercepted IJN messages decrypted by a special unit of Navy codebreakers based at Pearl Harbor. Nimitz's decrypt team had elicited from this supersecret source a remarkably detailed picture of Japanese forces assembling for the Midway operation. From this finding, CINCPAC (Commander in Chief, Pacific Fleet Command), as Nimitz was called, learned the names of key IJN warships in the support, occupation, and striking forces

1

projected to converge on this remote coral enclave. Nimitz possessed, in effect, something very close to the Imperial Navy's order of battle for this engagement.

But early Sunday morning, 7 June, King's mood suddenly changed. An aide suggested he check page four of Sunday's *Washington Times-Herald*. When King did so, he exploded. He was even angrier when he looked at Sunday's *Chicago Tribune*. An observer said it was "one of King's most violent reactions during the entire war"—and King was infamous for having a low boiling point.[2] The story that bothered him on page four of the *Times-Herald* was also with slight variation on the front page of the *Tribune*: "Navy Had Word of Jap Plan to Strike at Sea."[3] The headline was bad enough. Equally unnerving, the information in the story paralleled almost precisely that assembled by Nimitz's cryptanalysts. The *Tribune* article did not actually state that the U.S. Navy had broken the Japanese naval code. But King worried that newspaper readers, and possibly the Japanese as well, would jump to that conclusion. Somehow, somewhere, there had been a horrendous leak: the *Tribune* had revealed facts it was not supposed to know.

What the *Tribune* writer had done, even if unknowingly, was direct public attention to one of the U.S. government's most fabulously successful military programs. It was called ULTRA, and few people in either the Army or Navy had ever heard of it. Next to the Manhattan Project, organized to build the atomic bomb, ULTRA and its companion program MAGIC were easily the U.S. military's most closely guarded secrets. MAGIC represented the joint Army-Navy effort to decipher Japan's highest-grade diplomatic communications, successfully accomplished in late 1940 with the aid of the so-called PURPLE cipher machine. ULTRA denoted the Army-Navy drive to decode Axis military radio traffic; after a two-year quest, the U.S. Navy penetrated the IJN's main operational code in the spring of 1942.[4]

ULTRA was a secret weapon of enormous importance. "Without it," observed World War II historian Waldo Heinrichs, "the war against Japan would have been far more perilous and difficult than it was."[5] The U.S. military thus went to extraordinary lengths to safeguard this secret. During the presidential campaign of 1944, General George Marshall, the Army chief of staff, dissuaded the Republican candidate for president, New York governor Thomas E. Dewey, from making the MAGIC and ULTRA programs a political issue. "The conduct of General Eisenhower's campaign and of all operations in the Pacific are closely related in conception and timing to the information we secretly obtain through these intercepted codes," Marshall told Dewey. Dewey had received an incorrect tip that MAGIC had revealed in advance Japan's intention to strike Pearl Harbor on 7 December 1941; he was going to use that report against Roosevelt in the campaign. When he got Marshall's letter, he backed off.[6]

The Navy was already known for its culture of secrecy. It kept a tight lid on ULTRA findings; they could be accessed only by those with a Secret clearance. At his Pearl Harbor headquarters, Admiral Nimitz was especially security conscious. He shared his ULTRA material—data supplied by his shore-based decrypt unit, the famed Station Hypo—with only a few trusted aides. During meetings he would rarely, if ever, divulge the source of his insights—"He would merely say that information had reached him," Hypo's lead cryptanalyst recalled years later. He would send updates to forces at sea based on decrypts from Hypo, but in disguised form so captains on the receiving end would not know the origins of those reports.[7]

Ironically, from all that could be learned, it was the contents of a 31 May CINCPAC radio dispatch that showed up in the *Chicago Tribune's* distressing 7 June article. Despite all of Nimitz's precautions, a CINCPAC message intended to alert Pacific Fleet task forces afloat to the impending action at Midway reached a ship not intended to get that information. The ship was *Barnett*, a transport carrying back to the United States survivors from the carrier *Lexington*, shattered on 8 May by Japanese warplanes during the Battle of the Coral Sea. On board that transport was a *Tribune* war correspondent named Stanley Johnston. A flamboyant, Australian-born globe-trotter, Johnston had been on the carrier during its demise. Also on board *Barnett* was *Lexington's* executive officer, Commander Morton T. Seligman. Seligman had daily access to incoming radio dispatches from CINCPAC. Seligman and Johnston shared a suite on board *Barnett*.

Before 7 June ended, Admiral King established one indisputable fact: the *Tribune* story, though unsigned, had been written by Stanley Johnston. No one knew how Johnston got the story, but his friendship with Commander Seligman was not overlooked. Did Seligman show him the dispatch? Or did Johnston steal it? Privately, King and his aides suspected that Seligman, in some unexplained way, had let slip into Johnston's hands the Navy's priceless ULTRA secret. However the leak occurred, they believed that the IJN, upon discovering the *Tribune* story, would, as a matter of course, change its code, closing off this crucial window into IJN planning.

Convinced there had been a flagrant breach of security, King ordered a Navy probe into the source of the Johnston story. So did Attorney General Francis Biddle; he instructed FBI director J. Edgar Hoover to mount a massive investigation. Biddle brought on board President Herbert Hoover's onetime attorney general, William D. Mitchell, to prepare a case for the grand jury, should the matter go that far, which it did. At the behest of President Roosevelt and Secretary of the Navy Frank Knox, on 7 August Biddle convened a grand jury to examine the incident. Roosevelt wanted the jurors to return criminal indictments against Johnston; *Tribune* Managing Editor J. Loy "Pat" Maloney; and possible others, such as the *Tribune*'s conservative publisher, Robert R. McCormick, one of FDR's most strident and implacable foes.

Now the media were intrigued. The grand jury announcement grabbed their attention; Biddle's action became a national story. The *New York Times*, the *Washington Post*, and other big city newspapers, as well as *Time* and *Newsweek*, covered it. Gossip writer Walter Winchell got into the act; he highlighted the episode in his *New York Mirror* column and put on the air some ill-considered words during one of his Sunday broadcasts. Even with all the publicity, many people could not figure out what the case was about. Neither King nor Biddle stated publicly that the matter involved codebreaking or the disclosure of the Navy's ULTRA secret. Biddle revealed only that it concerned the "possible violation" of a criminal statute, presumably the Espionage Act of 1917, which barred the communicating of national defense documents to people not authorized to receive them. That was a serious charge. Conviction under the Espionage Act carried maximum penalties of a $10,000 fine, ten years in jail, or both.

The *Chicago Tribune* did not remain silent. It defended Johnston's story and vigorously rejected all the administration's charges. Johnston vehemently denied that he ever had in his hands any sensitive documents; Maloney ridiculed any notion of wrongdoing on his part. McCormick denounced the case as an FDR-inspired effort to smear the *Tribune* and aid a rival newspaper, the *Chicago Daily News*, whose publisher just happened to be Navy Secretary Knox. The *Tribune* promptly turned its editorial burp guns on the Roosevelt administration; it accused Knox of venality (he was drawing paychecks from two sources), and it slammed FDR for playing politics by seeking to punish the paper for its attacks on his conduct of the war.

There was more to the case. There were also allegations that the *Tribune* had flouted censorship directives that obligated the paper to get prior approval for military stories. The paper dismissed that accusation, contending the censorship rules, as written, did not apply to that particular *Tribune* story. (The director of censorship, Byron Price, actually agreed with the paper on this point.) *Newsweek* caught the essence of the brouhaha with an article that reprinted the *Tribune*'s 7 June headline and much of its original story; *Newsweek* added, "the scoop" blew the lid off Navy Department reserve. Infuriated officials called for the investigation on the ground that the dispatch violated the Voluntary Censorship Code and tipped off sources of Navy information to the Japanese, thus making such sources useless.[8]

Newsweek, like most of the press, played down the codebreaking angle. The Navy was fortunate in this regard. COMINCH quickly came around to the view that the last thing he wanted was journalists delving into the Navy's ULTRA activities.[9] That may have been good for the Navy, but it was not helpful for Biddle's case. Thus, the charges against *Tribune* staffers remained ill-defined and vague. Too vague, apparently, for the grand jury. After a few days of hearing testimony from a handful of Navy officers and newspaper editors, the grand jury threw out the case. It refused to return an indictment against Johnston, Maloney, or anybody else associated with the *Tribune*. Johnston was off the hook; he was free to go about his life.

The Johnston case may have been closed, but it was not forgotten. Over the years historians, Navy observers, and others pondered how Johnston obtained that story. Theories abounded. One widely circulated tale imagined Johnston filching Nimitz's dispatch while on board the carrier *Saratoga* as it steamed toward Pearl Harbor in early June 1942. Unfortunately for this yarn, Johnston never traveled in *Saratoga*.[10] The late Adlai Stevenson, the former governor of Illinois and two-time Democratic candidate for the U.S. presidency, reportedly told a friend he learned the truth while serving as special assistant to Navy Secretary Knox in 1942. Stevenson was alleged to have said Johnston got the dispatch off the cruiser *New Orleans*. He, too, was mistaken; ships' records show that the correspondent never sailed with *New Orleans*.[11]

Johnston proved to be a slippery character. He was hard to pin down and remained for years something of an enigma, almost a phantom. If not quite forgotten, he was nevertheless fading from view, his case deemed by many to be no more than a historical curiosity. But Johnson didn't entirely disappear. Events soon conspired to rescue him from oblivion: with the passage of time, his story acquired historical importance. After all, Johnston was the only mainstream journalist the government sought to prosecute under the

Espionage Act during World War II. This distinction enabled him to be seen in a new light: as a pioneer. Indeed, his brush with criminal law foreshadowed the more adversarial relationship between journalists and the government that emerged during the Cold War. Echoes of that 1942 controversy resound in recent cases involving reporters and whistleblowers who have published, or caused to be published, leaks of sensitive national security material. As with similar confrontations today, Johnston's skirmish with the federal government raised fundamental issues at the core of American democracy; it concerned defining the scope of press freedom during wartime, exploring the limits to the public's right to know, and raising questions about secrecy and its place in a free society.[12]

A question arises: does the Johnston matter shed any light on the explosive cases commanding headlines today? The answer hinges, in part, on solving vexing puzzles about the correspondent that have persisted over the years. Just who was Stanley Johnston and how *did* he get that story? Did he lie about its origins? Did he disregard Navy and civilian censorship rules? Why did the grand jury dismiss this case? Did grand jurors understand it involved codebreaking and the possible giveaway of a vital military secret? Did the Roosevelt administration seek to persecute the *Chicago Tribune*? Or did it have good reason to go after Johnston and his newspaper? Did the Japanese ever read Johnston's story and change their naval code? Was any harm done to U.S. national security? Key grand jury and FBI records released in recent years permit some conclusions to be drawn and some judgments to be made about Stanley Johnston.

CHAPTER 1

A DATE WITH LADY LEX

Our departure from Honolulu was a lazy, lackadaisical one.
We just drifted over the horizon apparently engaged
in some routine maneuver.

—*Stanley Johnston*

PEARL HARBOR REPAIR BASIN, 0700 ON 15 APRIL 1942

Running late, Stanley Johnston paused just long enough to behold the awe-inspiring vessel before him. Then he hastened on board. Johnston could not believe his luck. For weeks the tall, easygoing journalist, a dashing figure with his smartly trimmed mustache and Australian accent, had been making a nuisance of himself at Pearl Harbor, pestering Navy brass for posting to a warship and getting nowhere. But late the previous evening, he had gotten a phone call from Pacific Fleet headquarters: if he wanted a ship, he had better quickly wrap up his affairs in Hawaii. Now, ten hours later, Johnston was astonished to be standing where he was: on the hangar deck of one of the U.S. Navy's vintage carriers, the famed *Lexington*. He was also pleased to be greeted by a crisp, businesslike officer who identified himself as Morton Seligman.[1]

Commander Seligman was the executive officer on the carrier. As such he was second in command to the Lex's skipper, Captain Frederick C. "Ted" Sherman. Seligman bid the newcomer a hearty welcome, but he had to admit he had not known Johnston was coming until the day before. That was when Sherman received a hand-delivered letter from Admiral Chester Nimitz, Commander in Chief, Pacific Fleet Command (CINPAC), informing him he would have journalistic company on his next operation—a vaguely defined mission that seemed to promise action somewhere in the South Pacific. Nimitz closed his note with an appeal, one that, events would show, Seligman took seriously: "Your cooperation in assisting Mr. Johnston will be very much appreciated."[2]

Extending Johnston the first of what would be many courtesies, Seligman escorted the correspondent to his quarters. Duffel bag in hand, still a little shaky after his breakneck morning, Johnston followed the officer through the ship's labyrinthine passageways, up metal stairs and into the forward part of ship. This was where he was to be billeted—a region of the ship called Admiral's country, a suite of comfortable and spacious rooms reserved for the highest-ranking officer on board. That would be Rear Admiral Aubrey W. "Jakey" Fitch, who agreed to share his rooms with the reporter. Fitch was important: he commanded the entire Task Force 11. *Lexington* was his flagship. Sherman, in contrast, was responsible only for the carrier.[3]

Johnston could finally relax. This spot had not come easily. For a time, he had practically despaired of getting on board any ship, let alone "Lady Lex," as crew members had affectionately nicknamed the carrier years earlier. He had not been idling his time away. He had been beseeching Navy officials for such a slot since 3 March 1942, when he first showed up at Pearl Harbor as a newly minted war correspondent for the *Chicago Tribune*. Over and over, he told Navy officials exactly what he wanted to do—go out with the Pacific Fleet and see the U.S. Navy in action against the Imperial Japanese Navy. Weeks passed and he heard nothing.[4]

∼

Johnston had no idea what broke the logjam. All he knew was that the night before, while relaxing at his hotel in Waikiki, he had received an unexpected phone call from the Pacific Fleet's public relations staff. He could go out with the fleet the next morning but he had better not dally. He had to report to Pearl Harbor's main gate no later than 7 a.m., ready to sail. He should take care of any business he had in the islands; he might be gone for weeks. Johnston said he would be there. Out of breath, a little disheveled in his slightly worn khakis, he arrived at the gate on time, although just barely.[5]

Exiting his taxi, Johnston found waiting for him, sitting in his jeep, an officer he recognized as an assistant in the Fleet's PR office: Lieutenant James Bassett. Bassett was there because he had been told to be there; drive Johnston straight to *Lexington* were the orders he had received from his boss, Lieutenant Commander Waldo Drake, the fleet's director of public relations. Johnston and Drake were well acquainted; they got on extremely well in the hothouse atmosphere of Navy press relations. Johnston had no way of knowing it, but Drake had smoothed Johnston's way on board the carrier, first by seeing to it that CINCPAC's letter of introduction about Johnston reached *Lexington*'s top officers on 14 April, then by following up that letter with a phone call to Commander Seligman. The message: welcome on board *Chicago Tribune* correspondent Stanley Johnston. As we have seen, Seligman got the message.[6]

Drake would play a critical role in Johnston's future. He seemed the ideal officer to handle press relations and help people like Johnston. Drake had a solid newspaper background, having worked as a reporter and editor for the *Los Angeles Times*. He was a naval reservist; early in 1941, he joined the Pacific Fleet's PR staff. But as Johnston had learned weeks earlier, Drake was no ordinary PR man. He was also the fleet's chief censor, a thankless job given him by CINCPAC. His charge was to make sure that no information reached the Japanese that could aid their war effort. This was not an easy task. He and his small staff were granted heavy authority to prevent any useful morsel from reaching the Japanese navy; they could, if they saw the need, change or reject all copy produced by reporters covering the fleet. Disagreeable as this job might have seemed to some, Drake embraced it and did not hold back in exercising his power.

Correspondents assigned to the Pacific Fleet generally recognized the need for some form of censorship. They understood there was a war on. But they did not like the way Drake did his job. They complained he performed his duties too aggressively and, making matters worse, they often found him rude and insensitive to their needs. Some accused him of playing favorites; it was even rumored he kept a little "black book" of journalists he disliked. Others griped that he "sat" on copy too long, or wielded his censor's pen promiscuously, sometimes emasculating their stories beyond recognition.[7] Drake's defenders said the officer was simply doing his job. In fact he may have been, but the negative perception persisted, leading many reporters to believe he could make or break their careers at Pearl Harbor. Some grudgingly decided that if they wanted fast action on the stories submitted for censorship, they had better handle Drake with kid gloves.

Johnston did not treat Drake with kid gloves; he did not see the need. He and Drake were on good terms. They had hit it off when the two first met in early March in CINCPAC's public relations office. Genial and outgoing, irrepressibly good-natured, Johnston made friends easily, and he made friends with Drake. Drake, in fact, served as Johnston's mentor during the correspondent's first days at Pearl Harbor. He introduced Johnston to the fleet's multilayered and sometimes convoluted system of censorship. There were a lot of rules, most covered in a directive handed out to all journalists assigned to Pearl Harbor: the Navy's *Memorandum for War Correspondents*. From this rule book, Johnston learned he should not report the strength or composition of U.S. naval forces, the location or movement of those forces, plans or orders for future operations, armament or equipment of any kind, the sinking of enemy submarines, or the results of enemy action or American casualties.[8]

There was one more thing. As a condition for receiving the press credentials that would allow him to cover the Pacific Fleet, Johnston would have to obey an edict the Navy considered sacrosanct: mandatory censorship. Any article involving the Pacific Fleet, whether written on land at Pearl Harbor or on board a warship, had to be cleared by a representative of the fleet. Johnston readily agreed.[9] Having accepted all the Navy's terms, Johnston got his credentials around 11 March; he could now write stories about the fleet from Pearl Harbor. His new papers did not, however, automatically entitle him to posting on board a warship. That privilege would require separate Navy approval and adherence to yet another layer of censorship.

Virtually every reporter or photographer assigned a warship signed a four-paragraph pledge, or *Agreement for War Correspondents*, as the document was officially called. The terms required the journalist to submit to a fleet representative, "*for the purpose of censorship all statements, written material, and all photography intended for publication or release . . . based on any observations made during the period or pertain to the places visited under this authority*" (emphasis added). Another paragraph required the journalist to waive all claims against the United States for losses, damages, or injuries that might be suffered as a result of outbound passage with the fleet. Reporters embarking on warships considered the agreement routine, a necessary formality. On 7 April 1942, one week before Johnston boarded *Lexington*, Richard Tregaskis, a soon-to-be-famous correspondent with the International News Service, signed such a pledge before boarding a vessel heading for the central Pacific on a separate operation. Waldo Drake signed the agreement as a "witnessing officer."[10]

No one knew what Drake's assistant, Lieutenant Bassett, was thinking when Johnston hopped into his jeep at 7 a.m. on 15 April at Pearl Harbor's main gate. Bassett was, however, pressed for time. Whatever the reason, he disregarded two long-established rituals. First, he dispensed with the customary briefing in which he or Drake reviewed the ground rules spelled out in the Navy's *Memorandum for Correspondents*. That did not matter much; Johnston already knew those strictures. Second, more puzzling and certainly more consequential, he did not require Johnston to sign what had become the obligatory *Agreement for War Correspondents*. True, Johnston had already agreed orally to comply with all the rules of censorship. But the *Agreement* was considered by the Navy to be an additional safeguard. This seeming lapse on Bassett's part would raise eyebrows in Washington in just a few weeks.[11]

Anxious to get going, Bassett speedily chauffeured Johnston over to the berth that housed the huge carrier, scheduled to exit Pearl Harbor in about an hour. *Lexington* had been in dry dock three weeks, on the receiving end of a top to bottom overhaul. That work done, Lex was being readied to move. Soon after Johnston met Seligman and settled down in Admiral's country, he felt the ship budge. Through a porthole he could see several tugs, attached to the ship by mooring lines, easing the carrier out of its berth and into the harbor. Falling in line behind several destroyers and a cruiser, with other ships taking up the rear, the carrier started to advance. The ships proceeded slowly, single file, into the narrow channel toward the Pacific some two miles away. This was Fitch's Task Force 11. It consisted of seven destroyers and two heavy cruisers, *Minneapolis* and *New Orleans*, all there to support *Lexington*.

Soon the small flotilla passed through Pearl Harbor's narrow entrance and out into the Pacific. "Our departure from Honolulu was a lazy, lackadaisical one," Johnston remembered later. "We just drifted over the horizon apparently engaged in some routine maneuver. We disappeared in a direction almost opposite to that in which we intended going. This apparent aimlessness was continued until we were 50 miles or more from land, well out of sight of any islands. Then, and only then, did the ships close up, turn on their southerly course and gradually pick up speed."[12]

～

Johnston was a bizarre addition to the 2,951 officers and men assigned to *Lexington*. Standing more than six feet, he towered over most. With his dark brown hair combed straight back and just beginning to gray at the temples, he looked distinguished, almost like a country gentleman. He was not especially handsome; one colleague remembered him as having "a long, thin, horseface." But thanks to that William Powell mustache and distinctive Aussie accent, he projected an air of worldliness and urbanity. His accented voice seemed to permeate the ship as he wandered about talking to everyone he could find. He loved to chatter, and to many shipmates it seemed like he never stopped. A Navy report later described him as a "voluble talker."[13]

Gabby as he may have been, his Navy colleagues liked hearing him talk, and they relished his amazing stories. They were pleased to find that he was a man of many parts and that earlier in his life he had mastered such disparate skills as Morse code and sculling; indeed, he had been a champion sculler in Australia.[14] They probably did not know, or care, that he was a relative newcomer to journalism, having been added to the *Tribune*'s staff only in recent months. Just a few months earlier, in fact, he had described himself as a mining engineer, a label that reflected his business interests in gold mines in New Guinea and similar ventures elsewhere.[15] In truth, he was not so much a journalist as a professional gadabout—a soldier of fortune who had traveled widely in search of adventure and treasure. He had turned to newspapering only in desperation—when global war dried up opportunities in his usual area of activity.

The officers and men who enjoyed Johnston's company had no way of knowing that his way of doing journalism would propel some of them into an unwelcome spotlight. They would find themselves trapped in what was probably the Navy's most embarrassing scandal of the Pacific War. Johnston would be the target of a federal probe, and a number of his shipmates would be interviewed by FBI and Navy investigators. But that unhappy development remained many weeks away. In the meantime, Task Force 11 had a war to fight: crews went about their business: planes were put in the air and brought back; guns were tested; machinery was oiled.

And Johnston, for his part, traversed nearly every nook and cranny of the massive carrier, asking questions, seeing how things functioned, getting to know the workings of a warship. Seasoned as he was in many different fields, Johnston was still learning the craft of journalism. Although he had worked briefly, and capably, as a stringer for the *Tribune*'s London bureau in 1940, tracking the early phase of the war, he had no real background in this line of work. He had never served the apprenticeship typically required of beginning reporters. He had never worked on a newspaper as a cub reporter, covering city hall and cops and learning the trade from the bottom up. He had not written his first news story until age forty. He still had some rough edges.

∼

Johnston may have been a greenhorn at newspapering, but he was no stranger to military service. Or to questions about his wartime experience and personal history. Stanley Claude Samuel Johnston was born 27 March 1900 at Palmers Island, New South Wales, Australia. He was the son either of a civil engineer (the story he gave the *Chicago Tribune*) or a local fisherman (the version unearthed by the FBI).[16] He attended Australian schools until age fourteen. Then, ten days after Great Britain declared war on Germany, he quit school and, unlikely as it might seem, joined the Royal Australian Naval Reserves (RANR). He pulled off this coup, he told people later, after running away from home (and presumably lying about his age). With war raging in Europe, he was now in the Australian Armed Forces. He would go on to give many colorful accounts of his military career. In reports to *Tribune* editors and chats with U.S. naval officers on board *Lexington,* he painted a striking picture of his military action. In 1915 he saw service with the ANZAC (Australian and New Zealand Army Corps) forces in Egypt, then participated in operations in Gallipoli and France. He was wounded twice. He received a commission with a New South Wales artillery unit.[17] Years later, while living in Paris, he passed himself off as a former officer in the Australian army.[18]

Almost none of this was true. He did, incontestably, enlist in the RANR at age fourteen, but he did not do so after running away from home.[19] Joining up turned out to be surprisingly easy. Australia's armed forces had a history of recruiting Boy Soldiers and Boy Sailors—youths age from fourteen to seventeen—to perform various kinds of war work, sometimes even to serve as combatants (minimum age for regular service in the Australian military was eighteen years). Enlistment, however, required parental approval, which Johnston almost certainly had when he signed up on 14 August 1914, just days after Allied forces captured a German steamer off Melbourne (one of the first shots fired by Allied troops in the war). Johnston thus became one of 3,092 cadets in training with the Royal Australian Naval Brigade, an arm of the RANR. About six hundred members of the brigade were, in fact, deployed to the Mediterranean theater, where some saw action in Egypt and Gallipoli.[20]

Stanley Johnston was not among them. Shortly after enlisting, he joined some five hundred trainees ordered to the Royal Australian Navy's New Guinea Expeditionary Force, a combat group that, in September 1914, seized German wireless stations near Rabaul in the Bismarck Sea. But his duty did not take him near the fighting. In mid-1915, when the Gallipoli campaign was heating up, Johnston was assigned to shore duties in the RAN's naval staff office in Brisbane, Australia. What he did there does not show up in his records, although one muster list described his trade as "pastry cook." Whatever his duties, he remained at the naval office through 5 April 1916 (the Gallipoli campaign had ended 9 January 1916). Rotated back to sea, he was assigned to the cruiser *Gayundah*, on patrol between Australia and New Guinea. Nine months later, after he turned seventeen, Johnston was transferred to the regular Australian navy. Attached to the RAN's Home Service, he was now sent to the Signal School at HMAS *Cerberus* for a special course in convoy signaling.[21] With the war nearly over (Germany signed the armistice on 11 November 1918), Johnston, on 25 October 1918, was ordered to the British cruiser HMS *Suffolk*, where records show he served as a yeoman of signals. He remained with the *Suffolk* for three months, during which time the cruiser steamed to Vladivostok, Yokohoma, and Hong Kong.[22] There, on 24 January 1919, he disembarked, ending his regular navy stint. Back with the reserve force, he finished his naval career on board the *Cerberus* in Australian home waters; he was discharged on 30 June 1919.[23]

Johnston's naval career was perfectly honorable. He did everything he was asked to do. But he did not do the many things that he claimed to have done. He did not serve in Gallipoli or Egypt or France. He did not serve as an officer in a New South Wales artillery unit. He was not wounded, nor did he ever serve in combat, a fact disclosed by his World War I "medal card" maintained at the National Archives of Australia in Sydney. The card shows that after the war he received only the War Medal—a decoration for those who served with the Australian Armed Forces from 1914 to 1920 but not in a theater of war. Had Johnston so served, he would also have received a Victory Medal and a 1914–15 Star; his card shows he was not entitled to either medal.[24]

Still, Johnston clearly acquired many useful skills with the RAN Brigade, Morse code and signaling being just two. After his discharge in 1919, he settled in Sydney, where in 1921 he married and studied at the University of Sydney. He graduated in 1923 with a degree in mining engineering. With his new credential in hand, he found consulting work that took him all over Australia and East Asia; he seized opportunities that led him to traverse the Arafura, Celebes, and South China Seas. But after four years of consulting, he wanted to try something new. His curiosity was piqued by accounts of gold strikes in the Bulolo Valley in New Guinea. Making his way through dense mosquito-infested jungles and lush mountains, he staked out several claims. He later sold them and joined the Bulolo Gold Dredging Company in the early 1930s.[25] This venture worked out for Johnston, at least for a time. The company flew its mining machinery, men, and supplies in from the New Guinea coast, and its gold out by one of the world's first and most successful air freight lines. He helped establish this air freight service.[26]

By the mid-1930s, Johnston was again getting restless. He was intrigued by events in Europe; he thought there might be opportunities there. In 1936 he headed in that direction but traveled by way of America, stopping for a time in New York City. Johnston liked the city, especially its nightlife. While out on the town one evening at one of Manhattan's lively nightspots, a club called the Paradise Cabaret, he took an interest in one of its dancers. She was Barbara Maria Beck, an attractive young woman nine years his junior.[27] They had much in common. Like Stanley, Barbara was a traveler; she was born in Wurzburg, Bavaria, Germany, in 1909. She emigrated to the United States in 1926. A talented dancer, she soon joined the Broadway dance troupe George White's Scandals. In 1934 she became a naturalized U.S. citizen. When the two met at the Paradise Cabaret, Stanley was single; he had divorced his first wife in 1935. Barbara was married but separated from her husband, a musician named Albert Incagnoli. (He had apparently abandoned her in the early 1930s; she would divorce him in 1941.)[28]

Stanley and Barbara would eventually join forces, but not right away. Stanley proceeded alone to London, where he worked approximately a year for a company building experimental gas turbines. He returned to New York in late 1937 and reconnected with Barbara. On 30 July 1938, they boarded the ocean liner S.S. *Washington* bound for Hamburg. Traveling falsely as man and wife, they settled for a time in Germany, where Barbara's parents still lived. (Stanley told U.S. authorities later that they picked Germany because Barbara's mother was dying and they wanted to see her.) Along the way, they met a German banker who helped Stanley begin a small enterprise, to which Stanley gave the name Ersinger and Company. It was headquartered at Muncher-Gladbach, a city on the northern Rhine. There he manufactured and sold plastic hair curlers.[29] The business flourished, enabling Johnston to build up a sizable bank account. Barred from exporting his earnings, he invested in Germany. He acquired an estate that, he claimed, included a castle on the Rhine. His prosperity did not last, however. Johnston's property was confiscated as Germany moved closer to the world war it would launch in

September 1939.[30] Stanley and Barbara thought they had better get out of the country—fast.

Now on the move, the couple landed in Paris. Preternaturally self-confident, Stanley introduced himself to Louis Huot, the European representative of Press Wireless, Incorporated, a news and photo transmission network headquartered in Chicago. Johnston had no previous experience in that business, but he had a way with words. He was a gifted storyteller, a natural salesman. He could be very persuasive. He apparently also fibbed a little. Wanting to burnish his military résumé, he gave Huot the impression that during the European War he had served as an officer in the Australian army and seen action in France.[31] Huot was impressed by Johnston's background in engineering as well as his training in Morse code. Huot hired him. In late 1939, he transferred Johnston to Amsterdam to supervise the opening of a Press Wireless operation in that city.[32] The job seemed ideal, but Johnston soon found himself in trouble.

His frequent trips back and forth between Amsterdam and Paris brought him to the attention of Dutch and British authorities. With both the Netherlands and Britain braced for attack by German forces, officials of those two countries believed Johnston might be an Axis intelligence agent.[33] Their investigation turned up nothing incriminating, but concerns about Johnston's activities would follow him. They surfaced when Johnston turned up in London in March 1940 traveling with Press Wireless president Joseph Pierson. During this trip, Pierson learned from Australian authorities that Johnston's claim to have been an officer in the Australian army was false—his name did not turn up on the register of that country's officers. When Pierson mentioned this to officials in Britain's Ministry of Information, the British again focused on Johnston. They again wondered who he really was. They were worried enough to cancel the visa that would have allowed him to return to Amsterdam, where Barbara waited for him. Under the circumstances, Pierson felt he had no choice but to dismiss Johnston.[34]

Stranded in London, Johnston looked around for a job. Barbara, meantime, had no reason to remain in Amsterdam; she left the city just weeks before the Wehrmacht invaded the Netherlands on 10 May. She returned to Paris to await news from Stanley. In fact, he had news. Pierson, before returning to Paris, did Johnston one good turn: he introduced him to Larry Rue, the London bureau chief of the *Chicago Tribune.* Rue looked Johnston over, apparently liked what he saw, and decided to hire him as a stringer. Johnston told Barbara that she should stay tuned, waiting for news of his activities and how he might retrieve her from Paris.[35]

Johnston now got his first taste of professional journalism. He seemed to have a knack for it and clearly had a gift for being at the right place at the right time. Working for the *Tribune* that summer, just as the Battle of Britain was heating up, he was assigned to Dover to cover the German air raids believed to be a prelude to a land invasion. His job was to search the horizon for incoming planes and ships, a task for which he prepared by reading *Jane's Fighting Ships* and other technical manuals. He pleased his new bosses. "[He is] an excellent observer and knows modern war mechanics and technique," Rue wired the paper's headquarters in Chicago. "I am paying him 1 pound sterling a day temporarily, just enough to cover his living expenses, but may give him some kind of bonus later."[36]

Johnston also showed tremendous courage and valor when, on 11 September, a bomb fell on his Dover hotel. Johnston, another *Tribune* reporter, and two British naval officers were occupying a room on the fourth floor when the bomb hit, severely injuring his *Tribune* colleague and killing the two naval officers. Johnston escaped serious injury, and probably death, by riding a wooden bureau down to ground level as the building collapsed. He then tunneled through the wreckage looking for survivors and still found time to file a story before deadline.[37]

Later, back in London, Johnston continued to satisfy Larry Rue with weighty backgrounders on a variety of naval and military subjects, getting paid, as always, on a piecework basis. But once again he was getting restless. He wanted a permanent staff position, but the *Tribune* did not have one to offer in London. Given that situation, Chicago seemed a likely place to job hunt. It was not only the home of the *Tribune*, which clearly liked his work, but also the offices of Press Wireless (headquartered in the Tribune Tower). Maybe, if the *Tribune* did not work out, Press Wireless would hire him back and give him another chance. He started writing letters to the president of Press Wireless, Joseph Pierson, with whom he had traveled to London early in 1940 and who was now back in his home office in Chicago.

Crucial as landing a permanent job surely was, it was secondary to an even more pressing concern: he needed to extricate Barbara from Paris. She had found herself trapped there when German tanks rolled into Paris in June 1940, beginning the German army's long, grueling occupation of that city. She seemed to be all right, though. Stanley told friends his German-speaking wife had found part-time work as an interpreter at the scaled-down American consulate (formerly the U.S. Embassy). This job supplemented her other employment as an interpreter and typist at the Paris bureau of the *New York Times*, still in place during the early days of the occupation. Welcome as these positions were, they did not serve the couple's long-term goal: to reconnect and resume their life together, preferably in the United States. That would not be easy. There were complications.

The most daunting one facing Johnston boiled down to a four-letter word: visa. He could not get an exit visa for the United States. The problem was different from the one that had vexed him in March, when authorities were perplexed by his story that he had served as an officer in the Australian army. Johnston had cleared up that problem; he said the erroneous report was the result of a misunderstanding. British officials accepted that and assured him that he was no longer under suspicion.[38] But there was a new difficulty. British law forbade its citizens—as an Australian, he was considered British—from traveling to foreign countries during wartime except for a good reason, such as employment, proof of which had to be demonstrated.[39] If he had wanted to, he could have, under British rules, obtained an exit visa for Australia. But he did not want to go there; he wanted to go to the United States.

Johnston did not have a job in the United States. The *Chicago Tribune* would keep him on as a stringer in London, but it had no position to offer him in the United States. Press Wireless was not any help. The letters he received from its Chicago office were discouraging. It seemed the United States, too, had laws that got in Johnston's way. One prohibited companies from making promises of work to noncitizens abroad. "I am advised that it is a penitentiary offense to bring a citizen of another country into the United States on a labor contract," Pierson wrote Johnston in January 1941.[40] Pierson seemed sympathetic but said his hands were tied.

Johnston's problem with Press Wireless went beyond the rigidities of American law. They extended to Louis Huot, the Press Wireless executive who originally had hired him in Paris. Now living in London, Huot—having heard that Johnston was seeking reemployment with his company—weighed in against his former employee. He reminded Pierson that Johnston had embarrassed Press Wireless in London and Paris by his "bragging" that during the European War he had served as an officer in the Australian army. "His serious fault is an extravagant, heedless, and reckless way of talking,"

Huot wrote Pierson. "I remain convinced he is a dangerous employee for us and a person with whom we can hardly afford to entertain formal business relations."[41]

Now it was Johnston who was trapped. The only good news he got was that Barbara, in January 1941, had pulled some strings and managed to make her way to Lisbon, the capital of a neutral country where she would be safe. There she waited for Stanley. They had hoped to meet in Lisbon, then head for the United States.[42] The only thing holding them back was that Stanley lacked proof of employment there. "I MUST have a letter," he implored Pierson in an 11 March note. Without one, he feared he would be "doomed to rot [in London] until the war ends."[43]

Johnston redoubled his efforts to break free of London. He called everyone he knew in the War Office and at the Admiralty: "I went after them through the best channels possible," he wrote Pierson on 17 March. He even contacted Lord Louis Mountbatten, a high-ranking naval officer and a favorite of Prime Minister Winston Churchill. "Lord Louis Mountbatten and I had a connection some years ago so I wrote him,"[44] Johnston said. What Mountbatten may have done for him is not known. Nor did Pierson help; he did not provide the letter Johnston wanted. The *Tribune*'s Larry Rue may have put in a good word for him, but nothing more. In the end, Johnston took the exit visa he could have had all along: he was going to Australia—via the United States.

Stanley and Barbara reconnected in Lisbon in May. After a few days, they returned by ship to Britain and then proceeded to the United States on board the American transport ship *Siboney*. The couple arrived in New York on 26 May; Stanley was admitted as a temporary visitor in the United States for business purposes with a visa good for six months. In fact, he had no job lined up. As far as the London bureau of the *Tribune* was concerned, he was just another unemployed stringer. When *Tribune* officials in Chicago got wind of Johnston's journey, they queried Rue, "What's Johnston's mission to America?" Rue answered on 23 May: "Stanley Johnston is not connected with the *Tribune* whatsoever. He probably is taking up reemployment with Press Wireless."[45]

He was not. He had received no job offer from Press Wireless; he thought if worse came to worst, Pierson might hire him to open a Press Wireless office in Australia. But he was off on his own, gambling he could talk his way into a congenial, lucrative position once he reached his target city: Chicago. Of course, what he really wanted was a job with the *Tribune*, not Press Wireless. That did happen, but not right away. Showing up at Tribune Tower (where both Press Wireless and the *Tribune* were housed), he searched out *Tribune* editors. He received a cordial welcome, surprising in light of Larry Rue's dismissive note. The *Tribune's* managing editor, J. Loy "Pat" Maloney, thought Johnston showed promise, as did the paper's legendary and rather forbidding publisher, Colonel Robert R. McCormick. McCormick even took Stanley and Barbara to lunch; they seemed to get along well. "One of the reasons [McCormick] liked Johnston, he was a big man," remembered *Tribune* editor W. D. "Don" Maxwell. "The colonel always admired [physical] stature."[46]

Aside from their height (the publisher stood six feet, four inches), McCormick and Johnston would seem to be an odd pairing. McCormick was the publisher of the largest isolationist newspaper in the United States. Johnston was a man of the world. But McCormick, too, had traveled widely. As a neophyte publisher, he had journeyed to Russia in 1915 to observe the European War on the eastern front. Two years later, he got caught up in that war when, as a member of the Illinois National Guard, he was called to active duty. He was ordered to France, where he served first as a major, then as a full colonel, in an artillery unit with the 1st Infantry Division. After the war, he let it be known that he liked being called "colonel." He enjoyed the company of admirals and generals, and he prided himself on his grasp of military issues. By the late 1930s, the *Tribune* had emerged as one of the Franklin Roosevelt administration's most vehement critics. It condemned FDR's New Deal domestic policies, and it bitterly opposed any U.S. involvement in European or Asian affairs that might draw the United States into war. If Johnston had strong political views at this time, they do not show up in his surviving letters or public statements, but there is no reason to believe he ever felt uncomfortable at the *Tribune*.[47]

Expansive and ebullient, always radiating good cheer, Johnston seldom had trouble winning over the people he needed to win over. He won over *Tribune* editors now. They did not, however, offer him a regular staff position; instead, they presented him with the kind of deal he had come to the United States to avoid: piecework. He would be paid for each individual story, as he had been while covering the Battle of Britain in Dover. Disappointed, he nevertheless accepted and was glad he did. The paper's editors used their influence to have his visa extended a few months. They also teamed him with aviation editor Wayne Thomis; the two produced a number of solidly researched articles on a variety of naval and military issues. The articles put Johnston in a good light. His copy showed that while he was not a polished writer, he knew his stuff. He possessed expertise the paper could use. Colonel McCormick was impressed.

As the weeks passed, Johnston's stock at the *Tribune* rose. By the end of the summer, he had achieved a long-sought goal: he was added to the paper's permanent staff. Other milestone events followed. On 11 September 1941, Barbara's divorce from Incagnoli became official. Stanley and Barbara married on 22 September. On 13 November he filed a petition for naturalization as a U.S. citizen; on 16 December his petition was granted.[48]

Johnston's career took another turn after 7 December 1941, when Japanese war planes attacked Pearl Harbor and propelled the United States into World War II. A 30 December memo from the Department of the Navy to the *Tribune*'s Washington bureau chief, Arthur Sears Henning, provided useful information. The memo pointed out that since the U.S. Fleet was operating from Hawaii, "it looks as if that is where [the *Tribune*] should have a man to cover any warship operations that may develop in the Far East." McCormick thought Johnston should go and approved the submission of his name to the Navy Department for accreditation.[49]

Told his Navy papers were in the works, Johnston in January proceeded to San Francisco, hoping the Navy would let him take Barbara to Hawaii "as my personal secretary." However, Barbara got as far as San Francisco but no farther. Because the Navy was now evacuating all the civilians it could from the islands, it rejected Johnston's bid. With Barbara staying behind, Johnston caught a transport ship to Hawaii on 21 February 1942. He arrived thinking himself a fully-accredited war correspondent but soon ran into the first of what would be a number of unpleasant surprises. Appearing at the Pacific Fleet's press office on 3 March, he found his papers had not arrived. He would have to resubmit his application for accreditation. He did not receive his press card until 11 March, and then he discovered the card had limitations. It was good only through 1 July 1942, after which it would have to be renewed. And it was primarily for identification purposes. It entitled him to cover fleet news from Pearl Harbor; it did not, however, entitle him to be on a warship. He would need another clearance for that, from the Pacific Fleet commander and the Secretary of the Navy. He submitted such a request.[50]

While waiting for a "deep sea" assignment, Johnston assured his bosses there were plenty of stories he could write from Pearl Harbor. He got off to a rocky start. The *Tribune*'s editors wanted anything they could get from their new war correspondent, but three weeks after his arrival in Hawaii, Johnston had yet to file a single article. "When can we expect stories?" they wired him on 21 March. Seven days later, they wired him again: "Want reply message 21 March." A day later, Johnston answered that his copy had hit a snag at the fleet censor's office but that the problem had been cleared up: "Cabled story filed today; should flow evenly now."[51]

Johnston knew what his editors were looking for. As one astute observer of the *Tribune* put it, "McCormick was not interested in detailed background stories—what he wanted in a foreign news story was the exclusive interview, the dashing exploit, exposes, scoops, something to make big headlines."[52] Even when he tried to produce such stories, his bosses were not pleased. They did not like the way he handled the Butch O'Hare story. Lieutenant O'Hare was the *Lexington* fighter pilot who, on 20 February 1942, became the Navy's first fighter ace; soaring over the Bismarck Archipelago, he single-handedly attacked nine Japanese bombers approaching his carrier, shooting down three and damaging three others.[53] Shortly after the Lex returned to Pearl Harbor on 26 March, O'Hare's exploit became widely known. The *Tribune* wanted a story. Johnston wrote one, but it reached the paper late. "Your O'Hare story arrived three hours after opposition, missing all editions," he heard on 30 March. He blamed the delay on transmission problems on the mainland.[54]

Johnston's editors were getting impatient. On 31 March they wired him again: "What chances going with Fleet?" A few days later he replied that he had been promised a ship, "but owing to inactivity and other delays, it is indefinite when I will have an eyewitness story."[55]

More time passed. Johnston was getting anxious. The home office was putting greater pressure on him to produce front-page stories. By mid-April he had little to show for the six weeks he had spent in Hawaii trying to cover the Pacific War from Pearl Harbor. He clearly had not proved himself. So when Nimitz's staff called the evening of 14 April, asking whether he could join *Lexington* the next morning, he was elated. Of course he could be there. He started packing.

∽

Once on board *Lexington*, Johnston enjoyed the prerogatives accorded war correspondents. Under Navy policy, journalists were to be treated like commissioned officers in such matters as messing, living conditions, and transportation.[56] He certainly conducted himself like an officer. Those who might have doubted that he was officer material would see their concerns melt away very soon. They would see Johnston at his swashbuckling best during the playing out of a time-honored naval ritual—it would be performed when the carrier, for reasons that would be clear later, unexpectedly changed course.

For three days *Lexington* had sailed uneventfully, proceeding on what appeared to be a training mission. On 18 April, the carrier paused briefly near Palmyra Atoll, the site of a U.S. Naval Air Station, roughly one thousand miles southeast of Pearl Harbor. After delivering fourteen Marine Buffalo fighters to the remote, almost godforsaken post, Lex resumed steaming, but on a different course. It had been originally scheduled to link up with a flotilla of battleships as part of an exercise. But late on 18 April, Fitch received new orders from Admiral Nimitz canceling that meeting. He was directed to take Task Force 11 deep into the South Pacific to an area near New Caledonia. The change led to speculation about operations in the Coral Sea.[57]

To reach that region, Lex would have to drop below the equator—no routine occurrence. Crossing the equator—known in nautical circles as crossing the line—was a very big deal in the Navy. As Johnston later put it, "The Line is the equator and in war or peace the American Navy makes its crossing an occasion for celebration whenever there are Lowly Pollywogs on board its ships."[58] Pollywogs were those officers and enlisted men who had never before served on board a ship that had crossed the equator. They were to be at the mercy of the Shellbacks—old salts who had served their time as Pollywogs and now thoroughly relished the role reversal.

During the evening of 19 April, Johnston watched as 130 Shellbacks and Pollywogs gathered in the ward room, now turned into a "court" headed by Commander Seligman. The court consisted of a Grand Inquisitor—Commander Walter Gilmore—surrounded by a five-man Jury: Commander Arthur J. White, senior surgeon on board Lex; Lieutenant Commander William Ault, Lex's air group commander; Commander Heine Junkers, the ship's chief engineer; Lieutenant Commander Weldon Hamilton, skipper of one of Lex's two dive-bomber squadrons; and Lieutenant Commander Bob Dixon, skipper of the other dive-bomber squadron.[59] Dixon—described by Johnston as the personification of a Navy airman—would turn up again in the correspondent's story.

Johnston watched intently as Pollywog after hapless Pollywog was called before the court; subjected to merciless questioning from the Grand Inquisitor and the Jury; and, invariably, found guilty. The court handed down a witches' brew of sentences that, depending on the individual and, of course, the mood of the court, might require defendants to wear winter clothes on the flight deck to look for icebergs, don outlandish costumes and face "fiendish" tortures, or run the gauntlet down the whole length of *Lexington*'s flight deck. It was all in good fun, but if the sailor happened to be a Pollywog, not necessarily to be welcomed.[60]

Then it was Johnston's turn. "You may be sure my own case was soon called," he wrote later. "I had heard something of what was coming and had made certain preparations. There had been outspoken glee over the opportunity of initiating a newspaper correspondent. I was warned I was to 'get the works,' in fact, and I had helped things along by appearing very ignorant of what was coming." Johnston presented his documents. "And I startled the Court by promptly claiming my rights and putting my foot on the Court's table," he wrote later. "By this I indicated I had crossed the Line in the Pacific, the Atlantic and Indian Oceans. In fact Line-crossing has been something I've been doing frequently ever since I was born." The Court did not drop its case easily. Seligman, Gilmore, and the others scrutinized his papers for flaws. Eventually, however, the correspondent was recognized as a Shellback—"to the disappointment of all in the room," Johnston added. Johnston now took his place at the judgment table.[61]

For the Lex's Pollywogs, the ceremony served as a memorable rite of passage, signaling their initiation into the Navy's elite circle of truly hardened naval veterans. But for Johnston it was something more: it marked his entry into *Lexington*'s culture. He was now accepted, albeit unofficially, as a full-fledged member of the ship's crew. Officers from Rear Admiral Fitch on down to the greenest ensign enjoyed his line-crossing performance; they appreciated not just the spunk, but also the savvy he displayed outsmarting the ship's brightest officers.

The chunky, easygoing Fitch liked having Johnston on board; they were both outliers in their respective worlds. At age fifty-eight, Fitch was one of the few experienced aviation flag officers in the Pacific Fleet. He led the air task group with the carrier *Saratoga* during the Pacific Fleet's abortive attempt to reinforce Wake Island in December 1941. He wanted to remain at sea, but on 30 December he was rather unhappily assigned to shore duty at Pearl

Harbor, in charge of organization, supply, and matériel for all of the carrier squadrons shore-based on Oahu. On 1 April 1942, he was pleased to be back at sea, taking over as commander of Task Force 11 on board *Lexington*.[62] He felt liberated.

Johnston also got along well with Captain Sherman, possibly because the captain knew something about reporters—both his grandfather and father had been newspaper publishers. Also with a background in aviation, Sherman had commanded the Lex for two years. Regarded as one of the Navy's sharpest thinkers, he was among the first to advocate concentrating multiple carriers into a single task force, a concept that would be used in the campaign ahead.[63] Usually all business, he did permit himself one eccentricity: he brought on board his pet cocker spaniel, Wags. He had a nest, or bed, not far from Johnston's room in Admiral's country. Sherman would go on to be a highly decorated admiral; he would also remain a Johnston loyalist through all the clamor over the correspondent's reporting in the weeks ahead.

Johnston formed an especially close friendship with Sherman's executive officer, Commander Seligman. Seligman had a distinguished history. Born in Salt Lake City on 1 July 1895, he hailed from a family of rugged pioneers who had helped open up the American Southwest to commerce in the mid-nineteenth century. The Seligman family ran a business that delivered merchandise from Kansas City across the Old Santa Fe trail using wagons drawn by oxen, mules, and horses.[64] Morton Seligman, however, lit out in a different direction; on 13 June 1914, he was appointed to the Naval Academy by New Mexico's U.S. senator Thomas B. Catron. He entered the academy in 1915, a member of the class of 1919. Because of the European War, he and other members of his class graduated a year early, in 1918, just in time to join the Atlantic Fleet. He was first assigned to destroyer duty. Then, as the war ended, he was ordered to command a force of twenty-four submarine chasers charged with clearing mines out of the North Sea. For "distinguished service" during this hazardous duty, he was awarded the Navy Cross, at that time the Navy's third-highest decoration. After the war, he entered flight training at the U.S. Naval Air Station in Pensacola, Florida, where he earned his wings in 1922. He went on to command Fighting Squadron 6 on board the carrier *Saratoga*; later, on board the *Ranger*, he commanded that carrier's air group.[65] Since January 1942, he had been serving as *Lexington*'s executive officer, a nonflying post that could have prepared him to command his own carrier.

At first glance, Seligman and Johnston seemed to have little in common, except perhaps the sporty mustache that was the trademark of each. Johnston's was black and bushy while that of the forty-six-year-old Seligman (four years Johnston's senior) was starting to gray. There the similarities seemed to end. Short and wiry, Seligman stood barely five feet eight inches tall, while Johnston, standing above six feet, eclipsed him in height. Seligman was an intense, serious-minded officer who was on the reserved side. Johnston was an exuberant, outgoing chatterbox who loved socializing and telling tall tales. But Seligman was impressed by the fact that Johnston had shown up on written orders from Nimitz. This gave Johnston an eminence he might not otherwise have had. Seligman assured the correspondent he would help him in every way he could—and he let Johnston know that, within reason, he would have the run of the ship.[66]

~

Lexington steamed closer to the Coral Sea, a great expanse of water bounded by Australia on the west, Papua New Guinea and the Solomon Islands on the north, and New Caledonia on the east. Early in April, the Navy's codebreaking unit at Pearl Harbor, known later as Station Hypo, decrypted a highly revealing Imperial Japanese Navy radio transmission. The message pointed toward Port Moresby on New Guinea's west coast as Japan's next target for conquest.[67] If the Japanese succeeded in this action, the consequences for Allied strategy would be dire. Japanese occupation of Moresby, now controlled by Australia, would put Japanese fliers within easy striking range of key Australian cities and deepen Japan's penetration of the southwest Pacific.

At first Nimitz resisted Hypo's estimate. He thought the Japanese might instead be contemplating targets in the Solomon, Ellice, and Gilbert Islands, far to the east of Port Moresby. But soon the evidence piled up. New decrypts showed unmistakably that a massive invasion force was assembling at Rabaul, Japan's base on the northeastern tip of New Britain consisting of troop transports and numerous warships, including three and possibly as many as four aircraft carriers.[68] The coded geographic designators for Moresby appeared more frequently in Imperial Navy radio traffic.

On 17 April, Nimitz accepted Hypo's Moresby prediction as "a working hypothesis," and he so informed his testy, mercurial boss in Washington, Admiral Ernest J. King. Drawing on Hypo's intelligence, Nimitz calculated that the big Japanese armada would move south, sail around the southern tip of New Guinea, turn west into the Coral Sea, and then proceed north up to Port Moresby. In time, King's estimates aligned with Nimitz's, and King flashed CINCPAC a green light to take appropriate counteraction. One day later, on 18 April, Nimitz ordered Fitch to take Task Force 11 to a point 250 miles northwest of New Caledonia and there rendezvous with Task Force 17, a small squadron of seven warships commanded by Rear Admiral Frank Jack Fletcher on board the carrier *Yorktown*. Nimitz directed Fletcher, in tactical command of the two task forces, to intercept and smash the Imperial Navy armada, which was expected to show up during the first week of May. The combat that Stanley Johnston wanted to see was just a few days away. He would be in the middle of it.

CHAPTER 2

GUTS AND GLORY

Johnston . . . was observed everywhere lending aid to
the wounded, procuring life jackets,
chatting cheerfully with the men on deck.
—*Morton T. Seligman*

Johnston felt practically wired to the ship. His quarters happened to be right under the flight deck and just ahead of the forward airplane elevator. The hinged steel flap that covered the groove between the elevator and the flight deck was just above his cabin. "Every aircraft that took off had to run across this metal flap," Johnston wrote later. "And each time, there was a loud metallic 'whang,' as the flap slammed down on the steel plate of my ceiling."[1]

Johnston used to lie abed as the pre-dawn scout and fighter patrols took off. Half asleep, he found himself counting each aircraft, ultimately reaching the point where he could distinguish between bangs made by different types of airplane. "When I went down to the wardroom for breakfast I could always tell just exactly how many planes had taken off," he said. "I won so many arguments on this point that finally my reports were accepted as official." Crew members got even with Johnston by needling him: "Is it too noisy for you there, Stan?" He always gave the same answer: "Well, no. It's the same for the admiral as it is for me."[2]

Johnston's extraordinary niche in Admiral's country did more than help him win wardroom arguments: it gave him an uncanny feel for *Lexington*'s operations. He was well placed for just about any eventuality. From the ship's strange rumbles and sometimes chilling vibrations, he could usually tell what was going on. When he registered those pulses, or heard the gongs that periodically sounded, sometimes as part of a drill, sometimes in earnest, he could move quickly. He had easy access to the steel ladder that led to the precincts above, the action areas in *Lexington*'s large island structure that loomed over the flight deck.

Each officer, indeed, each crewman, had his own battle station. Johnston's station was on the signal bridge—a six-foot-wide "open verandah" twenty-five feet above the flight deck. He liked his spot. It was in prime real estate dubbed Captain's country, so-called because it was the area where Captain Sherman conned the carrier and controlled the flying, landing, and general activities of the ship. This zone was the heart and brain of the Lex. Every compartment in the ship was connected to it by phone lines or voice tubes. Everything that happened on the vessel was reported directly to the captain.[3] Also, putting to use his knowledge of Morse code, he could read the blinkered messages passed between ships. Johnston would know what Sherman knew.

He settled in. "Every time the battle stations call was sounded," he said later, "I dropped my loafing, writing or gossiping, and tramped up to the open deck twenty-five feet above the flight deck from which one could see everything happening on and around the *Lex*."[4] The scene was spectacular. From his perch he could watch the action below on the long, narrow flight deck that stretched away toward the bow and stern, extending a total of 888 feet. *Lexington* had a storied past. Originally designed as a battle cruiser, she was converted into one of the Navy's first aircraft carriers to comply with the terms of the Washington Naval Treaty of 1922, which for a time ended all battleship and battle-cruiser construction. She entered service in 1928 a formidable warship, able to carry close to eighty planes while making speeds up to 33.25 knots (38.26 miles per hour). The Lex could cover more than seven hundred miles in a single day and night.

Five months into the war, *Lexington* had already seen plenty of action. Venturing into waters near the Bismarck Archipelago on 20 February 1942, fifteen Wildcat fighters and Dauntless dive-bombers from the Lex faced seventeen long-range Mitsubishi G4MI "Betty" torpedo bombers, launched in two waves from Japan's base at Rabaul. Five of the nine Bettys in the first wave were shot down before reaching the carrier, and the other four were splashed after making an abortive bombing run. A second wave of nine bombers was thwarted when Wildcat pilot Butch O'Hare, as noted, shot down three and damaged three others. Three weeks later, steaming in the Gulf of Papua in company with *Yorktown*, Lex directed fifty-two planes to fly over the Owen Stanley Mountains on New Guinea to strike Japanese shipping anchored off the villages of Lae and Salamaua, on the northeast coast of New Guinea. While Lex did lose a plane, its aircraft, along with those from *Yorktown*, inflicted on the Imperial Navy its heaviest losses since the outbreak of the war.[5] Two weeks later, on 26 March, the carrier returned to Pearl Harbor for a refit.

~

At dawn on 5 May, Johnston rolled out of his bunk, awakened by the "clang, clang, clang, clang" of the steel hinged flap on the flight deck just over his head. The first squadrons of scout planes were racing down the deck for their takeoffs. But it was not only the rumble of Lex's planes that caused Johnston to rise promptly this morning and make his way to the flight deck: the oiler *Neosho* was making a scheduled visit. By the time he was topside, the smaller ship was already delivering mail and passing oil into the carrier's thirsty tanks. He had mail of his own for *Neosho*, expected to reach Pearl Harbor well ahead of the carrier. Johnston was following orders; he was doing what CINCPAC's censor, Waldo Drake, expected him to do: use whatever means he could to get his copy back to Pearl Harbor for review. "[I] beat out a series of dispatches covering the latest action," Johnston said. "My stories went off with the confidential mail to the Naval censors at Pearl Harbor."[6]

Then, watching *Neosho* break off and steam away, Johnston felt uneasy. As do many war correspondents assigned to cover distant combat, he wondered if he was getting through. "Although mine was a correspondent's paradise, there was a thorn in my garden," Johnston wrote later. "I had to send my stories to the Navy without ever knowing what the censors did to them—whether they were killed, *in toto*, or whether they were going through untouched. In fact, I was never sure they were getting to Pearl Harbor, or to the mainland at all." As the days passed, his sense of isolation deepened. "It was trying to go suddenly to sea and find oneself cutoff completely," he said. "I couldn't even cable, 'Dear Editor, am I still with you?'"[7]

Johnston consoled himself with one extremely pleasant thought: "The good feature of the whole thing was that there was no other correspondent with any of the ships in the fleet [and] therefore I couldn't be scooped." Reassured by this certainty, he relaxed a little. He found new ways to engage himself and stay abreast of the action. He spent a lot of his time in *Lexington*'s air-plot room, where loudspeakers relaying aviation chatter were located. He learned the routines of the airmen aloft when they communicated with each other or with the fighter director—the central radio control of the carrier's airplanes. The various airplane circuits were connected to amplified speakers in the room. "Sitting in comfort I could hear the pilots out on their patrols far over the horizon," Johnston said.[8]

Early in the morning on 7 May, the room's loudspeakers came explosively alive. "Gangster near fleet," blared a radio call about 7:30 from a *Yorktown* scout plane. A few moments later, the pilot augmented his initial report. "It's a Kawanishi snooper," he said, referring to one of the Imperial Navy's huge Kawanishi H6K4 flying boats.[9] Officers in the radio room reasoned that if a U.S. Navy plane had seen this big aircraft—dubbed the "Mavis" by U.S. naval airmen later in the war—it had almost certainly spotted the American fleet.[10] The Japanese plane also had had plenty of time to report the American presence. "Well we're in the soup," one officer commented. "The Japs know we're here and we haven't found them. If they're as good they are supposed to be they'll be taking off right now to give us a pasting."[11]

But the Japanese did not paste either *Lexington* or *Yorktown* this day. Like their American counterparts, IJN attack planes were having trouble locating their targets. Receiving confusing reports from many different scouts, flight directors on board two Japanese fleet carriers now in the Coral Sea, *Zuikaku* and *Shokaku*, ordered seventy-eight warplanes to a position where they thought they would find the American carriers. Instead, they found the oiler *Neosho* and its escort, the destroyer *Sims*. Japanese planes made short work of *Sims*—sinking it almost instantly—and left the *Neosho* a drifting hulk.[12] (It was finally located on 11 May by the U.S. destroyer *Henley*, which took off survivors and then torpedoed her, sending to the bottom all *Lexington*'s confidential mail and, of course, Johnston's precious dispatches.)

America's strike planes fared better, but they, too, were misdirected. The ninety-three aircraft launched by *Lexington* and *Yorktown* actually were led away from their primary objectives, *Zuikaku* and *Shokaku*. Failing to find the two big carriers, they did come across a worthy consolation prize: the light carrier *Shoho*, escorting the Main Body of IJN transport ships moving around the southern tip of New Guinea en route to Port Moresby. American SBD (Scout Bomber Douglas) Dauntless dive-bombers and TBD Devastator torpedo planes pounced on *Shoho*, scoring seven torpedo hits and thirteen bomb hits. *Shoho* turned out to be the first Japanese carrier sunk by U.S. naval aircraft.[13] During his return flight, *Lexington*'s SBD pilot Bob Dixon sent a prearranged message back to his ship, interpreted as *Scratch one flat top!* Dixon's words became one of the iconic phrases of the Pacific War.[14] It evoked cheers in the radio room.

The stories told by Dixon and the other pilots after landing back on Lex gave Commander Seligman and Johnston an idea. Using a Dictaphone that happened to be on board, they decided to make a recording the next day of the fighting around *Lexington*. They rigged a microphone line from the commander's cabin up to the signal bridge (Johnston's battle station) and had about forty feet of loose line there—to enable Johnston to move freely around the bridge and see everything that might happen. If everything went according to plan, Johnston would be able to put on discs a play-by-play account of the action. Seligman and Johnston thought a great deal would happen on 8 May. Both knew the day would be pivotal for the U.S. Navy in the Coral Sea. They knew each of the opposing fleets now had a pretty good idea of the other's location; they doubted that Imperial Navy attack planes would miss the American carriers two days in a row.

∽

Johnston had a hard time getting to sleep that night. "I finally fell asleep at 4 a.m.," he recalled. "So exhausted was I that when the pre-dawn 'battle stations' call came at 5:30 I just rolled over and dug into the pillow again. But the 'clang, clang, clang' of the scouts going off finally roused me. And suddenly I was wide awake. I had just remembered there was a very good reason for getting up this morning—there were Japs around and about us and a battle in the offing." Glancing out the nearest porthole, he saw a beautiful, clear morning with the sun sparkling just over the horizon. His heart sunk. "It was a marvelous day—exactly the kind everyone in the fleet would have gladly done without," Johnston mused later, "for an aircraft carrier . . . is safest when it is running through fog and heavy rain squalls."[15]

Starting out quietly, the day did not remain calm for long. At 8:20 a.m., a *Lexington* scout pilot, Lieutenant (jg) Joseph Smith, radioed a contact report. Having just reached the limit of his 225-mile outbound course and now heading for home, Smith ran into an IJN armada; he sighted two carriers, four heavy cruisers, and three destroyers, steaming some 170 miles northeast of Lex. Twelve minutes later, Lex's radio room intercepted a Japanese transmission giving the U.S. carrier's position, course, and speed.[16] Evidently an Imperial Navy scout plane had observed the American force and escaped unnoticed. "We knew definitely we had been located," Captain Sherman said. He predicted the attack would come in at about 11:00 a.m.[17]

General quarters were sounded. Sherman ordered the ship into "condition Zed," whereby every watertight door and hatch is bolted down. There was a lot of slamming and banging, unavoidable considering the carrier's six hundred separate compartments. But the work had to be done. The idea was to make the ship as close to unsinkable as it could get. Obeying orders from Fitch and *Yorktown*'s Frank Jack Fletcher, in tactical command of the two carrier groups, Sherman held off launching his own attack planes. Task force leaders wanted to make sure their scouts did not turn up Japanese carriers anywhere else. They did not want any nasty surprises. When no other reports came in, they decided it was time: between 9:00 a.m. and 9:20 a.m., Lex put in the air fifteen SBD Dauntless dive-bombers, twelve TBD Devastator torpedo planes, and nine Wildcat fighters. They joined *Yorktown*'s twenty-four SBDs, nine TBDs, and six Wildcats, all heading northeast.[18]

Comforting as it was watching those planes take off, no one expected they would catch the Japanese napping. "I feel that at the present time an air attack group cannot be stopped," Sherman told Johnston on the bridge, while both men stood looking out. "It's likely that the position will be similar to that of two boxers, both swinging a knockout punch at the same time, and both connecting."[19] Sherman's forecast proved correct. At 11:00 a.m., radar reported many enemy aircraft approaching from the north, distance about seventy-five miles. The enemy planes were first sighted visually at 11:13. They were torpedo planes, flying from about six thousand to seven thousand feet. They split into two waves and came in from both bows.[20]

The Japanese planes did not arrive unmolested. Twenty-three SBDs, on anti-torpedo plane patrol, circled on station at two thousand feet and roughly six thousand yards out—a distance that reflected pilots' intention to intercept the enemy planes well before they got near the U.S. task force. In this instance, they were too far out and too low; the Japanese planes roared over them at high speed. Still, the SBDs managed to shoot down three torpedo planes, but five SBDs were lost. Many enemy planes got through and attacked from both sides of Lex. Torpedoes started coming from both starboard and portside; Sherman maneuvered with full rudder both ways. Some torpedoes from starboard crossed ahead; two others ran parallel to the ship, one on each side. Some from port ran ahead; two ran under the carrier without hitting it.[21]

Lex's luck did not hold. At 11:20 a.m., the first torpedo struck the carrier and exploded near the port forward gun gallery. One minute later, another torpedo smashed into *Lexington* from the port side, just opposite the bridge. The situation got more critical when Japanese dive-bombers showed up. They flew in at seventeen thousand feet, eluding, at least for a time, Lex's Wildcats that had been patrolling at ten thousand feet. The Wildcats were not able to attack the bombers before those IJN planes reached the "push-over" point. The bombers made their dive. One bomb estimated at 550 pounds smacked the after end of the port forward gun gallery, in the ammunition locker just outside Admiral's country. Another bomb battered the captain's boat on the port side, and yet another hit the stacks and exploded inside. Several near misses on the port and starboard sides spewed fragments that killed or injured many in machine-gun and signal stations.[22]

At 11:32 a.m., the last Japanese dive-bomber screamed over *Lexington*, raking the ship with machine-gun bullets and dropping a bomb that fell close but did not land on the carrier. Then there was silence. The attack was over. From the moment the first torpedo plane was sighted at 11:13 to the roar of the final dive-bomber, no more than nineteen minutes had passed. For twelve of those minutes, the ship had been turned into a shooting gallery; between 11:20 and 11:32 seven explosions rocked the carrier, two from torpedoes and the remainder from direct bomb hits or near misses. The ship listed six degrees to port. Damage control parties tried to control the list by shifting oil. Fire control parties fought fires, while still other teams pumped water out of compartments that were partially flooded.

The situation could have been worse. Not only was the Lex still afloat, there were signs that damage control teams were getting on top of the problems. The ship's steering gear remained intact; it was making twenty-five knots. The carrier returned to even keel; it soon started to bring in and service attack planes just back from their raids on *Zuikaku* and *Shokaku*. Then, at 12:47 p.m., a mighty explosion staggered the ship. The blast came from amidships well down in the bowels of the vessel. The ship's communication system immediately broke down; all telephones except one line went out. Rudder indicators on the bridge ceased to work. Still, Sherman and his staff managed to jerry-rig the controls sufficiently to let him steer the ship.[23]

Despite the crew's best efforts, Lex's condition worsened. A raging fire broke out from the main deck down to the forward area of the hangar deck.

Fire control teams dragged hoses to the areas that were blazing, but they were not able to do much good. The fires continued to spread, now to the rear of the ship. Minor explosions recurred at frequent intervals, intensifying the fire and trapping many of the crew members in engine rooms and other remote compartments. Commander Seligman was in the middle of it all, heading efforts to rescue stranded seamen and directing the firefighting work below deck. He constantly put himself in harm's way.[24]

"I came across Commander Seligman several times in different parts of the ship with his fire and rescue squads," Johnston wrote later. "Every explosion killed or burned some of his men; others were getting their lungs full of the smoke or blinded by the fumes. As the injured or blinded men were brought up to the flight deck for treatment, other men stepped forward, donned the smoke helmets taken from the casualties, and went below in their places." Seligman continued to go below. He took more chances; everywhere he went the ship got hotter. One explosion occurred just as he was starting through a manhole. One of Seligman's men who had witnessed his narrow escapes said, "The Exec was continually being blown through doors and out of scuttles like a cork out of a champagne bottle."[25]

Johnston, too, was busy that afternoon. He found it impossible to carry out the plan he and Seligman had devised the previous day; dictating into a microphone while bombs were falling and torpedoes hitting proved futile. There was too much noise, too much chaos. He thought he could be of greater use below deck where people were in trouble; he turned out to be of considerable help. His effort didn't go unnoticed. "When it became apparent the *Lexington* was in a bad way, Johnston went below decks for his personal effects," remembered dive-bomber pilot Weldon O. Hamilton. "He came up a little later lugging a badly wounded seaman. He dashed down again. Pretty soon he returned, carrying another injured man. I don't know how many times he repeated the performance. Every time he insisted he was going after his own stuff, and every time he came back with a wounded or burned sailor. He risked his life time and again."[26]

Seligman observed that when Lex was at its moment of greatest peril, Johnston jumped in and did everything he could to aid the wounded, procure life jackets, and make himself useful. As the day wore on, he would do more.[27]

By 4:30 p.m., Sherman saw that the situation was irretrievable. His staff later established that small gasoline leaks from storage tanks, weakened by the heavy pounding the ship had taken from torpedo hits, caused the buildup of gasoline vapors in the lower regions. The vapors were ignited by a spark of unknown origin. The fires that ensued, fed by gasoline and breaking out from ruptured vents, proved difficult to quench. Then the water main broke in the area of the explosion. Long hoses led from distant parts of the ship proved of little use because of very low water pressure. It turned out to be a losing battle.[28]

Over a weakening phone, Sherman ordered personnel in the engine rooms to secure the plant and get up on deck. Firefighting efforts now ceased. The ship came to a stop. Sherman ordered life rafts made ready. He asked the destroyer *Morris* to come alongside and provide assistance. Lex personnel not immediately needed—those not involved in damage control or rescue efforts—made their way down knotted ropes to the deck of the destroyer. Sick and wounded were evacuated by whaleboats to other task force ships standing by. Still, Sherman resisted the idea that Lex's days were over. "It seemed outrageous that we could do nothing to put out the fire and save our ship," he said later.[29]

But they could not. There was only one decision left, and it was made by Admiral Fitch. At 5:07 p.m. Fitch, unperturbed and cool, leaned over the flag bridge and told Sherman he had better "get the boys off the ship." "It was heartbreaking, but it seemed to be the only thing left to do," Sherman said. "Reluctantly I gave the order to abandon ship. It was the hardest thing I have ever done." The men disembarked in an orderly way. Some of the crew, seeing it was not yet their turn to slide down the ropes, went below to the ship's store, which was not in the fire area. They filled their helmets with ice cream and stood around the flight deck eating it. With *Morris* able to handle only so many, ropes were dropped over the side. Men slid down into the water, where they looked for rafts or waited for whaleboats to pick them up.[30]

As his men evacuated the ship, the captain remembered Wags. "Hadn't seen him since before the battle," Sherman later wrote in his diary. "The door from [the] bridge to my emergency cabin was closed. I opened it and dense smoke poured out. I thought well if Wags is in there he is suffocated." Then Ensign R. A. Martin, Lex's assistant navigator, appeared; he had a gas mask and offered to look for the dog. Sherman told him not to but Martin went in anyway, only to return empty-handed, unable to find Wags. "Just then I looked aft past the signal bridge and there was Wags standing on the walkway to the radar, looking scared and shaking. I grabbed him and carried him down to the flight deck." A marine orderly found a life jacket. "Between us we put it on him and lowered him on a rope over the side where a boat picked him up."[31] Sherman and his dog were reunited several days later in the Tonga Islands.

Johnston was among the last off the ship. After taking a final walk around the flight deck, he transferred all his notes to the breast pocket of his shirt, where he hoped they would stay dry. A few officers lingered on deck. Despite the tragedy befalling their ship, they were in a light-hearted, joking mood. So was Johnston. "Johnston asked what he was supposed to do," Lieutenant Commander Hamilton recalled later, smiling. "I told him to cable his editor for instructions."[32] Johnston didn't cable Maloney. Selecting a rope with a big knot at its end, he cautiously lowered himself down hand over hand. He climbed into a raft and then across into a whaleboat already loaded with Lex personnel. The boat towed several filled life rafts to the cruiser *Minneapolis*, standing by to collect survivors. The men disembarked, but Johnston stayed on board the small craft with the coxswain. They started back for another load but this time ignored the rafts; they noticed dozens of men in the water who had been swimming. Many were near exhaustion. With the coxswain handling the engine and rudder, "I began heaving swimmers in the boat," Johnston wrote later. In all, he and the coxswain pulled on board nearly sixty men; then they went back for the rafts.[33]

On board *Lexington*, Fitch and Sherman remained on the bridge, watching silently as the evacuation proceeded. By 6 p.m. they could see only a few stragglers on the deck; they decided it was time to take their leave. They made their way down to the flight deck. Fitch went first, slipping down a rope on the port side. He was almost instantly picked up by a cutter. Sherman made a final inspection. He encountered Seligman, who reported all men were off the ship. They were the last two men on board when a tremendous explosion shook the carrier; they had to duck to avoid falling debris. Sherman ordered Seligman to disembark, which he did. Sherman saw him swimming toward a whaleboat. Then Sherman went down a line hand over hand and dropped into the water, where he was scooped up by a cutter and transported to *Minneapolis*.[34]

Seeing that hundreds of *Lexington* men had made it to *Minneapolis*, Sherman now did a roll call. That took some time. Survivors were scattered among nearly all the ships of Task Force 11. Checkups by signal disclosed an astonishing total of 2,735 survivors. From what Sherman could find out, no one had drowned owing to abandoning ship. All losses were the result of air combat or bomb explosions and fire on the ship. According to Sherman's preliminary count, out of a total complement of 2,951 men, 26 officers and 190 men had lost their lives. In other words, 92 percent of the men had been saved. "This in itself is considered to be a remarkable achievement," Sherman told Nimitz.[35]

Less clear was the success of the American raids on *Shokaku* and *Zuikaku*. Together, *Lexington* and *Yorktown* that morning had unleashed seventy-five attack planes against the two carriers. Sherman initially believed the U.S. planes had sunk *Shokaku* and damaged *Zuikaku*. He was wrong about that. Although America's two task forces had indeed achieved a victory, it was not as decisive as Sherman thought. *Shokaku* survived the mauling administered by U.S. planes. It was, however, severely crippled and headed slowly for home; *Zuikaku*, which had found haven in a rain squall during the attack, remained behind for a couple of days with the rest of the IJN striking force. (It rejoined *Shokaku* later in Japan.)

The Imperial Navy, of course, described the Battle of the Coral Sea, as the engagement came to be known, as a Japanese triumph. In a narrow tactical sense the Japanese may have come out ahead. Against the loss of a light carrier, IJN planes had destroyed the oiler *Neosho*; the destroyer *Sims*; the big carrier *Lexington*; and as it thought at the time, put out of action *Yorktown*. The carrier that morning had been jolted by a 550-pound bomb hit, but *Yorktown*'s crews quickly doused the flames and the ship righted itself. It headed eastward for the Navy's base at Tongatabu in the nearby Tonga Islands.

Despite their greater losses in tonnage, U.S. naval forces scored a major strategic victory in the Coral Sea campaign. It was the first decisive naval battle in history in which surface ships did not exchange a shot; it was fought entirely by aircraft. As a result of this fight, the Japanese abandoned their drive to seize Port Moresby—the first time, Sherman noted, that "a modern Japanese Navy had been defeated." Also, while the U.S. Navy lost 81 aircraft and many pilots, the Japanese lost 105 planes, with an additional 90 heavily damaged, plus a sizable portion of its elite flying corps. Sherman called Coral Sea "a milestone in history."[36]

∾

One hour after all Lex survivors had been safely evacuated, the carrier contin- ued to blaze and remain afloat. "The picture of the burning and doomed ship was a magnificent but sad sight," Sherman said. But with evening coming on and the carrier turning into a torch, Sherman and other officers worried it could serve as a beacon for Japanese snoopers. Fitch ordered the destroyer *Phelps* to sink *Lexington* by torpedoes. The tin can fired five torpedoes, three of which hit. Those blows had their intended effect. The carrier did not go quietly. As *Lexington* disappeared under the waves, a tremendous explosion erupted in the bowels of the vessel that rocked ships for miles around.[37] But she did not turn over; she went down with her head up. "Dear old *Lex*," an officer whispered. "A lady to the last."[38]

On board *Minneapolis*, the carrier's survivors were received like conquer- ing heroes. They were shepherded to bountiful mess tables and soon were relaxing as guests of the cruiser's officers and men. Johnston was treated like one of the crew. He was fortunate in another respect. While waiting for a dry change of clothing, he fished out of his pockets sheaves of loose-leaf notes and his little black notebook. By drying them in the laundry's steam presser, he saved every one, discovering to his surprise that his hen pecks were still legible. He would have material, after all, for the *Tribune*'s news pages: he would be the first reporter to tell the full story of the Coral Sea engagement.[39]

Now an integral part of *Yorktown*'s Task Force 17, the remaining ships of *Lexington*'s old task force (once Task Force 11) started to move. On 11 May, the ships split up. *Yorktown*, steaming slowly and trailing an oil slick, headed toward Tongatabu.[40] *Minneapolis*, joined by the cruisers *New Orleans* and *Astoria*, each carrying a sizable load of *Lexington* survivors, proceeded to Noumea, New Caledonia, the southernmost island bordering the Coral Sea. Thanks to an agreement with the Free French, who had ousted the previ- ous Vichy-oriented regime and now controlled the island, the United States had an excellent base there. Reached quickly and easily on 12 May, Noumea afforded the battered and bruised men of *Lexington* a place to catch their breath and even relax for a day.

Johnston had business of his own—a meeting with Navy censors. During the three-day trek to Noumea, he banged out his first stories on the Coral Sea battle. He turned them in to the censorship office in *Minneapolis*, which was soon to return to Pearl Harbor. The ship's designated censors (officers representing the cruiser's captain) assured Johnston they would deliver his articles to Waldo Drake.[41] Making the most of his friendship with the CINCPAC censor, Johnston attached to his articles a jolly little note:

> Dear Waldo: Please see if you can get this stuff censored and have commercial cables send it as fast as you can arrange to have the news cleared. What a pal you turned out to be—wait till I get back to Honolulu—hope to see you inside next ten-twelve days if the luck holds.[42]

Johnston did not yet know it, but he was not going back to Honolulu. The 750 Lexmen on *Minneapolis*—a group that included Fitch, Sherman, Seligman, and Johnston—were going someplace else. Shortly after arriving in Noumea, they transferred to *Astoria* for the second stage of their exodus. They were joined by 780 Lex survivors who had been on board *New Orleans* and the destroyers *Dewey* and *Phelps*. Carrying, in all, more than 1,500 of *Lexington*'s officers and men, *Astoria* departed Noumea on 13 May for Tongatabu Island, 1,080 miles due east.[43] Two days later, the cruiser pulled into the lush, tropical harbor at Nukualofa, the capital of the Polynesian kingdom of Tonga.[44] It arrived shortly after *Yorktown* and its escort vessels had made port, bringing with them hundreds of additional *Lexington* survivors. Happy to be on dry land, many of Lex's refugees headed for town—"a tiny, hot and dry little place," as Johnston described it.[45] They took full advantage of a four-day layover; Johnston found a Dutch sea captain who treated him to a bountiful dinner.

But for Lex's senior officers—Fitch, Sherman, and Seligman—Tongatabu was not so much a respite as an opportunity to catch up on work. They had reports to write. They had to tell Nimitz, and through Nimitz, King, what had happened to *Lexington* on the 7–8 May. They also had a somewhat more pleasant task: deciding which of the officers and men on board the carrier during those fateful days demonstrated extraordinary valor, thereby entitling them to special recognition, meaning a decoration or a citation of some kind.

The three leaders singled out a number of officers and men for awards. One of those selected, ironically, was not a member of Lex's crew, or even in the Navy: they agreed that Johnston had earned a citation. Fitch and Sherman prepared a recommendation stating just that and routed it through Fletcher to Nimitz at Pearl Harbor; Nimitz quickly endorsed it when he got it and forwarded it to King. COMINCH would find it sitting on his desk in

Washington in a couple of weeks. The Fitch-Sherman proposal has not survived, but in all likelihood the document used wording similar to that found in Seligman's 14 May report to Sherman:

> Mr. Stanley Johnston, representative of the Chicago Tribune, behaved with conspicuous courage throughout the action and during the subsequent trying period. He rescued at least one seriously burned and blinded man from a smoke and flame filled compartment. He was observed everywhere lending aid to the wounded, procuring life jackets, chatting cheerfully with the men on deck and otherwise assisting with great efficiency. He was among the last to leave the ship.[46]

King, of course, would have the final say in the matter. But that decision was weeks away. In the meantime, Johnston and his *Lexington* colleagues had more pressing matters to think about: they were going home.

CHAPTER 3

A ROOM WITH A VIEW

I saw a lineup of Jap ships versus American ships.
—*Edward J. O'Donnell*

Johnston was among *Lexington*'s 2,700 survivors reshuffled to different vessels at Tongatabu. The six warships that had brought them to the island were needed elsewhere. *Astoria* turned around and headed back to Pearl Harbor. *Minneapolis, New Orleans,* and most other ships engaged in the Coral Sea rescue effort had already gone back. The banged up *Yorktown* would linger a few days in port then follow them. Only two transports and a cruiser remained behind to take Lex's personnel home. Johnston, Seligman, and more than a thousand others were assigned to an aging transport ship acquired from the British in 1940; it was called *Barnett*.

The usually prompt Seligman was among the last to clamber on board. Most of his shipmates had arrived early to get the best lodging they could on what was sure to be a crowded ship. But Seligman did not have to worry about quarters. Fitch arranged to return to the U.S. mainland on the cruiser *Chester,* making it his flagship; Sherman joined him on board *Chester* as his chief of staff. Seligman thus became *Barnett*'s highest-ranking guest—a status that earned him the most desirable space available, a suite of rooms in what the ship called "commodore's quarters." Normally reserved for a task group commander, the suite consisted of a bedroom and an adjoining pantry (Seligman's private space), a separate dining room with a large table, and a second bedroom big enough to hold two bunks. Seligman could bring in two guests. He reserved one bunk for Commander Winthrop C. Terry, Lex's communications officer who had contracted a severe case of hives; he would spend almost the entire trip bedridden and heavily sedated. Seligman reserved the other for his friend Stanley Johnston.[1]

Another unusual courtesy Seligman accorded the correspondent played out in the ship's wardroom. As the senior officer among Lex's emigres,

Seligman followed Navy custom in being seated at the head of the table. Navy custom also prescribed that the second highest ranking officer be seated on his left. Seligman did not follow that rule. He asked *Barnett*'s billeting officer, Ensign O. T. Olson, to place Johnston to his left, instead of an officer. There Johnston remained during *Barnett*'s mess events throughout the voyage.[2]

Early in the afternoon of 19 May, four days after reaching the Tonga Islands, *Barnett* exited Nukualofa's fine harbor. In addition to its own complement of 490 officers and men, it carried 1,251 *Lexington* survivors, most of whom had jammed their way into every open space they could find. *Barnett* sailed with two other laden vessels—*George F. Elliott*, a transport ship packed with 1,032 Lexmen, and the fast cruiser *Chester*, billeting seventy from the carrier, Fitch and Sherman among them.[3] With *Chester* leading the way, the ships ventured into the Pacific and headed north. They were joined briefly by *Yorktown* and its escorts, now steaming back to Pearl Harbor. The small caravan proceeded on its northerly course. But on 21 May, Fitch's three-ship flotilla peeled off sharply to starboard and headed east. Next stop: San Diego.[4]

On board the banged-up *Yorktown*, Frank Jack Fletcher had not planned on returning to Pearl Harbor so quickly. He had arrived in the Tonga Islands thinking he was on the last lap of a voyage that would end at the Bremerton, Washington, shipyard, where he hoped his badly damaged carrier would get the extensive overhaul he believed it needed. Fletcher learned otherwise on 18 May, when he received orders from Nimitz to return to Pearl Harbor fast. He picked up a whiff of impending action somewhere in the central Pacific. How sailors learned these things would always be a mystery, but there were rumors the IJN might be moving against Midway Atoll.[5]

Whatever the Japanese were up to, *Lexington*'s survivors would not be part of any action that resulted. They were going in the opposite direction, riding slow-moving vessels that would need more than two weeks to traverse a 5,300-mile route. There was nothing anybody could do. *Barnett* could not make much more than thirteen knots, requiring *Elliott* and *Chester* to adjust their speeds accordingly. To Lex's action-oriented men the cruise seemed interminable. They were restless. They were curious about the rumors they had heard. They wanted news. Seligman thought they should work. He volunteered their services to *Barnett*'s skipper, Captain William B. Phillips. "We offered to assist the ship in any way we could en route," Seligman said later. "We had officers standing gun watches, and an officer below deck on watch."[6]

Seligman also presented Phillips with a request: he wanted to read—and he wanted his top officers to read—all radio traffic generated by Pacific Fleet headquarters at Pearl Harbor, even if it was not intended for *Barnett*. The captain did not immediately agree. It was not his practice, he said, to decode messages not addressed to his ship; moreover, he lacked the communications personnel required to handle such a large volume of traffic. Seligman persisted. He pointed out, rightly or wrongly, that it was the custom on all Navy ships to decode all messages for which the ship is equipped with a code. Also, with the war in the Pacific heating up, he believed that it was vital that he and his department heads keep up with operations in the Pacific. Then he threw in the kicker; he would provide five *Lexington* communications officers to receive and decrypt the additional traffic: Lieutenant F. C. Brewer, communications watch officer; and four ensigns, James B. Johnson, George Y. McKinnon, Robert E. Hebbler, and E. H. Railsback, all decoding watch officers. Brewer would head the team.[7]

Phillips could hardly say no. But he stipulated that message handling by Lex personnel follow *Barnett*'s procedures, and that all the work be done under his oversight. He would have veto power over circulation of messages. He forbade Seligman, or his staff, to make pencil duplicates of "secret" messages routed to them. Seligman welcomed the arrangement. As always, two copies would be made of every incoming message received by *Barnett*'s radiomen; there would be a "raw" file copy that would go instantly into the ship's safe and a "working" copy that would be handed to the decoding watch officer. Once the message was decrypted and typed, it would be put in a folder and passed to *Barnett*'s communications officer, Lieutenant (jg) Daniel Bontecou. Bontecou would deliver it to Phillips for review; the captain would initial it and return it to Bontecou. If Phillips had no objection, the message folder would be delivered to Lex's Lieutenant Brewer for circulation to Seligman and his department heads: Commander Herbert S. "Ducky" Duckworth, air officer; Commander A. F. Junker, chief engineer; Lieutenant Commander Edward J. O'Donnell, gunnery officer; and Lieutenant Commander Terry, who was laid up and actually in no condition to read anything. With Brewer standing by, officers would read and initial each message, then return it to its folder. No message would be permitted to be left behind. Brewer would then return the folder to Bontecou, whose orders were to destroy the messages as soon after their return as possible. Only the "raw" file copy would remain intact.[8]

Not every message was circulated. Early one morning, around 22 May, Phillips called Seligman and Duckworth to his quarters to discuss what seemed to him to be a highly sensitive message. Since *Barnett* sailed on 19 May, Phillips had tried to keep his visitors at arm's length. But now he wanted a second opinion about a dispatch he suspected should not have been decoded, let alone typed and prepared for distribution. Originating at Pacific Fleet headquarters, the message concerned Nimitz's order to deploy a new task force—Task Force 8—to waters near the Aleutian Islands, presumably to counter a Japanese armada bearing down on those islands. As Phillips remembered the message, it contained details about the composition of Task Force 8. Phillips wondered if circulation of this information would not be a breach of security. Seligman and Duckworth seemed not to have an opinion, but Phillips acted anyway. "I destroyed the message myself," Phillips said later. "And I considered it wrong for it to be deciphered."[9]

Somehow word of the message got around, exciting officers' curiosity and heightening awareness of the drama unfolding in the central Pacific.

~

Johnston had plenty to do. Working at a small table in his alcove, punching keys on an old typewriter he had dug up, he polished his Coral Sea copy for the *Tribune*. At Seligman's suggestion, he put together a battle history of *Lexington* from Pearl Harbor through the Coral Sea campaign. The project turned out to be controversial because Johnston was granted access to classified information to complete the brief narrative, which touched on Lex's role in combat near Rabaul, Lae, and Salamaua as well as in the Coral Sea. Believing a chronicle of the carrier's deeds would boost morale, Seligman distributed copies to *Lexington* crew members. He did so with the proviso that Lexmen return their copies before leaving the ship. Most did. But one seaman did not; his copy was found in a San Diego taxi, causing Seligman some embarrassment later.[10]

As he did on board *Lexington*, Johnston enjoyed the run of this ship. With two exceptions, he could go just about anywhere he wanted to go; the exceptions were the code and radio rooms. They were off limits to Johnston and, for that matter, most others. Still, he was allowed remarkable freedom of movement. One place he visited was the chart room. For maps of the Coral Sea needed for his various projects, he dropped in on that cabin around 22 May and there met Lieutenant Bontecou. Johnston now encountered Navy resistance for very nearly the first time since boarding *Lexington* on 15 April. Bontecou took a dislike to the correspondent; for some instinctive reason, he doubted that Johnston could be trusted, a concern he confided to Captain Phillips. The captain told Bontecou to keep an eye on the newcomer. He did. "Johnston just struck me as a man who talked a lot," Bontecou said.[11]

Bontecou gave Johnston the Coral Sea maps he requested, but he did not feel good about it. He wondered how far he should go providing material to the newspaperman. He consulted Seligman for advice and was astonished by what he heard. Seligman said it was okay to show Johnston some restricted information, because authority to do so had come from higher up. Or so Bontecou recalled the conversation. Bontecou quoted Seligman telling him, "On *Lexington*, we were authorized to show Johnston secret and confidential messages and letters. If Johnston talks too much when he goes ashore, he will be blackballed by his newspapers."[12]

Seligman denied telling Bontecou any such thing. "The conversation to which Bontecou refers is entirely a misunderstanding," he told Navy investigators later. Lex's radiomen, he protested, did not take their orders from him, but from Admiral Fitch. "Bontecou completely misunderstood me as to saying I had any such authority," Seligman insisted. "Even if I had said so, it would have been ridiculous."[13] Bontecou, however, had a witness: Ensign W. D. Stroud, also a *Barnett* communications officer. Stroud was standing by, listening in during the exchange. He told an FBI interviewer that Seligman declared that Johnston could be trusted and could see secret or confidential material. If Johnston did not keep these matters to himself, "it would ruin his career as a correspondent," Stroud quoted Seligman telling Bontecou.[14]

Whatever Seligman did or did not say during this conversation, Bontecou's version of it blemished the commander's reputation. Reports of this and other FBI interviews were circulated among Navy chieftains in Washington. They gained an impression of lowered standards, even of laxity, on *Barnett*. The picture omitted some extenuating circumstances. Bontecou and his Lex counterpart, Lieutenant Brewer, did their best to control the highly restricted radio traffic that streamed daily into the transport, but this was not always easy on board a ship teeming with restless, unemployed officers who wanted to get the latest information and hash things over.

The nerve center for information was Seligman's cabin. It was always open. It served as a combination neighborhood hangout, local watering hole, and general-purpose gathering place. Of the things that brought them in, few were more important than coffee. Anyone could always get a cup of coffee in Seligman's den. "The room was used during the day as a sort of little corner for [officers] to come and get coffee out of hours," Johnston said. "There was nothing served on the ship [except] in meal hours, but they did arrange to serve coffee in this room." Beginning around 10 in the morning, he recalled, officers would start dropping in and out of Seligman's suite and continue doing so until around 11 at night. "It was usually crowded."[15]

Hungry for all the news they could get, officers followed with particular interest the comings and goings of Lieutenant Brewer, Seligman's designated courier. He might appear in the exec's suite anytime during the day, depending on the flow of radio traffic and the moods of Captain Phillips, who might take his sweet time before initialing a dispatch. Once Phillips signed off on a decrypted message, or a batch of them, they would be put in a folder and handed to Brewer, who would then make his rounds. Proceeding by rank, in descending order of importance, Brewer always headed first to "commodore's quarters." There he found Seligman sitting at the big table, surrounded by coffee drinkers. Seligman was not always in the best of spirits; he still suffered from wounds sustained during the *Lexington* rescue effort. He would undergo several back operations upon his return to the U.S. mainland. But he was usually there.

Not all of Seligman's visitors came to gossip or even drink coffee. Some came to work. They joined Seligman on a project assigned by Sherman: develop a chart of the Coral Sea showing the movements of *Lexington* during its final days, then depict the location of the various torpedo and bomb hits sustained by the carrier. Papers were often strewn all over the table. Arriving in the middle of a working session, Brewer would hand his folder to Seligman, stand nearby and watch, always careful to keep the folder within eyesight. Typically Seligman would read the message, or messages, initial them, and hand them back. Sometimes he would do more. If a lot of people were in the room, he might read aloud part or all of a message. If a message struck him as especially important, he might make notes about it on a piece of scratch paper, or so said some observers.[16] He might even pass the folder to another officer at the table, if he thought that officer had some responsibility or specialized knowledge that justified him seeing it.[17] These departures from standard procedure violated Phillips's security rules, but in the context of *Barnett* they seemed warranted, at least to Seligman and other officers present.

Once Seligman relinquished the folder, Brewer would move on, after dropping by Terry's bunk. If the officer was alert, Brewer would tell him what was in the folder, then initial the messages on his behalf. This done he would continue his rounds. Upon tracking down Seligman's department heads, Brewer returned the folder—with all messages initialed by readers—to Lieutenant Bontecou, who would temporarily place it in the ship's safe. Bontecou in a day or two would remove the messages from their folder and destroy them.

Back in Seligman's quarters, Brewer's bulletins touched off lively discussions; increasingly they were about the action looming in the Pacific. Johnston was usually nearby; even in his alcove he could easily hear every word of what officers had to say. "This newspaperman was nearly always in there," Brewer reported.[18] Although Johnston had gained the confidence of *Lexington*'s executive officer, as well as that of Fitch and Sherman, some officers now started to have doubts about the correspondent. They wondered about the propriety of Johnston's close proximity to these "secret" and highly confidential messages. SBD pilot Robert Dixon noticed that when Brewer showed up with his latest traffic from the radio room, officers would close the folder when Johnston approached.[19]

Two *Lexington* officers—Ensign Johnson and Ensign McKinnon—were especially alarmed by Johnston's presence. They complained about the correspondent to their immediate superior, Lieutenant Irving E. Davis, serving as Lex's chief communications officer during Terry's illness. About a week into *Barnett*'s voyage, they took Davis out on the deck where they could not be overheard. What troubled them, they told Davis, was that Seligman had read a "secret message" aloud while Johnston stood by within easy earshot. As *Lexington* decoding officers assigned to *Barnett*'s radio room, they knew full well the sensitivity of CINCPAC traffic pouring into the transport. They worried that because of Johnston's presence, this information might get out, a slippage they feared could have dire consequences for fleet security and, for that matter, their own careers. They thought they might be held responsible, and they asked Davis for advice on what action should be taken. "I told them," Davis said later, "that no action could be taken by us inasmuch as the senior officer, and presently the commanding officer of the *Lexington* personnel on the *Barnett*, saw fit to read this message to others." Davis added, however, that in the event anything came of this incident, he would back up the two ensigns, and he did do that.[20]

If Johnston now seemed a security threat to some, he became a nuisance to others. Lex's chief engineer, Commander Junker, was annoyed when Johnston requested that he be allowed to see one of Junker's reports on the Coral

Sea engagement before it was handed in to Seligman. Junker told Johnston he would have to get Seligman's permission first.[21] Johnston let the matter drop. Even Seligman got impatient with Johnston when the correspondent looked over his shoulder and started copying the executive officer's diagram showing where the Japanese torpedoes had hit the carrier. He forbade Johnston from copying this document.[22] Of course, Johnston was doing what any good reporter would do; he was pursuing his story, getting critical facts from the most knowledgeable people available: officers on the scene. Irritating as it was, reportorial snooping could be construed as standard journalistic practice—annoying but simply what reporters do.

But other aspects of Johnston's conduct aroused concern. His penchant for storytelling was starting to wear thin. Some officers now rolled their eyes when the correspondent launched into one of his tales. He had told a good many over the weeks. Some proved true; he had, after all, lived an adventurous life: He had indeed searched for gold in New Guinea, he had definitely sold hair curlers in Germany, and he had demonstrably covered the blitz from Dover for the *Chicago Tribune*. But many of his yarns strained credulity. He told one officer he was on board a British ship that was sunk during the German attack on Crete (Johnston was in London seeking a job with the *Chicago Tribune* bureau during that military debacle); he told another that he had been present during at least part of the Libyan campaign (that engagement lasted from 1940 through 1943 but no evidence surfaced that Johnston had covered the war from North Africa).[23]

Johnston seemed to have been everywhere. Lex gunnery officer Edward J. O'Donnell remembered doubting Johnston early on. "From questioning him about the Gallipoli campaign I gathered he was familiar with it," O'Donnell said. "[But] I was a little bit suspicious of it and voiced my suspicions about him." For this officer the last straw was Johnston's hair-raising tale about the time he outwitted Prime Minister Winston Churchill in obtaining some highly confidential information. Johnston had gone too far. So when he asked O'Donnell about a secret new projectile the Navy was using on *Lexington*, the officer clammed up. He refused to tell Johnston anything. From these and other encounters, O'Donnell judged that the reporter was "not very scrupulous" and was interested first in the *Chicago Tribune*, with all other considerations being second. "I feel that Johnston used his contacts and friendships with the officer personnel to further his newspaper career," O'Donnell told FBI investigators later.[24]

Johnston's credibility clearly had ebbed. From the hero who had helped rescue several dozen Lex swimmers from the Coral Sea two weeks earlier, he had turned into a source of anxiety for many on *Barnett*. Officers who had previously enjoyed his company became more guarded. Johnston seemed unfazed by the skepticism, if he even noticed it. He remained amiable and chatty, telling stories and jumping into naval discussions with officers when the opportunity arose. He also retained the confidence and goodwill of Commander Seligman. And he remained in commodore's quarters for the few days that remained before *Barnett* reached San Diego. A reporter could not have asked to be in a better place.

∾

Back at Pearl Harbor, installed in the dank, windowless basement of the Navy Administration Building, some two dozen cryptanalysts and Japanese-speaking language officers struggled to read Imperial Navy messages. They had started making headway against that fleet's main operational code in late February. Then, in April, under the leadership of their quirky but brilliant boss, Commander Joe Rochefort, they scored a breakthrough. Rochefort's team, the legendary Station Hypo, had pinpointed the timetable and movements of the Japanese armada heading into the Coral Sea en route to Port Moresby. The result was the 7–8 May Coral Sea campaign in which the *Lexington* and *Yorktown* task forces played decisive roles, and by so doing blocked the Imperial Navy's advance, albeit at the expense of *Lexington*.

Five days after that engagement, on 13 May, Hypo's codebreakers decrypted another critical dispatch; this one purported to show a massive IJN force gearing up to seize and occupy Midway Atoll, situated some 1,200 miles northwest of Pearl Harbor. Subsequent decrypts showed multiple fleet units bearing down on Midway, spearheaded by a striking force composed of carriers, battleships, and cruisers. Hypo also projected that a second Japanese force would operate against the Aleutian Islands. Though Army and Navy brass in Washington initially rejected Hypo's estimates, Admiral Nimitz believed them. After overcoming the resistance of his Washington superiors, Nimitz deployed to waters near Midway a counterforce consisting of three carriers—among them a rapidly patched-up *Yorktown*—to intercept the IJN striking force. Nimitz also put into play a much smaller force—Task Force 8—to check the IJN thrust in the Aleutians. Hypo forecast that Japanese carrier-borne planes would strike their first blows against Midway and the Aleutians on 3–4 June.

As the day of battle approached, Nimitz thought all Pacific Fleet warships should be alerted to the impending action. On 31 May he circulated a dispatch, based on Hypo's decrypts, describing the composition of Imperial Navy forces arrayed against Midway. Not being, strictly speaking, a task force warship, *Barnett* was not among vessels addressed by Nimitz, but the transport picked up the message anyway: it was message 311221.[25]

CINCPAC's dispatch arrived at 3:52 in the afternoon, classified secret. The classification did not deter *Barnett*'s radioman, Seaman First Class George Zinser; many messages received by the transport's radiomen since 19 May had been stamped secret. Zinser copied this one; he had it typed by a machine onto paper tape. As always, it was encrypted in the Pacific Fleet's distinct code. The tape in hand, Zinser took it next door to the code room. One of *Lexington*'s decoding watch officers, George McKinnon, started working on it. Decrypting the message would not have taken long, probably less than an hour. It was then typed anew, put in readable form, and inserted in a folder along with several other recently decrypted messages. At this point the protocol established by Captain Phillips for routing CINCPAC's secret messages broke down.[26]

Under Phillips's rules, the completed message should have gone first to *Barnett*'s communications officer, Lieutenant Bontecou, who then would have taken it to the captain.[27] If Phillips had followed his usual practice, he would have reviewed the dispatch and then decided whether it was okay to circulate. His approval would not have been automatic. Just a few days earlier, he had burned a similar CINCPAC message announcing the deployment of Task Force 8. Whether this very cautious officer would have cleared for distribution an even more detailed message describing the strength and disposition of the massive Japanese force approaching Midway can be doubted. But Phillips did not see Message 311221, at least not on 31 May. For reasons that were never clear, it was not brought to him until 10 a.m. the next day.[28] Instead of being passed initially to Bontecou, the message folder was handed directly to Lex's Lieutenant Brewer. Brewer started out on his rounds; he headed first to commodore's quarters.[29]

When Brewer reached Seligman's cabin, it was late in the afternoon, nearing the dinner hour. Lex's executive officer was sitting at his big table, hunched over a large sheet of thin tracing paper copying the carrier's route during the Coral Sea campaign. He was busy. A number of officers were in the room; some, with questions, were trying to get his attention. Others milled about. Seligman was not in the best of moods; he only dimly remembered Brewer's visit. "We were all very much in a state of a mental turmoil," he told Navy investigators later. "We were loaded with a terrific amount of work that we wanted to get accomplished before we arrived in San Diego. Some of us were not particularly well." Seligman counted himself among those who were not well: "I was in sort of a state of confusion and thousands of people a day asking me questions about this and that and the other things and I wouldn't be able to remember a conversation to save my life."[30]

Preoccupied as he was, Seligman accepted Brewer's folder. What he said after taking his first look at Message 311221 was never recorded, but he could have been amazed at what he saw. He probably had never seen a decrypt quite like this one; few people had. The decrypt was not perfect; CINCPAC's message contained garbles, either because of errors in transmission or due to miscues in the decrypting. As a result, the names of some IJN ships in the *Barnett* decrypt did not exactly match those in Nimitz's original (see Appendix c for Nimitz's original and Appendix D for *Barnett*'s decrypted version). But the essential information was there.

As itemized in the CINCPAC dispatch, the IJN had put to sea not one fleet but three. In the vanguard was a striking force consisting of four fleet carriers (*Akagi, Kaga, Hiryu* and *Soryu*), two *Kirishima*-type battleships or battle cruisers (the decrypt was not clear which), two *Tone*-class cruisers, and twelve destroyers. Linked to this lead group but cruising separately was another muscular assemblage, a support force, or invasion force, spearheaded by two light carriers, two *Kirishima* warships, four *Mogami* cruisers, an *Atago*-class cruiser, and ten destroyers. Steaming in concert with this conglomerate was an occupation force; it was made up of four cruisers, two to four transports, four to six troopships, eight to twelve supply vessels, twelve destroyers, and sixteen submarines.

Seligman probably stared at the message a while, just to make sure his eyes had not deceived him. He may not have remembered what happened next but others did: he read parts of the dispatch aloud.[31] He did more: he took notes off this dispatch.[32] Responsible for the security of the message file, Brewer might have been uncomfortable with this, but he had seen Seligman share messages and make notations before. He had gotten used to it; he did not know how detailed Seligman's scrawls might have been this time. He did not say anything; he stood near the door out of the way.[33] When Selig-man relinquished the folder, Brewer continued his rounds. On the other side of the ship, in a stateroom occupied by six officers, he found Commander Junker and Lieutenant Commander O'Donnell. They read the dispatch and initialed it. Then Brewer tracked down Commander Duckworth in the ward-room. He also initialed the document. Brewer returned to the radio room, where the folder was placed in the ship's safe.[34] Then he headed back to the wardroom where officers were assembling. It was the dinner hour.

⁓

By early evening Seligman's suite was filling up. O'Donnell showed up late, around 9 p.m. He and one of his five roommates, Lieutenant Commander Edward H. Eldredge, had been playing bridge. But they were curious about Message 311221; they ended their game and headed over to Seligman's place for a cup of coffee. When they arrived, three or four officers were already sitting around the big table with Seligman. Eldredge noticed that on the table in front of them was a handwritten outline—it itemized, in paragraph form, the composition of the various IJN Navy forces. The memorandum was writ-ten in pencil on a blue-lined piece of scratch paper about 4 by 8½ inches; Eldredge did not recognize the handwriting.[35] O'Donnell saw the same out-line; it was handed to him by dive-bomber pilot Bob Dixon, sitting at the far end of table. O'Donnell glanced at the paper and found it familiar; it was the same document Brewer had brought to his quarters earlier and which he had initialed. The scratch paper listed the names of twelve Japanese ships divided into three groups: a striking force, a support force, and an occupation force.[36] He was looking at a duplicate of what seemed to be Message 311221.

Dixon had arrived early. He started off the evening squeezed in at the far end of Seligman's big table, listening to the discussion about Midway. Unlike O'Donnell, Dixon was not a department head; he was not authorized to see CINCPAC's classified decrypts. But he had regularly seen them during *Bar-nett*'s voyage. He was handed what appeared to be one now; it was actually a piece of scratch paper. When he looked at it more closely, he saw a list of many Japanese warships, all carefully organized into three groups: a strik-ing force of carriers and cruisers, a supporting force with battleships, and a follow-up force with transports. He thought the list was not just interesting, but potentially of staggering importance. He thought O'Donnell, as Lex's gunnery officer, should see it and, as noted, passed it to him.

Dixon did not feel good about the scene in Seligman's suite. He felt uneasy seeing a document of such obvious gravity being circulated from hand to hand so casually. He looked about. He made a point of locating Johnston. He did indeed see the correspondent, walking around the room, chatting with officers. He did not, however, see Johnston at the table, nor did he see him at any time perusing Seligman's valuable piece of paper.[37] That was the story Dixon would tell an FBI investigator in just a few weeks. In truth, he may have seen more. Forty years later, an article would appear in a widely circulated naval magazine under the byline of a close Dixon friend; the writer would report that Dixon had seen a great deal more.[38]

Nobody knew what Dixon had or had not seen that evening. The officers in commodore's quarters had questions of their own. They were puzzled about things. They did not know the meaning of certain terms or the types of all the Imperial Navy warships named in the CINCPAC dispatch. In particular, they did not know what to make of *Kirishima*: was it a battleship or a battle cruiser? A *Barnett* officer happened to be in the room, Lieutenant Commander B. M. Coleman. Did *Barnett* happen to have a "silhouette book"? That was the generic name given the Navy's version of *Jane's Fighting Ships*, the standard volume used to identify ship types of all navies. *Barnett* did have such a book. Coleman fetched a copy from the ship's chart room.[39] The silhouette book was restricted but that did not seem to matter; it was passed around to everyone, including Johnston. The book did settle the argument: *Kirishima* was a battleship. O'Donnell shuddered. He remembered thinking that stopping that Japanese force would be a formidable task for whichever U.S. ships were assigned the job. He must have said that out loud because Johnston came over and said to him, using his nickname, "It will be some fight, Mac."[40]

Eventually the discussion ended, the group broke up. Dixon, O'Donnell, Eldredge, and others present lost track of Seligman's well-thumbed scratch paper. They would tell FBI and Navy investigators they had no idea what happened to it.[41] That piece of paper simply vanished.

$\sim$

On 2 June, two days after Lex's officers had hashed over Message 311221 in Seligman's suite, *Barnett* sighted San Diego. Following *Chester* and *Elliott*, the transport made its way into San Diego's spacious harbor. It was around 8 p.m. Because of the late hour, Johnston did not expect *Lexington* personnel would be allowed to go ashore until next morning. He had commodore's quarters to himself. The ailing Terry had been helped out early. Seligman was away on ship's business. Johnston decided to do a little more work on his *Tribune* articles. Using the typewriter in his alcove, shuffling his notes around, he noticed on his desk a blue-lined piece of paper on which someone had written the names of Japanese warships; they were listed under three headings: "striking force," "occupation force," "support force." Johnston copied the names off the list onto another piece of paper.[42]

About that time one of Lex's Marine orderlies came by the suite to inform Johnston that Commander Seligman wanted him to pack quickly, depart the ship, and report to him on the pier. Johnston threw together his few possessions, carefully putting the newly copied list of Japanese ships in his pocket and leaving behind the original scrap of paper.[43] Making his way down the ship's gangway, Johnston spotted Seligman and, not far away, Lieutenant Bontecou, his old nemesis. Bontecou was standing by, keeping his promise to Captain Phillips that he would personally walk the correspondent to the customs office, strictly as a preventive measure, apparently to make sure Johnston did not get away with anything.[44]

Johnston did not have much to declare; the "raw" newspaper copy in his possession seemed innocuous. A folded piece of paper in his pocket did not attract attention. Johnston got through customs and met Seligman. The two had a final talk; it was about censorship. Seligman pointed out the steps Johnston needed to take to get his Coral Sea copy cleared. First, he should contact Lieutenant Harold P. Requa, assistant public relations officer, Eleventh Naval District, San Diego. Late as it was, Johnston called Requa, explaining that he had many pages of roughed-out newspaper articles that needed to reach Washington right away. Requa proposed he bring his material by district headquarters at 10 a.m., 3 June.[45] That sounded good to Johnston.

Requa was impressed with Johnston's attitude: he thought the reporter's desire to get his copy to Washington through proper channels indicated that he knew he could publish nothing without the Navy Department's approval.[46] Johnston, too, was pleased. He had a system in place for moving his work closer to publication. He was also delighted that the Navy had made reservations for him (and for officers as well) at the sprawling, and very luxurious, Hotel Del Coronado, in nearby Coronado. He got a lift from a Navy officer. Johnston was off and running.

CHAPTER 4

HOLD THE PRESSES!

Mr. Maloney, I have got some good dope for you.
—Stanley Johnston

By the time Johnston arrived at the del Coronado, he was out of every-thing: money, clothes, personal items. All that was at the bottom of the Coral Sea. The first thing he did was call the *Chicago Tribune*. Late as it was in Chicago, somewhere near 2 a.m., he knew somebody would be there. He got the night editor, a gentleman who in the argot of the *Tribune* was known as the dog-watchman.[1] The dog-watchman was not immediately helpful; he wanted to know why Johnston did not have any money. "I said, 'Well, I don't have any money but I must have some.'" When the gentleman remained doubtful, Johnston raised his voice. "I said: It is urgent. I would like to get somebody to attend to it today." That seemed to work. The gentleman on the other end of the line said he would see what he could do.[2]

That matter taken care of, Johnston next asked the hotel's front desk to provide him a typewriter. It delivered one to his room.[3] Before turning in, he typed out on fresh stationary his notes from the crumpled scratch paper he had carried in his pocket from *Barnett* to the del Coronado.[4] Replicating his notes almost exactly, he shaped this material into a memorandum to his boss, the *Tribune*'s managing editor, J. Loy "Pat" Maloney.[5] He put the memo in an envelope with some other items, discarded the scratch paper on which he had scribbled his notes, and called it a night. He did not awaken until around 9 a.m., when the front desk rang him up with the news his money had arrived. The dog-watchman had come through.

Johnston did not take his Coral Sea copy over to the Naval District Head-quarters on Wednesday, as Lieutenant Requa had proposed. He had too much else to do. The first thing he did was try to reach Maloney. Ordinarily the *Tribune*'s managing editor did not show up at the office until around 2 p.m.

(the usual pattern for a morning newspaper). But when Maloney learned (from the dog-watchman) that his missing war correspondent had not only returned from the Pacific but wanted to report in, Maloney came in well ahead of schedule. The two finally caught up with each other by phone late Wednesday morning.

Like everyone else at the paper, Maloney had been worried. Other than a terse note from Pacific Fleet headquarters that Johnston was alive and well and on his way home, no one had heard anything about Johnston for weeks. Johnston had not communicated because he was not allowed to. The stories he had filed from the South Pacific had not been forwarded to Chicago.[6] The Navy had clamped a tight lid on news from, and about, the Coral Sea action. Aside from a brief communique in which the Navy reported a major battle in that area—one that appeared to go extremely well for the Americans—little information had been released.[7] The Navy had not disclosed the sinking of *Lexington* and would not until mid-June. With the Midway campaign nearing, it did not want the Japanese to know what ships the Americans might, or might not, have lost in the Coral Sea. *Lexington* personnel going ashore at San Diego were under orders not to divulge the fate of the carrier or any other details of the Coral Sea engagement.

When Maloney finally got Johnston on the phone and heard his reporter blurt out, "I'm back," it was like hearing a ghost. He felt both relief and, good newspaperman that he was, curiosity. He had many questions. Maloney knew that Johnston had been assigned to a ship departing Pearl Harbor 15 April, but he did not know which one or where it was going. (Johnston did not know himself until he arrived at Pearl Harbor that morning.) Now he wanted to find out everything: Where had Johnston been and what, if anything, had he seen? Most important of all, did his reporter have any copy for the *Tribune*? Johnston did not waste any time getting the words out: "Mr. Maloney, I've got the greatest story of the war so far."[8]

Maloney quizzed him but could not get anything else out of him. "Finally, he told me he was in the Battle of the Coral Sea," Maloney told investigators later. "That is all I got. I finally asked him if I recall with a little petulancy: 'Who won the battle?' He said: 'We did.' I said: 'What did the enemy lose?' He said: 'That I cannot tell you, Mr. Maloney, until I see you.'"[9]

Johnston adhered to the strict censorship rules laid down by the Navy. Still, Maloney kept pressing him. Asked how many ships the Navy had lost, Johnston replied curtly, "I cannot discuss it." When Maloney tried to find out what ship he was on, his reporter refused to tell him. Johnston said, "I must conduct myself as follows: I must take my stories, outlines of the stories that were notes, sentences and paragraphs but not really ready for publication, and give them to the Navy in San Diego. And they must proceed to Washington through the regular channel."[10]

Somewhat exasperated, Maloney wondered if the clearance process could not be sped up. Could he not at least cable his copy to the *Tribune* and let his editors deal with the Washington censors from Chicago? "I can't telegraph it," Johnston said.[11]

Maloney was almost frantic. He had a reporter sitting on a scoop, possibly "the greatest story of the war so far," and he could not see it. At least not until Johnston arrived in Chicago and Maloney could look at Johnston's raw copy. Then there was the censorship issue. He would have to wait for Johnston's stories to make their way through the Navy's many layers of censorship: first, the San Diego bureaucracy, consisting of Lieutenant Requa and his superiors. If all went well, they would review Johnston's copy in a timely fashion and ship it off to Washington. In this instance that meant the Navy Department's Office of Public Relations, doubling as the Navy's censorship bureau. All this would take time.

Maloney was concerned about losing his scoop or, more precisely, seeing another news organization stumble across the same story and run with it before he could get the *Tribune*'s version into print. Maloney asked Johnston a question: "There must have been a lot of people that came home with you, were there not?"

"Yes, lots of them," Johnston said.

"Well, they are going to talk."

"No, they are under strict orders, the same as I am. We have got the story, we have got it alone. Don't worry about it, Mr. Maloney."[12]

There was nothing Maloney could do but wait. The conversation ended, with Johnston promising to call his boss later that evening. In the meantime, there were things Johnston had to do. He used his new money to stock up on clothes. He tried unsuccessfully to reach *Lexington*'s skipper, Captain Sherman, residing temporarily in the San Diego area. Both men had reasons to want to chat. Johnston probably hoped to continue their conversation about naval censorship, begun two weeks earlier on board *Astoria* as it steamed toward Tongatabu.[13] Sherman had an issue of his own; earlier he had loaned Johnston an advance copy of his report on the Coral Sea battle marked secret.

"I had let him have [it] to look at and [it] was to be returned," Sherman noted in his private diary. "He had failed to contact me at San Diego and failed to return the copy." (Johnston told Sherman later that he destroyed the document before leaving San Diego.)[14]

Unable to reach Sherman, Johnston now called Requa and Seligman and arranged to meet them at his hotel that evening. Chatting with the two officers at the del Coronado that night, the subject, needless to say, was censorship. Once again they worked out a schedule for Johnston to deliver his Coral Sea copy to the Naval District Headquarters; he would bring his stories by first thing in the morning, 4 June. He asked that Navy censors in San Diego forward the copy directly to Washington, without examining the articles first. He undoubtedly would have quoted Sherman on the urgency of the matter; Seligman would have backed him up.

Then Johnston got back in touch with Maloney. Exaggerating a little, Johnston told his boss that he had left his stories with the Navy in San Diego; from there they would be transported to Washington. Maloney seemed satisfied, although by this time he knew there was nothing he could do to hasten things along. But as the two men talked, another topic came up: a Navy bulletin that afternoon reported that Japanese bombers had just pounded Dutch Harbor in the Aleutian Islands. The *Tribune*'s managing editor asked Johnston if he had an opinion about that. Johnston did. He thought the attack might be a feint to deflect attention away from Japan's larger goal to strike Hawaii. "Mr. Maloney, I have got some good dope for you," Johnston said.[15] "I've got some dope on the whole picture in the Pacific that I would like to talk about."[16]

But Maloney did not want to pursue Dutch Harbor. He had his mind on one thing, and he wanted to keep Johnston's mind focused on the same thing. "I was chiefly interested in the Battle of the Coral Sea, as managing editor of the *Tribune*, in getting it in." As for Johnston's dope about the Pacific, "I rather passed this off as unimportant," Maloney said. "Reporters often go down the byway, when I wanted to keep him on the main track." Johnston, as Maloney recalled later, persisted: "I am writing it out for you. I am going to mail it to you." Okay, Maloney said, that was fine. But what he really wanted to know was Johnston's schedule: when could he expect him in Chicago. His reporter assured him he would leave first thing the next day, Thursday, 4 June.[17]

Johnston was up early on Thursday, but he did not do everything he had promised. He did not, for example, take his copy in person to Naval

District Headquarters in San Diego. Instead, he arranged for a hotel messenger to deliver the copy in a sealed envelope, with a letter in which Johnston explained to Requa why he could not come be there personally: he had to be somewhere else. When the package arrived on Requa's desk, Johnston got lucky. As requested, Requa did not subject Johnston's work to the usual time-consuming review; he simply put his stories in a pouch and expedited them to Washington by plane.[18] Whatever Johnston said to Requa on Wednesday evening about the importance of haste apparently had the desired effect.

Nor did Johnston go to Chicago. The "somewhere else" he had to be that day was not Chicago but Los Angeles. Even before calling Maloney early Wednesday morning he had fired off a wire to Barbara, still waiting for her husband in San Francisco. She had not heard from Stanley for more than six weeks and was almost sick with worry. She had heard from the *Tribune* that he was okay but that was all she knew. So when she received his wire instructing her to call him at the del Coronado, she did so right away. They talked off and on during the day and arranged to meet the next day in Los Angeles, midway between their two cities.[19]

Johnston was on the move Thursday. After arranging for the hotel's messenger to deliver his envelope to the Navy, he checked out of the del Coronado and caught an early train to Los Angeles. Stanley and Barbara met at the Clark Hotel around 11 a.m. and stayed there until early Friday morning. The only other person Johnston saw in Los Angeles was an old friend, Tim Turner of the *Los Angeles Times*. Turner had been on the British battle cruiser HMS *Repulse* when it was torpedoed and sunk by the Japanese on 10 December 1941; he was among the fortunate survivors. Apparently feeling guilty about not proceeding directly to Chicago, Johnston asked Turner not to publicize his presence in Los Angeles.[20]

Friday, 5 June, was another moving day. Barbara returned to San Francisco and Stanley caught an early United Airlines flight to Chicago. He marched into the *Tribune*'s newsroom in the early afternoon to the applause and hosannas of the paper's staffers. Johnston was home.

❧

Maloney was more pleased than anybody else by Johnston's arrival. "By that time, we, in the *Tribune* office, were, I might say, nuts about this story," Maloney said later, referring to the Coral Sea pieces he knew Johnston was carrying. "We began to realize how great it was, and we could hardly realize that we had it alone." Now Maloney could look at Johnston's copy and see what he had. He saw that his reporter did indeed have a great story. It was more dramatic, more riveting, than his reporter had led him to believe. Maloney wanted to see his notes turned into stories fast—as fast as Johnston could write them, and as fast as Navy censors could clear them (Maloney understood that the *Tribune*'s Coral Sea copy would be reviewed by Navy censors).[21]

Johnston needed a place to work undisturbed, a quiet den away from the jangling of newsroom phones and the pesky questions of fellow reporters. Maloney assigned him to a private office down the hall from the newsroom—a small, out-of-the-way space he called the booby hatch.[22] The room was perfect. It was a spare, bare-bones office. It had a typewriter and a telephone, but little else. A guard nearby was instructed to let no one—no one except Maloney—enter that room. "So I was locked in there rewriting all of the Coral Sea story," Johnston recalled.[23] Maloney, of course, did enter. "I spent most of Friday afternoon with him," Maloney said later, "and some of Friday evening, some of Saturday afternoon with him, arranging to have his stories rearranged and rewritten, planning out whether they should run chronologically, and all the things a newspaperman would do handling a story of this kind."[24]

Preoccupied as they were with the Coral Sea, neither man remembered Johnston's pronouncement from San Diego that he had "some dope" concerning the Japanese attack on Dutch Harbor. Johnston never mailed his memo; the envelope was still in his pocket, apparently forgotten. Johnston worked Saturday night in the booby hatch, if not quite alone. Earlier, Maloney had assigned Johnston's old friend, aviation editor Wayne Thomis, to work with him on the Coral Sea story. Around 9 p.m. on Saturday, bleary-eyed and tired, wanting a cup of coffee and some company, he left his little room and ambled into the *Tribune*'s newsroom. The Associated Press machine was clacking over in one corner. He took a look. The machine was printing out a communique issued by the Pacific Fleet commander, Admiral Nimitz. It read, in part, "Through the skill and devotion to duty of their armed forces of all branches in the Midway area our citizens can now rejoice that a momentous victory is in the making."[25] Johnston read a little farther down. Nimitz proclaimed, "Pearl Harbor has now been partially avenged." His communique added,

> The battle is not over. All returns have not yet been received.
> It is with full confidence, however, that for this phase of the

action the following enemy losses are claimed: two or three carriers, and all their aircraft, destroyed; in addition one or two carriers badly damaged and most of their aircraft lost; three battleships damaged, at least one badly; four cruisers damaged, two heavily; three transports damaged. It is possible that some of those wounded ships will not be able to reach their bases. One of our carriers was hit and some planes lost. Our personnel casualties were light.[26]

Johnston was elated. He looked around the room and saw Maloney and his subeditors reading the same communique but not saying much—"they seemed rather calm about it." Johnston was troubled by their blasé attitude, he would tell federal investigators later. "I have an enthusiasm for the United States Navy," Johnston said. "I think it is good, and I'm afraid I was a little excited about this victory, and they did not seem to me to be suitably impressed with the magnitude of this battle." He recalled trying to explain to Maloney and his editors that "the biggest naval battle in history had been fought, much more damage than at Jutland, and the United States Navy had won it."[27] He got little reaction.

Johnston approached Maloney's desk. He tried again: "This must be the biggest fleet the Japanese could get together." His managing editor seemed interested: "Well, what could they get together in the form of a fleet today?" Johnston remembered the memo in his pocket that he had meant to mail to Maloney but never did: "I have some dope on what the Japanese have got left in the form of a fleet." He showed Maloney the memo with the list of Japanese ships. Maloney's curiosity was piqued. This could be another scoop. He ordered Johnston to shape the memo into an article. What seemed significant about this episode to Johnston was that Maloney and his editors did not realize the huge significance of America's Midway victory until he presented his memo, typed up at the del Coronado. The memo had served a patriotic purpose. Or so he would suggest to his interrogators. He had practically a patriotic duty to show it.[28]

～

Maloney recalled the events of Saturday evening, 6 June, a little differently. He well remembered Nimitz's communique. "There was a great stir to get in with this tremendous story," Maloney would tell investigators in a separate interview. Contrary to Johnston's version, in which *Tribune* editors seemed unmoved by the Midway saga, Maloney recalled that "we in the *Tribune* regarded it as a great victory." To give the story more space, "We took the cartoon off page one"—something the paper as a rule did only on election days. Given this story's high priority, "I was avid for all the information I could get about it," he said. "Naturally, as was every good newspaperman in the United States, we were patriotically thrilled."[29]

Around 9:30 in the evening, Maloney said, Johnston wanted to see him. His reporter handed him the memo he had intended to mail from San Diego but, for one reason or another, did not. Maloney recalled their conversation this way:

Johnston said, "Mr. Maloney, here is the stuff I mentioned to you on the telephone in San Diego."

"I said: 'What stuff?' —not remembering it. He said: 'Don't you remember? I said I was going to write you a letter.' 'Yes, that is right, said I.' 'Here is the letter,' said Johnston."

Maloney liked what Johnston showed him: "This is fine; this is great," the *Tribune* managing editor said. "It enhances the victory and supplements the Nimitz communique in grand style. It shows what a helluva force the American Navy whipped out there."[30]

Maloney did have one concern. "Where did you get this?" he asked. His reporter had no trouble answering: "I got it from the same place I got all my information, from what I can figure out in my own head and from conversations with the men I have been with on the boat." He did not tell Maloney everything. He did not report his close relationship with *Lexington*'s executive officer, Commander Seligman. Nor did he mention the naval dispatch itemizing the Imperial Navy's order of battle at Midway that had been passed around Seligman's quarters; nor did he cite the blue-lined scratch paper with the names of Japanese ships that he had copied. But Maloney did not press him for more details on his sources. He had a very good reason, he would later tell investigators: he respected Johnston's reportorial skills. "He knew ships," Maloney said. "I have heard him, and had heard him before we sent him over there, mention every capital ship in the Japanese navy, every battleship, every cruiser, even some of the big destroyers."[31]

Moreover, Maloney said, Johnston was a close friend of Francis E. McMurtrie, editor of *Jane's Fighting Ships*, the reference book of detailed information on all the world's warships. As it happened, McMurtrie's office in London was in the same building and on the same floor as the London bureau of the *Chicago Tribune*. McMurtrie was a frequent visitor to the *Tribune* office. According to Maloney, whenever McMurtrie and Johnston both happened to be in town at the same time, they would "go out to tea together, go to some wine shop and sip tea or wine or both and chew the fat on boats."[32]

Maloney accepted Johnston's explanation without further questioning. He thought he had another scoop: "This is a fine story to play on page 1, along with the Nimitz communique," he remembered telling Johnston. He wanted the story, but time was running out. The *Tribune* went to press late Saturday night at 11:30. The deadline for copy was 10:30 p.m. It was now around 9:30; Johnston would have little more than an hour to write the article, polish it, and get it through the editing process before the rapidly approaching deadline. Maloney did not think Johnston could do it. He knew his reporter to be a slow writer, and not a particularly good one. "Johnston does not write well," the *Tribune* editor told investigators. "He gets all his facts in, but he lacks smoothness, clarity, and color."[33]

Convinced Johnston could not write the story alone, Maloney got him some help. He ordered Thomis, already working with Johnston on the Coral Sea story, to switch gears and now help him write the Midway story. To Maloney this made sense. Thomis had a reputation as a stylist, a smooth writer who could make a drab, matter-of-fact story come alive. Maloney ordered the two men not to reappear until they had a finished product. They were told to get busy; time was short.[34]

Tackling Johnston's memorandum, they divided up duties, with Thomis reworking the "lead" paragraphs, or introduction, while Johnston thumbed through *Jane's Fighting Ships* in search of key characteristics of the IJN ships named in the memo (their tonnage, size, and caliber of their guns). In fashioning a new intro, Thomis made one critical change that would come back to haunt the *Tribune* in future weeks; he attributed the material in the story to "reliable sources in the naval intelligence." ("I'm the stupid jerk who attributed the story to naval intelligence," a rueful Thomis admitted later. "That was the dumbest possible thing to have done.")[35]

With a lead that satisfied him, Thomis quickly transformed Johnston's bureaucratic-sounding memorandum, with its coded abbreviations and odd naval expressions, into readable newspaper copy. He carefully organized the Japanese ships in the same order as they appeared in the memo: striking force ships listed first; followed by those in the support force; and, last, those in the occupation force. Under each heading, he incorporated some new information—tonnage and armaments for many of the ships identified—dug up by Johnston during his perusal of *Jane's*. The two men handed in their story with time to spare.

Maloney was pleased by the prompt delivery of the story but not by the story itself. Or at least not by the introduction, the part written solely by Thomis. "The lead of it did not suit me," Maloney said. "I thought the lead was muddy and unclear, and I clarified it somewhat." He rewrote the first two paragraphs but left the body of the story unchanged. He also left intact Thomis' unique contribution: the attribution to naval intelligence. Then Maloney added a controversial element of his own, another variation that would cast a cloud over the *Tribune* story. He slapped a Washington dateline on the article so it would look like it originated in Washington. Maloney thought this change made perfectly good journalistic sense. "The most authoritative place you can pin a thing like that is on Washington," he would tell investigators. He also approved the attribution to naval intelligence: "Johnston was not enough of an expert, in my mind, to be quoted having said this." Maloney in effect admitted that Johnston's article would have appeared shaky without the fictional foundation cobbled together by *Tribune* editors.[36]

By the time Maloney finished his rewrite, Johnston was out of the picture: he had lost control of his own story. He would later disavow the "Washington dateline" and "naval intelligence" changes made by Thomis and Maloney and even profess ignorance about how those amendments came about. "I don't know who did that," Johnston would tell federal investigators. "I had nothing to say in that way at all," he said, trying to explain the mysterious workings of the editorial process. In rewriting his copy, editors were just exercising their prerogatives as editors. "That is the normal thing in the newspaper office."[37]

Removed from the writing and editing process as he now was, Johnston failed to raise an issue of singular importance in wartime American journalism: censorship. He did not bring up the matter because he could not. Or felt he could not. He was no longer in a power position. He recognized that his status in the *Tribune* newsroom was very different from what it had been in *Lexington* and *Barnett*. On those ships he had been a sort of celebrity, a one of a kind—a man of the world who had owned gold mines in New Guinea, covered the Battle of Britain, and was even married to an American showgirl (this morsel had gotten around both ships). All this gave him a mystique among men not easily taken in. Somewhat awed by Johnston, Commander

Duckworth called him "a smart man" who knew his job, and *Barnett's* Captain Phillips described him as "a very clever individual with a thorough knowledge of the Navy."[38] Johnston turned his stature into clout; he used it to persuade people to help him with his fact gathering, and sometimes even to push people when he wanted to get his way.

But Johnston did not have that kind of standing in the *Tribune* newsroom. He was a relatively junior member of that newspaper's reporting team; he had been a regular staffer for less than a year. Aside from his Coral Sea adventure (which had not yet been translated into newspaper stories), he had not done anything special. He was just a promising newcomer in a large newsroom full of established veterans, some of them star reporters. He was not yet a star. He was still on trial as a beginning newsman. He certainly could not push Maloney—although, of course, no one could.

As the managing editor of the mighty *Chicago Tribune*, a newspaper that billed itself as "The World's Greatest Newspaper," Maloney was a force unto himself. Short, balding, and a little on the sassy side, he was a hands-on, shirtsleeve editor who kept his office door open so he could see just about everything going on in the *Tribune's* spacious newsroom. From his perch, he ran the news operation with a firm hand. Blunt spoken and scrappy, he sometimes rubbed people the wrong way. But for all his rough edges, he knew how to get the best out of his staff. He was highly intelligent and well educated (a Dartmouth Phi Beta Kappa); he had traveled widely and had served in the European War as a combat pilot (he flew as part of Eddie Rickenbacker's famed 94th Aero Squadron).[39] After the war, he rejoined the *Tribune* (resuming a reportorial career he had started earlier) and worked his way up to managerial authority, earning every promotion through hard work. He prided himself on his patriotism and enjoyed the full confidence of the *Tribune's* legendary publisher, Robert R. McCormick. He was not somebody who could easily be nudged to do something he did not want to do.

Johnston did not try to nudge him. "Well, you see," Johnston explained, "I looked on Mr. Maloney as the managing editor of the paper, the same way as if I was in the Navy as a junior officer and turned something in to the captain." Johnston added, "It is his responsibility, he runs the newspaper and he knows what censorship is, and I figured he would attend to whatever was needed to be attended to that way."[40]

～

Maloney did attend to the censorship issue, albeit in his own idiosyncratic fashion. He was familiar with the domestic component of the Roosevelt administration's system of voluntary censorship. He had been working cooperatively with Washington's censors ever since the president on 19 December 1941 signed an executive order creating an Office of Censorship (OC). Exercising its new authority to censor war-related information in the media, the OC on 15 January 1942 published its *Code of Wartime Practices for the American Press* consisting of guidelines for the press. The regulations were considered voluntary because they had been agreed to earlier in the year by the nation's editors and broadcasters. They were spelled out in a five-page, church-bulletin sized pamphlet circulated to virtually every newspaper and radio station in the country.[41]

Maloney had a copy in his desk and looked at it.[42] Under OC's rules, editors were supposed to seek clearance in advance for any article or broadcast that might be in conflict with the regulations. But submitting the Johnston article to the agency's censors would take time, and Maloney did not have a lot of that. He was right on deadline: it was close to 10:30 p.m., the deadline for copy intended for the Sunday morning *Tribune*. Even assuming he could rouse an OC staffer at that late hour, too much time would pass. He would lose the story for Sunday, and there would be little point running it Monday; it would be stale news by then. Even worse, censors being censors, Washington might kill the story altogether. Maloney did not want that to happen. He re-read the guidelines on ships in the *Code of Wartime Practices*. It forbade printing the following types of information: "The location, movements and identity of naval and merchant vessels of the United States in any waters, and of other nations opposing the Axis powers, in American waters; the port and time of arrival or prospective arrival of any such vessels, or the port from which they leave; the nature of cargoes of such vessels; the location of enemy naval or merchant vessels in or near American waters."[43]

Maloney relaxed. He did not think these strictures applied to the *Tribune* story. The Johnston piece did not, after all, report the movements of U.S. naval vessels. And while it did address the activities of enemy ships, it did not reveal them to be "in or near American waters," a disclosure that would have transgressed OC's code. The Midway campaign was fought in an area northwest of that atoll, many miles away from American waters. "It seemed clear to me that way out there in somewhere west of Midway was not American waters," Maloney told investigators. "I could not possibly see how that could be helping the Japanese in any way by telling them where their boats were."[44]

Other factors played into Maloney's thinking: the *Code of Wartime Practices* was, as noted, a voluntary code; it was designed for news organizations gathering information inside the United States. Editors were expected to observe the guidelines on the honor system; if they were uncertain about whether an article contained material in violation of the code, they were supposed to ask the Office of Censorship for an opinion or, better yet, wire the article to Washington for review by OC's small staff (it examined hundreds of articles during the war). In other words, editors were required to use their own judgment regarding the need for official clearance of particular articles. If they judged incorrectly, the penalty would be relatively light; the OC lacked authority to do little more than direct negative publicity at the offending party. Maloney exercised his judgment now: Johnston's story did not breach OC guidelines.[45]

The *Tribune*'s acting city editor, Stewart Owen, was not so sure. Owen was the last stop in the *Tribune*'s intricate editorial process as copy moved inexorably to the printer. Maloney handed him the story around 10:45 p.m.—late but not too late. Owen read the story and promptly raised the question of censorship. "Well, I have looked it up," Maloney said, showing Owen a copy of the code. Owen was subordinate to Maloney, but he was a seasoned editor with many years on the paper; he was not afraid to challenge his boss. "Why don't you ask Henning about it?" Arthur Sears Henning was the paper's longtime Washington bureau chief and a highly respected presence in the *Tribune* world. He had served as an effective liaison in the past between the Chicago team and the Office of Censorship. Maloney agreed. "I was cocksure at this time, having interpreted [the code] myself," he said. "So I thought there would not be any harm."[46]

Late as it was, Maloney called Henning at his home in Washington. He described Johnston's story fleetingly as some "information and dope" his reporter had brought back from the West Coast about the probable makeup of the Japanese ships defeated at Midway. "You don't think, Arthur, that I would be in the wrong with censorship in any way if I print that?" he asked. "No, I don't think so, in any way," Henning replied, "because it is about the enemy." They agreed the story would not be telling the Japanese anything they did not already know. They concurred that this was one naval story that did not require any scrutiny by censors.[47]

As Navy and Justice Department investigators would tell them shortly, they were wrong. Confident as they had been about the meaning of the censorship code, the two journalists had missed an important subtlety—one that would elude many players in the drama about to unfold. They erred in thinking that the Office of Censorship was the appropriate agency to consider Johnston's article. It was not. The OC had no jurisdiction over this article. The Office was established to review articles about wartime issues developed inside the United States. But Johnston had obtained his material while at sea, first in *Lexington*, then in *Barnett*. Under the Navy's policy, which Johnston had pledged orally to observe,[48] any article using information acquired in a war zone, or at sea with a U.S. Navy ship, was subject to mandatory Navy censorship. As for the Office of Censorship, whatever its reviewers might say about the story would be irrelevant. It was not "their" story; their opinion would not matter.[49]

Such considerations were far from Maloney's mind late Saturday, 6 June 1942, as the hour hand closed in on 11 p.m. He had to quickly move this story to the presses. As always on a large metropolitan newspaper, makeup of the front page was a collaborative effort among top editors, with Maloney's the lead voice. Headlines were scrawled out, refined, and put in place. The writer of the controversial headline atop the Johnston story was never named, but it was probably someone on the *Tribune*'s copy desk—one of the regular headline writers. Maloney scanned a mock-up of the page: "I OK'd the heads and subheads myself, looked them over, took the entire responsibility for the form the story was in."[50]

The story squeezed in under the wire. When the presses rolled at 11:30, Johnston's article was in, prominently displayed on page one—"above the fold," as newspapermen like to say. Maloney even had time to transmit Johnston's "scoop" to the roughly two dozen newspapers that subscribed to the *Tribune*'s news service. In addition to the *Tribune*, three newspapers—the *San Francisco Chronicle*, the *New York Daily News*, the *Washington Times-Herald*—would carry the article. The *Tribune* ran Johnston's story, without his byline, as a sidebar to the paper's lead article on the Nimitz's communique. The controversial and heavily rewritten first two paragraphs read as follows:

NAVY HAD WORD OF JAP PLAN TO STRIKE AT SEA

WASHINGTON, D.C., June 7 – The strength of the Japanese with which the American Navy is battling somewhere west of Midway Island in what is believed to be the greatest naval battle of the war was well known in American naval circles, reliable sources in the naval intelligence disclosed here tonight.

The Navy learned of the gathering of the powerful Japanese units soon after they put forth from their bases, it was said. Although their purpose was not specifically known at the time, the information in the hands of the Navy Department was so definite that a feint at some American base, to be accompanied by a serious effort to invade and occupy another base, was predicted. Guesses were even made that Dutch Harbor in the Aleutians and Midway Island in the Hawaiian group might be targets.[51]

The article proceeded to list the names of Imperial Navy ships assigned to the striking, support, and occupation forces as they appeared on the blue-lined scratch paper Johnston had found in his room on board *Barnett* on 2 June (see Appendix B for the entire Johnston story).

～

When Johnston and Thomis handed in their copy to Maloney sometime after 10 p.m., their work for the *Tribune*'s Sunday edition was done. But their day was not over. Johnston still had other work to do. He was struggling to finish what eventually would be a nine-part series on the fate of *Lexington* and the Battle of the Coral Sea; it was scheduled to start running in just a few days (Navy censors willing). Maloney wanted Thomis to continue working with Johnston. He ordered both back to the out-of-the-way cubby hole down the hall; they worked through the night. Around 5 a.m., they called it quits. The two men walked through the lobby on their way out of the building. There Johnston noticed the freshly printed Sunday edition sitting in a pile in a little vestibule. He picked up a copy of the paper and saw his story on the front page. "My goodness," he said to Thomis, "to get the story down to Washington and censored and back in this time." Johnston thought that was pretty amazing; he did not know how Maloney had done it. "I was surprised," he said later, "to find you could get it censored late at night in Washington."[52]

Maloney also had put in a long night, although he had gone home much earlier than Johnston and Thomis. He was pleased by how the Sunday edition had turned out. "I recall—and this is not sob stuff—but I recall telling Mrs. Maloney the next day what a helluva swell, nice work that was," he would tell federal investigators. "That was one of the best *Tribunes* I ever participated in."[53] Not all readers would share Maloney's enthusiasm for that issue of the *Tribune*.

CHAPTER 5

AID AND COMFORT TO THE ENEMY

We're going to hang this guy higher than Haman.
—*Charles M. "Savvy" Cooke Jr.*

President Roosevelt began each day reading newspapers. This morning ritual went back to the earliest days of his presidency. He would awaken around 8 a.m., turn to the edge of his bed and hit the button for his valet, who would help him into the bathroom. Then he would return to his bed, throw his old blue cape over his pajamas, and start his day with breakfast in bed. While eating his breakfast, Roosevelt would first look through dispatches that had come in from abroad and then skim a few selected newspapers: the *New York Times* and *New York Herald Tribune*; the *Baltimore Sun*; Washington's two morning dailies, the *Post* and *Times-Herald*; and, unfailingly, the *Chicago Tribune*.[1] FDR did not read that paper because he liked it. "Roosevelt was a constant reader of the *Tribune*," observed the *Tribune*'s White House correspondent, Walter Trohan. "His insatiable curiosity impelled him to peek at what his enemies were saying."[2]

Roosevelt had grown accustomed, if not reconciled, to the steady stream of criticism that poured forth from that newspaper, published by his most embittered foe, Robert R. McCormick. By June 1942, there was very little McCormick could put in his paper that would shock the president. But the story that appeared on the front page of the *Tribune* and on page four of the *Times-Herald* on Sunday morning, 7 June 1942, seemed to go too far. It crossed an invisible line in FDR's mind. Whether Roosevelt actually read the story that morning and instantly grasped its significance, or whether Navy Secretary Knox or some other Navy official phoned and briefed him on it will never be known. But what is indisputable is that before the morning ended, Roosevelt had set in motion a White House–backed campaign geared not only at silencing McCormick, but at putting him behind bars as well.

The showdown between the two men had been building for much of FDR's presidency. It was the culmination of years of bare-knuckle squabbling and political jousting between the publisher and the president. Given McCormick's conservative politics and his daredevil style of political attack, a final face-off was probably inevitable. By the early 1930s, McCormick had molded his newspaper into one of the country's strongest voices for private enterprise and laissez-faire economics. Even so, it looked for a time, early in FDR's presidency, like the two men might get along. They knew each other personally, having been classmates years earlier at Groton. After Roosevelt's inauguration, they invited each other to visit. During the first days of the New Deal, McCormick backed FDR's demand for half a billion dollars in spending cuts, and he praised the Civilian Conservation Corps as "relief at its best."[3] This amity, however, did not last.

As the New Deal moved more aggressively to help the jobless and promote economic recovery, the *Tribune* turned sharply critical. When Roosevelt proposed creation of a National Recovery Administration, an agency that would establish codes of fair competition for business, the *Tribune* opposed the scheme, branding it as "fascistic." Other New Deal initiatives now came in for a similar pasting. Beginning around 1934, FDR and members of his cabinet were continuously described in scathingly abusive terms; in editorials and front-page cartoons, they were depicted at various times, incongruously, as both communists and fascists.[4] To the *Tribune*, the New Deal had become a giant conspiracy to subvert the "American Way of Life."[5]

The Roosevelt-McCormick rift widened in the late 1930s as the world moved toward war and FDR looked for ways to bolster the Western democracies against would-be aggressors. The *Tribune* blasted these efforts, rejecting any form of intervention in Europe or Asia. Backing the America First movement, McCormick envisaged a Fortress America, strong enough to resist enemies but not strong enough to fight offensive wars in far-off places. Although not pro-Hitler, McCormick thought the German threat was exaggerated. In the Pacific, he called for U.S. withdrawal from China and the Philippines to reduce the likelihood of conflict with Japan. He attacked the government's call for conscription, likening FDR to a "panty-waist Hitler" for borrowing an idea from the German youth movement. He editorialized against Lend-Lease supplies to Great Britain and the Soviet Union, arguing such aid would turn America into a dictatorship. He characterized Roosevelt as a nervous charlatan "hell bent for war."[6]

FDR was not McCormick's only target. He frequently denounced Navy Secretary Frank Knox, publisher of the *Chicago Daily News*, the morning *Tribune*'s hated afternoon rival. The two men detested each other even though both were Republicans, strong conservatives, and ardent patriots with impressive military records. As noted, McCormick served as an artillery officer in France during World War I; he ended the war a full colonel. Knox served as one of Theodore Roosevelt's Rough Riders in the Spanish American War; then, during the World War I, he served (like McCormick) in an artillery unit, ascending to the rank of major.[7] Knox had been the Republican vice presidential candidate in 1936, running with Kansas governor Alf Landon. Throughout the 1930s, the *Daily News* consistently opposed the New Deal. But in July 1940, just before the Republican Convention, Knox joined FDR's cabinet, as did another prominent Republican, Henry Stimson. Stimson had been Herbert Hoover's secretary of state; he now joined the Roosevelt administration as secretary of war. FDR's coalition government embarrassed Republicans, and it served another purpose. As both Republicans and internationalists, Knox and Stimson, by their presence in the cabinet, conferred a bipartisan aura on the Roosevelt administration's military buildup. McCormick was appalled by the appointments; he now stepped up his onslaught against Knox, accusing him, among other things, of using his high position to benefit the *Daily News*.[8]

Knox got in some licks of his own. Ignoring what most people would consider a blatant conflict of interest, Knox encouraged the creation of a morning paper, the *Chicago Sun*, to compete against McCormick's paper. With FDR cheering him on, Knox leased the top three floors of the *Daily News* building to investment banker Marshall Field III, who was bankrolling the *Sun*. Field, the wealthy heir of the Marshall Field department store fortune, had recently launched a liberal afternoon paper in New York called *PM*. Now he wanted to start a liberal paper in Chicago. Knox helped him every way he could; he even let Field use his paper's presses. Field scheduled the *Sun*'s debut for 4 December 1941. Many people in Chicago, dissatisfied with the isolationist and fiercely anti–New Deal *Tribune*, looked forward to the new arrival. McCormick hoped to spoil the *Sun*'s first day. Earlier, he had let his staff know he wanted a hot scoop to deflect attention away from the *Sun*'s birth. His staff did not disappoint.[9]

On 4 December 1941, the *Tribune* published a sensational story purporting to reveal Roosevelt's secret plan to take America to war. The front-page article ran under a banner headline—with the largest print ever used by the newspaper—screaming FDR'S WAR PLANS! A subhead blared: GOAL IS 10 MILLION ARMED MEN. The story unveiled a government document called the Victory Program, described as "a blueprint for total war." Written by Chesly Manly, the *Tribune*'s Capitol Hill correspondent, it divulged details of a plan to create an American expeditionary force of some five million men that would invade German-occupied Europe by July 1943. In time, the article said, U.S. armed forces would total more than ten million men. Manly said the report on which he based his story "represents decisions and commitments affecting the destinies of peoples throughout the civilized world."[10]

The story caused a furor in Washington. Carried the same day by the *Times-Herald*, published by McCormick's cousin, Cissy Patterson, the article was read by diplomats; journalists; military chieftains; and, of course, lawmakers. At first glance, it seemed to make a mockery of FDR's pronouncements that he was doing everything he could to keep America out of war. McCormick called the story "the greatest scoop in newspaper history."[11] If corroborated, it might have been. But the *Tribune*'s "exposé" did not turn out to be the scoop that McCormick claimed it to be. What Manly had gotten hold of was no more than a contingency plan framed by the War Department to be used in case the United States found itself at war with Germany. FDR ordered the plan on 9 July 1941, instructing Stimson and Knox to explore "at once the over-all production requirements to defeat our potential enemies."[12]

Queried about the story at a press conference the following day, Stimson fumed. While conceding the document was authentic, he stated it was merely a study formulated for the fighting of a possible war. The July 1943 date was not an actual timetable for conflict; it was simply the first date on which planners believed that the United States could be prepared for action. "What would you think," Stimson asked rhetorically, "of an American General Staff which in the present condition of the world did not investigate and study every conceivable type of emergency which may confront this country and every possible method of meeting the emergency?" He heaped scorn on McCormick, raising questions about the publisher's patriotism and accusing him of giving "gratification" to America's potential enemies.[13]

McCormick's intention, of course, was not just to eclipse the *Sun* (which readers initially found rather dull) but, more importantly, to sabotage Roosevelt's military buildup. That was a real possibility. Congress had just begun considering Roosevelt's request for $8 billion in additional military appropriations to accelerate defense production.[14] Now, in the wake of Manly's story, isolationists in and outside Congress were charging that the president was trying to trick the country into war. The appropriation and, indeed, FDR's entire Victory Program could be imperiled. "The *Tribune's* scoop," one historian years later wrote, "was one of the most sensational and potentially damaging in the history of American journalism."[15]

Faced with what they believed was a breach of national security, Roosevelt's lieutenants wanted to prosecute the *Tribune* and *Times-Herald* editors along with the individual or individuals—presumably government officials—who leaked the information to Manly. "Nothing more unpatriotic or damaging to our plans for defense could very well be conceived of," Stimson said. He called on his War Department colleagues "to get rid of this infernal disloyalty which we now have working in America First and in these McCormick family papers." Later in the day on 4 December, at a cabinet meeting convened by the president, Attorney General Francis Biddle came around to the same view, declaring that, in his opinion, the papers' editors could be indicted under the Espionage Act of 1917.[16]

Surprisingly, Roosevelt would not go along. Though he at first supported the hard-liners, he soon changed his mind. For reasons no one quite understood, he thought pursuing a legal case against the two papers would be a mistake. He directed his press secretary, Steve Early, to let reporters know that the administration would not challenge the right of their newspapers to print whatever they regarded as news, whether it was accurate or not. FDR did, however, authorize probes by the FBI and Army into the source of the leak.[17] Federal sleuths ultimately grilled more than one hundred military and civilian War Department employees. Among them was Lieutenant Colonel Albert C. Wedemeyer, the Victory Program's overseer and, curiously enough, a strong isolationist and ally of America First leader Charles Lindbergh. But investigators were unable to tie him, or anybody else, to the leak, at least officially.[18] (Manly refused to divulge his source.) Very soon the case was rendered moot. When Japanese war planes bombarded Pearl Harbor on 7 December, the United States found itself engaged in a world war against the Axis powers: Japan, Germany, and Italy. FDR and his team now confronted the life and death issues of national survival. Punishing errant editors, or identifying misguided leakers, vanished as an issue.[19] The country had other business.

Like everybody else, McCormick was surprised by Japan's attack on Pearl Harbor. The *Tribune* blamed "an insane clique of Japanese militants" for launching the war the newspaper had sought to avert. As for its feud with FDR, the paper let bygones be bygones. It dropped its virulent antiwar campaign and joined other newspapers in calling for national unity and the strongest possible effort to defeat America's Axis enemies. This tack did not last. When McCormick learned that America's commanders in Hawaii, Lieutenant General Walter C. Short and Admiral Husband E. Kimmel, privately faulted Washington for their inability to mount a defense, he again turned his fire against the Roosevelt administration: the *Tribune* demanded Knox's resignation.[20]

While the newspaper continued to support the Army and Navy and the overall military effort, it lashed out at the administration's conduct of the war. It charged that FDR was running the war as "a bigger and gaudier WPA [Works Progress Administration] project." It cried that military strategy had been entrusted to "nuts and dreamers" like Harry Hopkins, whose spending policies as relief administrator allegedly contributed to America's weakness. McCormick continued to hope that Hitler and Stalin would destroy each other. Doubting the feasibility of attacking Germany, he urged that American forces be concentrated in the Pacific and not be squandered in wasteful forays in Europe and North Africa. When some of the *Tribune*'s slams were played back by an approving Radio Tokyo, FDR pounced. He assailed "a few bogus patriots who use the sacred freedom of the press to echo the sentiments of the propagandists in Tokyo and Berlin."[21] The feud resumed with renewed force.

～

Late Sunday morning, 7 June 1942, Roosevelt had before him a *Chicago Tribune* article that seemed to divulge secret information. The story had already raised eyebrows at Navy intelligence. Intel officers noted the headline: "Navy Had Word of Jap Plan to Strike at Sea." That wording by itself, they said, signaled to readers something they were not supposed to know: U.S. Navy cryptanalysts had broken into Japan's main naval code and thus were able to furnish Nimitz the "advance word" without which his Pacific Fleet forces could not have routed the Japanese fleet at Midway. The fact that the Navy had accomplished such a breakthrough was one of the crown jewels of U.S. military achievement; it was easily among the two or three most carefully concealed secrets of the war. Any leak that compromised that secret, FDR's war planners feared, would find its way to the Japanese. The revelation would lead them to instantly change their naval code, a development that, Navy officials figured, would set back U.S. codebreakers many years in their efforts to fathom Imperial Navy moves. Nimitz's capabilities would be weakened in the Pacific, his drive against Japanese naval forces slowed. Because of the *Tribune* article, some Navy brass deemed this grim scenario virtually inevitable.

Six months earlier, Roosevelt had grappled with a similar question: what to do about the *Tribune* after it ran a "scoop" exposing "FDR's War Plan"—a plan that, on closer inspection, turned out to be no more than a contingency plan setting out possible moves the United States might make in case it found itself in a global war. FDR's closest advisors thought that story benefitted potential enemies by putting on display the highly classified details of American military planning. They wanted to charge the newspaper with treason. Roosevelt, as noted, rejected that course, deciding it would be ill-advised to take vigorous action against a newspaper. Not this time, at any rate. After hearing that the *Tribune* article could cause the Navy to lose a vital source of information about the Imperial Navy, FDR was boiling mad. According to one prominent historian, Roosevelt briefly contemplated sending a detachment of Marines to Chicago to occupy the Tribune Tower and close the paper.[22] If he did propose such drastic and constitutionally suspect action, wiser heads quickly deflected him from that path. Marines or no Marines, FDR did impart to Navy Secretary Knox and other members of his team one resounding, overriding message: explore every avenue that might lead to the prosecution of Robert McCormick.[23]

Four blocks from the White House, sitting in his large, bare-bones office on the third deck at the old Navy Department building, Ernest J. King discovered the *Tribune* story early Sunday morning. Shortly after arriving to put in his usual full day, the commander in chief was tipped off about it by an aide in the Office of Naval Intelligence (ONI), located just down the hall at Main Navy, as the Navy Department was then called.[24] He read it in the *Times-Herald* under the headline, "U.S. Navy Knew in Advance All about Jap Fleet." The hot-tempered King didn't need any nudging from the White House to form a strong opinion about this story. After seeing everything that was in it, King's main biographer wrote, the admiral flew into a "white fury."[25]

King quickly assembled his top staffers to assess the damage. They all held pretty much the same view: while the article did not explicitly state that U.S. Navy codebreakers had cracked the IJN's cryptographic system, it nevertheless crossed a very dangerous line. There was so much rich detail in the story about the identity and makeup of the Japanese naval forces approaching Midway, all harvested by the Navy's decrypt units at Pearl Harbor, Melbourne, and Washington, that people could be expected to figure it out. As one of Pearl Harbor's intelligence analysts put it, "Any informed reader could only conclude that Japanese codes had been broken."[26] But if that much was clear, there still remained much that was not: where did the story come from, and who, or what group, leaked that information? Since the story carried a Washington dateline and was attributed to "reliable sources in naval intelligence," that indicated King's own bailiwick. Suspicion fell immediately on ONI.

But who in ONI would do such a thing? King's people wanted to talk first to the chief of ONI's Far Eastern Section, Commander Arthur McCollum. "I came down to the Navy Department," McCollum recalled years later, "and my goodness, the place was shaking." He was told to report right away to King's chief of war planning, Rear Admiral Charles M. "Savvy" Cooke Jr. Entering Cooke's office, he was instantly besieged by questions, like "who do you know on the *Chicago Tribune*?" McCollum said he did not know anyone on that newspaper. Cooke was not satisfied: "Mac, you've been talking to reporters some damn place." McCollum asked the admiral to calm down but Cooke was in high dudgeon. He was not backing off. He flashed a copy of the Sunday *Tribune*'s front page and barked, "What do you think of that?"[27]

Now McCollum lost his temper. "Wait a minute, admiral!" McCollum said, and the two exchanged words for a minute. Then McCollum made what he thought was a constructive suggestion. He would take the *Tribune* article back to his office and compare it with Nimitz's original dispatch. "All right," Cooke said. "Take the damn thing out of here. You'd better be right." McCollum returned to his office and compared the contents of the *Tribune* article with his own "bootlegged" copy of Nimitz's original message—a raw copy with all the "mistakes and garbles" that routinely turn up in dispatches and usually are corrected by the radio officers on the receiving end. As the communication process worked, the dispatch would be "cleaned up" and edited before being circulated around the Navy Department and ultimately filed.[28]

In juxtaposing the unedited dispatch with the *Tribune* article, McCollum found the same "mistakes and garbles" in both. "The names of the ships were misspelled in the dispatch and they were misspelled the same way in the paper," McCollum said later. He reached two conclusions. His first judgment was that whoever wrote the *Tribune* story had seen the original, unedited dispatch. If so, he could not have gotten it from the Navy Department, because copies in Navy Department files had been cleaned up and corrected. "This reporter had obviously seen that specific dispatch, and he wasn't here in Washington," McCollum reasoned. "He couldn't have been."[29]

McCollum showed his findings to his boss, ONI's director, Rear Admiral Theodore S. "Ping" Wilkinson. Wilkinson was very much on the spot. His people were the first to be suspected of leaking Nimitz's message, and King did not have a reputation for letting mistakes go unpunished. Wilkinson grabbed the newspaper clipping and the dispatch out of McCollum's hand and charged down the hall toward King's office with McCollum running after him hollering, "Wait, wait, wait, don't take that down there." "He paid no attention," McCollum recalled, "he was a little deaf anyway. He went charging through the outer office and into King's office." There they found Captain Carl Holden, acting director of naval communications. Holden was protesting his innocence. "Well, they can't point the finger at me," Holden told King. "There are only five copies of that dispatch in existence and I've got all five of them."[30]

Now it was Wilkinson's turn. He noted there were actually six copies, counting McCollum's bootlegged copy (obtained by McCollum out of channels). Savvy Cooke showed up just as Wilkinson explained—apparently to King's satisfaction—why McCollum and, indeed, all of Navy intelligence, could not have been the source of the leak. Cooke and King calmed down as far as ONI was concerned, but Cooke was still fuming. He was adamant that McCormick should be prosecuted. "He's a goddam traitor, that's what he is," Cooke said. "Going to give it to the Department of Justice. The president is buying this thing and we're going to hang this guy higher than Haman."[31]

⟨∾⟩

ONI was off the hook. So was naval communications. From the evidence King gathered, the entire Navy Department looked clean. Where, then, had the story come from? King called in a *Tribune* reporter with whom he was acquainted, Walter Trohan, the newspaper's White House correspondent who also covered military affairs. King started to berate Trohan about the story. "I was taken to task by the icy Admiral Ernest King," Trohan wrote later. But Trohan, a diehard conservative who shared McCormick's anti–New Deal and isolationist sentiments, couldn't be pushed. "I gave him as good as he dished out, being confident the story was not the *Tribune*'s because it had not been submitted to censorship through the [Washington] bureau. I assumed it had been picked up and rewritten from the wires or another paper."[32]

For all his bluster, Trohan did not know any more about the source of the story than did the Navy. He did, however, offer to make inquiries and call back if he learned anything. Also, in the course of Trohan's heated conversation with King, a critical issue surfaced: How did this story get through censorship? If the *Tribune's* Washington bureau had not submitted it, who did? And if it was submitted to a censor, which one? There were, after all, two censors. There was the Navy's Office of Public Relations, which performed censorship duties in Washington for stories reported in Navy combat zones. And there was the civilian Office of Censorship, headquartered in an old federal building downtown; it had jurisdiction over war-related articles developed inside the United States. Because the *Tribune* piece contained classified information on Midway, King's people figured the censor should have been the Navy itself. They got in touch with Captain Leland P. Lovette in public relations. He said he would look into it.[33]

Very quickly Lovette established that his office had neither reviewed nor received any copy from the *Chicago Tribune* concerning Midway. It did have in its possession, however, a 3,500-word article by a *Tribune* war correspondent named Stanley Johnston, with sixteen photographs, on the Coral Sea battle. The piece had been sent over by the Office of Censorship on 6 June for review by Navy censors. The Navy promptly placed the story and all the pictures in escrow pending release of further details of the Coral Sea campaign. (As of 7 June, the Navy still had not informed the American public about the loss of *Lexington* a month earlier.)[34] Stanley Johnston seemed worth checking out.

Lovette's assistant, Commander Robert W. Berry, called Waldo Drake in Honolulu, reaching him around 7 a.m. local time (it was around noon in Washington). Yes, Drake knew Johnston. He filled in Berry on what authorities in Washington probably already knew but had lost track of: Johnston sailed out with *Lexington* on 15 April. He was known to have lived through the carrier's ordeal on 8 May and, as far as Drake could tell, had been on one of the transports that conveyed Lex's survivors to the U.S. mainland on 2 June. Drake gave Johnston high marks for reliability; he had always faithfully submitted his copy to fleet censors. He didn't think the Navy had anything to worry about as far as Johnston was concerned. He assured Berry that, before Johnston had departed Pearl Harbor, he had signed the usual correspondent's agreement to submit to Navy review everything he wrote while at sea.[35]

Despite Drake's assurances, Lovette thought Johnston probably wrote the *Tribune* article. But he had no idea how Johnston got the story or, for that matter, how it got into print. He next called his civilian counterpart, Nat Howard, assistant director, Press Division, at the Office of Censorship. Did he, or anybody in his office, clear the *Tribune* story or know anything about it? When Howard professed ignorance, Lovette briefed him on the matter. He told Howard about Stanley Johnston, and he closed with a kicker: information in the story was known to no more than ten men in the entire Navy Department.[36] In other words, papers printing the Midway story had transgressed every rule the Navy had put in place to safeguard its secrets and in the process had laid bare one of the government's most scrupulously veiled military activities: codebreaking.

Howard was not a typical censor nor was he an ordinary bureaucrat. He was the editor of the *Cleveland News*, on leave from the paper to serve with the Office of Censorship. He took the post out of a sense of patriotic duty. He believed in freedom of the press as much as Robert R. McCormick. He hated to tell editors what they could and could not print. He also thought that in time of war, the military needed certain latitude to protect secrets—types of information spelled out in the OC's voluntary code. The code was voluntary because it was not imposed; however, the newspaper industry earlier in the year had agreed to observe it.

As shaped by the Office of Censorship, restricted information fell into categories such as Troops, Ships, Planes, Fortifications, and Production. Under the OC's guidelines, newspapers could print information under those headings only if they had obtained "appropriate authority" to do so from a government or military official.[37] Howard regarded the whole idea of censorship as odious, but he believed the only way to preserve the government's system of voluntary censorship was for the press to cooperate. If it did not, he feared the alternative would be worse—a form of mandatory censorship that he and other journalists would find even more abhorrent.

Howard now proceeded with a task he dreaded. He had to ask a bunch of newspaper editors how they obtained a certain story and why they printed it. The article in question troubled him; it appeared to be a flagrant violation of the OC's code. He judged that it had breached the code's Ship's Clause that, among other things, ruled out publishing information "*about the location of enemy naval or merchant vessels in or near American waters*"[38] (emphasis added). Such information could be published only if the newspaper had gotten "appropriate authority" from a responsible official. Howard wondered how any official could have sanctioned the *Tribune*'s Midway story.

He first called the *Times-Herald*, ultimately reaching a top editor, Frank Waldrop. Waldrop was contrite. He noted that the story was circulated by the Chicago Tribune Press Service and had arrived in his office around midnight while he was editor in charge. Waldrop put the story in the paper because he thought it "must have been cleared" before it was distributed. He said he was beginning to realize his mistake; in all likelihood, the story had been circulated without prior clearance—at the *Tribune*'s risk and the risk of its press service clients.[39]

The Waldrop conversation confirmed that the Midway story had originated outside Washington, almost certainly in Chicago. Howard now called the *Tribune*'s Washington bureau chief, Arthur Sears Henning. Howard was testier with Henning. As Howard always did, he asked Henning where the *Tribune* got the story. He also asked him to provide the "appropriate authority" for publishing this highly sensitive information—material that seemed clearly to contravene the code's Ship's Clause. He mentioned Stanley Johnston. If the story had come from Johnston, did the *Tribune* not know that the correspondent was required to submit his copy to a Navy censor? Yet the article had been circulated to no censor, Navy or civilian. Why? Howard told Henning that unless he received satisfactory answers to these questions, the Office of Censorship was prepared to officially, and publicly, cite the *Chicago Tribune* for violating the OC's *Code of Wartime Practices for the American Press*. The citation might be announced as soon as the next day. Henning did not give an inch; he simply replied that he would refer the matter to the *Tribune*'s managing editor, Pat Maloney, and get back to Howard later in the day.[40]

Henning reached Maloney at his golf club around 1 p.m. Maloney was not pleased. "So it was with a very sad heart that I got the message from Mr. Henning—I was over to play golf, that is my day off, Sunday—that the Censorship Bureau was objecting to our story," Maloney told federal investigators. "I believe the word was 'cited,' or something."[41] Strictly symbolic as it may have seemed, a citation against the *Chicago Tribune* would be no small matter. True, the OC had no enforcement powers; the citations it issued carried no civil or criminal penalties. But the office did have moral authority. Through its citations, the office could direct unwanted publicity at a recalcitrant newspaper or radio station, and by so doing create the impression that a

particular media organization was flouting the rules other papers respected. Such a citation would not help the *Tribune*, already under fire for its relentless attacks on Roosevelt. McCormick would not be happy. A citation would also reflect on Maloney's leadership. Ironically, up until this point, the *Tribune* had one of the best records among big city dailies for cooperating with Washington's censors.[42]

With much at stake, possibly even Maloney's job, the *Tribune*'s managing editor and the paper's Washington bureau chief started collaborating on a statement they hoped would clear them and their newspaper with the Office of Censorship. They worked off and on for hours, talking through the *Tribune* switchboard and a telephone booth out at Maloney's golf club. With only a few timeouts to deal with occasional distractions, they worked late into the afternoon.[43]

∼

Nat Howard had a new problem. Shortly after talking with Henning he learned, as did the Navy, that the *Tribune*'s controversial Midway article also had appeared in the *New York Daily News*, published by another one of McCormick's cousins, Joseph M. Patterson, and the *San Francisco Chronicle*.[44] To keep the story from showing up in other papers, Howard acted decisively. At around 1 p.m., he released to the four press wires—Associated Press, United Press, International News Service, and Trans-Radio—the following special message: "The Office of Censorship calls special attention to provisions in the 'ships' clause of the censorship Code that nothing be published of movements of United States naval ships in American waters of the Pacific, or of tactical disposition of naval forces indicating *any prior knowledge* of enemy movements or strength, or of enemy ship locations, movements or identities in American waters of the Pacific, other than is contained in the official communiques of Navy or War Departments or their commands" (emphasis added).[45]

The note purported to cite the language of the Ships Clause to cover enemy vessels wherever they might be. Unfortunately for the argument Howard was trying to make, there was no such wording in the clause. That provision did not tell editors to refrain from indicating prior knowledge of enemy movements or strength. That was Howard's invention. His note actually amended the code. The Office of Censorship would soon adopt Howard's new wording and incorporate it into the Ship's Clause, but as of

6 June the old language had been the official version—the version editors were expected to observe. This discrepancy did not prevent Howard from sending the following telegram to the managing editors of the *Los Angeles Times*, the *St. Louis Globe Democrat*, and other clients of the Chicago Tribune Press Service: "DID YOUR NEWSPAPER THIS MORNING PUBLISH CHICAGO TRIBUNE PRESS SERVICE STORY CONCERNING LOCATION MOVEMENT AND IDENTITY OF ENEMY NAVAL SHIPS IN AMERICAN WATERS MIDWAY AND OAHU ISLANDS AND INFERENTIAL MOVEMENT UNITED STATES NAVAL SHIPS TO MEET THESE? STORY TRANSGRESSED SHIPS CLAUSE PRESS CENSORSHIP CODE APPARENTLY WITHOUT APPROPRIATE AUTHORITY."[46]

Henning called Howard at 3:28 p.m. to complain about the telegram. He said his managing editor wanted to know how the *Tribune* story violated the Ships Clause. He argued that by Howard's idea of "location," the entire Pacific Ocean could be defined as "American waters." Howard snapped that he could define "location" for himself. He said his overriding point was that the Office of Censorship regarded the *Tribune* story "a highly dangerous" story. He reiterated that the office remained ready to announce the citation discussed earlier, and he stated that he was still waiting for the *Tribune*'s explanation. Henning said he would have the newspaper's statement by the end of the day.[47]

∽

By early afternoon, Ernest King had learned a lot about the *Tribune* story. The answer to the question of authorship had been sitting on his desk for days. It turned up in a memo to the commander in chief from Nimitz endorsing a recommendation from Fitch and Sherman that *Chicago Tribune* correspondent Stanley Johnston be awarded recognition—possibly in the form of a decoration—for his courageous conduct rescuing *Lexington* officers and men during the day of that carrier's demise. King would have noted that the recommendation was based on the eyewitness testimony of *Lexington*'s executive officer, Commander Morton Seligman. He also would have noted that Fitch and Sherman proposed a Distinguished Service Medal for Seligman, citing that officer's exemplary conduct that day. A call by King's staff to the Eleventh Naval District in San Diego confirmed that Johnston and Seligman, along with 1,250 other *Lexington* survivors, were on the transport ship *Barnett* that made port on 2 June.

Any lingering doubts King may have retained about the origins of the story were resolved when the *Tribune*'s Walter Trohan called back, as he said he would if he found out anything. According to Trohan, the story was written in Chicago with the Washington dateline added later to give the impression it was based on sources at the Navy Department.[48] Stanley Johnston was based in Chicago; he would have had plenty of time to make his way from the West Coast to the *Tribune* office by Saturday, 6 June, to write the story. King suspected that while in *Barnett*, Johnston had somehow gotten hold of Nimitz's 31 May dispatch: Message 311221. He did not know why the dispatch happened to be in *Barnett* or how the correspondent had obtained it, but he believed Johnston had read it and then recklessly used it as the basis for an article.

The commander in chief now put in place a sweeping Navy investigation to determine the source of the leak. He ordered the Eleventh Naval District in San Diego and the Twelfth Naval District in San Francisco, where *Barnett* was now moored, to do some investigating. They were to find out everything they could about Stanley Johnston, reconstruct his every move on the West Coast, interview all the *Lexington* officers and *Barnett* crew members they could round up, including *Barnett*'s captain, and of particular interest Commander Seligman, now residing in a San Diego suburb and awaiting back surgery. Also, King authorized his chief of staff, Vice Admiral Russell Willson, to bring Johnston to Washington for questioning by Navy officials.

King also wanted to bring the press into line with Navy thinking. He thought something should be done to prevent publication of another story like the *Tribune*'s. He did not know exactly what step to take; he did not have great relations with the press. Although he respected some journalists personally, he did not share their creed that the public had a right to know the details of important war developments. King's attitude toward the press had already ruffled feathers in Washington. When the administration's Office of War Information (OWI) weeks earlier had requested an expanded flow of Navy-related news, King refused. OWI's people mused among themselves that if King had his way he would issue but one statement—an announcement that the war was over: The United States had won.[49]

While King pondered his next move, he heard from Army Chief of Staff George Marshall. Marshall was just as furious as King about the Midway article. After reading the *Times-Herald* that morning, Marshall dashed off a two-page memo to King. It stated that "the way to handle this thing is for you to have an immediate press conference," during which King could warn reporters against stories that put vital secrets at risk. "I am strongly of the opinion that this should be done today," Marshall declared. The mercurial King did not always agree with Marshall, but he did agree this time.[50] He invited reporters—except those representing the *Tribune*—to attend a rare 5 p.m. press conference in his office. The assembled journalists were treated to a virtuoso King performance. It consisted of two messages. The first was intended for the American people—and the world. Everyone should realize, he asserted, that the U.S. Navy's presence near Midway was not strange. It was the result of routine legwork, not the consequence of any magical or esoteric fact gathering.

To support this fairy tale, King conjured out of thin air a seemingly logical scenario of Navy scouting. Chatting amiably, affecting a helpful air, King addressed the newsmen the way a benign schoolmaster might talk to a room full of schoolchildren. He continued in this jocular, bantering vein, finally getting around to the workings of intelligence. It was a rather pedestrian business, he insisted, just a matter of piecing information together "after the manner of a jig saw puzzle." He explained how the U.S. Navy played the game before the Battle of Midway. Anticipating a Midway strike was no big deal; it required no unusual genius; it was just a matter of fitting together the pieces in the right way, the way a schoolboy might. After all, the United States has many submarines scattered about the western Pacific, and they were able to provide a good deal of information. Also, it was clear after the recent engagement in the Coral Sea that the Japanese would have to go somewhere and do something. Looking at the map, King mused that almost anybody could see that among America's various important outposts, Dutch Harbor and Midway offered the Japanese their best chance of an action. "So to this extent we were prepared for the assault upon Midway," he continued reasonably, "and recognized that Alaska might also be attacked." America's Navy just worked out a simple puzzle.[51]

But jigsaw puzzles can be dangerous, King indicated, now warming to his main point. Puzzles are a game that two can play—Japanese as well as Americans. So the American military cannot lightly divulge critical information, or sometimes even routine information, because in context, that material could be a useful piece in the puzzle. "It is not necessary to complete the 'jig saw puzzle' in order to gain vital information," King noted, "but only to fit together a key part or parts thereof, in order to become possessed of important military information."[52]

King let that sink in before switching gears. Suddenly a different King materialized; it was the old commander in chief, stern faced and finger wagging. Adopting a far harsher tone, he told reporters that everything he was about to say was strictly off the record: "The *Washington Times-Herald* published, this morning, an item which purported to give 'chapter and verse' as to the composition and functions of Japanese forces advancing toward Midway," King stated. "This information came unmistakably, from a 'leak' that may involve serious consequences." He described those consequences in blunt terms: "It compromises a vital and secret source of information, which will henceforth be closed to us. The military consequences are so obvious that I do not need to dwell on them—nor to request you to be on your guard against, even inadvertently, being a party to any disclosure which will give 'aid and comfort' to the enemy."[53]

There it was in less than one hundred words: the *Chicago Tribune* article, carried also by the *Times-Herald*, had blown a secret critical to America's successful conduct of the Pacific War. He reproached the *Tribune* without mentioning it by name. He laid out the worst-case scenario that could result from the *Tribune*'s "leak," presenting it as indisputable fact: *a vital and secret source of information will henceforth be closed to us.* And he put American correspondents on notice that if they, or their brethren in other news outlets, in the future wrote stories like this one, they would be giving "aid and comfort" to the enemy—possibly even committing treason.

❧

Henning was now ready to confront Howard. After consulting back and forth all day by long-distance phone, he and Maloney finally completed their statement by around 6:30 p.m. Henning promptly messengered it over to the OC office. It was short but hard-hitting. The two newsmen contended that the *Tribune*'s story conformed "to the Censorship Code of January 15, 1942 in every respect" because "there is nothing in the Censorship Code forbidding the publication of the identity of enemy ships wherever engaged." Moreover, they went on, "the story contains no statement of the location, movements and identity of U.S. ships not contained in previously published Navy communiques."[54]

Howard was taken aback, but not only by the Henning-Maloney statement. He had heard earlier from a *Tribune* source that the Navy was incorrect in its assertion that Johnston had signed an agreement pledging to submit all his copy in advance to Navy censors. He learned from Navy PR sources what the Navy's top brass did not yet know: neither James Bassett nor Waldo Drake had required Johnston to sign a censorship pledge. Apparently, Johnston was *not* committed to Navy censorship in any way.[55] Unlikely as this seemed, Howard paused. He thought that without confirming proof that Johnston had signed a censorship agreement, the *Tribune*'s claim could not be dismissed. The case was starting to look murky. Howard prudently decided he had better hold his fire and consult with his boss, the director of the censorship office, Byron Price.

Like Howard, Price was a seasoned journalist. He had been executive editor of the Associated Press until late December, when FDR recruited him to run the censorship office. Now he was on an indefinite sabbatical, committed to somehow making workable the concept of voluntary censorship. The *Tribune*'s transgression—if that, in fact, was what it was—would seem to be a test case of the OC's ability to bring about newspaper compliance with its code. Price was of two minds. "As a professional newspaperman I despised McCormick's egotism and arrogance and was convinced that the *Tribune*'s studied distortion of the facts on some occasions was doing great harm to American journalism," Price said later. "But as director of censorship I could not let that enter into my thinking."[56]

Price and Howard took a new look at the issue before them. They put the *Tribune* article and the OC's code side by side; they saw that the case was not as clear-cut as they had at first thought. There was only one thing to do. Howard called Henning. He let Henning know that he agreed with the Navy's view that the *Tribune* story was dangerous and could do great harm to America's war effort. Consequently, the OC that day had amended the Ships Clause—henceforth, the code would rule out stories that hinted at *prior knowledge* of Japanese ship movements, and it would not sanction reporting of Japanese ship movements in *any* waters, unless previously included in an official Navy communique. But, Howard admitted, the new wording was not in effect on 6 June, so it could not be used as a measure for stories written on or before that date. Howard told Henning the case was borderline.[57] The *Tribune* had violated the spirit of the code, but not the letter.[58] The OC would issue no citation against the *Tribune*.

Maloney was jubilant when he got the news. He felt vindicated. He interpreted the OC's newly announced amendment to its Ship's Clause "as

tantamount to an admission that it was not covered in the original code"—
the "it" standing for Japanese ship movement activity reported in the *Tribune* story. Maloney now got on the phone to the *Tribune*'s publisher, Robert
McCormick. He had not called earlier because he did not want to bother
McCormick unnecessarily about a dispute that could soon blow over. It did
blow over, or at least it seemed to. "I called Colonel McCormick's attention
to it," Maloney said, "and told him I had the word that the censor had cleared
us, and I had some good word along with the bad, and so informed him."[59]

Maloney overstated the censor's position. Howard and Price had not
precisely cleared the *Tribune* story; they simply decided to refrain from pursuing a citation against the newspaper. There was also another player—the
U.S. Navy—to be heard from. So if Maloney and McCormick enjoyed a sense
of relief after the OC's decision, it proved short-lived. The Office of Censorship may have decided to drop the matter, but the Navy had not. In truth, the
OC did not have jurisdiction over the *Tribune* article. The information in it
was gathered in a combat zone; it was a story for Navy censors to review and
clear, if it was to be cleared. So when Navy officials learned of the OC's action,
or nonaction, they had mixed feelings. Lovette understood Howard's reasoning and called to thank him for blocking further circulation of the story.
But he noted the Navy was not through with the matter. Lovette's superiors
did not want to let it drop. King wanted to know the source of the leak; the
commander in chief may have been exaggerating only slightly when he told
Trohan earlier that if the leak was found in the Navy, the guilty man would
be shot.[60] King thought the best way to find the "leaker" was to grill Johnston,
now understood to be the story's author. Russell Willson called Henning to
let him know the Navy was continuing its investigating; he wanted to see
Johnston in his office the next day.

Shortly after finishing his chat with Maloney, McCormick got another
call, this one from Henning. McCormick was flabbergasted. He thought the
matter had been resolved. Yet it appeared a *Tribune* staffer, Stanley Johnston,
was in serious trouble with the Navy. Although an unyielding isolationist,
McCormick had always supported the military; he had taken pains over the
years to cultivate close relations with both services. He did not want those
bonds to fray; he did not want a cloud hanging over the *Tribune*. He took two
steps. First, he called back Maloney and told him to tell Johnston to get on
the next plane to Washington. Then he fired off a rather remarkable telegram
for Henning to deliver to Admiral King. It read,

I had only heard of the newspaper story at 7 o'clock tonight. I had not read the story before that. The news of the battle coming in at 8 o'clock last night shortly after I had been told that we could not hold Alaska, filled my day. I think it also affected our managing editor Maloney's judgment. As a former staff officer, of course I fully appreciate the impropriety of attributing the source of news to any anonymous staff officer, but Maloney, having been a pursuit pilot in Rickenbacker's squadron, did not see it that way. That was the only blunder I see in the story, which was creditable to the Navy, disclosed no information whatever to the enemy and was most helpful to public morale. Having been thru war and battle, as you have, I am sure you know the intimacy they engender among comrades. It is quite natural that our correspondent, Stanley Johnstone [sic], knew all that was going on. His entire bona fides was shown by his sending his story and his pictures to Washington, and, of course, not breathing a word of the Japanese movement until after the victory had been announced last night. As soon as I heard of the misunderstanding, I ordered that full information be furnished to you, of course. I have sent Stanley Johnstone [sic] to Washington with orders to tell you everything you wish to know. I hope the matter is cleared up satisfactorily. If such is not the case I wish you would communicate either with me directly or with Arthur Sears Henning, head of our Washington bureau.[61]

A very agitated Maloney now called Johnston at his home. He was to drop what he was doing. He was to get moving right away, make whatever arrangements by plane or train he could, but he was to arrive on time, 9 a.m., at Admiral King's office, Navy Department, the next day. The reporter said he would be there. Johnston was going to Washington.

CHAPTER 6

MOMENTS OF TRUTH

I lied to you this morning.
—*Stanley Johnston*

Johnston did not have an easy trip. After a jolting and disagreeable phone call from Pat Maloney around 9 p.m. Sunday, he did what he was ordered to do. He started calling airlines. Since there were no direct flights out of Chicago to Washington that night, he did the next best thing. He snared a flight to New York, but just barely. He showed up at the gate minutes before it closed at 10:30 p.m. By the time his plane touched down in New York, his only option for reaching Washington was a late train. Running well behind schedule, he finally showed up at the *Tribune*'s Washington bureau around 10:30 in the morning, tired, rumpled, and baffled by the Navy's urgent and seemingly unreasonable demand to question him. He was told to get over to Main Navy, where Arthur Sears Henning was waiting for him. The two made their way up to the third deck, appearing in King's office at 11 a.m.; they were exactly two hours late.[1]

The commander in chief did not receive them, as by now he had other business. They were met instead by King's chief of staff, the dour and sometimes prickly Russell Willson. Vice Admiral Willson ushered them into his nearby office. Henning and a bleary-eyed Johnston found themselves face-to-face with a roomful of brass hats—some of the highest-ranking officers at Main Navy. Besides Willson himself, the group included Vice Admiral Frederick L. Horne, Vice Chief of Naval Operations; Rear Admiral Wilkinson, director of naval intelligence; and Rear Admiral Arthur J. Hepburn, director of the Navy's Office of Public Relations, along with three Hepburn subordinates.[2] They constituted a formidable-looking group.

For all that Navy firepower, the session was remarkably informal, almost relaxed. At least it started out that way. The interview was not recorded. No written statements were submitted. There was no sworn testimony. No notes were taken, although Wilkinson later circulated a memorandum summarizing the main points of the meeting. This was to be a friendly chat. Henning started things out by introducing Johnston who, he said, was appearing on the express orders of the *Tribune*'s publisher, Robert McCormick. McCormick, Henning commented, just wanted to give Navy officials any information that would help them resolve their concerns about the article in question. Willson kept the spirit of amiability alive by noting that he had just received a heartfelt report from Admiral Fitch; the admiral recommended that Johnston receive a citation for the bravery he displayed assisting wounded personnel while *Lexington* was under fire during the Battle of the Coral Sea.[3] The admirals nodded approvingly.

If Willson brought up Fitch's citation proposal to disarm Johnston and possibly soften him up, he succeeded, but only to a limited extent. Johnston readily admitted there were serious errors in the story. Putting a Washington dateline on the article was a mistake, as was the statement that the information was derived from "reliable sources in naval intelligence." He said he wrote the article in Chicago relying solely on material he obtained on board ship and from *Jane's Fighting Ships*. He said he did not know anyone in naval intelligence. But if those were bloopers, they were not his bloopers. They were aspects of the story inserted by "someone else" during the editing process—a process that, at least at the *Tribune*, excluded the reporter. He did not know who put those things in, whether it was his rewrite man or his editor. Whatever he might be guilty of, he was not liable for those particular miscues.[4]

Well, maybe not, but did Johnston not know that the agreement he had signed before boarding *Lexington* required him to submit all his copy to a Navy censor? Johnston said he had no trouble with Navy censorship. He said that while based at Pearl Harbor, and while on board *Lexington* and rescue ships in the Coral Sea, he had unfailingly submitted his stories to Waldo Drake for review. As for his Midway story on the *Tribune*'s front page early Sunday morning, he recalled how surprised he was that his editors had gotten the piece cleared by censors so quickly; he simply assumed they had submitted it for Navy scrutiny. He did not contest the Navy's right to examine his copy, but he took issue with the admirals' claim that he was obligated to obey this rule because of a written agreement. He had signed no such pledge—an assertion that contradicted what the admirals had heard from Drake. He observed censorship, he said, because of oral instructions from Drake and others. But he had not actually signed anything—a point that would loom large in the weeks ahead as the Navy proceeded with its case.

Of course, the admirals had no way of knowing whether Johnston was telling the truth or not. It was just his word against Drake's. Suspending judgment on the censorship issue, Willson got around to the heart of the matter: How did he, Johnston, acquire the information set forth in his *Tribune* article? Was the story based on a dispatch, possibly one prepared by the commander in chief, Pacific Fleet, Admiral Nimitz? Had he received that CINCPAC message from any member of *Lexington*'s crew? Had he even seen it? If not, from where did he get all those details about the Imperial Navy force approaching Midway?[5]

Willson and his colleagues now confronted a different Johnston. Candid and forthcoming at first, he was now evasive and guarded. They ran into the same Johnston the *Tribune*'s managing editor, Pat Maloney, encountered Saturday night when he asked his reporter where he got his information about Japan's Midway force. Either because of fatigue or some other reason, he started to give stock answers. He affected surprise that such concerns should even be raised. There really was no mystery about how he got his material, or dope, as he called it. On board *Barnett* he shared a suite of rooms with Lex's executive officer and another officer. Day after day *Lexington*'s men jammed their way into the suite either to see the exec, Commander Seligman, or just sit around and chat and enjoy a cup of coffee. Eventually, Johnston said, they noticed a large map of the Pacific Ocean pinned to the bulkhead above a desk in his nearby sleeping quarters. They congregated in front of this map and discussed possible Japanese, and American, moves in the northern and central Pacific, where the Imperial Navy was known to be planning an invasion. "It was natural that I would hear the discussions," he said.[6]

From those conversations, along with a thorough study of *Jane's Fighting Ships*, Johnston said he pieced together the composition of the Imperial Navy's order of battle for Midway. That is all there was to it. No, he had not seen any secret dispatch from Nimitz. He had not seen any list of ships similar to the list that appeared in his article. He would not have used it if he had. He recognized that certain documents were off limits. Nor had any Lex officer provided him this information. There was nothing questionable in the way he did his work. Hearing this, the admirals rolled their eyes.[7]

Thoroughly exasperated, Willson interrupted Johnston. He glared at the correspondent and asked him if he expected the officers present to believe that such a meticulously detailed list could be constructed almost entirely from old manuals and casual, coffee-table conversation. Willson's aggressive questioning was not merely a piece of theater; he knew the intricacies of codebreaking backward and forward, having served as the Navy's first leader of its Code and Signal Section in 1917. He was virtually one of the Navy's cryptologic pioneers. So when Johnston hesitated, Willson pressed on. The admiral said he was intrigued by several aspects of Johnston's article. It was curious, he thought, that the ships cited in his article matched up almost perfectly with those named in Nimitz's dispatch. Not only that, they appeared in the same order, and under the same headings: strike force, support force, occupation force. From where did Johnston obtain that organization if not from Nimitz's secret dispatch?[8]

Willson found other anomalies in Johnston's article—spelling, for example. He could not help but note that when Nimitz misspelled the name of an IJN ship, so did Johnston. If Johnston had relied so heavily on *Jane's Fighting Ships* for his information, why did he not use *Jane's* correct spelling for the battleship *Kirisima*, rather than Nimitz's incorrect *Kirishima*?[9] And how could Johnston explain that his story named three cruisers—*Chitore*, *Chakas*, and *Choda*—that do not even show up in *Jane's*, although they did appear in *Barnett's* decrypted version of Nimitz's dispatch? Where did those names come from? Surely not from a wardroom bull session.

Johnston could not answer Willson's questions. He said he had no explanation for the alleged similarities between his story and the CINCPAC message. Willson then asked Henning if it was reasonable to believe that the two documents could be so strikingly alike if the article's author had not copied the Imperial Navy's order of battle from a master list. Henning agreed that it was hard to believe, if the actual comparison was as precise as Willson stated.[10]

Willson halted the meeting. He and the other officers present were clearly displeased with Johnston's presentation; they did not believe he had told the truth, or at least the whole truth. The admirals and the two newspapermen bid rather icy farewells. Almost as an afterthought, Willson asked Johnston if he would be available to appear before a future investigatory tribunal if the Navy Department set one up. The reporter said he would be there.[11] The *Tribune* staffers rather glumly departed Main Navy, each feeling the meeting had not gone well. Henning returned to his Washington office, while Johnston checked into a hotel to get some rest but did not get much. "Mr.

Henning telephoned me and said Admiral Willson was not satisfied," John-ston recalled later. "I said: 'Well, I will go back and see him again.'"[12]

By the time Johnston reappeared at Willson's office, it was late after-noon. This time Willson talked with Johnston alone. The admiral thought he had heard everything, but nothing prepared him for Johnston's opening comment: "I lied to you this morning."[13] No stenographer was there to write that down; the meeting was not recorded. Willson did not take notes, but he remembered Johnston's words and circulated them to King and King's staff. Whether Johnston used those exact words or similar language that meant the same thing could never be confirmed. The quote shows up in Wilkinson's memo and FBI memoranda based on conversations with Willson. The quote does not show up, however, in Johnston's version of the meeting. But from the correspondent's summary of this talk (the only written record of his sec-ond conversation), it is clear he had changed his story very nearly 180 degrees from his morning account.[14]

The Navy now had confirmation that Johnston had seen some kind of list. As Johnston explained it, he came across the list accidentally late in the evening on 2 June just after *Barnett* had docked in San Diego. "I was using the typewriter to clean up my stories and on moving some old papers from my desk saw a piece of paper with light blue lines on which someone had written the names of Japanese warships and listed transports etc., under headings of 'striking force,' 'occupation force,' and 'support force,'" Johnston told Willson. "The large number of ships and their groupings suggested to me that this evidently referred to something big. I noticed that someone had scratched out several names and written in other names as if to trying to straighten out errors." Then he added a kicker: "I copied the names off the list." That night, after exiting *Barnett*, "I examined the copy again and typed out a memo to send to my editor just in case some news broke to indicate an attack by such a force," Johnston said. It was the information on that list, embellished by additional material culled from *Jane's Fighting Ships*, that appeared in Johnston's story in Sunday's *Chicago Tribune*.[15]

Johnston defended his story. He maintained that it could not have told the Japanese anything they did not already know. Articles in other news-papers, as well as a lengthy dispatch by the Associated Press, suggested that "we had expected an attack," he said. "The fact that our navy forces were at sea and in the right place to intercept the enemy was proof both to me—and for that matter, the Japanese also—that we had prior warning of their intentions," Johnston wrote, recounting his words to Willson. "I insisted that the enemy would certainly not believe they were there by coincidence."[16] So where was the harm in his article?

How Willson responded is not known. Johnston did not report Willson's comments, and Willson in his own brief note to his fellow officers did not provide a blow-by-blow account of the conversation.[17] But he might have pointed out that none of the other articles, including the in-depth piece by AP, intimated that the U.S. Navy possessed a detailed description of the Imperial Navy's order of battle in advance of the Midway campaign. That was the rub. Not that the U.S. Navy knew Midway might be invaded, but that it had in hand, well ahead of time, the organization of the IJN's attacking forces, along with the names of many Japanese warships that would be engaged in that struggle. Willson might have repeated his earlier question: from where could the U.S. Navy have gotten this information? He thought the Japanese would have no trouble figuring it out, assuming Imperial Navy commanders came into possession of the *Tribune* article.

Whatever Willson did or did not say to Johnston, he concluded with one final question: why had the correspondent not delivered a full and honest report during the morning session? Johnston did not hold back on this one. He said his first realization that "something was brewing" registered Sunday night when he was ordered to Washington. "Naturally I immediately realized that this matter might get some of the men with whom I had recently been associated with into trouble and I naturally had a desire not to do this," he said.[18]

With this admission, Johnston's Washington interlude ended. He returned to his hotel and, first thing Tuesday morning, 9 June, typed up his best recollection of what he had said the previous afternoon. He prepared two copies of his "confession," if that is what it was. He dropped off one at the *Tribune*'s Washington office, with a request that Arthur Henning deliver a copy to Admiral Willson later in the week. Upon his return to Chicago, he handed the other to Maloney, who, he presumed, circulated it to McCormick.

∾

After hearing Willson's report, a profoundly disgusted King concluded the obvious: the flagrant security breach that had upset the White House and confounded the Navy Department had occurred on an obscure transport ship called *Barnett*. That much was clear. Less clear was how, and why,

Nimitz's secret dispatch—intended to alert all task force commanders about an impending action in the central Pacific—materialized on that ordinary vessel. Acting communications director Holden solved part of the riddle. He told King that CINCPAC's message was enciphered in a crypto channel held by all Class 3 vessels and above. Such ships are entitled to carry an electronic cipher machine (ECM), a highly classified device able to decrypt the Pacific Fleet's highest-priority dispatches. For reasons no one could understand, the lowly *Barnett* fell into Class 3. *Barnett* thus had the capability to receive and, if appropriately trained radiomen were on board, decipher the Pacific Fleet's top-secret messages. It did so on 31 May 1942.[19]

King gleaned two things from Holden's news. While there may have been a slipup on the receiving end, on *Barnett*, there also was a problem on the sending end: Pacific Fleet headquarters. To prevent another leak of this magnitude, COMINCH took corrective action. Late Monday he fired off a radiogram to CINCPAC, in part to close a loophole in CINCPAC's communication system and in part to lecture Nimitz on the fine points of radio security:

> CONTENTS OF YOUR THIRTYONE TWELVE TWENTY-ONE MAY REPEAT THREE ONE ONE TWO TWO ONE WERE PUBLISHED ALMOST VERBATIM IN SEVERAL NEWSPAPERS YESTERDAY X ARTICLE ORIGINATED WITH CORRESPONDENT STANLEY JOHNSTON EMBARKED IN BARNETT UNTIL JUNE SECOND X WHILE YOUR DISPATCH WAS ADDRESSED TASK FORCE COMMANDERS IT WAS SENT IN CHANNEL AVAILABLE TO NEARLY ALL SHIPS WHICH EMPHASIZES NEED OF CARE IN USING CHANNELS X COMINCH INVESTIGATING ON BARNETT AND AT SAN DIEGO[20]

COMINCH was not through. A day later, on 9 June, he dispatched a follow-up message to all ships in the U.S. Fleet, whether in the Atlantic or the Pacific:

> A VERY RECENT INCIDENT LEADING TO PUBLIC DISCLOSURE OF THE CONTENTS OF A SECRET NAVAL DESPATCH REQUIRES EMPHASIS ON THE FACT THAT THE BURDEN OF PROOF IS ON ANY FLAG OR COMMANDING OFFICER WHO CAUSES ANY DESPATCH TO

BE DECODED WHICH IS NOT REPEAT NOT ADDRESSED TO HIM.

ORIGINATING OFFICERS ARE ENJOINED TO SEE TO IT THAT ACTION AND INFORMATION ADDRESSEES ARE RIGOROUSLY RESTRICTED TO THOSE WHO NEED REPEAT NEED TO KNOW AND THAT THE TRANSMITTING AND CRYPTO CHANNELS USED ARE SUITED TO CARRY OUT SUCH RESTRICTION.

CONTENTS OF SECRET DESPATCHES MUST BE COMMUNICATED ONLY TO THOSE WHO NEED TO KNOW AND UTMOST CARE MUST BE TAKEN TO SEE THAT SECRET INFORMATION IS NOT DISCLOSED TO ANY OTHERS WHATEVER EITHER DIRECTLY OR INDIRECTLY.[21]

Unlike many officers in authority at Main Navy, King never doubted the immense value of cryptanalysis, or codebreaking, as a reliable source of information about enemy activity. So while some officers tended to be blasé about the *Tribune*'s 7 June article, King was horrified. As days passed, he continued to hammer away at the issue. He nagged his commanders relentlessly on the potential of cryptanalysis and the dangers of leaks. Weeks after the *Tribune* story appeared, he was still sending out reminders to his commanders to take every possible precaution "with regard to controlling the dissemination and use of radio intelligence in order to avoid drying up its sources."[22] He went so far as to circulate to the commanders of his Atlantic, Pacific, and Southwest Pacific forces new rules for securing radio intelligence. These were among his edicts: (1) radio intelligence should be passed on to subordinates only in the form of operational directives; (2) radio intelligence must be given out without any reference to its secret source; and (3) officers must avoid linking the outcome of operations with radio intelligence.[23] Clearly, if Stanley Johnston's article accomplished nothing else, it galvanized Admiral King to instill in his commanders a greater appreciation for the significance of radio intelligence.

∽

Thanks to Captain Holden, King now understood how Nimitz's high-priority message turned up on a marginal vessel like *Barnett*. He remained mystified, however, by how Stanley Johnston, a little-known rookie in American journalism, and an Australian at that, found his way on board *Lexington*.

After all, Pearl Harbor was teeming with accredited correspondents who would have killed for a slot like the one Johnston held on that carrier. Why Johnston? Ironically, Johnston's bosses in Chicago also wondered how their reporter wangled such a plum assignment. They buzzed about Johnston's coup for years. McCormick speculated implausibly that other reporters were not available because Navy Secretary Knox was treating them to various junkets to butter them up.[24] A *Tribune* lawyer, John F. Floberg, thought it was "really only a fluke" that Johnston was on any U.S. Navy ship, given his controversial history before the war.[25]

They were both wrong. Johnston's presence on *Lexington* was not a fluke. He was there because Admiral Nimitz wanted him on that ship. The admiral's decision followed weeks of protests from correspondents at Pearl Harbor regarding a wide range of issues. They were upset about the way censorship worked at the harbor, feeling it was needlessly complicated, arbitrary, and time-consuming. They did not like the Navy's requirement that they submit their copy to two different censors—fleet censors plus those onshore at the Fourteenth Naval District. They said that slowed down the review process to a crawl. Whole stories were sometimes thrown out without any explanation. Nimitz did something about this; he relieved the Naval District of censorship duties and ordered the fleet censor, Lieutenant Commander Drake, to provide "each correspondent a copy of all censored material."[26] The changes helped, but Navy censorship remained a sore point with reporters throughout the war.

Censorship, however, was not the only irritant vexing correspondents. They also griped about a pattern of Navy behavior they found just as infuriating: favoritism. Early in the year, reporters for the *New York Daily News* and other morning papers accused the Navy of favoring the afternoon *Chicago Daily News*, owned, of course, by Navy Secretary Knox. They argued that the release time for stories concerning major Navy operations was usually set for noon, a time that clearly favored evening papers. That problem was solved when the Navy changed the release date, pushing it up to a time when both morning and evening papers got the same break.[27]

The favoritism issue did not go away, however. Correspondents could not help but notice that the *Daily News'* respected and widely traveled reporter, Robert J. Casey, seemed to get all the choice assignments. To be sure, other reporters snared slots on warships. Foster Hailey of the *New York Times* joined *Lexington* for a patrol in January. James Joseph Custer of the

United Press and Bill Hipple of the Associated Press were, along with Casey, on board ships during the Halsey-Fletcher raids against Japanese bases in the Marshall and Gilbert Islands in February. But Casey seemed to be constantly at sea, invariably on board the cruiser *Salt Lake City*. Even Casey admitted that his frequent excursions had stirred chatter among journalists. In April, Casey said later, "Waldo Drake took me aside to inform me in a mysterious fashion that 'everybody' had been complaining about my being aboard the same ship continuously—'because you get all the good stories.'"[28]

Nimitz listened to these complaints. They coincided with Johnston's relentless clamoring for a posting to a U.S. Navy warship. CINCPAC wanted to end all the grousing about favoritism. How better to do that, he may well have thought, than to find a coveted sea assignment for the noisy newcomer from the *Chicago Tribune*, Knox's bitter rival? As a courtesy, Nimitz on 13 April let Knox know what he was contemplating. Knox could hardly say no. Early in 1942, Knox had told Navy public relations that no special privileges should be extended to *Daily News* reporters that were not granted to correspondents of other news organizations.[29] He continued that policy now. On 14 April, Knox via a radiogram authorized Johnston's passage on board *Lexington*.[30] As noted, Nimitz dashed off a letter to Captain Sherman, telling him of Johnston's pending arrival and asking that officers "assist" the correspondent in the performance of his work. Lex exited Pearl Harbor on 15 April with Johnston on board.

❧

CINCPAC's well-intentioned note to smooth Johnston's way on board the carrier may have had unintended consequences. Many correspondents over the months had been granted permission to join this or that warship. But rarely had their posting been preceded by a letter of introduction from the commander in chief, Pacific Fleet, let alone one requesting the captain to proffer cooperation to the newly arriving journalist. Nimitz's letter thus conferred on Johnston an eminence not usually associated with reporters assigned to warships. But thanks to the high-level players involved in his posting, Johnston, through no fault of his own, now found himself *a very important person*, somebody to be handled with courtesy and caution. Johnston's VIP status may well have clouded the judgment of some people at Pearl Harbor, even some on *Lexington*. Gradually the ripple effects of Johnston's strange position began to wash ashore in Washington.

Late Monday afternoon, on 8 June, Commander Bob Berry at Navy public relations received some unwelcome news from Waldo Drake at Pearl Harbor. In a telephone conversation, Drake said he had erred the day before when he assured Washington that Johnston had signed a censorship pledge before boarding *Lexington*. He said Johnston had told the truth when he insisted he had signed no such form. A very chagrined Berry sent the news up the chain of command at Main Navy; as a heads up, he notified Price's staff at the Office of Censorship. He told an OC staffer he would have to "get after" Hawaii.[31] Drake was now in the hot seat.

The FBI got to Drake before Berry did. Pressed by an agent about why he had not asked Johnston to sign the usual censorship accord, Drake conjured up a host of reasons. For starters, he said his hands were tied. He argued rather bafflingly that the rules requiring war correspondents to sign censorship agreements were not "promulgated"—a word Drake used—until after Johnston took passage on *Lexington*.[32] This explanation seemed lame. More than twenty war correspondents and news photographers attached to ships had already signed censorship contracts, even though regulations compelling them to do so had not yet been officially promulgated.[33]

But Drake said another factor figured in his thinking. Before Johnston even showed up at the carrier, he said he assumed all censorship rules relating to the *Tribune* correspondent had been complied with. He thought so, he said, because of the remarkable circumstances surrounding Johnston's posting to the ship: the fact that Nimitz assigned him to *Lexington* on the explicit authority of Navy Secretary Knox. The involvement of all these brass hats apparently led Drake to believe that Johnston was not subject to the usual censorship procedures at Pearl Harbor.[34] He was a VIP, and VIPs apparently do not sign censorship agreements. Drake thus conferred on Johnston a dubious distinction: he became the only correspondent assigned to a warship up to that point who had not signed a full censorship commitment.[35]

Drake strongly defended his actions with regard to Johnston. He told the FBI back in March, when Johnston was accredited to the Pacific Fleet, that he had personally provided the reporter with a copy of the Navy's *Memorandum for War Correspondents*. That document, he said, bound the journalist to Navy censorship, a commitment he claimed Johnston recognized and fully embraced. Of course, every journalist at Pearl Harbor had received a copy of that memorandum yet was still required to sign a written censorship agreement before boarding a warship. Drake nevertheless felt comfortable waiving

this requirement for Johnston. He trusted the reporter. "Mr. Johnston emphasized," Drake said, "that his experience as a war correspondent in Europe
[had] given him a true appreciation of the necessity for stringent security
measures in handling press copy, concerning military naval operations."[36]

As the Navy Department would discover shortly, vows exchanged orally
do not carry the same legal force as written contracts. Drake's oversight
would come back to bite the Navy and, for that matter, Drake himself, in the
weeks ahead. But his act of negligence, if that correctly describes it, was not
the only unpleasant surprise in store for King and his team.

❧

Early Tuesday, 9 June, COMINCH received another piece of disturbing news,
this one courtesy of his naval intelligence personnel on the West Coast. Vice
Admiral John Greenslade, commanding the Western Sea Frontier from San
Francisco, conveyed to King the results of a preliminary investigation conducted by *Barnett*'s captain, W. B. Phillips. Phillips reported to Greenslade
and Greenslade relayed to King that *Lexington*'s communications personnel
had assumed decoding duties while on board *Barnett*, at the request of Lex's
executive officer, Commander Seligman. Phillips went on to say that Nimitz's secret dispatch—Message 311221—had been decoded and circulated to
Seligman and three other *Lexington* officers (Junker, Terry, and Duckworth).
Then Phillips dropped a bomb on Seligman. He reported that *Barnett*'s communications officer—Lieutenant (jg) Daniel Bontecou—claimed that Seligman told him "he had been authorized on the USS *Lexington* to show all
secret messages and letters to Mr. Johnston."[37]

Greenslade's memo filled in the last piece of the puzzle. COMINCH now
understood, or thought he did, every essential aspect of the *Tribune* leak: how
Nimitz's dispatch reached *Barnett*; why a little-known reporter happened to
be on board; and now, from this new evidence, the name of the individual
who may have passed, or caused to be passed, this dispatch to the *Tribune*
reporter. King's attention turned to Morton Seligman. This was not easy for
King. He and Seligman were acquainted. In 1935, when King was chief of
the Bureau of Aeronautics, he brought the Navy pilot to Washington for a
two-year stint in that unit.[38] He knew Seligman to be a longtime officer with
an honorable record that included a Navy Cross from World War I. But King
was not a patient man. He was a perfectionist and an exacting taskmaster; he
did not like slackness nor did he suffer gladly what he regarded as ineptitude.

He also was known for his flare-ups and was feared by many for his displays of temper. He could be unjust and volatile; he was almost never idle. In tough situations he always did something, and he did something now. What he did was eminently reasonable: he ordered Russell Willson to get on the phone with Seligman and find out what in God's name had happened on *Barnett*.

By the time Willson reached Seligman on Wednesday, 10 June, the officer was already starting to feel beleaguered. Still at his home in Coronado, he had just delayed back surgery so he could attend, in San Francisco, a conference of *Lexington* and *Barnett* officers the next day, Thursday, 11 June. He had been summoned by Vice Admiral Greenslade.[39] On top of that, he had agreed to be interviewed by the FBI on Friday. He knew he was the subject of talk; he had heard through the grapevine what Bontecou had told Phillips. Now, with Willson on the phone, he learned more about Johnston's verbatim account of Nimitz's secret dispatch. No transcript was made of this phone conversation, but Seligman probably told Willson the same things he said at Greenslade's Thursday conference. No, he did not tell Bontecou that Johnston could see sensitive material. Message 311221? He only vaguely remembered seeing the dispatch. Neither it nor any of the other CINCPAC messages circulated on board *Barnett* were shown to Johnston. How could he explain the Johnston article? He could not. He said he and his fellow officers were stumped as to the origins of the article: "We've been wracking our brains,"[40] he said.

Seligman did not think he had done anything wrong. But when detailed accounts of the San Francisco meeting reached Washington, they reinforced King's doubts about Seligman. The conduct of officers in the suite that Seligman shared with Johnston was unsettling. The get-togethers there were chaotic—hardly an ideal environment in which to receive highly classified dispatches. Officers sometimes read the messages aloud for all to hear. Sometimes documents fell on the floor and had to be collected. Sometimes notes were taken. The communication watch officers delivering the messages were not always watching. Johnston was always around. Seligman said that was unavoidable and not a problem. In this and subsequent interviews, Seligman conceded that he had given Johnston a lot of latitude on *Lexington* and *Barnett*, but he said this was justified. "Johnston came to *Lexington* with the highest kind of recommendation right from CINCPAC," Seligman told Greenslade.[41] He exaggerated a bit: Nimitz sent Sherman a letter of introduction for Johnston, not a letter of recommendation. Again, the VIP factor seemed to be at work.

Rightly or wrongly, it seemed to King that Seligman had not sufficiently protected a vital secret. He had helped foster an atmosphere in which a high-value document could be compromised. This infraction alone justified disciplinary action. But Seligman's faulty judgment on board the transport now created a separate problem for King. Coupled with Drake's negligence at Pearl Harbor, it suggested the Navy itself had been remiss in the leak episode. Drake and Seligman appeared to make the U.S. Navy complicit in an offense that Navy officials regarded as a severe breach of national security. Some people feared this could weaken any case the Navy, or anybody else, might try to bring against Robert McCormick and his newspaper.

∽

The growing awareness in some quarters that the Navy's case against the *Tribune* might be fatally flawed did nothing to slow down the White House drive for action. On Tuesday, 9 June, Knox and King met with Roosevelt in the Oval Office.[42] One big topic of conversation was the *Tribune* leak matter. FDR wanted something done; he gave Knox a green light to take the case to the next level. Knox was pleased to do so. By this time, however, King was beginning to have second thoughts about the wisdom of such a course. In truth, he was more interested in plugging holes in the Navy's communications apparatus than in mounting a quixotic foray against a newspaper. But he, too, had been appalled by what seemed to him to be the paper's virtual contempt for America's basic security interests. He voiced no objections, at least not then.

That afternoon Knox wrote a milestone letter to Attorney General Biddle. He recommended that "immediate action" be taken by his department to obtain indictments under the Espionage Act against Johnston, Maloney, and other individuals implicated in the "unauthorized publication" of the article that appeared in the Sunday *Times-Herald*, on 7 June, under the headline "U.S. Navy Knew in Advance All about Jap Fleet." Knox charged that the article "involved the disclosure of secret and confidential information pertaining to the national defense of the country" for which all those to blame should be prosecuted.[43]

Knox did not attempt to set forth all the facts of the matter. He noted only that "our evidence" would, at the right time, be placed before the Justice Department. He did point out, however, that Johnston had been on a vessel returning from the Coral Sea when a "secret and confidential" dispatch was received on board. The content of the article, Knox charged, "leaves no room for reasonable doubt in the mind of any intelligent person that Mr. Johnston 'lawfully or unlawfully' came into possession of the said dispatch and willfully communicated the same to his publisher who, in turn, disclosed it to the world." Knox was alleging Johnston had violated clause (d) of section 31, Title 50, U.S. Code, Espionage Act.[44]

The charges could have been worse. At first Knox wanted to charge the *Tribune* personnel with treason, but Navy lawyers told him his case was not strong enough to sustain such a contention. But the Espionage Act itself was no laughing matter. Congress passed it in 1917, shortly after U.S. entry into World War I and amended it 1940; the law made it a crime to willfully publish secret naval or military information. Violators could be imprisoned for up to ten years, and they could be fined, if the court so desired, up to $10,000.[45] But many things had to happen before FDR and Knox could see Robert McCormick behind bars. Biddle would have to agree to move forward with the case. He would have to order J. Edgar Hoover's FBI to mount a full-scale investigation, sure to be time-consuming. Biddle would have to be satisfied the evidence gathered was strong enough to submit to a grand jury. If he were satisfied, the grand jury would have to indict. And if it did indict, a criminal court would have to convict.

Biddle did agree to proceed. He did not really have a choice (he knew FDR wanted him to), but he had decidedly mixed feelings about the case. He set tough terms for going ahead. "I told Frank Knox that the essence of the case was the harm done to the national safety," Biddle wrote later. "Except for that, the violation of law was purely technical. It would be necessary therefore for me to put on witnesses to testify that the newspaper stories showed that we had broken the Japanese code." Knox initially demurred, arguing it would be a mistake to make all this public. He apparently had heard from King, who—at least privately—was questioning the advisability of a public trial. When Biddle then said he would not prosecute without intel witnesses, Knox met again with King. King grumbled and voiced the concerns he shared with other officers, but in the end he consented to Knox's request. Knox assured Biddle he would have his witnesses.[46]

Knox and Biddle seemed to have an agreement, but their accord papered over deep cleavages within the Navy about the whole idea of a public trial. The issue of witnesses would come up again in Navy–Justice Department strategy sessions. The question had not really been settled. In Chicago, Robert McCormick had questions of his own.

CHAPTER 7

THE GATHERING STORM

If [Knox] intends to be tough, I can be just as tough.
—*Robert R. McCormick*

McCormick did not like the way things were going in Washington. He had been wary from the start. Ever since Arthur Sears Henning informed him on Sunday evening, 7 June, that Admiral King's people wanted to see Johnston, McCormick had wondered what the Navy was up to. He suspected Frank Knox was plotting something. "I hope the matter is all cleared up satisfactorily," McCormick wired Henning, just after ordering Johnston to Washington. "But in view of the many times Knox has used his position as Secretary of the Navy to help the newspaper he's interested in and hurt the *Tribune*, I cannot but be apprehensive that he'll do it once more." Then he gave Henning a preview of what he had in mind for Knox. "If he intends to be tough, I can be just as tough. If misrepresented, [I] will demand a Senate investigation not only of this but of all Knox's conduct as Secretary of the Navy."[1]

Still, McCormick did not think the situation was beyond repair. He had hoped that dispatching Johnston to Main Navy to tell his story would assuage King and his associates. They would see that nothing improper had occurred on board *Barnett*, and that would be the end of the matter. But early Tuesday, McCormick heard from Henning that the Navy remained dissatisfied: the admirals doubted Johnston's account. "As I think over the Johnston matter I am inclined to be indignant," McCormick wired Henning later that day. "He and his friends had been through hell fire together and were even contemplating a new battle. Naturally he knew what was going on." McCormick continued to defend his correspondent. "It is ridiculous to say any military information was given away. I understand Johnston was cited for heroism. It is pettifogging for these desk admirals to pick on him."[2]

McCormick seemed to be in Johnston's corner, but Pat Maloney wondered if the publisher would stay there once he read his reporter's 9 June Washington statement. Maloney read it Wednesday, learning for the first time that Johnston had copied the list of Japanese ships off a piece of scratch paper he found on his desk on board *Barnett*. Maloney, for his part, was not troubled by the revelation. But McCormick could be unpredictable. So when Maloney forwarded Johnston's statement to the publisher, he attached a cover note putting in a good word for the correspondent. "I had an interesting talk with Johnston on his return [from Washington]," Maloney wrote. "He knows his business and in my opinion is as clean as a whistle."[3]

Maloney need not have worried. McCormick never did believe that Johnston had pilfered a privileged document or improperly copied names of Japanese ships from a top-secret message. Either he never read Johnston's 9 June statement or did not pay any attention to it. He did not think a classified dispatch, or its contents, would be lying around a Navy coffee room for all to see. That is not how a professional navy worked. He traced all the fuss to the machinations of Knox. He thought Knox was making things up to destroy the *Tribune* and using "pettifogging" desk admirals to do it. So he remained unmoved late in the week when Admiral King answered the publisher's note of Sunday, 7 June. Much to McCormick's distress, COMINCH took issue with his contention that Johnston's article "disclosed no information whatever to the enemy."[4]

On the contrary, King stated, the article quoted almost verbatim "a secret dispatch whose contents were of such a nature as to indicate, unmistakably, that we—the United States —had acquired information which could only come from a certain enemy source." King closed by imparting his fear that, through the *Tribune* article, the Japanese might well have grasped that the United States had gained access to this "enemy source"—and, if so, this "could only lead to the drying up [of] the source."[5]

McCormick thought that was nonsense, but he did not immediately reply. He briefly considered firing back a hard-hitting rebuttal prepared by the *Tribune*'s law firm.[6] The lawyers proposed that he take a hard line and state emphatically that Johnston "had no access to any secret document." He did not send that letter. He agreed with the sentiment expressed but decided that, for the moment, his response should be low-key. A couple of days later, he told King that it never occurred to him that Johnston "could have known more than ward-room conversation," and he closed quietly, "I am still completely in the dark."[7]

McCormick did not believe himself to be in the dark, but he was not ready to show his hand. He apparently wanted to appear the benevolent bystander, a neutral arbiter just trying to get to the bottom of the matter. In fact, McCormick was gearing up for battle. Under the tutelage of the *Tribune*'s law firm, Johnston already was backing away from his 9 June statement. McCormick's lawyers did not like that document, particularly Johnston's sentence reading, "*The large number of ships and their groupings suggested to me that this evidently referred to something big.* I noticed that someone had scratched out several names and written in other names as if trying to straighten out errors." "The underlined [emphasized] portion gives entirely the wrong opinion," *Tribune* lawyer Howard Ellis commented, "To me it connotes that somebody had a secret message; that these exact Japanese ships were engaged in some operation hitherto unthought-of and that Johnston surreptitiously thus got hold of something big."[8]

That impression could not be permitted to stand. On Thursday, 11 June, two days after seeing Willson, Johnston signed an affidavit in which he played down—indeed, reduced to a trifle—the significance of the copying he did on board *Barnett*. "In gathering my papers together to make a hurried departure I saw there amongst a lot of discarded scrap paper a list of Japanese warships," Johnston now stated in the affidavit. "It was quite apparent to me that this had been some memorandum made during our various discussions of the probable constitution of the Japanese fleet."[9]

Was this memorandum of any importance? No, Johnston swore. "It contained no information which I did not previously have and in exactly the same form as I would have made it up myself," he wrote. "It occurred to me that I ought to make a memorandum of my thoughts on this subject, which were already outlined on this piece of scratch paper, and I thereupon copied it off and threw the piece of paper in the wastebasket with a lot of other scrap paper which was on my desk."[10] He did not tell Maloney about this piece of scratch paper Saturday night "because it never had occurred to me it was of any importance," Johnston declared, adding, a bit disingenuously, "and I still think it was of no importance."[11] Even if scribbled on a piece of scratch paper, a roughed out description of the Imperial Navy's order of battle for Midway would have seemed to be of some importance. But in Johnston's telling, the piece of paper was, in an amazing serendipity, no more than a mirror image of his own thoughts. It therefore served simply as a mnemonic device to remind him of facts about ships and fleets he already knew.

How did Johnston come to possess so much knowledge about the IJN? That was easily explained in the affidavit. "I have long been a reader of the military and air manuals published in the English and German languages," Johnston wrote. "I have made a study of *Jane's Fighting Ships* and I am personally friendly with the editor, Mr. McMurtrie. I have frequently discussed with him and other naval experts the make-up of the fleets of the various nations, especially Germany, France, Britain and Japan." From these naval authorities, he went on to say, "I have received as good information as can be obtained concerning the secret construction and plans for construction of the Japanese navy and air force."[12]

Furthermore, thanks to his experience at sea, on his way to and from the Coral Sea engagement, he learned still more about the Imperial Navy: its probable objectives, its tactics and the strategy it would employ, and the probable countervailing measures likely to be taken by the U.S. Navy in response. While sharing a cabin with two officers returning from the Coral Sea campaign, he had no trouble holding his own with these gentlemen and their friends. Certainly there was discussion of the makeup of the Japanese naval forces, he recalled. There also happened to be on board an old edition of *Jane's Fighting Ships*. "I told them of the information given to me by the editor of the publication concerning the probable construction of new Japanese boats," he stated. From the affidavit, it appeared that Johnston told naval officers almost as much as they told him. His message was clear: he did not need any secret document to reveal to him how the Imperial Navy would be organized for battle; he already knew it.[13]

Reaching San Diego on 2 June and then hearing of the Japanese attack on Dutch Harbor, Johnston decided to write a memo to his managing editor, Maloney. He wanted to let his boss know what he had figured out, not to expose a secret but to "acquaint the American people with the alertness" of the U.S. Navy. For this memo, he said, he did not rely on notes scribbled from scratch paper in *Barnett*. Those notes just jogged his memory a bit. "I had no secret information regarding the make-up of the striking force, the supporting force or occupation force which must have been utilized by the Japs," he swore.[14]

Thus, when he arranged the Japanese ships into striking, supporting, and occupation forces, he was just dipping into his personal repository of knowledge—knowledge available to anyone who bothered to dig it out. "Any student of naval affairs would have made the same listing," Johnston declared. It was elementary: all the ships named in his story, he said, could be found in *Jane's Fighting Ships*, with the exception of four cruisers: *Chakas*, *Myoko*, *Chitore*, and *Choda*. Even those ships were no mystery to Johnston. "I have heard this class of cruisers discussed and the names mentioned time and again," he continued, although he did not say where and with whom he discussed them. But he was always studying, always asking questions. "When I heard this class of ships discussed and the names mentioned I have asked for the spelling; the spelling used in my article is the spelling given me in response to my requests."[15]

Johnston now had a new story. The carefully crafted ten-page affidavit essentially erased the statement he hastily typed out alone in a Washington, D.C., hotel room on 9 June. That document, with its more candid and confessional tone, for all practical purposes ceased to exist. But would his revised chronicle prove any more convincing than the "unsatisfactory" account he conveyed to Main Navy admirals on 8 June?[16] Very unlikely. If by chance Navy chieftains had convened a panel of cryptanalysts to examine it, they would have spotted a few holes. They would have argued, with considerable potency, that the material in his article could not have been obtained simply through diligent study of naval manuals or even conversation with learned officers. The Imperial Navy was not a riddle so easily cracked.[17] It entered the war an awesome force, boasting nearly 350 ships, counting everything from the mightiest battleships down to the lowliest torpedo boats. Those ships were assigned to various fleets (the IJN assembled seven), but how they were employed varied with circumstances—the particular campaign and the ebb and flow of war.[18] It would have been impossible to know in advance which ships would be where. The IJN used different configurations at different times. Fleet organization could be slippery.

How, then, did Johnston so neatly re-create a good portion of the IJN's order of battle for Midway? Contrary to his affidavit, *Jane's Fighting Ships 1941* would have been of no help.[19] *Jane's* was a useful book. It itemized virtually every ship in the Imperial Navy by type, and within the various types, by classes (one ship of a certain type might have many classes). It reported the size (displacement, length, beam), guns, armor, and speed of each ship, or as many of those details as it could obtain. It carried pictures of each vessel, usually in the form of silhouettes and, when available, photographs. But there was much that *Jane's* left out. It was silent about how Imperial Navy ships might be used or in what fleet configurations they might appear. The terms "striking force," "occupation force," and "support force" did not show up in *Jane's*. Johnston would have gotten those terms from somewhere else.[20]

Given the limitations of *Jane's* and other manuals describing the Imperial Navy, it was glaringly evident that Johnston, in composing his story, depended heavily on a piece of scratch paper left lying on a tabletop in Commander Seligman's suite. It was all he had. Admirals King and Willson thought so. They made a persuasive case, as a close comparison of Nimitz's dispatch with Johnston's article would seem to confirm. Message 311221 began by listing ships assigned to the striking force: four carriers (*Akaga, Kaga, Hiryu, Soryu*), two *Kirishima*-class battleships, and two *Tone*-class cruisers, plus twelve destroyers. Johnston's lineup paralleled this list ship for ship (including the misspelling of *Kirisima*), even down to the twelve destroyers.[21]

Johnston followed in this fashion with the support force, sometimes repeating errors in the Nimitz dispatch, sometimes making slight modifications. CINCPAC's message allocated to the support force a light carrier, unnamed; two *Kirishima*-class [sic] battleships; four *Mogami* cruisers; the heavy cruiser *Atago*; and ten destroyers. Again, Johnston's list paralleled Nimitz's. To identify the carrier, he checked *Jane's* and found a light carrier that seemed to fill the bill—the *Ryuzyo.* Here he made a telltale slip: Message 311221 erred in putting a light carrier with the support force. No light carrier cruised with that group; however, one did sail with the occupation force. That ship was not named *Ryuzyo.* It was *Zuiho*.[22] Johnston picked up and copied Nimitz's error. He called the unnamed carrier *Ryuzyo* because it was listed in *Jane's* and *Zuiho*, for some reason, was not. The correspondent was guessing about the light carrier's name but guessed wrong. (See below for how Message 311221 was decrypted on board *Barnett*.)

```
FROM CINCPAC INFO TO COMINCH

CINC PACIFIC FLEET ESTIMATE MIDWAY FORCE ORGANIZATION X
STRIKING FORCE FOUR CARRIERS (AKAGI KAGA HIRYU SORYU)
TWO KIRISHIMAL TWO TONE CLASS CRUISERS 12 DESTROYERS SCREEN
AND PLANE GUARD X SUPPORT FORCE ONE UNIT VICTOR OR XRAY
CAST VICTOR 2 KIRISHIMAS 4 MOGAMIS 1 ATAGO 10 DD SCREEN X
OCCUPATION FORCE 1 TAKAO ONE DASSWI TWO MYOKOS (QUESTION)
ONE CHITOMS ONE CHIYODA TWO DASH FOUR KAUIKAWA MARU JOIN
DASH SIX AFIRM KING EIGHT SLANT TWELVE AFIRM PREP TWELVE
DESTROYERS X APPROXIMATELY SIXTEEN SAIL SAIL ON
RECONNAISANCE AND SCOUTING MISSION MID PACIFIC DASH
HAWAIIAN ISLANDS AREA
```

He got into bigger trouble with the occupation force. As decrypted on board *Barnett*, Message 311221 put four, possibly five, cruisers in the occupation force: *Takao*, one and possibly two *Myokos*-class cruisers, *Chitoms*, and *Chiyoda*. As the decrypt shows, three names—*Chakas*, *Chitore*, and *Choda*— were written above the names of the original four (only *Myoko* was not crossed out). As cryptanalysts would be the first to admit, their activity is not an exact science. It is an art requiring intuition and educated guesses. "[The American Navy] did not have an accurate handle on the translation of [ship names] of many Japanese ships at that time," Pacific War historian Jon Parshall told the author. "For instance, we thought there was a Japanese carrier on the books called *Ryukaku* which was actually *Shoho*."[23] Whatever the reason, the codebreakers handling Nimitz's message had a hard time decrypting and translating it. Some of the words seemed garbled. In any case, Johnston found himself confronting a bewildering jumble of names. Faced with the need to choose, he picked out the three names written in over the crossed out names and went with them. His *Tribune* article stated the occupation force consisted of four cruisers: *Chakas*, *Myoko*, *Chitore*, and *Choda*.

Questioned later about where he obtained those particular names, Johnston claimed he knew of them. He swore in his affidavit that he had heard them mentioned "time and again," presumably in discussions with naval officers. This was strange. While *Myoko* did appear in the 1941 *Jane's* under "first class cruisers," the cruisers *Chakas*, *Chitore*, and *Choda* did not exist in the Imperial Navy, at least not under those names.[24] They never appeared on any list in *Jane's Fighting Ships* or any other list of Japanese ships at Midway compiled by historians. They did not exist; they were mistranslations by the ship's cryptanalysts. The codebreakers who worked on Message 311221 in this instance made a mistake decoding difficult code groups. Johnston repeated their error.[25] Yet Johnston would have people believe that Navy officers not only discussed with him these phantom ships but told him how to spell them as well.

Main Navy's admirals would have been unpersuaded by the Johnston affidavit. McCormick, however, would not have cared. He was not seeking the good opinion of the Navy's higher-ups. He was thinking long term, and he was thinking that if the *Tribune* found itself in a showdown with the Navy, he wanted public opinion on his side. He did not release the affidavit but decided instead to hold it until later. In the battle for public opinion, he had another very strong card to play. He played it now.

〜

On Saturday, 13 June, under a bold two-line banner headline, the *Tribune* ran the first of Johnston's eyewitness reports covering the Battle of the Coral Sea. As told by the correspondent from his perch on the embattled *Lexington*, the stories were riveting. They covered every aspect of life on the teeming carrier and vividly portrayed every action in which the ship engaged, including a gripping account of the carrier's valiant, if ultimately doomed, struggle against Japanese war planes on 8 May. It was the first news report of *Lexington*'s loss. It highlighted the heroic efforts of Lex's officers and men to save the ship. As the *Tribune* boasted justifiably in a front-page editorial, the nine-part series—which would appear on the front page of every issue through 21 June—was "a clean scoop," the work of a reporter who had "the great good fortune to be the only newspaper man present during the battle."[26]

The series was a smash hit. Navy officers and men who read the articles gave them high praise. "I consider it the finest war story which has come out of the present conflict," Lieutenant R. A. Winston, on duty at the Bureau of Aeronautics at Main Navy, told Pat Maloney. Pilots commended the articles for portraying realistically the perils of naval aviation.[27] Navy censors who had deplored Johnston's 7 June article on Midway quickly approved all nine Coral Sea stories with only minor changes. Censors saw the value in Johnston's articles, which told a dramatic story about Navy deeds in the Pacific War that had not yet been conveyed to the public. The Navy helped the *Tribune* by holding back official disclosure of *Lexington*'s sinking until Friday, 12 June, a release date that would prevent competitors from beating the *Tribune* with that piece of news.[28]

McCormick thought the stories were so good he should give them away. "The epic is too great to be looked upon as a personal matter," the publisher wired Henning. "I am going to give the stories to UP [United Press], INS [International News Service] as well as AP [Associated Press]; asking them to credit the Tribune."[29] In a 13 June front-page editorial, McCormick told readers what he had done and why. "[The series] has been given for simultaneous publication to the news services without cost to them," the *Tribune* stated. "To do so, we felt, was a patriotic duty, for we doubt if anything could go further to hearten the American people and our friends abroad than to read Mr. Johnston's narrative of heroism crowned with victory. We felt that the possession of the story was a public trust, to be shared as widely as possible."[30]

The *New York Times*, the *Washington Post*, and many other papers ran many or some of the nine stories.

Johnston now enjoyed a certain celebrity. He was in demand for all kinds of public appearances. He started giving radio interviews. People wanted to hear about the Coral Sea. Even the Navy wanted him. While he remained under scrutiny by Navy and FBI investigators in Washington, Navy officials lower down the command hierarchy sought him out for all manner of activities. He cut a record to aid the Navy's recruiting efforts.[31] He spoke at one Navy event in Chicago that drew ten thousand recruits. At the Navy's urging, he gave what the service called "morale" speeches at General Electric, Ford Motor, and other companies. He joined half a dozen of Lex's enlisted men in Moline, Illinois, thus aiding recruitment in that city. "I really think he has done a lot of good," Maloney told Russell Willson later.[32] Whatever good he did, the Navy soon halted his appearances at Navy-sponsored events.

If *Tribune* staffers thought that Johnston's efforts on behalf of the Navy would buy goodwill in Washington, they were quickly disabused of that notion. Maloney found that out when he tried to arrange a visit to Main Navy to tell his side of the story. Ever since Johnston had appeared before Admiral Willson's panel on 8 June, Maloney thought he should be given a chance to explain his role in the production of Johnston's article. He asked Washington bureau chief Henning to call Willson to set up an interview. But when Henning checked with Willson's office, he was told rather bluntly that "no one there desired to talk to him because the case was now at the White House."[33] Henning correctly surmised that the Johnston matter had been turned over to the lawyers at the Justice Department for action. He so informed a very sobered Maloney. Events actually were moving faster than Henning, or McCormick, realized.

On Friday, 12 June, FBI Director Hoover called his assistant director, D. M. "Mickey" Ladd, with some very hot news. Ladd promptly passed it on to top FBI investigators in a four-page memo: "The President has authorized and directed the Attorney General to initiate immediate investigation looking into indictment for violation of the espionage statutes of the *Chicago Tribune*, the *Washington Herald* [*sic*], the *New York Daily News*, and possibly the *San Francisco Chronicle*, for the publication of a story on [Sunday]."[34]

Hoover imparted to Ladd detailed instructions for proceeding. He ordered Ladd to contact Vice Admiral Willson immediately to obtain "full details and background of this case as carried out by the Navy Department." Hoover was specific about what he wanted Ladd to do: "When you are talking with Admiral Willson I want orders to be issued by the Navy Department to the naval authorities at San Diego to give us or take us in on their investigation out there." He also was specific about what he did *not* want: "I don't want any holding out on us, either at Washington or San Diego." Hoover apparently did not know that by 12 June, the Navy's probe had shifted from San Diego to San Francisco. It hardly mattered. The director was putting heavy pressure on his chief assistant to move and move fast and get results. "We've got to tie this down because obviously it's going to be a vitally important case if they are going to indict," Hoover lectured. Hoover was not through. Tell San Diego, he continued, and whoever else needed to know, that "we are going to be in charge from the civilian side," he told Ladd. "I don't want our fellows to just stand on the sidelines and be yes men—in other words, we've got to get all the facts." Above all else, he repeated, do not let the Navy bottle up crucial information. "This is something they cannot play cozy with," Hoover stressed. "It's a joint thing in which both Navy and we are interested and I don't want anything held out on us."[35]

Hoover had now jumped into the Johnston case with both feet. Until this point, the FBI had conducted only a few preliminary interviews, mostly in San Diego and San Francisco. Now the agency was to give the case its highest priority; investigators were to fan out across the country tracking down relevant naval personnel. During the next two weeks, FBI agents quizzed *Lexington* and *Barnett* crew members in Denver, Philadelphia, New Orleans, Honolulu, Seattle, Boston, and other cities, wherever they could find them. *Tribune* editors now got more concerned. Henning regularly called his sources at the Justice Department to find out the status of the case. From one of his calls he made another troubling discovery: Attorney General Biddle had just recruited William D. Mitchell, a prominent New York lawyer and former attorney general under Herbert Hoover, to serve as a special assistant in the Johnston matter. He had arrived in Washington on Sunday, 14 June, and was already working on the case.[36]

⌇

Mitchell was McCormick's worst nightmare—a recognized leader in the legal profession respected by both Democrats and Republicans: a man who could not be accused of political bias. At age sixty-seven, in the twilight of a distinguished career in public service and private practice, Mitchell had no political axes to grind. In both the public and private arenas, he had acquired a reputation for honesty, high-mindedness, and strict adherence to moral principles. Strongly conservative in outlook, he nevertheless was not a typical Republican. He had, in fact, listed himself as an "independent Democrat," but in presidential elections he had voted for Charles Evans Hughes in 1916, Calvin Coolidge in 1924, and Herbert Hoover in 1928.[37] He did not think much of FDR's New Deal policies, a leaning he shared with administration cabinet members and fellow Republicans Frank Knox and Henry Stimson. Mitchell's appointment had, in fact, been recommended by Stimson, who also had been a member of Hoover's cabinet; he served as secretary of state while Mitchell headed Justice. Biddle hoped bringing in Mitchell would give the Johnston case a bipartisan tone—an air of unassailable integrity.[38]

McCormick saw this danger right away. How Mitchell conducted the Johnston case, and how he assessed its merits and viability in a criminal proceeding, could determine McCormick's fate as publisher of the *Chicago Tribune*—and, for that matter, the *Tribune* itself. Seeing Mitchell as a potentially lethal adversary, McCormick had his editors find out everything they could about him. What they turned up was not reassuring. True, Mitchell had his quirks, but *Tribune* sleuths turned up no real cracks in his armor. The portrait of Mitchell that emerged from their work was that of a man whose politics and personal style contrasted sharply from that of their boss. And, as a lengthy memo from Arthur Sears Henning made depressingly clear, Mitchell could be tough, possibly as tough as McCormick himself, maybe tougher.[39]

As a case in point, Henning cited Mitchell's role in one of the more controversial actions taken by Hoover administration: disbanding the so-called Bonus Army Marchers. By July 1932, the very depth of the Great Depression, more than twenty thousand out-of-work World War I veterans, their families, and their supporters had crowded into Washington and set up camp sites in parks near the Capitol. They had come to demand advance payment of bonuses promised them by the government but not redeemable until 1945. Mitchell ordered the veterans removed from all government property. When local police met with resistance, Army Chief of Staff Douglas MacArthur directed three thousand infantry and cavalry forces, supported by six tanks, to move in. They drove out the marchers along with their wives and children, burning their shelters and belongings. MacArthur was much criticized for using excessive force, but Mitchell supported him, asserting it was "high time" action was taken against marchers he claimed were made up largely of criminals, nonservicemen, and communist agitators.[40] McCormick did not champion the marchers' cause, but he did see the veterans in a more sympathetic light.[41]

Another issue central to the Hoover administration revealed other differences between the two men. To McCormick's horror, Mitchell was a "constitutional dry"—an ardent believer in the principle of Prohibition.[42] As attorney general, he prosecuted Prohibition cases vigorously. He thought U.S. attorneys, marshals, and other enforcement officials should be personal drys, and he removed several U.S. attorneys for laxity in their efforts to enforce the Volstead Act, which implemented the Prohibition Amendment. He once proposed to make Washington a model dry city—an idea that gained little support in that wayward metropolis.[43] McCormick, on the other hand, regarded Prohibition as an evil greater than the sins it was enacted to prevent. During the Prohibition years (1920–33), the *Tribune* ran hundreds of editorials chastising those who would use the powers of the federal government to regulate private conduct. But the law did not regulate McCormick's conduct. As his chief biographer pointed out, the publisher kept the cellars at his Cantigny Park estate near Chicago "well stocked" with alcoholic beverages.[44]

After leaving public life in 1933, Mitchell returned to New York and settled down to practice law. He steered clear of politics and concentrated on building up his law firm, gradually turning it into one of the most prestigious on the Eastern Seaboard. As Henning noted, Mitchell's firm tended to represent "high class" clients; they included big corporations like the Bell System and leading bankers like J. P. Morgan.[45] Although just as pro-business as Mitchell, McCormick was unimpressed. As the quintessential midwestern isolationist, he detested big eastern banks for their internationalism and alleged stranglehold on American business.[46]

McCormick and Mitchell did share common ground when it came to Roosevelt's New Deal. Along with millions of Americans, McCormick among them, Mitchell condemned FDR's 1937 court-packing proposal. Making one of his rare public pronouncements, he denounced the idea as "absurd and unsound." However, while critical of many aspects of the New Deal, Mitchell was never as rabid in his opposition to the administration's domestic policies as was McCormick. The two men parted company entirely in the area of foreign policy. A committed internationalist, Mitchell was pro-British; he endorsed FDR's Lend-Lease bill as a legitimate attempt to help Britain survive.[47] McCormick, as will be recalled, fervently believed the bill was expressly designed to give Roosevelt dictatorial powers.[48]

Mitchell and McCormick both had military backgrounds. During World War I, McCormick earned a Distinguished Service Medal serving as an artillery officer (eventually a colonel) with the famed First Infantry Division. Five years older than McCormick, Mitchell served as a second lieutenant in the Fifteenth Minnesota Infantry during the Spanish-American War. He continued in military service until 1901 as captain and adjutant in the Minnesota National Guard.[49] Fiercely patriotic as each man was, the two defined their patriotism differently. McCormick defined it in terms of America First and freedom of the press. Mitchell defined it in terms of defense of U.S. interests abroad, maintenance of military security, and public service.

To Mitchell, his role in the Johnston case was an act of public service. He had taken leave from his lucrative law practice in New York City after what he learned about the *Tribune* incident from Biddle and Stimson. He read Johnston's article and what literature about it he could obtain from the Justice Department. The material was skimpy; there were gaps in the case. Key issues of fact had yet to be nailed down and turned into a coherent narrative. Certain aspects of the legal theory underpinning the case remained unclear. But what Mitchell had read about the matter left him appalled. He believed it likely that Johnston and the *Tribune* had given away a precious military secret, thereby violating the Espionage Act of 1917. Therefore, he believed he had a patriotic duty to take the case and see it through to the end.

❧

Mitchell had not, however, taken the case hastily. He had thought about it for a while. He noted a potential trouble spot. He laid down a condition that he felt had to be met before he could join Biddle in this effort. He believed that to be successful, he would have to convince a jury that the United States had been injured by the *Tribune*'s 7 June article. Would the Navy provide the evidence that would let him do that? When Biddle assured him of the Navy's cooperation, Mitchell's concerns vanished. He jumped into the affair with the same zeal he had brought to cases against racketeers and bootleggers during the Prohibition Era. He no doubt was delighted to find a legal team in place eager to tackle a newspaper that had been denouncing the administration's conduct of the war almost ceaselessly since Pearl Harbor. He might or might not have been pleased to find that the Justice Department for months had been quietly monitoring *Tribune* editorials and news content; it was doing so behind closed doors, as part of a separate probe into newspapers and periodicals considered by some to be violating the Espionage Act.[50]

The "sedition investigation," as it was called inside Justice, was unrelated to Johnston's controversial article. Biddle had launched the sedition probe months earlier. It stemmed from Roosevelt's concerns that certain publications were echoing the Axis propaganda line. FDR did not think the attorney general was doing enough about the problem. Beginning early in the year, Roosevelt started sending Biddle brief memoranda to which were attached some of the scurrilous attacks on his leadership, with a notation: "What about this?" or "What are you doing to stop this?" In meetings with the president, Biddle let him know that Justice's lawyers were studying the problem, and he also explained the inadvisability of indicting anybody unless there was evidence that recruitment was being interfered with or unless there was a link between speech and propaganda centers in Germany—activities prohibited by the Espionage Act.[51]

One White House memorandum in particular got Biddle's attention. In it FDR included a compilation of excerpts of editorial content from a number of newspapers and periodicals that he regarded as the chief culprits. "The tie-in between the attitude of these papers and the Rome-Berlin broadcasts is something far greater than mere coincidence," Roosevelt told Biddle. FDR thought these "subversive sheets," as he called them, were serving Axis ends by fostering, or attempting to foster, defeatism and interference with the war effort.[52] In March, Biddle formed a grand jury to hear charges against some newspapers and various other publications.[53]

Biddle's probe had numerous targets. One of the most notorious was *Social Justice*, an anti-Soviet, anti-British, anti-Semitic weekly paper published by the outspoken Father Charles E. Coughlin. *Social Justice* sounded themes that seemed to support some of the policies of Hitler and Mussolini. Biddle silenced Coughlin in a behind-the-scenes move. He asked Postmaster General Frank C. Walker to revoke the paper's second-class mailing permit on grounds the paper was violating the Espionage Act by obstructing the war effort. Before a hearing could be held, Catholic Church leaders ordered Coughlin to either give up his priesthood or his newspaper. He quietly scuttled *Social Justice*.[54]

Other targets included isolationist, anti-Semitic, and virulently anti-Roosevelt periodicals such as *Roll Call*, published by William Dudley Pelley, and *X-Ray*, founded by Court Asher. Pelley was charged with high treason and sedition in April 1942. Those accusations were later dropped, but he was convicted of other charges and sentenced to fifteen years in prison. Asher was indicted for sedition but did not stand trial.

While the government pursued those relatively obscure publications, the Justice Department was quietly, and very secretly, studying the editorial content of three well-known newspapers: the *Chicago Tribune*; the *New York Daily News*; and the Hearst newspaper, the *New York Journal-American*. Rationale for the study was FDR's intuition that there was a suspicious coincidence between the Axis propaganda line and the content of the three papers. To test this hypothesis, Justice Department lawyers conducted a content analysis of the editorials and news of the three papers from just after Pearl Harbor through April 1942.[55]

Government researchers found cause for concern after matching material from the three papers with the three overriding themes of Axis propaganda: (1) seeking to demoralize American opinion by discrediting the motives of America's allies; (2) appealing to Americans to fight a purely defensive war; and (3) promoting internal disunity among races, classes, and groups. "There has been an editorial campaign fashioned out of the same material— conducted by a small segment of the American press," opined a Justice Department writer. "Whether this is deliberately contrived by seditious elements or is the honest view of patriotic but blind Americans is of minor importance; the result is the same." This writer listed the *Tribune*, the *Daily News*, and the *Journal-American* as "representing the worst offenders."[56]

The editorials, or commentary, in the three papers were not "in themselves treasonable, seditious, or damaging to national unity and our effort," this Justice Department analyst conceded. But he insisted there was still a problem. "Taken together," he declared, "the accumulation can leave an average reader in doubt as to the purpose of our struggle, the good faith of our allies and even our government. Such editorial policy leads to a 'what's the use' attitude, the opposite from that needed for the vast struggle in which we are engaged."[57]

Subsequent study led Justice's analysts to tone down their judgments. Late in May 1942 one Department of Justice lawyer, Raymond P. Whearty, stated flatly that "no foundation exists" for any criminal or administrative action against the *Tribune*. True, he noted, the *Tribune* is rabidly anti-administration and caustically critical of the New Deal. Nevertheless, Whearty wrote, "The utterances of this publication, in my opinion, do not transcend the limits of allowable comment and freedom of speech or create a clear and present danger of effecting any of the prohibited results specified in the Espionage Act." Whearty also debunked FDR's concerns about a parallel between Axis propaganda and *Tribune* commentary. The *Tribune*'s attacks are "clearly attributable to its political complexion and any resemblance to Axis propaganda appears to be purely coincidental."[58] Whearty had just deflated FDR's pet theory about a conspiratorial link between Rome and Berlin and the *Tribune*. His thorough analysis could have ended Justice's preoccupation with the *Tribune* and the other targeted newspapers, but it did not.

The investigation sputtered on for months, thanks largely to Whearty's boss, Lawrence M. C. Smith, chief of Justice's Special Defense Unit. Smith reported directly to Biddle. And the attorney general labored under the White House hope—certainly an expectation—of eventual government action against the McCormick and Hearst newspapers. After Whearty's detailed report, Smith could not promise action, but he could not let the matter drop either. "It is apparent that the contents of publications such as above [*Chicago Tribune*, *New York Daily News*, and *New York Journal-American*] do not give us a really good basis for legal action," Smith told Biddle in late May. "Nevertheless, these contents are harmful in that wittingly or unwittingly they further certain of the objectives of Axis propaganda."[59] By early June, despite Smith's efforts, Justice's sedition investigation into the *Tribune* seemed to have run its course.

The department's attitude changed on 7 June, when the *Tribune* ran on its front page, for just about the whole world to see, Stanley Johnston's story about the U.S. Navy possessing advance knowledge of the Imperial Japanese Navy's order of battle at Midway. Suddenly, the government's campaign against the *Tribune* acquired new life. Roosevelt, Knox, King, and even Biddle himself all wanted action against that Chicago newspaper, or at least they did at first.

With the *Chicago Tribune* again in government crosshairs, Mitchell agreed to lead the case against Johnston and his Chicago superiors. The sedition investigation into the editorial content of the *Tribune*, the *Daily News*, and the *Journal-American* did not end; Justice's analysts would continue to monitor the content of those papers throughout the summer of 1942. But that probe was relegated to the department's back burner. The focus now was on Mitchell and the new case he was trying to build. Mitchell wanted to get on with it. He wanted to see Hoover and talk with King, and so he called a meeting.

CHAPTER 8

A BEAUTIFUL MESS

I am getting to the point in this case where I am afraid I will
have to call in somebody else.
—*William D. Mitchell*

William Mitchell was not an easy person to know. He was quiet, a man
of few words. A visitor to his office at the Justice Department during
his tenure as attorney general found him sitting behind a large flat-
top desk—"a lithe, slender man with a well-shaped forehead, soft-brownish
hair, touched with grey at the sides, deep brown eyes of an almost feminine
softness." He was considered harder to see than President Hoover. He carved
out free time for himself by shunting as many callers as possible to subordinates. Reporters did not like being put off by him, but they admired his courtesy, the very well-mannered way he conducted himself.[1] There was a severity
about him, but it was an iciness that suggested an unsuspected capacity for
anger and intense feeling. He was strictly no-nonsense. He prided himself on
seeing the world as it was, without blinkers. He certainly did not think that
building a strong case against Stanley Johnston and the *Chicago Tribune* was
going to be easy. In the unlikely event he entertained any such hope, it was
quickly dashed Monday, 15 June—his first full day on the job—during his
luncheon meeting with Biddle, J. Edgar Hoover, King, and Knox in Knox's
spacious Main Navy office.[2]

King was the first to give Mitchell a bad moment. The admiral restated
what he had told Knox earlier: the Navy was not "particularly desirous" of
disclosing in a public arena the fact that it had broken the Japanese code.
Mitchell thought this matter had been settled; Biddle, with Knox's okay, had
told him so. Be that as it may, they were all in the same room now. After
some discussion, King softened his stand. Just as furious as the others about
the *Tribune* article, he agreed the issue was sufficiently important to warrant

showing the evidence Mitchell wanted, but only if absolutely necessary. He came around, but it was like pulling teeth.[3]

Then it was Hoover's turn. "I pointed out to Mr. Mitchell that one outstanding point of significance is that Johnston did not sign any agreement when he boarded the *Lexington* at Hawaii," Hoover wrote later, recollecting the meeting. Johnston thus became, Hoover noted pointedly, "the only [correspondent] so far as the Navy Department knows who has not been required to sign the full agreement."[4] When King and Hoover finished, Biddle and Knox contributed some thoughts of their own; they called Mitchell's attention to still other complicating factors, the most irksome of which was that the Office of Censorship, appropriately or not, had cleared the *Tribune* story, albeit *after* it had run in the *Tribune*.

After watching King agonize over the case and then seeing Hoover, Biddle, and Knox squirm, uneasy about all the quandaries swirling around this project, Mitchell might have felt like packing his bags and heading back to New York. But Mitchell was not any fair-weather lawyer. He had proved that a decade earlier as Herbert Hoover's attorney general, when he doggedly pursued cases against violators of the nation's Prohibition law. He did not easily give up on causes to which he was committed, even if they were regarded by many people as misguided or unworthy. He could be stubborn. On the other hand, he was not a successful New York lawyer for nothing. He did not like wasting his time. He did not want to get bogged down in a doomed enterprise.

Comfortable as he was heading the Justice Department case, Mitchell had his limits. He imparted to Biddle, Hoover, and King a sobering message of his own: a great deal of fact-finding had to be done. That effort might drag on for weeks, but he needed to fully grasp every aspect of the case before he could take it to the next step: asking a grand jury to return an indictment or indictments. That was not a foregone conclusion. If he found the case deficient in some way, he might recommend against prosecution; he did not yet know enough to say. Of course, the final decision would not be his. He could only recommend. The decision on whether to prosecute would be up to Biddle, with a strong vote one way or the other likely coming from Roosevelt. Indeed, the president's vote might well be controlling; no one doubted he would be heard from.

Mitchell now went to work. Despite all the glitches besetting the case, he remained persuaded that two *Tribune* staffers had violated the Espionage Act.

He thought the *Tribune* article had harmed national defense and that Stanley Johnston, *Tribune* managing editor Pat Maloney, and possibly unnamed others at the paper, were responsible for the damage done. He worried about only one thing: would he be able to prove it to the satisfaction of a jury? He believed his success or failure would likely hinge on how he used the Espionage Act. If he thought the evidence was strong enough he could, for example, build his case on Subdivisions (a), (b), and (c) of Section 31 of the act. These subdivisions carried the harshest penalty. Like other provisions, they involved the unauthorized transmittal of information to people not entitled to receive it. But (a), (b), and (c) would have required Mitchell to prove that Johnston and his co-defendants *intended*, or had reason to believe, that "the information [would] be used to the injury of the United States or to the advantage of any foreign nation."[5]

A lot of people favored this approach. Roosevelt probably would have welcomed it. The assistant solicitor general of the United States, Oscar Cox, advocated it. In a memorandum to the attorney general, Cox conceded that Johnston probably did not have "specific intent" to injure the United States. But he contended that it was "fairly apparent" that Johnston had "reason to believe" the United States would be injured. "The reporter was skilled in naval matters, as shown by his ability to understand the [Nimitz] dispatch, which was couched in technical terms," Cox wrote. He believed Johnston knew the dispatch was secret. He remained silent in order to be sure of his scoop. "But a person in his position," Cox insisted, "should have realized that the information contained in the dispatch had been obtained by the naval intelligence in some remarkably efficient manner: it should have been clear to him that revealing the text or substance of the dispatch would jeopardize the method by which this information had been gathered."[6]

Cox also made clear his low opinion of Johnston. "The reporter's conduct in taking and copying a dispatch of immense importance—as this one seems obviously to have been—is characterized by real turpitude and disregard of his obligations as a citizen," Cox told Biddle. "It is hard to believe that any jury or judge would take a sympathetic view of his case, or seek to free him on any narrow view of the facts of the law. He thoroughly deserves punishment."[7]

Mitchell did not disagree with Cox's assessment of Johnston's character. And he did not disagree that the correspondent deserved punishment. But he did disagree with Cox's view of the case. He noted that Cox had gotten a key fact wrong. Contrary to Cox's chronology of events, Johnston had not submitted his article *before* the 4 June Midway battle; that could have had consequences for the IJN's conduct of the action. He filed it two days *after* that engagement. Mitchell thought a jury would take timing into account in deciding *intent*, or what the reporter had *reason to believe*. He told Biddle that Cox's contention would stand no chance in court. The article's history did not suggest anything ominous. From what he could tell, the story had been "hurriedly published" after Nimitz's Midway communique, cobbled together in the style of a "scoop" because it contained hot material not previously published. Yes, the article was harmful, divulging as it did the U.S. Navy's amazingly accurate knowledge of the Japanese fleet. But Mitchell admitted that the *Tribune* had no way of knowing this data was supersensitive. "I think a jury would conclude," he informed Biddle, "that the *Tribune* did not realize that the publication might injure the United States or aid the enemy."[8]

Nevertheless, the *Tribune* article still violated the Espionage Act. "The harm lay in the fact that it disclosed that prior to the attack the United States had accurate information as to the number and character of the Japanese vessels, and that disclosure in turn would suggest to the Japanese that the United States probably got those details by breaking the Japanese code," Mitchell hypothesized. "Naval intelligence officers would quickly see all the implications, but laymen would not. Indeed it is because these implied disclosures are not apparent that I have insisted a jury might not see them and that at a trial they should be emphasized at the cost of further advertising our success in breaking the Japanese code."[9] In other words, he would need King's intel witnesses if he was to get a guilty verdict. The Navy's codebreaking secret would have to be sacrificed to secure a courtroom victory.

～

Mitchell thought the road to judicial success lay through Subdivision (d) of Section 31 of the Espionage Act (originally proposed by Knox in his 9 June letter to Biddle). To wit, "whoever, lawfully or unlawfully having possession of, access to, control over, or being intrusted with any document, writing, code book, signal book, sketch, photograph, photographic negative, blue print, plan, map, model, instrument, appliance, or note relating to the national defense, willfully communicates or transmits or attempts to communicate or transmit the same to any person not entitled to receive it . . . shall be punished by a fine of not more than $10,000, or by imprisonment for not more than ten years, or both."[10] Mitchell liked this language because it involved no element of intent to hurt the United States. Also, under this provision, "it is immaterial whether the document, writing, or note has been lawfully or unlawfully obtained." The defendant simply must have been in possession of national defense material. No question about that, Mitchell thought. In his view, Johnston's published story was "inherent proof" that he had access to the Nimitz message of 31 May or access to a copy of it and opportunity to make a copy of what he had access to. "Any other assumption would require a feat of memory impossible to all but prodigies," Mitchell wrote. "The order in which the ships were listed both in the message and the article, the duplication of errors, etc. are enough [to prove he had the document]." Also, the correspondent had already admitted making a copy of a paper he found on his desk—a piece of paper that, Mitchell figured, was surely a copy of Nimitz's Message 311221. That aspect of the case seemed nailed down.[11]

So far, so good for Mitchell. But not every facet of the Johnston puzzle was so obvious or so clearly favorable to the prosecution. Hanging over Mitchell's head were two unresolved mysteries, either one of which could wreck his case. How, for example, did the correspondent get hold of Message 311221? And why was he not required to sign a censorship agreement? The questions concealed a trap—the dreadful possibility, at least from Mitchell's point of view, that Johnston's actions might have had the sanction of higher authority, even if that authority itself was acting alone, outside the rule book. Mitchell knew the implications. "I think the burden is on the prosecution to show the publication was unauthorized," Mitchell wrote Biddle.[12]

To clear up these and other questions, Mitchell called on Hoover. He sent the FBI director a seven-page list of detailed questions he wanted agents to ask officers at Pearl Harbor, as well as the men of *Lexington* and *Barnett*, wherever they might be. Mitchell wanted to know, for example, whether the Navy's failure to have Johnston sign the usual censorship pledge was an oversight or intentional—did the Navy want to show trust in him by not exacting the agreement? If it was an oversight—that is, the result of a Navy mistake—that would weaken the Navy's case and, of course, Mitchell's. Johnston would have been free, at least in a purely legalistic sense, to go about his work in the South Pacific without restraints. But if intentional—perhaps a gesture of confidence in his reliability—there emerged the very real possibility that Johnston had betrayed a trust. That would help Mitchell's case.[13]

As for Message 311221, Mitchell noted the various inconsistencies in Johnston's statements. First the correspondent denied seeing any such dispatch and attributed the content of his 7 June story exclusively to coffee-table conversation on board *Barnett* with officers—and, as always, his reading of *Jane's Fighting Ships*. Then, however, he admitted he copied the names of some ships he found by accident on a piece of scratch paper in his room in *Barnett*. Asked why he had not revealed this earlier, Johnston said he did not want to get any of Lex's officers in trouble. This point nagged at Mitchell. He worried that an officer, possibly Commander Seligman or some other officer, might actually have shown Johnston Nimitz's dispatch. "This will not help the prosecution," Mitchell told Hoover. "It is better for the prosecution if it rests on Johnston's last statement that he copied a document, carelessly left exposed, and left the ship without ever informing any officer that he had done so."[14]

Hoover had his marching orders; he was to find out what had happened at Pearl Harbor and on board *Barnett*. Mitchell had his own ideas. He thought Johnston was lying about a number of things. One moment the correspondent was stating openly that he was subject to censorship. The next he was informing the Office of Censorship, through Arthur Henning, that he never signed an agreement for censorship and was wholly free from any such restrictions. Then there were all the contradictions about whether he saw or did not see a list of the Imperial Navy's ships at Midway. "This is a beautiful mess," Mitchell confided to Biddle. "The solution will have to await completion of the inquiry I have suggested to Mr. Hoover."[15]

～

Not all of Mitchell's suggestions were favorably received. He got nowhere trying to convince the director of censorship, Byron Price, that a new paragraph should be added to the OC's *Code of Wartime Practices*. He wanted the code to state that it did not supersede existing requirements that correspondents in combat zones submit their articles to Army, or Navy, censors. Price thought such a paragraph unnecessary. "It seems superfluous to state that [a reporter] must honor his commitment," to either Army or Navy censors, Price wrote Biddle. Price pointed out that combat-zone articles showing up at the OC are already referred to Army or Navy censors. So nothing would be gained under Mitchell's notion, but something might be lost because it created the possibility that eventually all articles produced inside the United

States would have to be submitted to either Army or Navy censors. This, Price opined, "might indicate that we are crossing the bridge from voluntary to involuntary censorship"—a move the Roosevelt administration had tried to avoid. Mitchell's idea was quietly shelved.[16]

Mitchell soon received another piece of unwanted news. It came from FBI agent Mickey Ladd on Wednesday, 17 June, two days after Mitchell had met with King, Hoover, Biddle, and Knox in Knox's office. Ladd had just interviewed two of King's closest associates, his acting chief of naval communications, Captain Carl Holden, and his ubiquitous chief of staff, Admiral Willson. Questioning Holden in private, Ladd asked the officer to name Navy personnel at Pearl Harbor who could establish the source of the data contained in Nimitz's message: did it actually come from breaking the IJN code? For a moment, Holden did not say a word. Then he begged off, stating he would have to refer this query to Willson. He did so. Willson consulted King. Then Ladd met with both Holden and Willson. The conversation did not go well for Ladd.[17]

To Ladd's amazement, Holden downplayed the idea that Nimitz's ill-starred dispatch had much to do with codebreaking. Adopting a confidential tone, Holden said there had been a lot of "misunderstanding" about that message. He said many people had the mistaken impression that it was based on a single source. Nothing could be further from the truth, he insisted. On the contrary, the dispatch was the summation of "various bits" of information culled from many different sources: submarines scattered around the Pacific, aircraft patrols, and naval intelligence services exploiting their informants. Yes, some of the data in the message were undoubtedly obtained from Japanese radio messages, intercepted by American ships at sea in addition to those picked up at Pearl Harbor. But no one should think that intercepts constituted the bulk of the information available to Nimitz. They were just part of the mix. Holden came close to saying there had been a lot of fuss over nothing.[18]

None of this was what Ladd wanted to hear. He had essentially been treated to a replay of the Navy's cover story—aimed at deflecting attention away from cryptanalysis—that King had presented so artfully to reporters at his 7 June news conference. Given Ladd's familiarity with King's bravura performance that day, he probably did not appreciate being spoon-fed the pabulum COMINCH usually reserved for the press. When Ladd tried to bring the conversation back to codebreaking, Willson jumped in. He firmly closed the door to any discussion of that topic. He granted that some people might have read Johnston's story and concluded that the U.S. Navy had deciphered parts of the Japanese code. But King was emphatic in stating that under no circumstances would Navy personnel testify to that fact, Willson told Ladd.[19]

King had flip-flopped. Two days after reluctantly agreeing to provide Mitchell with expert Navy witnesses in the case, he now reversed himself. What Mitchell said when he got Ladd's report is not recorded, but he probably was not surprised. He had seen King struggle with this issue before. The only thing that had changed since Monday was that King was no longer in a room full of powerful government players. He was now back with his own people and could say what he wanted to. Mitchell did not make a fuss or complain to Biddle. He probably figured that King's superiors would ultimately prevail upon him to supply the necessary witnesses. He thought Knox and Biddle would live up to their agreement, avowed when they asked him to take the case. He did not think they would bring him down to Washington for nothing.

∽

By Friday, five days after entering the case, Mitchell had pinpointed what he thought were its critical elements. First, there was the piece of paper Johnston had found in *Barnett* that contained the names of Japanese ships. The next most important items were Johnston's notes from that piece of paper and the memo he typed out for Maloney based on those notes. Mitchell wondered what had happened to all that paper. He thought comparing Johnston's notes with Nimitz's dispatch would end the mythology about *Jane's Fighting Ships*—and reveal Message 311221 as the *real* source of his article. It would show that he had obtained it while in a combat zone—where he was subject to mandatory Navy censorship. Johnston had already admitted to copying that piece of paper. He made that quasi-confession in his heartfelt 9 June statement chronicling his second meeting with Willson. Johnston had initialed that memo but he had not signed it. No witnesses had been present at that meeting. Mitchell now wanted to get Johnston's admissions on the record, so they could be presented in a court of law.[20]

Mitchell thought the best way to get what he wanted was to bring Maloney and Johnston to Washington. For his part, Maloney had wanted to meet with Navy officials in Washington since Johnston had his encounter with them on 8 June. Without knowing precisely what the charges were, the

Tribune managing editor had gotten the idea that he, along with Johnston, was being accused of some wrongdoing. He was upset and wanted to clear up what he thought were unwarranted concerns about Johnston's story and his role in its publication. The previous week, Henning had passed on to Willson a note from Maloney requesting an audience in Washington. He followed up with a phone call to Willson's office. Neither overture got results. Maloney's effort seemed dead until Mitchell learned of it. "This is useful because it offers an opportunity to invite Maloney to Washington to make his explanation," Mitchell wrote Hoover.[21]

But Mitchell did not want to meet with Maloney and Johnston right away. He wanted the FBI to complete its fact-finding first so he could get his ducks in a row. He proposed that the two *Tribune* staffers come to Washington for separate interviews sometime in early or mid-July. That was fine with them. They would have several weeks to do some preparing of their own. They, too, realized that the piece of paper Johnston copied in his room on *Barnett* would be crucial to the case. They realized something else; it was not only that piece of paper that mattered. Equally important was the Navy's view that Johnston had received information, any information, whether from a piece of paper or from officers in conversation, while on board a Navy ship at sea. If he had, the Navy would exploit that fact. *Tribune* strategists devised what they thought was an answer. Maloney and Johnston could not wait to meet Mitchell.

$\sim$

Maloney showed up at Russell Willson's Main Navy office at 10:50 in the morning on Thursday, 9 July. He was joined as Johnston was, a month earlier, by Henning, always a comforting presence when a *Tribune* staffer was in a jam. Once again the room was full of Navy brass. Besides Willson the group included the director of naval intelligence, Rear Admiral Wilkinson; Wilkinson's deputy, Captain Russell Train; and the acting director of naval communications, Captain Holden. Also seated in a little circle around Maloney was Biddle's special assistant, William Mitchell. The only other change from the month-earlier session was the presence of a stenographer.

The interrogation—for that is what it turned out to be—proved a grueling experience for Maloney and a frustrating one for Mitchell. Each recorded some hits, but the *Tribune* managing editor probably won on points. Maloney bobbed and weaved just enough to keep Mitchell from scoring a knockout

nerally Navy information, that he was permitted to publish
hat without Navy censorship? Is that the position you take?
ONEY: If he evolved the information—not information but the
dope on what this fleet was going to look like, if he and the
officers evolved it together, it was as much his as theirs. It was
not secret, but merely dope, and I thought, and still do think, it
might well be printed.[24]

loney's words jibed with the affidavit prepared by *Tribune* lawyers and
by Johnston on 11 June. Serving as a blueprint for Johnston's defense,
cument portrayed the correspondent on *Barnett* not as a passive note
, dependent on Navy officers for his material, but as an information
er, telling officers as much or more than he learned from them. Maloney
nded this theme throughout his exchange with Mitchell. "Knowing John-
n as well as I do," he said, "and his knowledge of ships, I have no doubt in
y mind that he was the leader in the discussion, right or wrong, because he
alks nothing else but ships."[25]

The implication was obvious: how could Johnston's story be subject to
censorship if it reflected his own hard-earned savvy, acquired independently
of the Navy officers around him, regardless of how knowledgeable and well
informed they might have been? Refusing to accept this picture of Johnston,
Mitchell tried again to get Maloney to admit he knew where his correspondent got his material.

> MITCHELL: You understood . . . that at least part of the information
> he had given you about the formation of the Jap fleet at Midway
> had been obtained from naval officers?
> MALONEY: No, sir, I did not, because no information was obtained
> from them, but they all got together and chewed it over, as we
> might on who is going to win the pennant. This is the best
> information, the best dope—you can use the word "informa-
> tion" if you wish, and I have used it in there, and I have also used
> the word "dope." That is what I believed, gentlemen, from the
> bottom of my heart when I put that story in the paper.[26]

Mitchell told Maloney he could not understand why he would put data
in the paper that Nimitz, in his Midway communique, had clearly withheld
from publication.

blow. Mitchell stumbled early when
to all of Johnston's notes and memo.
not to inquire about those items becaus
staffers to their importance. He was afraid
tee their disappearance. He was too late, h.
vividly illustrates:

> MITCHELL: What became of the letter tha
> San Diego and handed you in Chicag.
> MALONEY: I went after it on Monday, to try .
> lost, thrown away.
> MITCHELL: You made no effort to get it before t.
> MALONEY: No.[22]

Mitchell next tried to get Maloney to admit that he k.
obtained key details for his 7 June article while conversing w
on board *Barnett*:

> MITCHELL: When he called you on the phone he said he h.
> dope he picked up about the Japanese fleet in the Norι
> or something like that?
> MALONEY: He did not say he picked it up, he said he had it.
> MITCHELL: He had it?
> MALONEY: That is right. "I got some good dope," he said, "about w
> is probably going on up there about the enemy forces"; some-
> thing to that effect.
> MITCHELL: I see. It never occurred to you, I suppose, that any of the
> dope he got as to what was going on then in the North Pacific,
> he picked up while he was on the fleet?
> MALONEY: No, sir, it did not.
> MITCHELL: He picked it up out of thin air?[23]

When Maloney ignored that question, Mitchell attempted to pin down
the editor on his obligation under Navy rules to have Johnston's article
reviewed by a Navy censor:

> MITCHELL: Was it your idea if Mr. Johnston was traveling as a cor-
> respondent on a naval vessel and if he got some information,
> not by purloining or stealing a secret document but by merely
> hearing the officers with whom he was quartered, discussing

MITCHELL: It did not occur to you if Nimitz had wanted the information disclosed he would have printed it?

MALONEY: We print hundreds and thousands of things in all the newspapers of the United States that we do not get from an admiral or a general. We get our information from the outside, and if it is not in violation of censorship maybe we print it, if it is dignified and newsworthy.[27]

Hard as he tried, Mitchell could not get Maloney to grasp, or at least admit he understood, the different functions of the two censorship activities: first, the Office of Censorship for articles put together inside the United States, and second, mandatory Navy censorship for all articles developed by a correspondent while at sea with the Fleet. To wit:

MALONEY: Mr. Mitchell, does it not appeal to you as reasonable, that [Johnston's story] was not in violation of the censorship code with which I deal every day in my life?

MITCHELL: It does not appeal to me at all. You will find, if this case ever gets into a court at all, that the court will charge the jury that the censorship code had nothing to do with it, that your representative had special privileges under special conditions, and certainly the Navy had the right to lay down those regulations to men it puts on its fleet, regardless of what the Wartime Practice Code says newspapers generally may publish or not publish. You will find, if you get to the bottom of this thing, and your lawyer will tell you, that that is the case, and that this running to this code does not help you.

MALONEY: I was not running to it. That is what the Government wants us to do, is run to it. God, that is what we have been brought up to do, Mr. Mitchell.[28]

Another theme voiced by Maloney was patriotism. Johnston's story, the *Tribune* editor maintained, "enhanced the glory of the Navy," a comment that earned a rebuke from Mitchell: "Let us forget about glory, Mr. Maloney; there is too much of that here." When Mitchell suggested that Johnston's article might have harmed the Navy by ignoring security concerns, Maloney took umbrage: "I do not think there is anybody here who thinks I would put it in the paper in order to give information to the Japs." He challenged Mitchell, "Do you believe that?"[29]

"Nobody is charging you with that," replied a thoroughly exasperated Mitchell. Fed up with Maloney's evasions and rambling digressions, Mitchell exploded. He treated Maloney to an old-fashioned tongue-lashing. "I would say, if you want my judgment about it: I think you had a scoop on some vital information that Nimitz had not disclosed, and nobody else had disclosed, and at midnight you had this thing handed to you and you realized it was such a scoop that you were crazy to publish it," Mitchell fumed. "You tried to find some way out of delaying it for censorship, so you looked at this code, which did not have anything to do with the situation of a special correspondent, and published it without censorship; and then to cover up the fact that it had been obtained from the fleet, some of it had been obtained from the fleet by Johnston, you left him out of the picture, you dated the article Washington, D.C. and said it had been issued by the naval intelligence here."[30]

Mitchell was not through. He admitted to a startled Maloney and two dumbstruck admirals he might leave the case. The Justice Department brought him in, he said, because "they thought they would get an outside man who was perfectly indifferent to the *Tribune*. In fact, I am," he stated. "I do not know anything about the *Tribune*, I never knew a man on it except Mr. Henning here. I do not know McCormick, and I have no political quarrel with the *Tribune*." But after listening to Maloney's implausible explanations for an hour, Mitchell said he was not sure he could maintain the professional objectivity expected of a prosecutor. "I am getting to the point in this case where I am afraid I will have to call in somebody else, because I have reached the point where I do not know whether I could exercise a fair judgment or not, being so disturbed about the story in the way it happened and the reckless way in which the article was published without proper consideration of the Navy. It is just pretty hard to keep your feet on the ground."[31]

Taken aback by Mitchell's seething anger, Maloney came as close as any *Tribune* staffer ever would to a mea culpa. "Let me say this, gentlemen: that I regret exceedingly that I printed the story," Maloney said. "I wish to God I had sent it to censorship now that I see the consequence of the thing." Mitchell's questioning of Maloney ended.[32]

∽

Mitchell did not quit. He stayed on his feet and readied himself for his interview with Johnston, set for Monday, 13 July, at Main Navy. Johnston showed up at 11 a.m., accompanied, as always, by Henning. There were fewer brass hats waiting for him than at his 8 June meeting, just Wilkinson and Holden. Willson for some reason could not attend, unfortunate because he was the only officer who had heard Johnston say "I lied to you this morning." With Mitchell in charge and a stenographer present, the group settled in an unused third-deck conference room. What Mitchell hoped to accomplish, first and foremost, was to somehow elicit from the correspondent the same admissions about his copying activity on *Barnett* that he volunteered to Willson two months earlier. That turned out to be impossible. He did not get even the muted apology he extracted from Maloney. Instead, he found himself grappling with Johnston's bizarre and mind-numbing brand of storytelling—a mishmash of logic chopping and who's-on-first doubletalk.

Mitchell started out trying to find out why Johnston said one thing during his morning interview on 8 June with four Navy admirals, then something quite different in the afternoon, when he returned for a second conversation with Admiral Willson.

> MITCHELL: You did not say anything in your first conversation with
>   [Willson] about any memo that you copied, did you?
> JOHNSTON: I did not, no, because I did not think it was important.
> MITCHELL: But you did think it was important to come back and tell
>   him that there was a memorandum that you copied?
> JOHNSTON: Only because I wanted to explain everything.
> MITCHELL: Why did you change your story?
> JOHNSTON: I did not change my story. It was just another item that I
>   remembered amongst a lot of other things.[33]

Johnston made little of his second conversation with Willson. Yes, he agreed, he went back to Main Navy after he learned that the admirals were unhappy with his answers during the morning session. But he had not returned to make any kind of admission. Mitchell asked how he accounted for the many similarities between his 7 June article and Nimitz's 31 May dispatch: the names of ships, the order in which they were listed, the punctuation, and even actual errors in the in the names of the ships. Mitchell quoted Willson stating that Johnston could not answer the question on 8 June.

> MITCHELL: Did that occur?
> JOHNSTON: Yes, but I did not say that I could not answer the question.
>   I said that I could not explain that, because I do not know now
>   even that such a document existed.[34]

Mitchell pressed him on what he called the "remarkable coincidence in many ways" between the two items: Nimitz's dispatch and Johnston's article. When Mitchell asked him to explain that coincidence, Johnston said he thought such a coincidence might be "possible" but agreed "it would be most unlikely."[35] Mitchell narrowed his focus, an approach that, for a moment, seemed to yield the admission he was looking for.

> MITCHELL: How do you account for the fact that there was some
>   misspelling in the article in the *Tribune* of June 7 that was dupli-
>   cated in the Nimitz dispatch?
>
> JOHNSTON: Because for the spelling of four ships I used, that I can
>   remember—four ships off this bit of scratch paper.
>
> MITCHELL: You used the spelling for four of the ships that you
>   obtained from the scratch paper on the *Barnett*?
>
> JOHNSTON: Yes.
>
> MITCHELL: So if there was a misspelling there that would account for
>   the duplication of it?
>
> JOHNSTON: Yes.
>
> MITCHELL: Did you tell anybody on the *Barnett* that you found this
>   memorandum and copied it?
>
> JOHNSTON: I did not copy it, and it was not a memorandum, to my
>   mind; it was a piece of paper that had been discarded and that
>   had no importance at the time.[36]

Mitchell concentrated on the piece of paper. Mitchell believed it was a fairly exact copy of Nimitz's Message 311221 and, in effect, the key to the whole case.

> MITCHELL: And you did not see the original of this dispatch from
>   Admiral Nimitz of May 31?
>
> JOHNSTON: No.
>
> MITCHELL: The first you came to it was to see this memorandum that
>   was lying on your desk there, that you picked up and copied at
>   the time you left the ship?
>
> JOHNSTON: That was not the memorandum at all, that was the kind of
>   a list written out in discussions. It was [like] some of the others,
>   some of which I wrote myself, from *Jane's*, a discussion of what
>   the ships had to fight with. It seemed to epitomize the subject of
>   the discussion.[37]

Mitchell bore down hard on this point, reminding Johnston again of the many similarities between the Nimitz dispatch and his *Tribune* article. Did this not indicate that Johnston had obtained the key facts that went into his article while he was on board *Barnett*?

> MITCHELL: And I want to hear what you have to say about it, whether you are willing to admit here that the material you got about the fact that the Jap fleet was made up in this way was very largely obtained from information you derived in one way or another, properly or improperly—conceded it was "properly" for the sake of the argument—on board the *Barnett*?
>
> JOHNSTON: I cannot see that it was information that I got on the *Barnett*, to my mind. It was just open discussion that went on for days, that would go on between naval men when they are at war.[38]

Mitchell turned to the censorship issue. Johnston readily admitted he was under Navy censorship for his Coral Sea copy and studiously followed it. But he felt less constrained with regard to his Midway material. Johnston said that matter fell properly into Maloney's area of responsibility, but with one caveat: if he, Johnston, tapped his own knowledge, "I would never figure that would be censorable."[39] The correspondent insisted that is how his *Tribune* article came about: it was a product of material he dug up on his own without help from anybody—it was the fruit of his own enterprise. Mitchell thought this an amazing assertion.

> MITCHELL: Now you just made the statement that you did not get any information that was published in this article while you were on the Pacific Fleet.
>
> JOHNSTON: Not information, no.
>
> MITCHELL: You did not get any of the material or statements contained in this article of June 7th while you were on the Pacific Fleet or on the *Barnett*?
>
> JOHNSTON: No, nothing definite, no definite information.[40]

Mitchell noted certain aspects of the *Tribune* article that seemed to belie Johnston's claim. Mitchell reminded him of the article's rather astonishing precision in describing the makeup of the Japanese fleet, along with the names of Japanese ships, and dividing those ships into a striking force, a support force, and an occupation force. Mitchell found the level of detail unusual.

JOHNSTON: Yes, sir, that was the story.

MITCHELL: That was your dope, was it not?

JOHNSTON: That was my dope that I compiled that night, 90 percent that night out of *Jane's*.

MITCHELL: You did it that night?

JOHNSTON: Out of *Jane's Fighting Ships*, yes.

MITCHELL: It was not the memorandum that you brought from San Diego that had anything to do with that?

JOHNSTON: Not 5 percent of the story was in that San Diego memorandum.[41]

Mitchell then brought up what some people regarded as the heart of the matter: the limitations of *Jane's Fighting Ships*. That volume said nothing about what ships might sail with which force. Nor did it even use the terms striking force, support force, occupation force.

MITCHELL: Is there anything in *Jane's* book that would tell you what particular vessel was in a striking force, or support force, or occupation force of a particular Japanese fleet headed for the Midway Islands around the first of June?

JOHNSTON: Only that for a striking force one would probably use their best ships, with certain reservations.

MITCHELL: I see.

JOHNSTON: For instance, they would use their best carriers, because it was an air fighting stunt, and the four carriers listed there are the four best the Japanese had, that I know of, after the ones we bumped off in the Coral Sea.[42]

Mitchell tried again, this time with a narrower question.

MITCHELL: Did you tell Commander Seligman at that time that you had seen this piece of paper, as you call it, and made any notes from it?

JOHNSTON: Because it had no importance to me, I did not, no. It then had no importance to me. As a matter of fact, it still does not seem to me to be important.

MITCHELL: It does not seem important although you got the information from it that you would publish in this article? You just said the article came from that memorandum.

JOHNSTON: I did not think it was information.

MITCHELL: You did not, eh?

JOHNSTON: No.

MITCHELL: You did not think the make-up of a particular Japanese
fleet around Midway was information at all?

JOHNSTON: If I had known there was a Japanese fleet around Midway
then I would have known it was information.[43]

Mitchell did not try to unravel the logic behind that answer. Like so much
of what Johnston had to say, it did not track with earlier answers. Johnston
had already admitted he and his *Lexington* colleagues had spent days discuss-
ing the impending action around Midway. Mitchell let it go. He and Johnston had a final exchange. When Johnston said his *Tribune* article was "not
an exact copy" of the scratch paper he found on his desk, Mitchell paused.
But as he did with Maloney at the tail end of that interview, Mitchell let his
emotions show. He made clear what he thought of the story Johnston tried to
tell that day. "You are right," he told the correspondent, "that article is not an
exact copy of the Nimitz dispatch, but I think when you see the articles and
compare them, that the man who wrote the article necessarily knew some of
the contents of the Nimitz dispatch, obtained by seeing the dispatch, a memorandum of it, or hearing it discussed by officers on the ship." Johnston did
not answer. The interview ended.[44]

∾

When Johnston departed Main Navy, Mitchell felt just about the same way
he did after the Maloney session four days earlier: disgusted. He was appalled
by Johnston, who he believed had lied to him. He was displeased by the interview itself; he felt he had not delivered the kayo punch he needed to smash
the case. The correspondent proved elusive. He would no sooner admit to
something than he would retract it. Okay, he would say, he got at least "some"
of the content that appeared in his *Tribune* article from a piece of scratch
paper he found in his *Barnett* room, but then, in his next breath, he would
say it was not really "information" at all, just scribbles from "general discussion" with his Navy colleagues, and that discussion, whatever it was about,
was not necessarily about Midway. Heck, he did not know there was a Japanese fleet heading for that atoll; he did not know about that until he reached
Chicago. Sure, he knew he was covered by Navy censorship; he assiduously
observed it for his Coral Sea copy. But that rule did not apply to the Midway
material he already had in his head. And how was anyone to know what he

had in his head and what he had derived from that piece of paper? No one would ever know because he had discarded the notes that would settle the matter. How would all this play in court?

Mitchell's interviews probably were ill-advised. He had asked Maloney and Johnston to admit to deeds that could have been unlawful; he tried, in effect, to get them to collaborate in their own prosecution. They declined to play along. *Tribune* strategists had done their job well. Mitchell now reached a new low in the case. His mood would bear on a recommendation he would make soon: prosecute Johnston and Maloney or drop the case. Whatever course he proposed, he had done his professional best. He had attempted to prevail against Johnston and Maloney by using their own words against them. That was one way to derail the Johnston defense. But it was not the only way. Another government actor tried a different path to discredit Johnston—a backstage attack using gossip and rumor. And so the affair was about to get ugly.

CHAPTER 9

JOHNSTON AND SELIGMAN
Men in the Middle

This is driving me nuts—
the whole Navy, FBI calling me all the time.
—*Morton Seligman*

J. Edgar Hoover liked good stories. He especially relished yarns—sometimes tall tales, sometimes tantalizing tidbits—about celebrities and other would-be dignitaries. He treasured these fables in part because they amused him, but also because they served a political purpose—in the quest for favor at the White House, they pleased the man who occupied the Oval Office. No less than any other normal human being, President Roosevelt could savor a juicy morsel at the expense of some big shot or adversary. As director of the nation's largest police agency, Hoover presided over a bountiful supply of rumors, rumbles, whispers, and buzz. Late in the spring of 1942, he came into possession of some particularly sensational material about a suddenly notorious couple of interest to the White House: Stanley and Barbara Johnston.

Hoover's document arrived at the White House on 18 June, conveyed by a special messenger. That was the way he usually delivered his missives, whether they were letters, one paragraph notes, or lengthy memoranda. He rushed them over almost daily, sometimes to FDR's foreign policy troubleshooter, Harry Hopkins, but more often to Major General Edwin M. "Pa" Watson, FDR's military advisor and appointments secretary. This one was a three-page memo addressed to Watson. Marked Personal and Confidential, Hoover's cover note said the enclosed might be "of possible interest to the President and you." The memo was decidedly of interest; it was titled "Re: Stanley Claude Samuel Johnston." If Watson followed his usual practice, he routed it into the Oval Office.[1]

Johnston had been a mystery ever since Navy officials identified him as the author of the *Chicago Tribune*'s controversial 7 June article. Until his nine-part series on the Coral Sea campaign started running on 13 June, few had ever heard of him. Except for staffers in the *Tribune*'s Washington bureau, he was largely unknown in the close-knit community of journalists who covered the nation's capital. Many people wondered who he was and where he came from.

For FDR and others with questions about what kind of person Stanley Johnston was, Hoover's memo would have removed all doubts. It purported to be a synopsis of the correspondent's life and career, but it made no attempt to present a balanced picture of either Stanley or Barbara. It scrambled truths and half-truths, exploiting every opportunity to portray the two as people of dubious character. Citing Johnston's trips to England, France, and Germany in the mid- and late 1930s, the memo said he was accompanied by his "so-called wife," Barbara.[2] It omitted the extenuating circumstance that Barbara's first husband had abandoned her in 1930.[3]

Hoover's memo highlighted some of Johnston's more regrettable traits—his tendency to exaggerate and inflate his own importance chief among them. His bragging in France that he had been an Australian army officer in the Great War—known to be false—was duly noted. The report embellished this shortcoming and, relying on rumors and gossip, invented others. According to Hoover, Johnston was "a ruthless, tough, heavy drinker, a 'phony', a confidence man, and a 'gaudy liar.'" The memo recycled the two-year-old canard that Johnston might have conspired with the Nazis during his years in Europe. It noted, correctly, that Dutch intelligence investigated Johnston while he worked for Press Wireless in Amsterdam, concerned about his frequent trips from the Netherlands to France in 1940. "It was thought," Hoover wrote, "that he was one of the individuals responsible for 'leaks' from the French general headquarters to Germany."[4] But the FBI director failed to point out that Johnston was later cleared of those suspicions by British intelligence. He would not have been let out of Britain otherwise.[5]

Barbara was not ignored in Hoover's screed. His grossly biased account focused on Barbara's supposed activities in Paris when she found herself stranded in that city after the German occupation in June 1940. With Stanley sidelined in London, she consorted "with German officers and alleged members of the German Gestapo," Hoover claimed. He went so far as to assert that during her seven months in that city—before she extricated herself early in 1941—she fell "under suspicion by the British authorities because of her frequent contacts in Paris with the German element."[6] The evidence for these allegations was thin, based as they were primarily on insinuations and gossip. But Barbara did have one important accuser: a *New York Times* writer living in Paris named Anne Marie Jungmann. As that newspaper's remaining correspondent in Paris after the capitulation of France, she managed to reopen the *Times* bureau there and keep it running for a while. She was in a good position to observe Barbara, recently hired by the paper's Paris business manager to serve as his secretary.[7]

Jungmann's impressions of Barbara surfaced two years later when the FBI interviewed her as part of its investigation into Stanley's background. The agency learned of Jungmann from U.S. Army intelligence, to which she had written a damning letter about Barbara in June 1942. In her letter, she described Barbara as "pretty and attractive" but with little or no knowledge of office work. She was, however, "very charming," and she possessed one attribute that would have been valuable in an English-speaking office in occupied Paris: she spoke perfect German. That skill would have been useful in Paris in 1941. Whatever the reason or reasons, she soon came to the attention of German officers. They usually showed up when the *Times* correspondent happened to be away, Jungmann learned from the building's concierge and various neighbors. "Whenever I went out on a story the office was filled with gay German officers," Jungmann wrote. "If I came in unexpectedly, there were always some of them there."[8]

Jungmann volunteered her thoughts on Barbara to Army intelligence because, as she put it, "I'd feel better about our national security if she were back in Germany."[9] Ironically, Jungmann wrote her letter on 3 June 1942, just four days before Stanley's *Tribune* article triggered a major FBI probe into his background and motives. With Barbara now a person of interest, Jungmann got caught up in the inquiry. The FBI wanted to know what she knew about Barbara and, if anything, about Stanley. Could she substantiate her insinuation that Barbara was "pro-Nazi"? As it turned out, she could not. When FBI agent P. E. Foxworth interviewed Jungmann in New York later that month, he learned nothing new or incriminating, leading him to conclude that "Miss Jungmann has nothing definite on which to base this opinion."[10]

Jungmann's observations did not constitute evidence. German officers may or may not have had legitimate business with the *Times*, but they probably were pleased to find a German-speaking employee in an American-owned company. Barbara was in a difficult spot, trapped as she was in a dangerous city occupied by a hostile power. Her language skills undoubtedly came in handy, even if using them required civility in her dealings with the hated occupiers. During this time she also put her language ability to good use as a part-time worker at the American consulate in Paris.[11] Whether Barbara had pro-Nazi sympathies would never be known; no concrete evidence ever surfaced to settle the matter. As for Hoover's allegations, in retrospect they appear to have been cheap shots—based almost entirely on innuendo and hearsay.

Not all of Hoover's contentions derived from Johnston's years in Europe. At least one stemmed directly from Robert R. McCormick. The *Tribune* publisher talked about Johnston with an FBI agent in the late summer of 1941, not long after the reporter arrived in Chicago. Johnston then was working for the *Tribune* on a trial arrangement, writing military pieces for the paper on a piece-rate basis. He hoped to sign on permanently with the *Tribune* and, to enable that to happen, had filed papers he hoped would lead to U.S. citizenship. The FBI investigated Johnston in the context of his application. According to the FBI agent who interviewed him, McCormick spoke disparagingly of Johnston, at one point characterizing him as a "phony" because of his overly ingratiating manner and his verbosity.[12]

McCormick could be maddeningly unpredictable in his attitudes and personal loyalties. Did he really view Johnston as a phony? Anything is possible, but it is not likely. Around the time of the FBI interview McCormick and *Tribune* editors, impressed with Johnston's work, were considering him for a post in Berne, Switzerland, where they hoped to open up a Press Wireless office. The *Tribune* and Press Wireless (based in the Tribune Tower) had a business relationship that could make that happen. "I rather lean to Johnston if the navy will guarantee him a full bill of health and if they are satisfied his more or less wife is not a spy," McCormick wrote Maloney in August of 1941.[13] Stanley and Barbara had already informed the publisher they were not married but would be as soon as Barbara's divorce was final. He also had learned, if not from the couple then from his London bureau, that Barbara's months in occupied Paris had raised eyebrows in certain circles. He did not regard this as necessarily incriminating, however.

Unacknowledged in Hoover's memo, McCormick did what any good employer would do: he ordered his editors to conduct their own security check into Stanley and Barbara. One piece of reassuring news came from the Chicago-based president of Press Wireless, Joe Pierson, who had met Johnston during the latter's tenure running PW's office in Amsterdam (see chapter 1). As noted, Pierson early in 1941 dismissed Johnston after he learned the Australian was being investigated by British intelligence. But a few months later, in the spring of 1941, Pierson heard that Johnston had been cleared. He got this news from J. H. Brebner, director, News Division, British Ministry of Information. "Stanley Johnston is doing well and he is all square now and can get his visa to Australia any day he wishes to do so,"[14] Brebner wrote. The letter removed one issue regarding Johnston.

More good news followed. At the *Tribune*'s request, Commander B. O. Wells, in charge of naval intelligence, Ninth Naval District, headquartered in Lake Bluff, Illinois, looked into the rumors surrounding Stanley and Barbara. Wells told the *Tribune* that information dug up about the couple was "old stuff," not grounds for any real security concerns. "So unless something unforeseen develops, the matter is closed," Wells said. He concluded his report: "DEDUCTIONS: No apparent naval interest has been disclosed by this investigation and a copy of this report is being forwarded to FBI in Chicago for such further action as may be indicated."[15] The FBI interviewed a number of people but, like the Navy, found no reasons to worry about Stanley and Barbara. Wells' report was followed on 30 August by a welcome message from Arthur Henning in Washington: "Navy gives clean bill of health (regarding Johnston)." He sent another message on 9 September: "War Department intelligence division reports all clear on Johnston."[16]

By September 1941 the clouds hanging over the heads of Stanley and Barbara had lifted. The couple was married on 22 September. In early December, the two traveled to Washington, where Johnston picked up visas for Switzerland, France, Spain, and Portugal. They were set to go to Berne, Switzerland, when on 7 December, the Imperial Japanese Navy raided Pearl Harbor. Johnston did not go to Berne. He picked up his U.S. citizenship papers on 16 December, and two months later, the *Tribune* directed him to Pearl Harbor.

None of this background appeared in Hoover's report. But if it was Hoover's aim to reinforce suspicions that Stanley and Barbara were shady people not to be trusted, he succeeded only modestly. The document "proves now that [Johnston] has a bad record with the British and has married a Nazi woman," War Secretary Stimson jotted in his diary.[17] Having just returned to Washington to serve as King's assistant chief of staff, Fred Sherman picked up the same rumors. "I heard Johnston had a thick dossier with the British, was a very questionable character," Sherman recorded in his own diary. He also noted that the reporter "had lived in Paris with a woman international spy whom he later married."[18] Troubling as this news might have seemed, Sherman continued to befriend Johnston and retain a favorable opinion of the correspondent.

At least one high-ranking member of FDR's team was decidedly unimpressed with the FBI director's memo: Biddle's special assistant, William Mitchell. Glancing through the memorandum with a cold eye, Mitchell noted in the margin, "We cannot make any use of this." Because of McCormick's effort to check out Johnston, "the blame for hiring [Johnston] hardly rests with the *Tribune*," Mitchell wrote. He added in his abbreviated style, "Nothing [in Hoover memo] to indicate that Johnston was trying to help the Axis in his trip on U.S. vessels."[19]

~

Johnston might have been in hot water, but he did not act that way. He regained his old swagger. He was as garrulous and high-spirited as ever. He went about his business with his usual air of nonchalance. He had plenty to do. He continued to give speeches (albeit not ones sponsored by the Navy), and he began work to turn his Coral Sea articles into a book. He moved temporarily out of town—to Waupaca, Wisconsin—into quarters where he could work undistracted. If Johnston carried himself as if he did not have a care in the world, he had good reason. He had the backing of a powerful organization. He was surrounded by admiring colleagues, supportive editors, clever lawyers, and a boss, the redoubtable Robert McCormick, who continued to champion his cause. McCormick was in a fighting mood or at least said he was.

Morton Seligman was not so fortunate. Still on medical leave in Coronado, living at home with his wife, Adelia, he was essentially alone. Aside from the call he got from Admiral Willson on 9 June, he heard little or nothing from his superiors. Periodically he would get a call from a fellow officer, but that was about all. His health was poor. He suffered from severe back sprain; swelling of the lower spine; and, to add insult to injury, chronically infected tonsils. He required occasional hospitalization.[20] The FBI continued to nag him for interviews and sometimes followed him into the U.S. Naval Hospital in San Diego. Seligman's physician on 23 June told an FBI agent that

When Special Prosecutor William D. Mitchell failed to call them to testify before a grand jury considering espionage charges against them, Stanley Johnston (left) and his boss, Managing Editor J. Loy "Pat" Maloney, went over to the jury room and asked to be heard. Mitchell turned them down, but a day later he relented and brought them in to tell their story to jurors. —HistoricalFindings

After the *Tribune* ran his series on the Battle of the Coral Sea, Johnston was in demand for all kinds of public appearances. He gave what the Navy called "morale" speeches at General Electric, Ford Motor, and other companies. He even gave talks to aid recruiting until the Navy halted his appearances at Navy-sponsored events. —*Courtesy of Robert G. Summers*

With his smartly trimmed mustache and Australian accent, Johnston projected an air of worldliness. He loved to chat with his Navy colleagues, and to many of his shipmates it seemed as if he never stopped talking. A Navy report described him as a "voluble talker." —*McCormick Research Center*

Johnston and his wife, Barbara, answer reporter's questions while a federal grand jury considers the government's charges that Johnston violated the Espionage Act. —*Acme*

This press card entitled Johnston to ride with the Pacific Fleet until 1 July 1942. But after the *Tribune* printed his controversial Midway article on 7 June 1942, his press credentials were revoked and never renewed. —*FBI*

After charges against him were dropped, Johnston joined the *Tribune*'s news staff. Denied the privilege to cover the Pacific Fleet, he for a time covered news and trends in Latin America. He ended his career as general manager of Robert McCormick's five-hundred-acre Cantigny Estate in Wheaton, Illinois. —*McCormick Research Center*

Paradise Girls
Gorgeous! Glamorous! Thrilling!
PARADISE CABARET RESTAURANT - 49th St. & Broadway, New York City

Passing through New York during his 1937–38 travels, Johnston met Barbara Maria Beck at the Paradise Cabaret, where Barbara was employed as a dancer. Born in Wurzburg, Bavaria, Germany, in 1909, she emigrated to the United States in 1926. Stanley and Barbara married in 1941.
—*Author's collection*

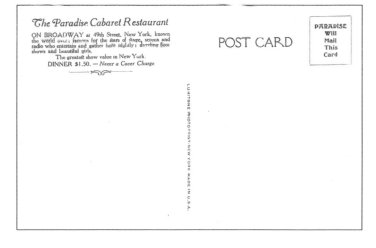

The Paradise Cabaret Restaurant

ON BROADWAY at 49th Street, New York, known the world over, famous for the stars of stage, screen and radio who entertain and gather here nightly; dazzling floor shows and beautiful girls.

The greatest show value in New York.
DINNER $1.50. — *Never a Cover Charge*

POST CARD

PARADISE
Will
Mail
This
Card

LUMITONE PHOTOPRINT-NEW YORK MADE IN U.S.A.

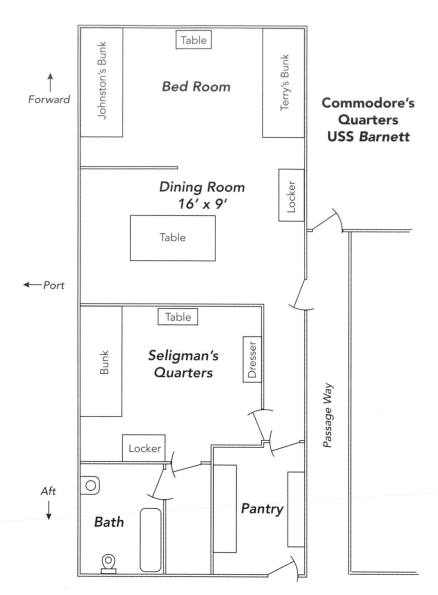

Forward ↑

Johnston's Bunk

Table

Bed Room

Terry's Bunk

Commodore's Quarters USS *Barnett*

Locker

Dining Room 16' x 9'

Table

← Port

Table

Bunk

Seligman's Quarters

Dresser

Passage Way

Locker

Aft ↓

Bath

Pantry

Commander Morton Seligman enjoyed desirable space on board the rescue ship *Barnett*. The space consisted of a bedroom with an adjoining pantry, a separate dining room with a large table, and a second bedroom big enough to hold two bunks. Seligman gave Johnston one of the bunks. *Lexington* officers housed elsewhere in the ship routinely dropped in to Seligman's quarters to drink coffee and socialize. Many of these officers, along with Johnston, were present on the night of 31 May 1942 when a secret message from CINCPAC was delivered to Seligman. Government prosecutors alleged that the contents of that message ended up on the front page of the *Chicago Tribune* on 7 June 1942, casting suspicion on Johnston. —*FBI*

Stranded in Tongatabu in the Tonga Islands, Stanley Johnston was among one thousand Lex personnel assigned to the aging transport ship *Barnett*. During *Barnett*'s two-week voyage to San Diego, Johnston was believed by federal investigators to have copied a secret CINCPAC message. —*Naval History and Heritage Command*

Banished? Morton Seligman was ordered in late 1942 to command a U.S. Naval Reserve Aviation Base near Peru, Indiana. Some officers thought the assignment—far from the action of the Pacific War—was punishment for his role in the Johnston affair. Not necessarily. His injuries sustained in the Coral Sea rendered him unfit for service in a combat zone. —*NARAII*

Navy Secretary Frank Knox (above) and Robert McCormick, as publishers of competing Chicago newspapers, were fierce rivals. After Johnston's Midway article appeared on the front page of the *Tribune*, Knox, backed strongly by President Roosevelt, called on Attorney General Biddle to seek indictments against Johnston and other *Tribune* staffers under the Espionage Act. —*Author's collection*

When the *Chicago Tribune* published Stanley Johnston's Midway article on 7 June 1942, the Navy's commander in chief, Admiral Ernest J. King, was outraged. He wanted to punish the *Tribune*. But when he considered the consequences of a public trial—wider disclosure of the Navy's codebreaking success against Japan—he reconsidered. —*Naval History and Heritage Command*

Attorney General Francis Biddle doubted the viability of the case against the *Chicago Tribune* from the beginning. He didn't think the evidence was strong enough. But when Navy Secretary Knox and President Roosevelt called for action against the *Tribune*, he relented. —*Getty Images*

New York lawyer William D. Mitchell was no fan of the Roosevelt administration. A strong conservative, he had served as Herbert Hoover's attorney
general. But when Biddle asked him to serve as his special assistant in the
Johnston affair, Mitchell felt he had a patriotic duty to take the case.
—*Minnesota Historical Society*

Admiral King, the Navy's blunt-spoken COMINCH, chafed under the civilian leadership of Navy Secretary Knox. Their relationship deteriorated further when King refused to provide the expert witnesses Knox had promised Biddle in the Johnston grand jury hearings. —*Naval History and Heritage Command*

FBI Director J. Edgar Hoover ordered his investigators to find out what happened on board *Barnett* during its voyage to San Diego. FBI sleuths fanned out across the country; they interviewed *Lexington* and *Barnett* crew members in Denver, Philadelphia, New Orleans, Honolulu, Seattle, Boston, and other cities—wherever the investigators could find them. —*Library of Congress*

The Navy's fears that news of its success breaking the Imperial Japanese Navy's code would leak out were nearly realized when gossip maven Walter Winchell, on 5 July 1942, told his radio audience that "intercepted and decoded messages" played a role in a recent military action.
—Author's collection

Rear Admiral Frederick C. Sherman remained loyal to his friends. With his carrier *Lexington* smashed and sinking, he saw to it that his cocker spaniel Wags was rescued and carried to safety. Sherman remained Stanley Johnston's advocate during the correspondent's time of travail. Sherman, in his testimony before a federal grand jury, vouched for Johnston's integrity. —*Author's collection*

~~SECRET~~

"UNITED STATES PACIFIC FLEET
FLAGSHIP OF THE COMMANDER-IN-CHIEF

A2-14/(27)
SERIAL 01166   April 14, 1942.

CONFIDENTIAL

From: Commander-in-Chief, United States Pacific Fleet
TO: Commanding Officer, U.S.S. LEXINGTON

Subject: Press Correspondent, passage for.

    1.   The Secretary of the Navy has authorized Mr. Stanley
Johnston, accredited representative of the CHICAGO TRIBUNE, to take
passage in ships of the Pacific Fleet, for the purpose of obtaining
news material, to be published after censorship of the Commander-in-
Chief, Pacific Fleet.

    2.   In accordance with the above authority, the Commander-
in-Chief, Pacific Fleet, is granting Mr. Johnston permission to take
passage in the LEXINGTON, during her next operating period, to obtain
material for news releases concerning operations of the LEXINGTON and
accompanying units.

    3.   All articles subsequently written by Mr. Johnston are
subject to existing security instructions and the provisions of General Order No. 96.

    4.   Your cooperation in assisting Mr. Johnston will be very
much appreciated.

    5.   In the event that the LEXINGTON is transferred to a com-
mand other than the Pacific Fleet, it is requested that the same
cooperation, consistent with military security, be accorded Mr. Johnston.

                                        /s/ C.W. Nimitz/

                                        C.W. NIMITZ

copy to:
    Comsowespacfor   CERTIFIED TO BE ATRUE COPY
    Comansacfor   /s/ W. W. DRAKE
    Comtaskfor ELEVEN   W. W. DRAKE
                                            Lieut. Comdr., USNR"

- 12 -   ~~SECRET~~

Admiral Nimitz went to a lot of trouble to see that war correspondent
Stanley Johnston got in *Lexington*. There's reason to believe that Lex's
executive officer, Commander Morton Seligman, accorded Johnston
special treatment because of this letter. —*FBI*

Pacific Fleet Commander Admiral Nimitz initiated the secret dispatch that was picked up by *Barnett*'s radio receivers and circulated among *Lexington* officers. Witnesses said they saw a rough copy of this message in Commander Seligman's quarters. —*Naval History and Heritage Command*

Dive-bomber pilot Robert E. Dixon was in Commander Seligman's *Barnett* stateroom on the night of 31 May 1942 when Nimitz's secret dispatch reached Seligman. Dixon told the FBI little more than that Stanley Johnston was in the room, but years later he was quoted posthumously telling a friend he saw Johnston taking notes off the Nimitz message. —*Naval History and Heritage Command*

Lieutenant Commander Waldo Drake was the Pacific Fleet's director of public relations and also its chief censor. He never satisfactorily explained why he didn't require Stanley Johnson, when he was assigned to *Lexington*, to sign the customary pledge that he would comply with the rules of Navy censorship. —*Harry S. Truman Library*

A former Associated Press executive, Byron Price directed the wartime Office of Censorship. He was disturbed by Stanley Johnston's article, but he opposed sanctions against the *Chicago Tribune*, believing that for reasons of national security the *Tribune*'s transgression should get as little publicity as possible. —*Wisconsin Historical Society*

"THE HARPIES OF THE SHORE (WOULD) PLUCK THE EAGLES OF THE SEA" —*Oliver Wendell Holmes.*

One day after Attorney General Biddle announced a grand jury probe into the *Chicago Tribune*, the newspaper mounted a counterattack: It launched the first of a series of sharp-edged articles assailing Biddle and Navy Secretary Knox for a wide range of misdeeds. It kept up the barrage of criticism until the case was dismissed two weeks later. —*McCormick Research Center*

Tribune managing editor J. Loy "Pat" Maloney approved a rewrite of Stanley Johnston's Midway article that carried a false Washington dateline and incorrectly attributed the information in it to naval intelligence. He also decided the article wasn't covered by censorship rules. The Justice Department targeted Maloney, along with Johnston, in its grand jury probe. —*McCormick Research Center*

The *Tribune*'s Washington bureau chief, Arthur Henning, advised Managing Editor Maloney that Johnston's Midway story didn't fall under the censorship rules of the Office of Censorship. He missed the larger point that Navy censors, not the civilian-controlled Office of Censorship, had jurisdiction over the story. —*McCormick Research Center*

As the *Tribune*'s military correspondent in Washington, Walter Trohan was acquainted with Admiral King. After reading Johnston's Midway article, a furious King summoned Trohan to his office and demanded to know where the story came from. Trohan assured COMINCH it wasn't produced by the Washington office. He was right about that. —*Harry S. Truman Library*

On 4 December 1941 the *Tribune* published a sensational "scoop" purporting to reveal President Roosevelt's secret plan to take America to war in 1943. Enraged by the story, War Secretary Stimson noted that the article was based on a "contingency" plan, not a "real" plan to go to war. The story created a furor. The FBI grilled the article's author, Chesly Manly, but he never revealed his source. —*McCormick Research Center*

Tribune aviation editor Wayne Thomis served as Stanley Johnston's personal rewrite man. Using Johnston's material, Thomis wrote the war correspondent's controversial 7 June 1942 *Tribune* article that identified Imperial Japanese Navy ships deployed for the Battle of Midway. Thomis admitted to government investigators that he was the editor who attributed Johnston's information to naval intelligence in Washington. *—McCormick Research Center*

President Roosevelt was the driving force behind the government's effort to prosecute *Chicago Tribune* personnel for allegedly violating the Espionage Act. FDR's targets were not only staffers Johnston and Maloney, but also the paper's publisher, Colonel Robert R. McCormick, a bitter enemy. Roosevelt wanted to put him behind bars. *—NARAII*

Chicago Tribune publisher Robert R. McCormick spoke regularly on the *Tribune*'s radio station, whose call letters, WGN, stood for World's Greatest Newspaper. McCormick used every medium at his disposal to defend *Tribune* staffers Stanley Johnston and Pat Maloney. He believed the government's case against them had been fabricated by his archrival, Navy Secretary Frank Knox, publisher of the competing *Chicago Daily News*.
—McCormick Research Center

Chicago Tribune publisher Colonel Robert R. McCormick, seen here on one of his rare visits to the *Tribune* newsroom. Usually he only ventured out of his spacious, twenty-fourth-floor office for a special occasion. One such occasion was the grand jury's decision on 19 August 1942 to throw out all espionage charges against *Tribune* personnel. When McCormick walked into the newsroom to share the good news, he received a standing ovation. *—McCormick Research Center*

More than 2,700 of *Lexington*'s 2,951 officers and men survived the pounding by Imperial Japanese Navy warplanes on 8 May 1942. Amazingly, no lives were lost during the evacuation. Stanley Johnston administered first aid to wounded sailors when the ship was in dire peril and later helped swimmers out of the water. He was one of the last men off the ship. *—NARAII*

the commander, then awaiting two operations, was not in a good condition to be questioned. Because of the injuries he had sustained in the Coral Sea, his doctor doubted whether Seligman's memory of events on board *Lexington* and *Barnett* could be relied upon. The agent put off this visit, but he did interview Seligman in the hospital on another occasion.[21]

By early July, Seligman was feeling abandoned. He worried about his naval career. He wondered if he had any friends. Out of desperation, Seligman called the *Chicago Tribune* during the evening of 15 July, trying to reach Johnston. He got the city editor, Don Maxwell, who was shocked by what he heard. Seligman seemed to be falling apart.

> SELIGMAN: Have him call me at 9 o'clock tomorrow morning, please. Say, they've got me over the barrel. I've been in the hospital—they're after me—the FBI, the whole Navy. I'm not going to stand for it. I want to tell Stan about it.
>
> MAXWELL: Who is after you, commander? What do you mean over the barrel? Who called you?
>
> SELIGMAN: Admiral Willson called me. The whole Navy has been after me. My wire's tapped. They're putting the bug on me.
>
> MAXWELL: Where are you talking from now?
>
> SELIGMAN: From my home.
>
> MAXWELL: Maybe the wire is tapped there, too.
>
> SELIGMAN: I don't care if it is. I got nothing to hide. If Stan got some secret stuff that's his business. I told him he'd get me in trouble if he used anything we talked about. That's why I want to talk to him. Say, publicity is the only way to fight them. Are you going to run out on me?[22]

Maxwell reported later that he had to interrupt an almost hysterical outburst from Seligman.

> MAXWELL: Stan never mentioned your name, in any investigation, commander, and we don't run out on anything. Stan will call you—why all he talks about is your heroism. You're one of his favorite heroes.[23]

Reading over Maxwell's account of his conversation with Seligman, Maloney wondered what the commander meant when he said something to the effect that "I told Johnston that if he mentioned any of the secret stuff he got from me he would get me in trouble." He called Johnston in Waupaca.

Johnston said that "secret stuff" was not in any of his stories. What Seligman had in mind, Johnston said, was the many secret aspects of the carrier *Lexington* that he, Seligman, had charge of and that Johnston understood to be off-the-record. Among those items were the range of *Lexington*'s guns and the method of pointing the guns; details about shell fuses; type of radio and the way the radio was used—"one thousand and one other secret internal Navy affairs." Johnston said he knew none of that could be published. "That is why so little was cut out of my [Coral Sea] stories by the censor and that is what Seligman apparently thought I might have been blabbing about," Johnston said. As for any dispatch from Nimitz, Johnston assured Maloney that Seligman showed him no such item.[24]

Johnston did phone Seligman. Calling from Waupaca the following evening, he reached a very distraught Seligman. Johnston was stunned by the commander's condition. The officer seemed exhausted and shell-shocked. They spoke for nearly an hour, with the writer's 7 June article the first topic of conversation. Johnston tried to relieve Seligman's anxieties, even if it meant mangling the truth. He told Seligman that none of the information that appeared in his *Tribune* story was obtained while he was at sea. In detailing the makeup of the Japanese fleet at Midway, Johnston said he based that on what he called "guesswork, surmise, opinion and judgment." He did, however, tell Seligman about the scrap of paper—with its doodles and scribbles—from which he had made a few notes before leaving *Barnett*.[25]

Whether Seligman caught the contradiction between "no information obtained while at sea" and the "scrap of paper" was unclear, but that item did pique the commander's interest.

> SELIGMAN: Who wrote the paper?
> JOHNSTON: I have no idea. As you know we all gathered for discussion over there in the corner.
> SELIGMAN: Yes, it was like a madhouse.[26]

Seligman proceeded to brief Johnston on what he had been through since 7 June. He had been quizzed by Admiral Willson, interrogated by naval intelligence in San Francisco, and hounded by FBI agents. They wanted to know, first, whether any secret messages were left anywhere in *Barnett* where Johnston could get hold of them. Second, they wondered if codes or signals were discussed in Johnston's presence. Seligman answered no to both questions. But he did not feel good about the situation. He felt he was being made a scapegoat for the "leak" of classified information. He worried about his career. He feared the Navy would exile him to some desert island where he would never be heard from again. He felt his chances for promotion were slim.[27]

Johnston tried to cheer him up. In Johnston's telling, very little of what was going on had anything to do with Seligman. It was all part of a nefarious "political effort" to smear the *Chicago Tribune*. He told the commander that Biddle's special assistant, William Mitchell, had tried to bluff him into confessing he had copied Nimitz's secret message. But when Johnston asked Mitchell to produce a copy of that message so it could be compared with his article, the lawyer had to admit the two were not "exactly the same." Johnston felt vindicated. He said the *Tribune* would not buckle under the pressure. Nor would it would abandon Seligman. The paper viewed him the way it would regard one if its own employees who had been unjustly accused of wrongdoing; the paper would bring to bear all the publicity it could to protect him. Seligman appreciated Johnston's comments: "I feel much better to know the *Tribune* is with me to see that I will get fair play."[28]

Johnston remained uneasy after his talk with Seligman. He felt the commander needed stronger reassurance that the *Tribune* was behind him. At Johnston's request, Maloney called Seligman the following afternoon to reaffirm the paper's support. Not to worry, he essentially told the officer, "The *Tribune* has always been damn strong for the Army and Navy." He commiserated with Seligman, letting him know that he had company in his struggle; he was not the only one being harassed by the Feds. "They tried all kinds of tricks on Johnston to get him to admit he copied some secret document," Maloney said. "That is what makes us sore and that is why we're going to fight."[29]

Feeling now more comfortable with *Tribune* personnel, Seligman launched into a rather elaborate explanation of his surprisingly relaxed attitude toward censorship and war correspondents on board ships in wartime.

> SELIGMAN: Here is the proposition. Actually, as I see it, when Admiral Nimitz sent a war correspondent to my ship—Stanley Johnston—obviously if the Navy gives people credentials—we are not mixed up in politics like they are—I don't care what paper this man may be from, if he comes from the admiral he comes to get correct information and to give the public the benefit of his knowledge and experience.[30]

In Seligman's unusually laissez-faire approach to press relations, that correspondent was entitled to full cooperation. Johnston, or any other journalist on board, was to be regarded as a kind of fly on the wall. He was to be almost invisible. He could hear anything. "I don't stop to discuss something merely because the reporter happens to be around," Seligman said. The reporter could have freedom of movement. He could see a lot—if not everything, close to everything (the radio room would always be off limits). He had a right to be there but could exert no claims. "I do not go around getting information for that correspondent," he told Maloney. "Obviously I have no time for that. If he happens to get information that is his business. You or I or anybody else wouldn't employ a man who could not get information."[31]

Seligman's view of his responsibilities did not include censorship. That activity was something handled by other people. "We had a system out on the west coast before I left for the western Pacific whereby we told the newspaper people everything and then the press relations bureau cut it down to what they thought should be published," Seligman said. "That [was] the end of that." Obviously, that approach did not work in this instance. Curiously, Seligman did not press Maloney on why he, as managing editor, did not submit Johnston's story to Navy censors. He expressed no fault with the *Tribune*. He lodged no complaint against Johnston's story.

> SELIGMAN: I don't think it did a damn bit of harm. I think the whole thing is purely political and I feel sore as hell about the whole thing but on the other hand I have had 28 years of service and I don't want to throw that away.[32]

Relieved as he was by Maloney's call and his earlier conversations with Maxwell and Johnston, Seligman still agonized. He continued to fret about his career and his health, and he resented the constant pressure from FBI agents. They seemed to never run out of questions.

> SELIGMAN: It is a hell of a note. I have been terribly ill and this doesn't do me any good.[33]

~

Given the disposition of his superiors in Washington, most particularly that of Admiral King, Seligman had good reason to fear for his future. But then, in a different kind of way, so did Stanley Johnston. He had no way of knowing whether he would ever work again as a war correspondent. On 17 June,

Commander Berry of Navy public relations dictated a memorandum suspending his Pacific Fleet credentials.[34] Acting on Johnston's behalf in Washington, Arthur Henning tried to find out what the reporter needed to do to have them restored. Navy Department officials always shrugged and said they did not know. Without those papers, of course, Johnston's days covering the Navy from Pearl Harbor, or anywhere else for that matter, would be over. He met with other setbacks. Johnston learned that the Royal Canadian Mounted Police had designated him as a "suspected enemy agent" and placed him on its Central Security War Blacklist. The listing required Canada to deny him access to all government facilities.[35] His career as a war correspondent was definitely in doubt.

Career issues aside, Seligman and Johnston faced a more immediate problem. By mid-July, William Mitchell had been on the Johnston-*Tribune* case just about a month. He had quizzed Johnston and Maloney, had studied the evidence, and was expected soon to make a judgment with regard to the case. A lot of people wondered what Mitchell would do. Would he recommend taking the case to a grand jury? Seligman dreaded that possibility; Johnston prepared for it. Both hoped it would not come to pass, and meantime they waited.

CHAPTER 10

FULL SPEED AHEAD

We shall make available all necessary witnesses.

—*Frank Knox*

The government's case against Stanley Johnston and the *Chicago Tribune* nearly crashed in mid-July. Biddle's special assistant, the redoubtable William Mitchell, expressed "serious doubts" about whether Johnston or anyone else at the *Tribune* could be convicted of espionage. In a carefully crafted, fourteen-page memo to Biddle and Navy Secretary Knox, Mitchell, on 14 July, recommended the criminal proceeding be dropped.[1] Mitchell's gloomy assessment coincided with Biddle's view, but it collided with Knox's. Knox was not ready to throw in the towel. Presumably, he would impart his thoughts to the president. Roosevelt, after all, would make the final call. Would he back Knox? The two usually seemed to be on the same page. Or would he take the unexpected advice of his trusted attorney general and his prima donna special assistant?

As of 14 July, no one knew how FDR would decide. One thing was clear, however: Mitchell's thinking had changed since he arrived in Washington. After four weeks on the case, during which time he had immersed himself in the government's contradictory evidence, tried unsuccessfully to extract a coherent story from Maloney and Johnston, and run afoul of a recalcitrant Admiral King, he reassessed the whole matter. He had come to respect King's point of view, even if he did not accept it. But he saw King's predicament. The problem was not only that a public trial would call attention to an activity the Navy wished to keep secret. There was another issue: King's intel experts— officers performing valuable duty elsewhere—would have to be uprooted and reassigned to a courtroom. The trial might drag on for weeks. "In light of all these conditions," he told Biddle and Knox, "I think the question whether the 'game is worth the candle' should first be submitted to the Navy," and let the Navy decide whether or not to go ahead. Mitchell made it clear where he stood on the question of a trial.[2]

In his pungent, crisply argued memorandum, Mitchell laid out the key factors that he thought would make it hard, if not impossible, to convict either Johnston or Maloney. He approached the matter elliptically, writing that "the evidence available justifies the conclusion that neither Maloney nor Johnston is telling the truth." He was especially critical of Maloney. He characterized the managing editor as greedy for a scoop—so greedy that he concealed the fact that Johnston was the author of the *Tribune*'s 7 June story. That sleight of hand enabled the paper to avoid Navy censorship. This was inexcusable, Mitchell thought, since Maloney knew that Johnston had collected at least some of his information while sailing with the Pacific Fleet. Attributing Johnston's disclosures to unnamed officers in the Office of Naval Intelligence was, in Mitchell's view, "a despicable thing to do as it cast suspicion of 'leakage' on ONI officers in Washington." Mitchell added, "Then Maloney published the article, with a total and reckless disregard of any possible injury to the cause of national defense."[3]

Culpable as Maloney and Johnston may have been, could they be convicted of breaking the espionage law? With the evidence at hand, Mitchell did not think so. One problem was the law itself. Deficiencies in the espionage statute, he believed, would make conviction especially difficult. As Mitchell explained to Biddle and Knox, the law did not penalize "wilful disclosure" [*sic*] of secret *information*; it penalized only the disclosure of the contents of a *document, writing,* or *note.* Mitchell said he doubted that a jury would regard the scrap of paper Johnston found on *Barnett* as a document, writing, or note as defined in the statute.[4]

Another problem—one the Navy already fully appreciated—would arise in the context of the defense likely to be employed by *Tribune* lawyers. They would tell a jury that the story, in ascribing Nimitz's ambush to "advance information," had disclosed little more than what had already been stated or intimated in press dispatches from Honolulu. They would argue that this information could have been gained by submarine and air scouting. "A trial would necessarily disclose the means by which the Navy obtained the information and a trial is public," Mitchell reminded his two colleagues. If perchance the Japanese had not yet been put wise by the *Tribune*'s story, he observed, the added publicity of a trial might have that result.[5]

Mitchell buttressed his analysis by bringing up an unpleasant issue—especially for Knox—that was sure to be a factor in any trial: the handling of "secret" dispatches on board *Barnett* by Navy officers. This would not help the government's case. The indisputable fact was that Johnston had gotten his hands on Nimitz's dispatch or a copy of it. If some officer had indeed left a copy of that message lying around, as now appeared likely, *Tribune* lawyers could fairly argue that there was as much carelessness by Navy officers on the ship as the *Tribune* was guilty of. Mitchell figured that a jury would probably agree.[6]

The case against Johnston, Mitchell regretted saying, was weak. In truth there apparently was nothing on that scrap of paper from which he took notes to indicate it was secret. The correspondent might have guessed it was pretty important, even recognized it as highly sensitive (why else would he have copied it?), but it was not stamped secret. The fact that it was sitting undisturbed on a desk gathering dust suggested there was nothing secret about it, or so defense lawyers would argue. Moreover, Johnston's decision to rely on his managing editor to have the article censored was natural under the circumstances. "Johnston's conviction is therefore doubtful," Mitchell wrote.[7]

As for Maloney, the outlook for conviction was equally grim. True, the evidence showed that he had reason to believe Johnston had obtained information while on *Barnett*—a fact that would have made his article subject to Navy censorship. But Maloney maintained—and Johnston supported him on this—that he did not know that his correspondent's information was obtained from any writing or document. Johnston did not tell him about the scrap of paper until later. "Maloney can claim that he did not 'wilfully' offend because he knew nothing about any document or writing and that defense seems likely to be sustained," Mitchell believed. And if neither Johnston nor Maloney could be found guilty, it was certain that the Tribune Corporation could not be convicted. Failure to convict would have consequences, he warned. It would be unfortunate, he wrote, if a prosecution should be begun and result in acquittal: "It would hurt the Administration and consequently the cause of national defense."[8]

The government's case seemed to have only one place to go. "In view of these doubts as to conviction and the interferences with Navy operations by using Navy officers as witnesses," Mitchell concluded, "it is my judgment that the case should not be prosecuted."[9]

Mitchell's unsparing analysis could have settled matters, but it did not. Mitchell did not have the last word. President Roosevelt did. And the president did not listen only to Biddle and Mitchell; there was also Knox waiting off stage. Mitchell had addressed his memo to both Biddle *and* Knox in order to give the Secretary of the Navy a chance to make his opinions heard. The extent to which Knox expressed a different view to Roosevelt is not known. Even if he did so, his comments, in all likelihood, did not matter that much. The president already had his mind made up, or so it seemed to Biddle when he met with Roosevelt in the Oval Office on 16 July to discuss the matter. Their conversation turned out to be pivotal.[10]

Held two days after Mitchell had urged that the case be shelved, the meeting was a difficult one for Biddle, although it should not have been. He and the president had known each other for years. But they had different political styles, different temperaments. Aristocratically fastidious, given to suave, double-breasted suits, sporting an elegant mustache, Biddle was not a fighter. He had no taste for rough-and-tumble combat. A newcomer to the cabinet, he was unsure of his standing in the White House. He was also impressed by FDR and, like many people, had a hard time saying "no" to him.[11] So when he brought up the problems raised by Mitchell, he got nowhere. He found Roosevelt incredulous, and a little angry as well. The idea that Johnston and Maloney could have transgressed Navy censorship without also trampling on the law seemed absurd. He would not accept the action favored by Mitchell, now endorsed by Biddle. He sent his attorney general back to the Justice Department, telling him that if he and his lawyers examined the case thoroughly, they would find that the law had been violated.[12]

❧

Biddle returned to a Justice Department deeply divided over the Johnston case. Biddle's assistant attorney general, Wendell Berge, opposed any move to prosecute the *Tribune* staffers. He cited Mitchell's analysis, agreeing "that it is quite improbable that a conviction could be obtained." He said this was a case the government could not afford to bring unless there was a reasonable chance of winning. He did not see a reasonable chance; there were too many problems. In the first place, he doubted that the public would ever understand the issues involved. Technical explanations would be needed to spell out the *Tribune*'s alleged wrongdoing. That effort, he said, would probably engulf the case in questions of freedom of the press and the arcane details of censorship. "I do not think," Berge wrote Biddle, "we could succeed in making our position clearly enough understood to accomplish any real public benefit."[13]

But Justice's assistant solicitor general, Oscar Cox, serving as the department's lawyer, sharply dissented. "In my opinion there is a good enough case to proceed against Johnston," Cox told Biddle. Cox had already challenged Mitchell's interpretation of the matter and he continued to do so. He conceded the case against the correspondent was not open and shut. Still, he thought the law and facts were sufficient to justify proceeding with the indictment and the trial. He was less sure when it came to prosecuting Maloney; his situation seemed murky. But not Johnston's. Cox wanted to move forward at full speed. "The public interest—the prevention of serious leaks—dictates the going ahead," Cox said. "In all probability, the indictment alone would have a salutary effect in preventing disclosures so dangerous to our war effort."[14]

Cox did not want Johnston to get away unscathed. If a full criminal proceeding proved unfeasible, he proposed the government take some lesser action against the correspondent. He should be censured in some way, Cox thought. As one possibility, he proposed that Admiral King issue a public denunciation of Johnston. Or if that idea did not pan out, he wondered if the Navy could convene a military tribunal and put the reporter on trial in a court-martial. "Under any of these alternatives," Cox wrote, "Johnston and other *Tribune* reporters should certainly be barred from the Fleet." Johnston, of course, had already been banished.[15]

Cox's sentiments coincided with growing controversy now swirling around the *Tribune*. Even though Biddle's investigation was secret and conducted behind closed doors, news of the probe was starting to seep out, and not always in ways that were helpful. As early as 23 June, the liberal New York tabloid *PM* ran a revealing story under the following headline and deck:

'News', Chicago 'Trib'
Betray U.S. Secrets
Leak Chokes Off Source of Navy's Information About Japanese Plans

Alluding to *Tribune* publisher Robert R. McCormick and his cousin, *New York Daily News* publisher Joseph Patterson, the article began bluntly: "The McCormick-Patterson press still is publishing vital information to our enemies and getting away with it."[16]

PM thus became the first newspaper to report the government's inquiry into the *Chicago Tribune*. *PM* writer Kenneth G. Crawford noted that "vital facts" of the case had been "common gossip" in Washington for days. Editors refrained from publishing anything at the request of government officials. But *PM*, for reasons that can only be guessed, decided to print what it knew, or thought it new. Crawford's story, however, went well beyond common gossip. It divulged many key details of the federal probe. It restated the thrust of the *Tribune* story—the Navy had "advance information" about the Japanese attack on Midway—and it chronicled the Navy Department's horrified reaction. Admirals were said to be "furious" about the story, and they reportedly demanded the Justice Department unearth the paper's source. *PM* stated that it had learned the article did not originate in Washington, as first believed; it surfaced somewhere else and was based on a Navy document, circulated possibly by a Navy officer. The FBI was said to be looking into the matter; the former attorney general William D. Mitchell had been appointed by Biddle to handle the case. None of this had been previously reported.[17]

PM's was the kind of story King and his lieutenants found particularly troublesome. It did not explicitly state that the Navy had cracked the IJN's code, but like Johnston's 7 June article, it brought that possibility to mind. Obviously, this was not the sort of coverage COMINCH wanted to see in newspapers around the country. The article probably reinforced King's concerns about what would happen in the event of an indictment and public trial of *Tribune* staffers: news about Navy codebreaking—linked to the Midway success—would explode as reporters descended on the trial. But the *PM* article did have an upside, at least from the point of view of Knox and the White House: it made the *Tribune* look irresponsible, even cavalier.

Crawford did not say how he got the story, but it was well-known that *PM*'s publisher, department store heir Marshall Field III, had good sources in the Roosevelt administration, especially in the Navy Department. Field and Knox were old friends. As noted, Knox had provided encouragement, and resources, when Field six months earlier had launched the *Chicago Sun*, a new morning daily to compete with McCormick's morning *Tribune* (see chapter 5). Field envisioned the *Sun* as a liberal alternative to the conservative *Tribune*. But if, as seems plausible, someone in Knox's circle leaked the Johnston story to *PM*, the informant passed on to Crawford an egregious error. His article stated that the Justice Department had decided *not* to take action against any of the *Tribune*'s executives or employees. "It was decided that the facts did not warrant any government action," Crawford wrote. Nothing could have been further from the truth; as of 23 June, no decision had been reached on what action, if any, to take against the *Tribune*.[18]

Off base as it was, the *PM* story nevertheless opened the media flood-gates. Scribes from all ranks of the newspaper and radio worlds noticed it and wondered. One whose curiosity was piqued was radio gossip commen-tator and newspaper columnist Walter Winchell. As it turned out, Winchell and Robert McCormick were bitter enemies; they had feuded for years. A onetime vaudeville hoofer, Winchell's usual fare was the indiscretions and misdemeanors of show business celebrities. But Winchell also was a Naval Reserve officer who claimed close ties with Admiral Hepburn, director of Navy public relations. As the war progressed, he began including in his broad-casts choice bits of military information, much to the consternation of Hep-burn and the Office of Censorship. In an effort to rein him in, censors would periodically call Winchell's bosses—NBC's Blue Network executives in New York—and point out his transgressions.[19] But he continued to confound the censors. He did so brazenly on his Sunday, 5 July 1942 broadcast when he ventured into the forbidden realm of codebreaking, telling his nationwide audience, "When the history of these times is written it will be revealed that twice the fate of the civilized world was changed by intercepted and decoded messages. I cannot enlarge on that, it is military information."[20] As far as the Navy was concerned, he had already said too much.

Winchell continued to play fast and loose with the censorship code in his syndicated column, *On Broadway*. He did in this one, printed in the 7 July *New York Daily Mirror*:

> The story all over Washington and Newspaper Row here con-cerns Col. R.R. McCormick's paper in Chicago. . . . It again tossed safety out the windows—and allegedly printed the lowdown on why we won at Midway—claiming that the U.S. Navy decoded the Japs' secret messages, etc. . . . True or not, we dunno. . . . Official Washington was so incensed at the pub-lisher's persistent disregard for military secrecy—it decided to teach him a lesson. . . . What one man saved him? . . . His dead-liest enemy in Chicago, publisher Frank Knox.[21]

Winchell got many things wrong. The *Tribune*'s 7 June story did not claim the Navy had smashed Japan's naval code, although it invited readers to draw that conclusion. And McCormick was not saved; the case against his *Tribune* staffers remained very much alive. Knox had not saved him. Winchell simply picked up *PM*'s notion that the case had been dropped and gave Knox the credit. The columnist also breached the censorship code. Under the Roosevelt administration's policy of voluntary censorship, writers and broadcasters were expected to let Washington's censors review in advance any and all articles, or column items, concerning military activity. Clearly, Winchell did not understand that rule; he failed to run his item by the Office of Censorship. If he had, the office would have referred it to the Navy Department, whose censors would have promptly killed it. In the wake of the Johnston affair, any mention of codebreaking was strictly forbidden. Censors let Winchell's bosses know.[22]

Winchell's column item represented one more rip in the veil of secrecy that was supposed to surround the Navy's cryptanalytic efforts. His item actually went further than Johnston's story: It expressly credited the Navy's Midway success to codebreaking. When challenged by censors, Winchell stated he had a special relationship with Admiral Hepburn that allowed him to write special items desired by the military. Hepburn denied any such relationship existed. Eventually, censors brought Winchell into full compliance with their code, but by that time a year had passed.[23]

In the meantime, Winchell continued to exasperate censors. He did not ease up on McCormick, getting in more digs at the publisher's expense. Some listeners could have sworn Winchell in his 12 July broadcast was referring to McCormick when, during a meandering digression on patriotism, he preached that while not every man born in Berlin hates democracy— "neither does every man born in Chicago love this Republic." McCormick was born in Chicago. If that comment was too subtle for some, Winchell made sure his meaning was clear when, a moment later, he noted that underground newspapers in Europe continued their attack on Hitler, while in this country there was a different phenomenon: "At the risk of nothing some American newspapers continue to underhandedly support Hitler's principles in America." No doubt many people, rightly or wrongly, interpreted Winchell's comment as an oblique slap at the *Tribune*.[24]

Winchell was not the only one directing ire at Robert McCormick and his newspaper. As the *Tribune* continued its attacks on the administration, Americans from different parts of the country started to turn their wrath on the newspaper. Other newspapers also found fault with FDR's war policies, but the *Tribune* led this onslaught, daily blanketing the isolationist Midwest with disparaging and sometimes abusive editorials.[25] By midsummer and early fall, letters and telegrams were pouring into the White House and Justice Department, all demanding that something be done about the *Tribune*. Citizens' groups and even labor unions weighed in. Local 103 of the United Electrical, Radio & Machine Workers in Camden, New Jersey, accused the *Tribune*, the *New York Daily News*, and the *Washington Times-Herald* of "engaging in a subversive and un-American propaganda policy." The United Automobile, Aircraft and Agricultural Implement Workers in Cicero, Illinois, demanded the *Tribune* be closed down—because it advocated "rebellion against the United States Government." The National Maritime Union expressed a similar sentiment.[26]

"Dislike for McCormick was by no means confined to New Dealers," censorship director Byron Price commented. "He had served as an artillery officer in World War I and he regarded himself as an authority on military matters. The ire of professional military men was aroused by his constant use of his newspaper and his Chicago radio station to instruct the Army and the Navy on the proper conduct of the war."[27]

If the government was to move against McCormick and his *Tribune* staffers, this seemed a perfect time to do it. There would be public support for some kind of action. Still, Biddle could not make up his mind. FDR had ordered him and the Justice Department to reconsider the case and find grounds for an indictment. But the attorney general continued to agonize. He sought the advice of people he trusted. One of those was Price, a longtime journalist and sagacious observer of the Washington scene. Price liked Biddle but had reservations about him as attorney general. "He never was a very strong character, especially when confronted with a concerted drive by the New Deal element in the administration," Price recalled later. "I never believed that Biddle favored prosecution [of the *Tribune*]. He asked for my opinion and I said I would expect nothing but humiliation for the government to come from such a proceeding." Days passed without Biddle deciding whether to go for the indictment or tell Roosevelt, once and for all, it could not be done.[28]

∾

Biddle's problem was solved by Frank Knox. Two weeks after Mitchell tried to scuttle the case, Knox finally reached what seemed to be a final, and unalterable, decision: "We shall make available all necessary witnesses just as soon as you are ready to proceed," he informed Biddle. In a 29 July letter to the attorney general (AG), Knox assured him that, after much deliberation, the Navy Department had reached a firm verdict. He reminded the AG that weeks earlier, the Navy's chieftains had considered it in "the best interests of national defense" that the case go to a grand jury. According to Knox, his leadership team had not abandoned that view: "Upon further consideration we are still of this opinion and therefore renew our previous recommendation."[29]

Knox said that he and the department's top officials had weighed the objections raised in Mitchell's skeptical memorandum and found them unpersuasive. Indeed, he and his colleagues were unburdened by doubts; they thought the evidence was strong enough to convict the *Tribune* defendants now identified. "In any event," Knox added, "we do not believe that the fear of possible acquittal should deter the responsible officers of the Government in laying a case of this importance before the courts." He thought that Mitchell and Biddle were being overly pessimistic, and he closed by lecturing them that courts should not be second-guessed, as Mitchell's memo attempted to do. What courts might do "cannot be anticipated with any degree of certainty," he mused; nor, presumably, should any prosecutor pretend to know the future.[30]

Biddle and Mitchell were astonished. True, Knox had never wavered in his desire for action against the *Tribune*. But his enthusiasm was only briefly shared among the higher echelons of the uniformed Navy. After a few hot-tempered days during which Admiral King and his fellow admirals let loose a good deal of fury at the newspaper, they cooled off once they saw the implications of a public trial—the certainty it would reveal to the world the Navy's success breaking the Imperial Navy's main code. They did not want that to happen. By mid-June, King was already backing away from any kind of legal proceeding, and in late June he issued an informal but seemingly firm policy statement: no Navy officer would be allowed to serve as a witness with regard to codebreaking and Japanese navy messages.[31]

The Navy had seemingly reversed King's edict. Biddle and Mitchell were not only surprised, they were also puzzled. How had this change come about? Had Knox and King, who had been feuding for months over the boundaries of each other's authority, patched things up? Had they reached a very improbable accord? Or had Knox simply overruled the obstreperous King in a final showdown? Had King even been consulted? No one knew. Nor, for that matter, did anyone know what factors dictated Knox's eagerness to mount a dubious, and very high-risk, legal action against the *Tribune*. Predictably, McCormick's allies imputed the worst motives to the Navy secretary; they saw him as an opportunist who had "egged on" Roosevelt against the *Tribune*, hoping to weaken, if not destroy, a competitor. They thought he would use his public office to demolish a hated foe.[32]

But those who knew Knox best did not view him as venal or unscrupulous. They pointed out that he was every bit as patriotic as McCormick, having served years earlier as one of Theodore Roosevelt's Rough Riders in the Spanish-American War. His defenders considered him a man of principle who would not put his own personal gain ahead of the security interests of the country. They saw him, as two historians put it, as "a bluff extrovert of rugged physique and big-hearted impulses, not a great intellect."[33] His motives were probably simpler than they seemed to his enemies. Like Biddle, Knox was somewhat in awe of the president. He once told a subordinate that even though his politics differed from Roosevelt's, he considered FDR a "great man" and was proud to serve under him.[34] In all likelihood, Knox's renewed commitment to the case stemmed from a desire to please the president. He was doing what he thought Roosevelt wanted him to do: he had gotten his marching orders.

So had Biddle and Mitchell. With Navy intel witnesses now seemingly assured, they could proceed with the case. They had mixed feelings about taking it forward. They were wary of King and Knox. Nevertheless, without any illusions about the difficulties ahead, Mitchell thought he now had at least a slight chance of prevailing in a grand jury proceeding, possibly even in a public trial. Because of the expert testimony that would be at his disposal, he could still, if all went well, demonstrate to a jury the harm done by the *Tribune* story. Biddle was less hopeful. He confided his doubts to his friend Byron Price. "[The attorney general] said he felt he had a weak case against the *Tribune*," Price wrote later. "He was reluctant to bring an action which might not only be lost but which might make a martyr out of Colonel McCormick and give him further ground for complaint that the administration was persecuting him."[35]

But the government could not turn back now. Mitchell and Biddle had work to do. They had to round up witnesses, not codebreaking experts (Knox would supply those later), but officers who could speak to the movements and activities of Stanley Johnston on board *Lexington* and *Barnett*. They had to set a venue and a timetable and did all that. On Friday, 7 August, Biddle informed the press he had ordered an immediate grand jury investigation, at Chicago, of the publication by "certain newspapers" on 7 June 1942 of confidential information concerning the Battle of Midway. Jurors would be asked to probe the "possible violation" of the Espionage Act of 1917. Biddle's special assistant, William D. Mitchell, would conduct the case. The panel would begin hearing testimony on Thursday, 13 August. Biddle did not name the newspapers, but Robert W. Horton, head of the news bureau of the Office of War Information, intentionally or unintentionally let the targets leak out. He said the investigation "involves the *Chicago Tribune, New York Daily News* and the *Washington Times-Herald*." They were singled out in the *Washington Post* the next day; soon Johnston's and Maloney's names got into the mix.[36]

Biddle's statement was historic. It marked the only time during the war that the government sought a criminal indictment against one of the country's large anti-administration publications.[37] Biddle was now irrevocably committed to the case, but he remained suspicious of Knox. In making his announcement, he took the unusual step of bringing the Navy secretary directly into the controversy. The AG stated that the investigation was ordered after preliminary inquiry and upon the recommendation of the Navy Department. If anything went wrong and blame was parceled out, Biddle wanted company; he did not want to take the heat alone. In the meantime, it was the three newspapers named in the *Post* that were feeling the heat. Two of the papers were stunned. Both the *Daily News* and the *Times Herald* declined to comment on the grand jury investigation. They would remain silent for days. Not the *Tribune*. McCormick's paper did not hold back. It soon told the country what it thought.[38]

CHAPTER 11

McCORMICK AND KNOX

Showdown

We have said and proved that we cannot be intimidated.
—Chicago Tribune

Oddly, McCormick was caught off guard by Biddle's announcement. He had been expecting the worst. He had no illusions about what Roosevelt, Biddle, and Knox hoped to do. He believed they aimed to disgrace his newspaper and, if they could, put him behind bars. Throughout the long, hot summer—when Winchell was attacking and rumors about the case were buzzing—he remained defiant. He told Arthur Sears Henning early in June that if Knox intended to be tough, he could be just as tough. He may have figured the hubbub over Stanley Johnston would blow over, that the government would see it had a weak case and move on to other matters. Whatever he thought, when Biddle's 7 August press release circulated and McCormick realized he faced a real grand jury proceeding, he was shocked and momentarily dumbfounded.[1]

Sitting alone in his mansion on North Astor Street—a stately, four-story abode used by the publisher from time to time as a retreat—McCormick was unsure how to respond. He did make two quick phone calls, both to the *Tribune* newsroom. First he talked to his hard-charging managing editor, Pat Maloney. His message was not one Maloney wanted to hear. McCormick instructed him to take a short leave of absence. He did not suspend Maloney, but he did relieve him, for the time being, of all editorial responsibility for the paper. He wanted his editor to prepare his testimony and concentrate all his energies on his defense and, for that matter, the paper's strategy going forward. Maloney reluctantly agreed.[2]

Then he called the paper's city editor, Don Maxwell, and summoned Maxwell to the mansion. "He was in a very dark mood," Maxwell recalled.

"Don, what are we going to do?" he remembered his employer asking. Maxwell answered, "We're going to fight it and prove that this is an attempt by the Roosevelt administration to get you and the *Tribune*." McCormick apparently liked what he heard; he ordered Maxwell to run the newspaper, at least for now. "I told Maloney that he ought to stay away from the office while the grand jury is debating his case," McCormick informed Maxwell, "so you're in charge." Maxwell quickly devised a plan of attack. His job was made easier by the fact that *Tribune* writers had been preparing copy for just such an eventuality. "I went right back [to the office]," Maxwell said later, "and got hold of Bill Fulton," the paper's lead political writer. "Bill Fulton then began to write the series of how the *Tribune* was being persecuted by the Roosevelt administration."[3]

The *Tribune* moved fast. Under a screaming, front-page banner headline, "Biddle Attacks the Tribune," the paper on Saturday, 8 August, launched the first of four prickly, sharp-edged articles blasting Biddle and Knox and sounding the persecution theme. It did so day after day. The grand jury probe was not a surprise, Fulton stated. It was part of an ongoing "wave of inquiries" aimed at the *Tribune*. The campaign started heating up a few months earlier, the *Tribune* claimed, when FBI G-men "invaded" the offices of newspaper editors and tried to coerce them into granting the Associated Press services to the new pro-Roosevelt newspaper in Chicago, Marshall Field's *Chicago Sun*. Now, with the current grand jury scrutiny, the administration this time was abusing the grand jury system to serve a vindictive and crassly political end: "Get the *Tribune*."[4]

The *Tribune* let loose a barrage of charges against Frank Knox. The Navy secretary was accused of bungling the conduct of naval affairs in the war; misusing his high official position to benefit his own newspaper; and for good measure, exhibiting garden-variety greed. The *Tribune* brought out that Knox was getting $60,000 a year from the *Daily News* to serve his newspaper in an "advisory capacity" while also drawing an annual government salary of $15,000 as Secretary of the Navy. The paper suggested that Knox, with his annual earnings of $75,000 a year, mocked the concept of wartime sacrifice. The paper also wondered how he divided his time between his two responsibilities. "There are spots where it is difficult to tell where the secretary of the navy Knox's paper ends and the Navy begins, or vice versa," the *Tribune* commented acidly.[5]

Knox's earnings aside, the *Tribune* concentrated its fire on the secretary's alleged "unfairness," contending that he discriminated against the *Tribune* in naval assignments and repeatedly favored afternoon papers and his own in particular by releasing Navy battle news to them first. It depicted Knox as "a clucking hen" who can sit on a big story until the publishing time of his own newspaper rolls around, adding as a fillip, "and he usually does."[6]

To illustrate its point, the *Tribune* cited the frustrations of newspapermen who were assigned to the U.S. Fleet during its February raid on the Marshall and Gilbert Islands. Their stories were held up, put on ice by an official release date that clearly favored the *Daily News* and other afternoon papers. The *Tribune* correctly pointed out that other newspapers also protested, namely, the *New York Times, New York Herald Tribune, New York Daily News,* and *Philadelphia Inquirer.*[7] The *Tribune* failed to point out, however, that the Navy Department responded by instituting a new policy for "release dates and times" of correspondents' copy to create a more equal playing field for morning and afternoon papers.[8]

But the *Tribune* was not deterred by contradictions in its presentation. In a front-page editorial on Sunday, 9 August, the paper stated it had only one regret—that the "effort to destroy the *Tribune's* independence" was directed at two "valued associates," its highly esteemed managing editor, Pat Maloney, and its much-praised war correspondent, Stanley Johnston. "These are the men who have been chosen as victims," the paper cried. Victims they may or may not have been, but in the hands of *Tribune* writers they were many things: ardent patriots and paragons of probity and the highest journalistic standards. They were men of conspicuous courage—"Johnston would sooner cut off his right arm than give information to the enemy."[9]

The hyperbole was unnecessary. The valor Johnston displayed during the Coral Sea campaign when, at considerable risk to himself, he rescued endangered men from the sinking *Lexington*, then pulled many from the sea onto a whaleboat, was well documented. The *Tribune* made the most of Johnston's feat. It correctly pointed out that he had been recommended for a bravery citation by Admiral Fitch, Admiral Nimitz, and Captain Sherman—a citation not yet granted by Admiral King. The paper was less forthcoming in describing how Johnston obtained his controversial 7 June story on the makeup of the Imperial Navy armada nearing Midway. According to the *Tribune*, the article stemmed almost entirely from Johnston's hard-won knowledge, his discussions with experts everywhere and officers on *Barnett,* and as always, his thorough reading of *Jane's Fighting Ships.*[10] The paper failed to mention the "scrap of paper" that even Johnston admitted he found on *Barnett* on

2 June, listing the names of some ships in the Japanese armada; those names turned up word for word in his *Tribune* article.

While ignoring this crucial admission, the paper meanwhile trumpeted the fact that its correspondent was the only newspaperman at the scene of the Coral Sea battle. The paper conveniently overlooked a critical aspect of that seeming achievement—that Johnston's presence on board *Lexington* came about because Frank Knox had personally approved it. Of course, recognition of Knox's role would have diluted, if not punctured, the paper's caricature of the Navy secretary as invariably biased in his naval assignments.

Both Johnston and Maloney were portrayed as worldly men with strong military experience. Johnston was said to have joined the Australian army at age fourteen and a half in World War I. (He actually entered Australia's naval reserves at that age.) And Maloney was accurately portrayed as a flier who had served twenty-six months in the European War, most of them with the famous squadron commanded by Captain Eddie Rickenbacker. Citing *Who's Who in America*, the *Tribune* noted that Attorney General Biddle served in the U.S. Army from 23 October 1918 to 29 November 1918, adding dryly that the Armistice was signed on 11 November 1918.[11]

In speeding Johnston's 7 June article into print, Maloney's motives were pure. He quite simply believed the article "would add to the glory of our armed forces and have a salutary effect on national morale." As the editor in overall charge of the story, Maloney "scrupulously observed censorship regulations," the *Tribune* said.[12] But in boasting of its commitment to voluntary censorship, the paper fuzzed over a lapse in Maloney's judgment: he failed to submit Johnston's controversial article to either the Office of Censorship or to U.S. Navy censors. Such conduct hardly constituted "scrupulous observance" of censorship regulations. Those rules called for pre-publication review of all articles concerning military operations, especially in those cases where the material was gathered at sea or in a war zone.

In fact, Johnston's article was not examined until *after* publication. As noted, the Office of Censorship briefly considered issuing a citation against the paper. It did not do so as censors came to realize there was a loophole in their rules. Because of that crack, Byron Price's censors judged that the *Tribune* story was not, technically, in violation of the censorship code. It had transgressed the spirit of the code, they thought, but not the letter. They certainly did not declare the paper "guiltless," as *Tribune* writers claimed. Censors simply said they had "no further quarrel" with the *Tribune*; they let the matter pass. Then they moved to close the gap in their guidelines that the paper had exploited. The paper accurately described what happened next: "A few hours later the censorship bureau issued a supplementary rule requesting newspapers hereafter to impute to the United States Navy no advance knowledge of the disposition of enemy ships. *This in effect, was an admission that the previously promulgated regulations did not forbid such publication*" (emphasis added).[13]

Hereafter, a story like Johnston's would be in violation of the code, but not this time. The *Tribune* escaped a rebuke from the Office of Censorship because of a technicality—and was bragging about it. Such newspaper practice certainly did not measure up to the high journalistic and patriotic standards the paper boasted it met. But the *Tribune* was not in a remorseful mood. "We have no apologies to make," the paper stated in a front page editorial. It rejected any notion that it might have breached the Espionage Act: "The charge is as false as it is petty and we welcome the opportunity which may come to us to prove how false and petty it is."[14]

~

The *Tribune*'s bombastic, highly slanted version of the Johnston case accomplished a critical McCormick goal: it deflected attention away from the newspaper. By Monday, 10 August, it was not McCormick and his editors who were on the defensive; it was Knox, Biddle, and the Roosevelt administration. During a stormy Senate session that afternoon in which he obviously relied on some of the *Tribune*'s bare-knuckle reporting, Republican senator Wayland Brooks of Illinois accused the administration of using the "Gestapo methods of Hitlerism" to "get the *Chicago Tribune*." He called the attack on the *Tribune* "vicious, malicious and constant"—part of a well-organized, well-financed "purge and smear campaign" aimed not only at the *Tribune*, but at himself and other members of Congress who opposed FDR's policies before Pearl Harbor and America's entry into the war.[15]

Majority Leader Alben W. Barkley, Democrat of Kentucky, challenged Brooks, objecting to his use of "smear." "The smear highway is not a one-way street," Barkley said. "It has become fashionable in recent years to describe anybody who opposes our views by saying they are trying to smear somebody," the senator added. "I don't like the word smear. I don't like to hear it because it is an insidious word. I do not think it is fair to use it whenever anybody opposes our views." Reasonable as Barkley's comments might have seemed, two senators, Robert A. Taft, Republican of Ohio, and Champ Clark, Democrat of Missouri, supported Brooks, telling their fellow senators they thought their colleague was justified in his protest. Alluding to Biddle's move against the *Tribune*, Taft predicted that if this newspaper could be indicted, "no editor in the United States will be able to print anything but the official communiques."[16]

If one thing bothered Taft more than anything else, it was the government's decision to name in advance the targets of the grand jury probe. "It is customary in the case of grand jury investigations not to announce publicly the name of the person against whom charges are being heard," Taft said. Referring to Barkley's earlier point about the dangers of "smearing" people, Taft turned it against the Kentucky Democrat, adding, "The proceedings before the grand jury are supposed to be secret, so that a man will not be 'smeared.' I do not use that term in any special sense; but the purpose of secrecy in grand jury proceedings is to avoid an attack on the reputation of the person involved."[17]

Did Biddle smear the *Tribune*? Barkley's reply was rather lame: he declined to pass judgment on the propriety of Biddle's 7 August announcement. He did assert, however, that if the Espionage Act had been infringed, neither the *Tribune* nor anybody connected with it nor any other newspaper should be immune from prosecution. "The point I wish to emphasize," Barkley declared, "is that if there has been any law violated by anybody involved in this episode the people are entitled to know it."[18]

❧

Three days before grand jurors heard their first witness, the Johnston case had turned into a political circus. In a gratuitous display of solidarity with administration critics, the longtime isolationist senator Burton K. Wheeler, Democrat of Montana, volunteered his legal services to McCormick at no charge. In the House, Representative Clare E. Hoffman, Republican of Michigan, called for the creation of a special House committee to investigate the *Tribune*'s charge that Knox was using his official position to benefit his own newspaper. Hoffman said that if Biddle wanted to render a service to the nation, he would investigate Knox. "We heard in days gone by not a little about driving the money changers from the temple," Hoffman fumed. "What about getting them out of the administration?" He also joined those contending that the Secretary of the Navy discriminated against morning newspapers in releasing war news.[19]

Knox's admirals scoffed at this notion. Hoffman's allegation was answered by one of the Navy's heavy hitters, Rear Admiral Hepburn, who had just been named chairman of the Navy's prestigious General Board, a policy body. As director of naval public relations, a position he had relinquished to head the General Board, Hepburn said he had never received an order from Knox to favor any particular correspondent or newspaper. Just the opposite, he said. In a telegram to Hoffman, Hepburn stated that on 5 February 1942 he got instructions from Knox that "under no circumstances should the representatives of the *Chicago Daily News* receive any more favorable treatment from public relations officers of the Navy Department than is received by the correspondents of any similar newspaper, under similar conditions."[20]

Democratic supporters of the administration also jumped into the fray, sometimes creating an even greater muddle. Representative Elmer Holland, Democrat of Pennsylvania, charged that the *Tribune*'s 7 June story had "tipped off the Japanese high command that somehow our Navy had secured and broken the secret code of the Japanese navy." Holland believed he was striking a blow on behalf of Biddle and Knox, but the news that the Navy had cracked the Imperial Navy's key cryptosystem wasn't a message that either official wanted broadcast from the floor of the House. Holland didn't ease up. He accused the *Tribune, New York Daily News,* and *Washington Times-Herald* of working "consciously or unconsciously" under Hitler's orders to secure American defeat and enslavement.[21]

Possibly the most vitriolic words reeled off were those of McCormick's sharpest New Deal critic, Secretary of the Interior Harold Ickes. Ickes and McCormick had hated each other for years. In his 1939 book on America's press moguls, Ickes ventured that McCormick ran his newspaper strictly for personal gain and "self-aggrandizement." Later, as the war erupted, he suggested in a note to FDR, not entirely tongue-in-cheek, that the ships carrying newsprint from the *Tribune*'s paper mills in Canada to their "place of defilement on the Chicago River, be requisitioned by the Army or the Navy." (FDR filed the note away unanswered.) Now, as the grand jury was about to hear its first witness, Ickes convened a press conference and, once again, slammed the *Tribune* publisher. He told reporters he was convinced the *Tribune*'s 7 June story had violated federal law. "Anyone who gives aid and comfort to the enemy, regardless of wealth, trade or profession, should be prosecuted to the full extent of the law," he thundered.[22]

In an editorial the next day titled "Mr. Ickes Sounds Off," the *Tribune* couldn't resist taking a personal slap at the secretary of the interior; it also scored a legitimate point. "Mr. Ickes was never able to earn his living as a lawyer, but he knows enough law to be aware of the gross impropriety of his statement," the paper commented. "He knows the grand jury is in session investigating a charge made against two employees of this newspaper. The conclusion is inescapable," the *Tribune* snarled, "that Mr. Ickes is doing his little best to create an atmosphere of prejudice and ill will."[23] The *Tribune* was right in this instance; Ickes' remarks were gratuitous and, in all likelihood, unhelpful to his own cause.

~

Amid the clamor of bitterly clashing antagonists, Biddle's grand jury convened on Thursday, 13 August. William Mitchell had arrived in Chicago two days earlier; he declined to say a word about the pending proceeding. That was hardly surprising, given his reputation for reticence. But the *Tribune*'s top executives were nervous. What troubled them was that they had heard nothing from Mitchell regarding Johnston and Maloney; his silence signaled they might not be called to testify. *Tribune* strategists deemed that unfortunate; they believed their cause would be helped if jurors could hear the two journalists in person. Maloney certainly thought so. Even though relieved of his editorial duties, he was still in the office; he exploded, "God damn it all, there is no other way. We've got to get in there."[24]

The *Tribune*'s lead lawyer, Weymouth Kirkland, agreed. He promptly fired off a letter to Mitchell, informing him that Johnston and Maloney were anxious to testify. Kirkland argued that Mitchell had an obligation to present the two journalists to the grand jury since the Office of War Information had already let it be known that the government's probe was directed at the *Tribune* Company and the two *Tribune* men. "Certainly the premises [of the case], as well as Johnston's record of bravery in the Coral Sea and Maloney's service in the last war with Rickenbacker, not to mention their characters and reputation, entitle them to be heard by the grand jury," Kirkland contended. He had the letter hand-delivered to Mitchell's office.[25]

Kirkland was asking a lot. He was seeking an unusual privilege by asking that prospective defendants appear as witnesses in a grand jury proceeding.

Mitchell didn't appreciate the letter; he regarded it as an unwelcome intrusion into his handling of the case. Unpersuaded by the lawyer's logic, he decided to ignore his request. Mitchell explained to U.S. Attorney Albert Woll that he couldn't afford to allow Johnston and Maloney to testify. "I've only a slim chance to get an indictment right now," Mitchell said. "If Maloney and Johnston testify there isn't a chance in the world to get an indictment." Woll advocated a different course. He told Mitchell that to get an indictment, he needed to convince only twelve of eighteen jurors. If Johnston and Maloney were so compelling they would keep him from getting those twelve, it was better he find out now. After all, to get a conviction in court he would need twelve out of twelve. Their testimony would let him know what he was up against, so Woll advocated letting the *Tribune* men testify.[26]

Mitchell didn't immediately agree. He returned to his room at the Blackstone Hotel only to have another troubling encounter. Answering a knock at his door, he opened it to find himself confronted by Pat Maloney's eighty-year-old father. He had come to protest his son's innocence and urge Mitchell to let him appear before the grand jury. Mitchell's response was courtly and conciliatory. He commended the older gentleman for his loyalty to his son, but he didn't make any promises.[27] Mitchell let days pass without answering Kirkland's letter.

～

Even before the grand jury started hearing witnesses, the government's case had taken a fatal turn. Neither Biddle nor Mitchell knew this. They weren't ignoring the difficulties ahead. They grasped that their call for an indictment against two *Tribune* employees was by no means assured. Mitchell was the more hopeful of the two. He had been heartened by Knox's renewed pledge to send Navy cryptanalysts to Chicago to serve as expert witnesses in the government's case. They would explain the Navy's codebreaking success at Midway; presumably, they would attest to the damage done to national security by Johnston's 7 June article. Their testimony quite simply was the central pillar of Mitchell's case. What neither Biddle nor Mitchell realized was that this pillar was crumbling. Behind closed doors, some Navy intel officers, prospective witnesses, had flatly refused to appear before a grand jury. Under no circumstances, the officers vowed, would they testify about a triumph they regarded as one of the nation's most crucial military secrets. They wouldn't even if ordered to do so by the Secretary of the Navy.

One such holdout was Lieutenant Commander Edwin T. Layton, chief intelligence officer of the Pacific Fleet based at Pearl Harbor. Interviewed by an FBI investigator, Layton admitted that he personally drafted Nimitz's Dispatch No. 311221, circulated to the Fleet on 31 May as well as to the transport ship *Barnett*. After confirming that fact, Layton proceeded to exasperate his FBI inquisitor; he put on an exhibition of stonewalling the FBI man wouldn't soon forget. Yes, he wrote the message, but he would say no more. Asked whether the information in the dispatch had been collected from codebreaking, Layton said he didn't know. Well, he was asked, wasn't the Navy intercepting Imperial Navy messages and decrypting them? Layton professed ignorance of any such activity, reiterating that he didn't know anything about the Japanese code. Pressed by his interrogator, Layton declared that he would not admit—privately or publicly, officially or unofficially—that he possessed knowledge of the Imperial Navy's code.[28]

The FBI man tried a different tack. If called before a grand jury to testify about how the U.S. Navy discerned IJN ships at Midway, wouldn't he divulge what he knew? Layton's questioner didn't know his man. Steeped in the Navy's culture of secrecy, possessed of a sarcastic streak and, clearly, an infinite capacity for jest, Layton said he would look the jurors straight in the eye and would say he was wholly ignorant of the Japanese code. If pushed to explain where the information in Dispatch No. 311221 came from, Layton had an answer for that: he would say he fabricated it out of his imagination. Or he might tell them he got it out of a "crystal ball." Could he at least indicate whether the IJN changed its code after Midway? Layton said he had no idea, uninformed as he was about any Imperial Navy code system.[29]

Not yet ready to give up, Layton's FBI "quizmaster" tried one more time. Did he, as CINCPAC's chief intelligence officer, have an assistant acquainted with the Japanese code? If so, would he testify about what he knew? Layton declined to furnish any names, maintaining that Message 311221 was simply something he invented. Frank Knox, trying to round up Navy witnesses knowledgeable about U.S. Navy codebreaking, had no idea what he was up against.[30]

❧

Recalcitrant intel officers weren't the only annoyance vexing Knox. British officials, America's closest friends in the war effort, were hearing reports of leaks in the U.S. Navy's security system. British intelligence, in fact, had picked up rumblings that U.S. naval officers had "let slip" to a newspaper the Navy's success against the Japanese code. Britain's director of naval intelligence, Admiral John Godfrey, was alarmed. He didn't like what he heard, but his source was good, a highly respected British officer, Captain Edward Hastings, then Bletchley Park's representative in Washington. Bletchley Park, near London, served as the home of Britain's massive codebreaking campaign against the Axis powers; Hastings was Bletchley's man in Washington.[31]

Serving as a British liaison officer with ONI, Hastings was in frequent contact with top Navy officials. He was in an excellent position to know their day-to-day problems. He was present at Main Navy when King, Knox, and members of their staffs first became aware of Stanley Johnston's 7 June *Tribune* article. Hastings may have been tipped off about the article by a naval intelligence officer, or he may have found out about it in some other way, but learn about it he did. As it turned out, he tumbled onto a particularly inflammatory version of the *Tribune* story. He put what he knew in a letter to Admiral Godfrey.

Godfrey was a longtime critic of American intelligence. He thought the component parts of the U.S. intelligence system—the Army, the Navy, and all the civilian elements—were poorly coordinated. He deemed the entire system "leaky" and untrustworthy. His negative impression of American intelligence had already slowed down information sharing between the British Foreign Office and the U.S. foreign policy establishment.[32] So when he read Hastings' letter, posted in early July 1942, it reinforced his worst suspicions of U.S. intelligence. He circulated the Hastings letter to appropriate officials in the Foreign Office with a cover memo of his own. "The sorry tale unfolded in this letter from Captain Hastings must surely be the worst case that has ever occurred of the mishandling of Special Intelligence," Godfrey wrote. "All the offenses seem to have been committed; the messages, after being repeated in a low-grade cipher, were handled by a newspaper reporter, who ran the gauntlet of the Censor and the Editor, and finally found their way into the *Washington Times-Herald*."[33]

Godfrey did, however, express confidence in Admiral King. He told officials that King was dealing "with the matter in the most executive and, under the circumstances, adequate way, and is truly aware of the implications of this incident." Indeed, King in July was trying his best to keep the Biddle-Knox probe into the *Chicago Tribune* affair out of the public eye.[34]

As King proceeded with that effort, reports of a breach of security in U.S. naval intelligence were showing up in various parts of the British Empire. A week after Godfrey circulated Hastings' letter in London, the director of military intelligence in India, Brigadier Walter J. Cawthorne, got wind of the same leak, this time from an American correspondent passing through New Delhi. In a memo to his superiors in London, Cawthorne noted that the journalist, in a conversation with British officials, casually volunteered the following: "You see they have broken down one of the Japanese codes." He added that Allied performance at the Coral Sea was helped by the U.S. Navy's ability to trace the movement of Japanese ships by intercepting messages. Cawthorne complained that "American correspondents here are given a good deal of secret intelligence information by American staff officers" but receive little guidance on how to treat highly sensitive material.[35]

Cawthorne didn't name the correspondent doing the talking, but he probably was referring to an American wire service reporter based in Australia and attached to General MacArthur's headquarters. Astonishingly, the general's staff permitted the reporter, never identified, to file an article that clearly violated the U.S. military censorship rules: it attributed the Coral Sea outcome to the success of U.S. intelligence officers in decrypting Japan's naval code. Irked by the wire story, Army higher-ups in Washington rebuked MacArthur's press officers, leading to a near shake-up of the general's staff. The incident was reported in the trade journal *Editor & Publisher* by John Lardner, a correspondent for the North American Newspaper Alliance and a columnist for *Newsweek*. Exasperatingly, from the Navy's point of view, Lardner's report in *E&P* revealed almost as much about codebreaking as did the errant wire service story.[36] But Lardner wasn't the only U.S. journalist venturing into this forbidden territory. Writing in the *New York Times*, Hanson Baldwin, on 9 June, cited "radio intelligence" as a key factor in the Navy's overwhelming victory at Midway.[37]

With so much juicy memoranda swirling about among agencies—and, indeed, among governments—it was only a matter of time before the "sorry tale" of the Midway leak found its way into the office of Winston Churchill. Churchill was not pleased. "There was immediate reaction by Churchill," one historian recorded, adding that the prime minister promptly lodged a protest with Washington about the infraction.[38] British officialdom was even more distressed when it learned the Roosevelt administration was taking its case against the *Tribune* to a grand jury, an action that almost certainly would lead to a public trial. Admiral of the Fleet Sir Andrew Cunningham, commander in chief, Mediterranean Fleet, dashed off a "most secret" note to Admiral King expressing the British Admiralty's "anxiety in the matter." Cunningham wrote that

> the Admiralty have been asking about the charge now being brought against the "Chicago Tribune" in connection with the release of information concerning the Midway Operations. Their concern is naturally not as regards the merits of the case, but about the danger that details of our special intelligence methods may be compromised during the course of the trial. The terms of the charge as given in the Press are themselves an indication that we had prior information, and it is probably this that has aroused concern in the Admiralty.
>
> I have replied that the Navy Department are already keeping a close watch on the proceedings. The importance of keeping this source of intelligence secret is, however, so vital that I thought it well to inform you of the Admiralty anxiety in the matter. I feel sure you will agree that the preservation of this invaluable weapon outweighs almost any other consideration.[39]

King well understood British concerns. Two days after getting Cunningham's communication, King addressed the Admiralty's anxiety: "You may be assured that the Navy Department in its consideration of this case will continue to give full weight to the security of our special intelligence," King wrote Cunningham. "It is to be expected that the matter will be handled so as not to increase the harm already done in the original newspaper article."[40]

Back in Chicago, the authors of that article had worries of their own. They saw the government's grand jury bringing in witnesses in a case that could decide their fate, perhaps the fate of the *Chicago Tribune*. They wanted to be heard.

CHAPTER 12

THE GRAND JURY DECIDES

I felt like a fool.
—*Francis Biddle*

By Monday, 17 August, four days had passed without a word from William Mitchell. Johnston and Maloney decided not to wait any longer. Late in the morning, the two *Tribune* men proceeded over to the Federal Building and showed up at Mitchell's office. In an adjoining room, the grand jury was in session; there, the special prosecutor was taking testimony from two newspaper editors involved in the case. For the bored newsmen filling up the corridor and outer offices, waiting for something to happen, the arrival of Johnston and Maloney created a welcome diversion. "We saw in the newspapers this morning that the grand jury was nearing the close of its investigation," Maloney told the group. "We came here to volunteer our services."[1]

Maloney and Johnston sent their cards to Mitchell and waited for a response, but none came. After cooling their heels for a while, the two approached Mitchell's secretary, setting up an exchange that bore some resemblance to a Marx Brothers routine. Maloney asked if "the grand jury does not wish to see us." The secretary replied, "No." Maloney said, "Then I gather the inference, that Mr. Mitchell does not wish to see us." The secretary said, "Mr. Mitchell says that if he does want to see you men he will notify you through your attorney."[2]

Maloney and Johnston returned to their offices. There, they waited.

The grand jury had started hearing testimony at 10 a.m. on Thursday, 13 August, at Chicago's Federal Building. There were twenty jurors, of whom eighteen had voting rights (two were alternates).[3] They were a motley group.

The jury foreman was a thirty-seven-year-old decorator and paperhanger from Joliet named John O. Holmes. Others included a janitor from Chicago, an electrician from Woodstock, a plumber from Frankfort, an accountant from New Lenox, a furniture store executive from Glen Ellyn, and a farmer from Monee. Starting out, they knew little about the case. They knew it involved an alleged violation of the Espionage Act of 1917. They knew that two *Chicago Tribune* staffers—correspondent Stanley Johnston and Managing Editor J. Loy "Pat" Maloney—and, in fact, the *Tribune* itself had been accused of violating the act. An article in the 7 June 1942 *Tribune*, written by Johnston and edited by Maloney, was thought to have contained national security information. The act makes it unlawful for such information to be passed on to people not authorized to see it, in this case, the readers of the *Tribune* and, as we shall see, the readers of three other newspapers.[4]

But there was much the jurors did not know, and were not permitted to know, at least in the early stages of the case. They did not know, for example, that the information contained in the *Tribune* article was believed to have been derived from one of the U.S. Navy's most closely guarded secrets: code-breaking, or cryptanalysis, as this activity is commonly called. They did not know that the U.S. Navy had broken the Imperial Japanese Navy's main operational code, a coup that made possible the Navy's success against Japan on 4 June in the Battle of Midway. Under Frank Knox's agreement with Francis Biddle, this background would not be shared with jurors until the following week, when, presumably, all the other pieces of the case were in place. When the time was right, Navy Secretary Knox had agreed, the Navy would supply expert witnesses—cryptanalysts based in Washington—who would explain the extreme sensitivity of the information in the *Tribune* article and why, if it was divulged to a larger audience, it might do irreparable harm to national security and the U.S. war effort.

To help jurors get started, Special Prosecutor Mitchell had arranged for them to hear on their first day no fewer than seven witnesses, all Navy officers, each of whom had at least some knowledge of war correspondent Johnston. Not one, however, was an intelligence officer; not one was there to speak to the merits of the charges, for example, that the *Tribune* reporter had possibly violated the Espionage Act. Jurors would hear about that later. They would hear the phrase "secret dispatch" many times this day, but they would hear no references to cryptanalysis or codebreaking. ("The Navy is very sensitive about it, even yet, and I want to be very cautious about it," Mitchell told jurors.[5]) Those words were forbidden; they do not appear anywhere in the litany of words the grand jurors would hear this day or in the next few days. Nor would they hear anything about damage to national security stemming from the *Tribune* article. That, too, would be later.

Officers appearing before the grand jury on 13 August were there for a different purpose: primarily to talk about Stanley Johnston. They were there to explain, if they could, how a "secret message" transmitted by Pacific Fleet Commander Nimitz—a message that later gained notoriety as Dispatch No. 311221—might have fallen into the hands of Johnston. Of course, they were there also to find out if the Navy's rules for handling top-secret documents had been violated, not only by Johnston but by the Navy itself, that is, by Navy officers responsible for safeguarding those documents. But mostly they were there to discuss Johnston. Having encountered him on board either *Lexington* or *Barnett*, or both, they were there to describe the correspondent's movements while embarked on the two vessels. They were there to report any behavior by the newspaperman that they regarded as suspicious. They were there to speak to Johnston's character. Was he a man of honor? Could he be trusted? After hearing from Frederick C. Sherman, they might have wondered why the grand jury had even been convened.

Rear Admiral Sherman had been in Johnston's corner from the beginning. Weeks earlier, Sherman had told the FBI he got to know Johnston well during their weeks at sea, first, on board *Lexington*, then, later, on board the cruiser *Astoria*. During those perilous voyages, Sherman said he found Johnston honest and trustworthy and, of particular importance, aware of the need for censorship and quite willing to obey the Navy's rules for clearing copy. Sherman thought Johnston may have learned the contents of some secret dispatches by overhearing conversations. But he defended Johnston against charges of duplicity and wrongdoing.[6]

Sherman went about as far as he could go in support of Johnston. He vouched for the journalist's integrity and said he did not believe Johnston would deliberately seize an official message and publish it. Johnston would realize the dangers of revealing sensitive information. If he possessed such a message, he might keep it for his own files, but he would not put it in the paper. If it did appear in print, it was because someone else on the *Tribune* found the material and published it without Johnston's consent. Johnston might be covering up for that individual. The admiral said you get to know a man at sea. From his close association with Johnston during the Battle of

the Coral Sea and his observations of him under fire, he believed the correspondent was, as FBI agent William Robinson paraphrased Sherman's words,
"absolutely loyal and a very high type of man."[7]

Now Admiral Sherman appeared before a federal grand jury in Chicago's
Federal Building, in the musty jury room set aside for such meetings. He was
the first witness in the case. Showing up in dress khakis, his decorations and
admiral's shoulder boards conspicuous, the recently promoted Sherman cut
an impressive figure. He was confident and forceful; he projected an air of
authority and his words carried weight. By the time he arrived in Chicago
he was practically a national legend, thanks in no small part to Johnston's
articles in the *Tribune*, which chronicled this officer's valiant effort to save the
carrier *Lexington* during the Battle of the Coral Sea. Johnston could not have
asked for a better witness.

The questions put to him by Mitchell were respectful but narrow, focus-
ing primarily on whether Johnston understood censorship procedures
while with the fleet, and of course, whether Johnston, to his knowledge, had
adhered to them. Sherman told Mitchell what he had stated to the FBI: on
board *Lexington*, he had reviewed the censorship rules with Johnston, heard
the reporter's willingness to comply; then, later, while on board the cruiser
Astoria, after the sinking of *Lexington*, he had talked to Johnston again, now
directing the reporter to take his articles to the Navy Department in Washington. He said Johnston agreed to do that.[8]

Sherman did not confine his remarks exclusively to the censorship issue.
Given an opening, he elaborated a bit on Johnston, substantiating to a certain extent the correspondent's picture of himself as a savvy naval person
who, possibly, could hold his own with officers. "I found Mr. Johnston a very
able man," Sherman testified. "He had been a correspondent on a lot of ships,
and he had very good ideas, he gave us some good information." The admiral
added, "He had been down to New Guinea, in the gold mining area, for four
or five years, and information of that part of the world was very difficult to
get, and he had it first-hand. That does not particularly apply to naval tactics,
but it gives the background of the man."[9]

Jurors had only minor questions. One asked whether it was true that
Johnston had been cited for bravery. "I recommended him for some kind
of an award," Sherman said, "for heroic conduct in rescuing wounded men
below decks, and for helping to pull swimmers out of the water, men who
were swimming in the water." Pressed on whether Johnston did more than

are not allowed to make any copy of the message, but you could not possibly avoid it, you could not fight this war without it, nobody could remember everything in every message." Contents of the message, yes, he emphasized, but not an exact copy—"that would compromise the code."[34]

Mitchell showed him a photostat of Nimitz's dispatch, retrieved from *Barnett*'s safe. The document showed what appeared to be Seligman's initials in the upper left-hand corner. "Don't misunderstand me, gentlemen," Seligman said. "I don't deny having seen this message—if my initials are on it, I must have seen it." But he still did not remember it, because, as he put it, "there were hundreds and hundreds of messages [coming] through, and you can't remember the details of every specific message." Mitchell asked Seligman whether he could have made a memorandum of the contents of Message 311221, and done so in a way as to preserve the information in it, but without copying it word for word—that is, without giving away the code? "Could you have done that?"[35]

> SELIGMAN: I could, sir, yes, sir.
> MITCHELL: And you might have done it without your having any
>   present recollection of it, is that right?
> SELIGMAN: Yes, sir.[36]

Recognizing the implications of what he had just said, he quickly amended his admission, insisting that he and other officers would always endeavor to destroy any such memorandum after they were through with it. "The contents of our waste basket were burned every day."[37]

> MITCHELL: It is unfortunate that didn't happen in this case.
> SELIGMAN: But if I made a note from this particular message, it would
>   have been in my own kind of hieroglyphics. Anybody could,
>   of course, read it. But it would not be a copy of the message,
>   because we are not supposed to make copies of messages.
> MITCHELL: It might have said "striking force," and then listed the
>   same ships, and it might have said "support force," and then
>   named the vessels or classes of vessels that were named that were
>   named in the dispatch?
> SELIGMAN: Yes, sir.[38]

Now Seligman had a question. He wanted to know the heading of Nimitz's message. Mitchell showed it to him: "CINC [Commander in Chief] Pacific Fleet Estimate Midway Force Organization." Seligman seemed to breathe a sigh of relief. "Ah! That is the thing you would not put on the piece of paper," he said. "The paper wouldn't mean anything unless you had on it what you read."[39]

> MITCHELL: In other words, if you just wrote down "striking force," and then a list of all these ships, and then "support force," and a list of all these ships under that, and then "occupation force" and listed under that all the names, but you didn't say commander-in-chief's estimate, then you would be on the safe side?
> SELIGMAN: Of course, because in that case it merely becomes a list of ships. However, if some . . .
> MITCHELL: Some smart fellow . . .
> SELIGMAN: . . . smart chap picked up that piece of paper, and knew what was going on, and of these discussions that had been going on, he could readily deduce, "Here is my information."
> MITCHELL: Inside dope, in other words?
> SELIGMAN: Yes, sir.[40]

Jury foreman Holmes jumped in, pointedly asking Seligman whether officers who left such information lying on a table had not been careless or negligent—in that they created a situation whereby "some smart chap might come along and deduct or make his own conclusions?" Holmes wondered, "In your opinion, would you consider that as negligence, carelessness, or what?" Not necessarily either, Seligman said. "Under ordinary conditions, I would say that if I personally left a paraphrase of a message that contained important information lying about, I would be very careless," he said. "However, if I merely left a list of ships accidentally on my desk, a list of ships doesn't mean anything, anybody can make a list of ships. But unless you know the list came from a message like this, it doesn't mean anything."[41]

Mitchell brought up Johnston. Given his laudable conduct during the 8 May attack on *Lexington*, would not it have been natural, he asked, to treat him as an honorable fellow. In other words, after all they had been through, did not Seligman have to treat him as one of the officers and simply rely on censorship procedures to pick up anything in Johnston's copy that should not be there? "That is perfectly correct, sir," Seligman said. "In this case, Mr. Johnston had the highest credentials he could get. Both Admiral Fitch and Admiral Sherman were very much impressed with him. They reiterated that statement on several occasions." What is more, the Navy Department vouches

for him, does it not? Mitchell asked. "And vouches for him," Seligman said. "We assume, as naval officers, that when he gets ashore, he is going to carry out his obligations to the Navy."[42]

Did he carry out those obligations? Was he honorable? Mitchell wanted to know whether Johnston, after exiting *Barnett* and meeting briefly with Seligman on the dock in San Diego, told him he had found this scratch paper, with a penciled description of the supposed Japanese fleet, with the three forces. "Did he ever mention that he had seen that document, or a copy of it?" Mitchell asked. "No, sir," Seligman said. "If he had, regardless of the fact that I was feeling very badly, and very ill, I would have immediately said, 'What is this?'"[43]

~

Seligman had probably told jurors more than he intended. After hearing this officer explain how he and his colleagues almost routinely took notes off decrypted messages, jurors would have seen the potential for those messages to go astray. They would have seen how Johnston could have come into possession of a document he was not supposed to have. But no one had actually seen Johnston copy that message; nor had anyone told them why it mattered all that much. What was the harm? Waiting in the wings to help them with the first question was another Navy witness: *Lexington*'s famed dive-bomber pilot, Robert Dixon. Dixon had been in Seligman's suite the evening of 31 May. He was there when O'Donnell and Eldredge arrived; he might have seen something they did not see. He was scheduled to testify later the following week, right after jurors were to hear experts from one of the Navy's most esoteric, and rigorously concealed, units: OP-20-G, the Navy's strange name for its codebreaking arm. They were being brought in to tell jurors why Nimitz's dispatch had been stamped secret. And why information from that dispatch, if it had appeared in a newspaper article, could have impaired national security.

But first Mitchell wanted jurors to learn more about another aspect of the case: the fact that Johnston's story appeared not only in the *Tribune*, but also in such newspapers as the *Washington Times-Herald* and the *New York Daily News*. How did that happen? Why were the Navy's strict censorship rules not observed? And how did Johnston's article get written in the first place? With editors from New York and Washington standing by, Mitchell tackled the second question first. On Friday, 14 August, he introduced the journalist who had written a major part of Johnston's article, *Tribune* aviation editor Wayne Thomis.

Thomis and Johnston were old friends. They had met in the spring of 1941 when Stanley and Barbara, ostensibly en route to Australia, passed through Chicago and dropped by the *Tribune*. The paper offered to take him on, albeit on a freelance basis. The *Tribune* teamed him with Thomis. Thomis knew a lot about airplanes, and Johnston seemed to be equally learned about ships. The two produced several solid articles about naval tactics and hardware. This output led to Johnston's eventual posting to Pearl Harbor as a *Tribune* war correspondent. Many months later, when Johnston returned from the Pacific, the paper teamed him with Thomis again, this time to help him write his Coral Sea series and, of greater interest now, his much-disputed Midway article. Mitchell wanted to know how Thomis and Johnston wrote that story. Thomis supported his friend's version on some points. But on other issues his testimony diverged markedly from Johnston's. Their significant difference concerned what happened in the *Tribune* newsroom on the night of 6 June 1942.

The two disagreed, for example, on whether they constructed the story working together or separately. "I got *Jane's Fighting Ships* and went to work with that," Johnston told Mitchell in their 13 July interview. "The first draft of it I turned out myself, and then it was given to somebody else to rewrite."[44] Thomis remembered the event differently. "I wrote the first draft of it," he testified. "He sat beside me. We talked, put down the paragraphs as they went." They were aided in their "collaboration"—as Thomis called their mutual effort—by a 1940 copy of *Jane's Fighting Ships*. "We went through this thing and picked out the tonnages and weapons."[45]

> MITCHELL: You used *Jane's Fighting Ships* to elaborate this abbreviated list, to describe the guns and tonnage and things of that kind?
> THOMIS: That is correct.
> MITCHELL: You added that material to the original more cryptic list?
> THOMIS: We took names.[46]

According to Thomis, the two writers got "a lot of names" out of *Jane's*. He said Johnston already had a couple; Johnston, as noted, said he got four or five off the list he found on *Barnett*. In Thomis' telling, the two had been working alone that night in a back office (the room Maloney called "the booby hatch"), preparing what would be the first of Johnston's Coral Sea articles. Then Johnston wandered out into the newsroom nearby, apparently to get some exercise. "A short time later he came back and said, 'The boss thinks this is a mighty fine story. We got some stuff here. He wants us to do a separate piece on it,'" Thomis testified. He said Johnston showed him some penciled notations. "He had a piece of scratch paper torn in half, and some notations on it, I assumed from the conversation with Maloney," Thomis said. "We sat down together."[47]

Thomis related Johnston's words: "Now, I have here approximately the probable Japanese fleet what is up there." They went to work. Thomis marveled at Johnston's grasp of the Japanese fleet. "There will be, undoubtedly, a striking force," he quoted Johnston saying. Johnston went through the list: striking force, support force, occupation force. "The notations on the paper which we had there were very sketchy," Thomis said. "'4CV,' which he meant is a carrier. That is the Navy designation for carrier." (Actually 4CV would have designated four carriers—the number the Japanese deployed at Midway.) "'BB' means battleship. 'DD' is a destroyer. Anyway, he had these things jotted down there. He said, 'Here it is.'"[48]

Asked by Mitchell where all those jottings and designations came from, Thomis cited the piece of paper Johnston brought back from his meeting with Maloney. Thomis said it was a piece of scratch paper belonging to the *Tribune*—"we use it for making notes." Mitchell expressed puzzlement. He informed Thomis of Johnston's version of that paper: it was not a piece of scratch paper at all, but a document he prepared in San Diego, a sort of memorandum that he had started to mail to Maloney but, instead, carried back to Chicago. "Did you see that?" asked Mitchell. "I did not see it," Thomis said. "He said something about having made a memo, I did not see the doggoned memo, because he did not have [it] with him, as far as I knew, in the office that night."[49]

Mitchell could be forgiven at this point for doubting that he would ever get a straight story out of anyone at the *Tribune*. None of the stories fit together; they were all different. Thomis was not through yet. He soon contradicted both Maloney and Johnston on a crucial aspect of their testimony—the authorship of the Washington dateline on Johnston's story and the decision to attribute the article to naval intelligence. Weeks earlier, in his interview with Mitchell, Maloney admitted he put a Washington dateline on the story, but not the attribution to naval intelligence. Johnston, for his part, denied having anything to do with either of those elements. He denied it forcefully in his conference with Navy admirals on 9 June and in his lengthy exchange with Mitchell on 13 July. To wit:

> MITCHELL: You are not in any way responsible then for what form the article took finally, being headed Washington, D.C., as emanating from there and containing the statement "reliable sources in the Naval Intelligence disclosed here tonight"?
>
> JOHNSTON: No. I had nothing to say in that way at all.
>
> MITCHELL: You do not know then whether it was Mr. Thomis or Mr. Maloney that put in the heading "Washington, D.C." and the statement that the information had emanated from Naval Intelligence in Washington?
>
> JOHNSTON: No.
>
> MITCHELL: You do not know which of the two did what?
>
> JOHNSTON: I do not know who did what.[50]

Under questioning from Mitchell, Thomis narrated a sketchy, maddeningly murky story that bore little resemblance to Johnston's. Drawing on his memory, which he admitted was confused, he seemed to recall that he and Johnston were under instructions from Maloney to add the Washington dateline and naval intelligence elements. He thought the order might have come in a phone call from Maloney, who had called them while they were working, to speed them up. Johnston took the call. The order did not bother Thomis; indeed, he indicated he might have made both changes on his own if left to his own devices. Johnston was not a good enough authority to quote. "He was small potatoes to most people," Thomis said, "his name meant nothing." As for putting in naval intelligence, "I think anybody who would have been writing this, a dope story like that, would have done that," he said.[51]

Exasperated with what he regarded as Thomis' vague and evasive answers, Mitchell blew up: "I am not asking you about what they would do. I want to know who did it." Somewhat taken aback, Thomis said he was trying to be frank: "My best recollection was that Johnston and I decided to put [the story] in the Washington dateline." Mitchell asked: "You are quite sure that as the article left your hands and went to Maloney, it had that Washington dateline and the reference to the Naval Intelligence department?" Thomis answered: "Absolutely."[52]

If Mitchell intended to dent Johnston's credibility, he probably succeeded. He need not have been concerned. Jurors thought Navy officers on board *Barnett* had been remiss in their handling of Nimitz's message, but they did not have any illusions about Johnston, either. During Mitchell's Friday morning, 14 August, colloquy with the grand jury, one juror declared that "it was carelessness [on the part of the Navy], but, nevertheless, Johnston had no right to take that information off the ship without the authorization of the naval officers." Added another: "He violated a confidence that was placed in him." When yet another juror asked Mitchell whether they could infer that perhaps Johnston had not been truthful in his 13 July statement, the prosecutor said they should wait until all the facts were in before drawing conclusions.[53]

For now, Mitchell said, he wanted jurors to get a broader view of the case; he wanted them to hear from the editors who put Johnston's story in several newspapers. On Friday afternoon, jurors heard from Thomis. They reconvened on Monday, 17 August, to hear two new witnesses: first, Frank C. Waldrop, foreign and political editor of the *Washington Times-Herald*, then Ralph Sharp, night editor of the *New York Daily News*. The Justice Department had not charged either editor, or paper, with wrongdoing; they were not under active investigation. Needless to say, neither paper was popular at the White House; both had been among the Roosevelt administration's harshest critics. They had family ties to one of FDR's most implacable enemies, Colonel Robert McCormick. The publisher of the *Times-Herald*, Mrs. Eleanor M. "Cissy" Patterson, was McCormick's cousin. The publisher of the *Daily News*, Joseph M. Patterson, was also a cousin.

A strong conservative who had served in Herbert Hoover's cabinet, Mitchell had not taken the case to score political points for the Roosevelt administration. He thought he had a patriotic duty to take it. He wanted representatives of the two newspapers questioned. He thought they could shed light on how Johnston's article came to be widely circulated; he believed they should be made to explain why they published it.[54] Both Waldrop and Sharp had been on duty at their respective newspapers late Saturday, 6 July, when around 11 or 11:30 p.m. the story arrived—with a Washington dateline but without a byline. It had come in over what newsmen called a ticker: an AT&T wire that distributed newspaper stories to clients of the Chicago Tribune Press Service. Waldrop put the story in his paper's midnight edition. Sharp did much the same in New York, placing the article in his 1 a.m. edition.[55]

Neither editor submitted the article to censors or even considered doing so. Mitchell wanted to know their reasoning. He examined Waldrop first. The Waldrop he quizzed on 17 August, however, was very different from the Waldrop questioned by Byron Price's Censorship Bureau early in June, just after Johnston's story had appeared in the 7 June issue of the *Times-Herald*. Then the editor was regretful, almost apologetic; he tried to help authorities understand where the story came from, how the process worked. But on this day he was prickly, at times aggressive. He put on display the power of newspaper loyalties and family ties. His answers roughly paralleled the very legalistic defense offered earlier by the *Tribune*'s Pat Maloney.[56]

Why did he not take steps to censor this Navy-oriented article? "For the simple reason that the story appeared to me to not require censorship," Waldrop said. Mitchell asked whether he had been influenced by the fact the story appeared based on naval intelligence: Did that reference give it an authority that smoothed its way forward? "Well, as a matter of fact, even if it did not say 'naval intelligence,' for the simple reason that this story dealt with enemy action outside United States waters, [it] therefore was not under the censorship code." Clearly Waldrop had become thoroughly familiar with Price's *Code of Wartime Practices*.[57]

But what if Waldrop had known the article had not come from naval intelligence in Washington but, instead, had been written by Stanley Johnston in the *Tribune*'s Chicago office?

Did he know that? He did not. "I only knew what the article says," Waldrop told jurors. "It was just an ordinary story that I put on page four of the paper, without attaching particular significance to it at all." But what if he *had* known it was Johnston? And what if he had known that Johnston had acquired some information for the story while traveling with the Pacific Fleet; under Navy rules, material obtained at sea had to be submitted, not to Byron Price, but to the Navy? Would he still have published the article without any effort to have it approved?[58]

Waldrop said he probably still would have published it because, as he put it, "it seemed to be wholly of Japanese activities known to the Japanese." What about the headline on the story: "U.S. Navy Knew in Advance All about Jap Fleet"? Did that not sound as if the article was disclosing what Navy knew in advance? Not necessarily, said Waldrop. "I think the Japanese discovered the Navy knew in advance, too, when they got there." Now Waldrop surprised Mitchell, veering off in a new direction. "As a matter of fact," he said, "the fact that the Navy knew this in advance was well known generally throughout Washington, and I had specific reason to know that."[59]

His knowledge, he said, stemmed from a phone call he had received shortly before the Battle of Midway concerning a column he had written about Alaska. The column called for better communication—better roads and airplane service—with Alaska. The call was from one of Price's censors, James Warner. Warner was passing on a request from Lieutenant General John DeWitt, commanding the Army's West Coast Defense. "General DeWitt has asked us to ask the newspapers not to say anything about Alaska," Warner reportedly told Waldrop, because "they have information that the Japs are about to attack somewhere in the Pacific." DeWitt was disturbed; he did not want anything said about defenses on the West Coast or roads in Alaska.[60]

Given all this "common talk," talk bandied about in Washington by newspapermen and government officials, what could be the harm in a headline saying there had been "advance knowledge"? Waldrop asked. Did the Japanese not already know? What could they learn from that? Quite a bit, Mitchell thought. Mitchell now became the stern prosecutor. "Let's get down to brass tacks," he said. Look at the article, he directed: it stated that the Navy had information, first, that there was a striking force of four aircraft carriers (*Akagi, Kaga, Soryu, Hiryu*). Was that generally known?[61]

> WALDROP: Oh, no, not so far as I know. I didn't know that.
> MITCHELL: And that there were two battleships of the *Kirishima* class.
>   Was that generally known?
> WALDROP: Not by me.
> MITCHELL: Two cruisers of the Tone class?
> WALDROP: As to those details, I can't say that I knew those.[62]

"Why, of course, not," Mitchell jabbed. "You don't mean to have us understand that that description of the Japanese fleet in detail, with the names of the Japanese ships in that article, was common talk in Washington?" No, Waldrop said; the "common talk" remark referred only to his newspaper's headline stating there had been "advance knowledge." In Mitchell's view, the headline was part of the problem. "The real point about the thing," he said, "was that the United States knew in advance and had some means of acquiring advance knowledge of the exact description of that Japanese fleet, and that is what your heading means, doesn't it?" Waldrop would not budge: "My heading means that the United States knew in advance all about the Jap fleet, just as it says."[63]

A juror entered the discussion, directing a hypothetical question at Waldrop. What if he had a correspondent who, as a condition for traveling with the Fleet, had been asked not to print anything unless it had been censored by the Navy? If he, Waldrop, knew this, would he still print the correspondent's article, if it had not been censored? "My answer on that would have to be that it would depend," Waldrop said, not yielding an inch, "because many times, in dealing with government agencies, newspapermen are confronted with the demand not to print anything. They have to act on their best judgment as to whether it is a reasonable demand or not."[64]

Mitchell pounced. He scolded Waldrop again, this time for thinking that questions of censorship were up to newspapermen to decide. They were not, under the government's rules covering war correspondents. Did the editor not know his wartime obligations? Mitchell put the issue to Waldrop in the form of a question: "in other words, you assert the privilege of acting as your own censor, not letting the Navy decide whether the material is damaging or not, is that your theory?" "No, not quite that, sir," Waldrop said. He said he would need to know more about the case before he could answer: "It would depend entirely on the circumstances."[65]

$\sim$

Mitchell also had differences with Sharp. As he did with Thomis and Waldrop, he approached the witness as if he were an adversary, grilling him the way he would a defendant in a criminal case. Sharp was less contentious than the other two, but he and Mitchell would have their share of heated exchanges. Sharp started out well, answering questions put to him reasonably and thoughtfully. Asked whether he would have printed the article in question if he had known that it was not, as it purported to be, based on naval intelligence, or that it had not originated in Washington, Sharp answered plainly. "If I had known it was a falsehood, no," he said.[66]

Mitchell questioned the editor about his policy toward articles coming in over the ticker. Did he assume those articles sent out by the various news services had been properly submitted to censorship? Or did he act independently, feeling he had an obligation to make sure those stories were cleared? Sharp's answer made sense. "The Tribune Press Service, to me, is a press service," he said. "I treat it exactly as I treat the Associated Press or the United Press.

I assume that the service has consulted the censorship requirements, and has made any investigation that the story requires." That being said, he made clear he also accepted responsibility to check any story that, in his opinion, might be censorable.[67]

If so, asked jury foreman John Holmes, why did he not think it was necessary to recheck a story that involved naval intelligence? Sharp may have been more restrained in his comments than Waldrop, but he shared that editor's general view of censorship rules. "The article was definitely outside the censorship code requirement," he said, referring to Byron Price's *Code of Wartime Practices*. Mitchell jumped back in, trying to explain to the editor that this story had nothing to do with general censorship as administered by Price. Did not he know that the Navy had separate regulations that applied to correspondents with the fleet. Did he not know that? No, Sharp said. "This story had no relation to any correspondent in the field."[68]

Sharp had a point. How was he to know that this material had been gathered by a reporter assigned to the Pacific Fleet? The dateline indicated it came from Washington. He thought his inquisitors would better understand his decision on the night of 6 June if they knew what kind of a story he was dealing with. "I recognize the story as what we call a 'dope' story, in the newspaper business," Sharp said. "I relied on the source of origin for having the story written by some person competent to make the guesses and estimates in the story. Does that answer your question?" It did not answer all of Holmes' questions.[69]

> HOLMES: Your confidence in the source through which you received
> this particular information is so great that you feel it is not
> necessary to investigate any further as to whether it has been
> censored?
> SHARP: Let me make clear there was no question of censorship in my
> mind. The story did not come under any censorship regulations
> that we had in the office, either naval or Mr. Price's office. As for
> relying on the service for the facts of the story, I have to. I can't
> travel around the world to substantiate every story.[70]

Mitchell ran into the same problem with Sharp that he encountered with Waldrop: neither one realized that the Navy had separate, and very different, censorship rules from those of Byron Price. Earlier, when a juror asked him whether he was familiar with the Navy's rules concerning the release of information, Waldrop answered, "Frankly, I am not. I am more familiar with Mr. Price's code, because that is the one we work with day by day." When Mitchell put essentially the same question to Sharp, asking whether he knew the Navy had regulations that applied to special correspondents, the editor had to admit, "I do not."[71]

Mitchell and his jurors might have wondered how these two big-city editors, eight months into the war, could be so uninformed about issues vitally related to the practice of their craft. They also might have marveled at how well *Tribune* managing editor Maloney and, for that matter, *Tribune* staffers Johnston and Thomis had pulled off their 6 June sleight of hand. By shifting the dateline from Chicago to Washington, then attributing to naval intelligence information gleaned surreptitiously from a mysterious piece of paper on board a transport ship, they had befogged the minds of all. They flummoxed Navy censors, sent editors and admirals scrambling down blind alleys, muddied the issue of journalistic obligations in wartime. In military terms, they had contrived an exquisite diversion, an almost perfect smokescreen.

Jurors wanted to talk about Maloney and Johnston. Mitchell listened.

～

After editor Sharp departed late Monday afternoon, Mitchell resumed his colloquy with jurors. Several had questions, primarily concerning Stanley Johnston. One juror could not grasp why Johnston, before boarding *Lexington*, had not been required to sign a form committing him to accept Navy censorship. "You put your finger on something very interesting," Mitchell said. He explained that the Pacific Fleet's censorship regulations, while not officially issued until 28 April, were nevertheless in preliminary form on 12 April, three days before Johnston joined the carrier. There would seem to have been time for Johnston to sign a form (correspondents based in Hawaii had been signing such pledges for months). As Mitchell understood the problem, the new regulations, issued in Washington, had not yet reached Pearl Harbor. "But the essential fact is that he was told about it," Mitchell said, "and he admits having been told about it."[72]

Foreman John Holmes, speaking for the grand jury, rather haltingly ventured a request, carefully phrasing it to express respect for the prosecutor. "Not that we don't have the utmost confidence in everything that has been submitted here," Holmes started out, "but I am suggesting, and I think you made some mention of it in the beginning, that for the clarification of some

elements involved in this particular case, being of an important nature, as it is, this jury would perhaps be interested in receiving or hearing verbal testimony from both Mr. Maloney and Mr. Johnston, if it is not asking too much."[73]

It was not asking too much. Of course, Mitchell had not wanted to bring them in. He thought their intrusion would weaken his chance for indictments. But his thinking about them had changed. He had been besieged by all manner of special pleading since the grand jury convened on Thursday, 13 August. He had heard Albert Woll's pragmatic argument, read Weymouth Kirkland's pleading letter, and listened to Pat Maloney's distraught father who had knocked at his hotel door. Whether or not any of these appeals influenced his judgment, he never unequivocally said. He had been irritated by the Kirkland initiative; he sensed he was being set up for a *Tribune* ambush. "Kirkland's letter was evidently framed for publication," Mitchell told Biddle later. "I am sure they expected me to refuse the request and put them in a position to make an outburst that the inquiry was unfair." Mitchell certainly did not want to appear biased.[74]

Now, along with all the other pressures pushing him in that direction, he confronted a new one: the jurors themselves. "The Grand Jury at first did not want to hear these men," Mitchell wrote Biddle. "They made the point that Johnston and Maloney had already made full statements to the Navy, which had been transcribed and presented to the Grand Jury in full, and to hear them would be a useless repetition of their explanations."[75] But on Monday, the jurors changed their minds. After three days of testimony, during which they heard seven Navy officers and three journalists give conflicting and often confusing accounts, they wanted to hear from the two *Tribune* men.[76] Mitchell dictated a note to Kirkland asking that he arrange to have the two appear at his office before 10 a.m. the next day, Tuesday, 18 August. Mitchell had the note hand-delivered to Kirkland's office. Maloney and Johnston polished their presentations.[77]

～

According to reporters who saw them, Maloney and Johnston looked "deadly serious" when they arrived at the Federal Building on Tuesday morning. Showing up slightly ahead of Johnston, Maloney greeted newsmen with a statement: "I am ready to go before the grand jury and tell all I know," he declared. "If anyone thinks I gave information to the Japs against my country, he's crazy." A few moments later Johnston appeared, carrying for all to see a copy of *Jane's Fighting Ships*. "I'll tell the jury the same bloody story I told the admirals," he said. Both men said they would sign immunity waivers, a move that would give the government the right to use their own testimony against them if they should be brought to trial.[78]

When the grand jury opened for business on Tuesday, one key player was missing: William Mitchell. He never explained his absence but, in all likelihood, the thought of having to listen to Maloney and Johnston for three or four hours was more than he could bear. He had listened to each for extended periods once before—Maloney on 9 July and Johnston on 13 July. Each session had been grueling. Subjected to what he regarded as Maloney's endless stream of evasions and self-serving protests, he then doubted his ability to treat the *Tribune* editor objectively; he very nearly quit the case. Johnston was worse; Mitchell ended up believing very little of what the correspondent had to say about crucial points in the case. He was happy to turn the proceedings over to Assistant U.S. District Attorney Laurence J. Miller, who asked most of the questions. Jurors had only a query or two. Miller just let his two subjects tell their story.

Mitchell thought that Maloney would say pretty much what he said on 9 July and say it in the same histrionic way. Except for a few embellishments, he was right. Maloney recounted the saga of Stanley Johnston, telling of his 1941 arrival in Chicago, his mastery of ships and naval issues, his posting to Pearl Harbor and his return from the Coral Sea, bringing back with him a story that was "so hot" he could not discuss it over the phone. He told of the evening of 6 June, when he put Johnston and Thomis in a back office to work together on the Coral Sea stories. Later, he said, Johnston came running out of this room, saying, "Mr. Maloney, do you remember that dope I told you about over the telephone, that I had on the situation up in the North Pacific?"[79]

As Maloney remembered the encounter, Johnston pulled a letter out of his pocket. It was not a piece of *Tribune* scratch paper torn in half, as Thomis had described it. It was an actual letter. "[It] had two paragraphs, and then it had the names of some ships, and classifications of ships, and he was talking all the time I read it," the editor recalled, "and I can't tell you exactly what he said, except in general that he thought the attack on Dutch Harbor was really a feint, and that the Japs were really after Hawaii." Maloney said he thought this would be a very fine story. "I said, 'Well, hurry back in there, Stanley, and get Wayne to fix this up for you, and write [it] in the form of a story.'" About thirty minutes later—after Maloney phoned the two writers to hurry them along—a copyboy delivered a finished article to his desk.[80]

Maloney did not like it. The writing was muddy, the first sentence too long; he felt a reader would not grasp it. He rewrote the story. "I didn't change any of the facts in it at all," Maloney said, "but I changed the order, and as I remember, split the paragraph from one long sentence into two sentences. I think I rewrote the first two paragraphs, and I also took a paragraph that was high up in the story, and put it down at the bottom." Maloney left unresolved whether it was he or the Johnston-Thomis team that first put a Washington dateline on the story (on 9 July he took responsibility for that), but he made it clear where the reference to naval intelligence originated. "I did one thing I'm sorry for," he said. "I passed—Wayne Thomis wrote it—I passed the word 'disclosed,'" he said, alluding to the clause in the first paragraph in the *Tribune* story that stated, "reliable sources in the naval intelligence disclosed here tonight."[81]

Maloney said he recognized that naval intelligence did not disclose anything. "I am apologetic on that point, but I knew the information was held there," he said, "and I didn't think it would be doing any harm, or would help the Japs in any way, to attribute it to the Naval Intelligence officers." Moreover, "I certainly thought it was complimentary to our Navy," Maloney said, adding, "That was the real reason I put the Washington dateline on it."[82]

Maloney defended his handling of the censorship issue. He stated again he felt justified moving the story along because Byron Price's *Code of Wartime Practices* forbade only referring to "movements or names of enemy ships in American waters." He did not think Johnston's story came under the code. Like editors Waldrop and Sharp before him, he did not know, or at least said he did not know, that Navy regulations took precedence over Price's code. "You understand, ladies and gentlemen," Maloney said, "that never in my life had I submitted a story to naval censorship, and I have submitted hundreds of them to regular censorship, the Price censorship, so-called, the Office of Censorship in Washington, D.C." He did not know about the Navy's veto rights. Nor did he know about any list of ships from *Barnett*; he said Johnston had not mentioned it on 6 June.[83]

"I must impress another thing upon you there, if you are not clear on it, and I have every confidence in Johnston, all I know of him," Maloney said. "I don't want to be considered as running out on him, but I want you to know this, that our conversation [that night] was just as brief as I have given it to you, and he never at any time mentioned any kind of censorship to me, and he never mentioned anything about where he got the information, except what I have told you," that is, he got information from *Jane's Fighting Ships* and his own general knowledge of the Japanese navy.[84]

Maloney protested his patriotism; he contended his reputation was at stake. "I want to tell you people that I would sooner lose my two daughters than give information to the Japanese against my government," he said. He showed jurors a stack of documents that he said were letters of recommendation, all written, he said, by admirals, generals, and others attesting to his probity as an editor. He asked if he could read them to the jury. Maloney had come loaded for bear. Jury foreman Holmes stepped in. He invited Maloney and Miller to leave the room while jurors considered the matter. The jury went into executive session. When the two returned, Holmes told them the jury's answer was no. "The jury has decided that it is perhaps not necessary and perhaps will have no bearing on the case one way or the other," Holmes said, "in listening to those letters of recommendation."[85]

But jurors did grant one of Maloney's requests. They let him read from another stack of papers he had brought in: articles published around 4–6 June in other newspapers that also gave the impression the U.S. Navy had "advance knowledge" of the Japanese attack. He cited a story in the *New York Herald Tribune* stating that the raid on Dutch Harbor had been "anticipated." He referred to an Associated Press dispatch that called the Japanese thrust "far from surprising," and he quoted from a Hanson Baldwin column in the 4 June *New York Times* that stated, "The Japanese raids yesterday upon Dutch Harbor were not unexpected." He wondered how those articles differed from the *Tribune's* much-maligned story on 7 June. "[Those stories] certainly let the Japs know how we were fixed," he said. Why pick on the *Tribune?* he seemed to say.[86]

As for all those details in the *Tribune* story—names of ships and classifications of ships expected to be present in the Japanese armada—Maloney said those all came out of Johnston's head, not from a piece of paper pilfered on *Barnett.* Jury foreman Holmes was not sure he had heard Maloney correctly: "Is it true, do you actually believe that Mr. Johnston drew this out of his knowledge of what he knew," Holmes asked, "rather than having taken it from some message?" Maloney said he had no doubts. "It is certainly true that I believed that he drew it from his experience, and not from any secret message of the United States," he declared. "I can't make that too strong."[87]

                      ~

The grand jurors decided to move on. The story they most wanted to hear was Stanley Johnston's. It was not as if jurors had not already heard it or, rather, many different versions of it. The portion of Johnston's story they were most concerned with—how and from where the correspondent acquired the material used in his 7 June article—they had heard in bits and pieces. They had heard two Navy officers, Commanders Eldredge and O'Donnell, talk about a mysterious piece of blue-lined paper circulated in Commander Seligman's stateroom on board the transport ship *Barnett*. They had heard both officers put Johnston in that room with the blue-lined paper, later identified by O'Donnell as a close approximation of a secret radio dispatch from Pacific Fleet Commander Nimitz. They had heard the *Tribune*'s Pat Maloney relate Johnston's excitement on the night of 6 June—two days after the carrier battle at Midway—when he showed his managing editor a memorandum he had prepared in San Diego purporting to show the makeup of the Japanese fleet. They had heard that paper's Wayne Thomis say he joined forces with Johnston to write a story based on that memo, and they had read, or at least been exposed to, a transcript of Johnston's 13 July interview with Special Prosecutor Mitchell. Now they were about to hear yet another version of all these events: Stanley Johnston's oral presentation.

    Johnston's talk would differ in key respects from other accounts, including his own; indeed, it would be unlike anything they had heard before during four days of testimony. Johnston wasted little time on preliminaries; he provided only a glimpse of his time in Amsterdam (Press Wireless) and London (*Chicago Tribune*), and he omitted entirely his period in France and Germany. He got quickly to the point, which by this time could be stated simply: How could he know so much about the Japanese fleet that he could write an article that paralleled almost exactly Nimitz's secret message? How did he do it? Really, not all that hard, Johnston said, in effect. Roughing out the Japanese invasion force was the most natural thing in the world, he said, at least for someone like him who had made a study of that fleet. It was just a matter of using common sense.

    True, he depicted this force somewhat differently in his 13 July interview. Asked by Mitchell on that date how he knew what ships were in the Japanese fleet, he could say little more than that they would use their "best ships" and "best carriers."[88] By 18 August his views were more nuanced. "You would not use your best battleships to bombard land installations, because you expect that you will lose one or two of them, either through defending submarines, or from defending aircraft," he told jurors. For lobbing shells at fortifications on shore all that is needed, he claimed, is an expendable platform. "That is why they use their old battleships for the attack," he said. "That is why they used their ships of the *Kirishima* class for the attack on Midway." As anyone who reads *Jane's Fighting Ships* would know, he said, *Kirishima* is an older class of battleship. Thus, he put the *Kirishima* class in the striking force; that was just logical.[89]

So was reckoning what particular carriers the Imperial Navy would deploy at Midway. "The Battle of the Coral Sea proved what a destructive thing a carrier was," Johnston said. "You could hit your enemy 200 miles away and destroy his ships, regardless of what ships they were." From that time forward, he said, the Japanese knew the basis of their strength was not the battleship, but the carrier. "So in making up the Japanese fleet, I had a very simple task," he said. After eliminating from his calculations the two Japanese carriers he believed were destroyed at the Coral Sea (actually only a light carrier was destroyed, a fast fleet carrier was severely damaged), Johnston said this left five carriers for use at Midway. He figured the Japanese would use four: *Kaga* and *Akaga* (their biggest) and *Soryu* and *Hiryu* (their newest). Nothing hard about that.[90]

Nor was it surprising that the Japanese would add two Tone-class cruisers to their striking force. "There is nothing very remarkable about that," Johnston said. "The Tone class cruisers are unlike any other cruisers in the world. They have been built for a special purpose. There are no other cruisers in the world that have got all of their guns in front of the funnel, before the bridge. This is a distinction they have." As Johnston put it, "They are built to come in fighting." Equally unremarkable, he said, was the fact that the Japanese organized their forces into a striking force, support force, and occupation force. "There has been a cry raised as if it was something wonderful and mysterious [that] I said the forces would come in three groups," Johnston said, affecting mock amazement. "Ladies and gentlemen, there is nothing mysterious about that."[91]

Johnston was in his element. He rambled on as jurors listened quietly. Whether they were benumbed by his rather breathtaking display of nautical erudition or simply put off by what they might have considered a particularly artful snow job, they never said. They asked no questions, made no comments. They did not challenge him. If Mitchell had not taken the day off, he might have asked Johnston, as he did during their 13 July encounter, whether there was anything in *Jane's Fighting Ships* that would indicate what particular vessel was in a striking force, or support force, or occupation force of a particular Japanese fleet headed for Midway Atoll around the first of June. If Johnston had answered truthfully (he changed the subject in July), he would have had to say no. The terms "striking force," "support force," and "occupation force" do not appear in *Jane's*.[92] The implication of Mitchell's question was that he got his answers from a piece of blue-lined scratch paper, copied off Nimitz's secret dispatch.

Johnston had anticipated this concern. He went to great lengths to debunk the idea there was anything questionable or illicit in the way he obtained his information. Yes, there had been discussions among officers on board *Barnett*. "I entered the discussions," he said. "There was nothing secret about them, because nobody that sat in those cabins knew any more than I did. We discussed the make-up of the Japanese fleet." And, yes, a couple of days later, when he was packing up to leave *Barnett*, he found a piece of scrap paper on his desk. "[On it were] the names of some Japanese ships written in pencil and scratched out and rewritten in and scratched out, as if somebody had been holding a discussion on the Japanese Navy," Johnston said.[93]

The item turned out to be a trifle: "It was of no importance, a piece of paper," Johnston said. "It was on an ordinary scratch pad, something like the very one in my drawer when I made my own writing on loose-leaf. Somebody had been doodling on it out there, and a picture which I took to be the *Lexington*, with planes diving on her, and so forth, and had written all other stuff on it." But in examining the writing on this piece of paper, Johnston noticed some things he could use: "[I found] the names of three ships I didn't know how to spell, the *Choda* and the *Chakas*. I made a hasty note of that. Underneath them was this *Kunikisma Maru*. I made a note of that and threw it away."[94]

Whether jurors took this "piece of paper" as lightly as Johnston did would never be known, but one thing he said would have made an impression: the piece of paper was not stamped secret. Jurors had indicated to Mitchell on 13 August that they regarded the absence of a "secret" marking on that scrap paper as significant. They thought that mattered. "There was nothing secret about that scrap of paper," Johnston now said. "They do not leave secret signals lying about amongst something else. A secret signal is not left on a scrap and a leaflet to be doodled on. I didn't think that piece of paper important. I still don't think it was important."[95]

Johnston did, however, think that piece of paper important enough to take names from, transfer them to a piece of paper of his own, and then carry that new piece of paper to his San Diego hotel. There, sometime after midnight, he copied it once again, carefully typing it out in the form of a memorandum, this time on good stationery. He planned to mail it to Maloney; instead, he put it in his pocket and carried it back to Chicago. It was in his pocket the evening of 6 June when he left the little office at the *Tribune* where he had been working with Wayne Thomis and wandered into the newsroom. He glanced at the news ticker and saw that Admiral Nimitz had announced a great naval victory at Midway. He approached Maloney and pulled out the memorandum.

By this time, jurors had heard several versions of how Johnston's memo from San Diego came to be a newspaper story. All parties agreed that when Maloney saw Johnston's memo, he wanted it turned into an article. Then accounts diverged. In Johnston's telling, he wrote the first draft alone. He said Maloney directed him to the little office down the hall—the little office Maloney called the booby hatch—to write the story. "[Maloney] said, 'Do your stuff on what you think the Japanese fleet consisted of,'" Johnston recalled, "and I went inside. Took *Jane's Fighting Ships* with me and set out to build up the Japanese fleet as I got here." Johnston added an aside: "[Maloney] called Mr. Wayne Thomis, I think, or some way they got together to write the story."[96]

Johnston seemed to be telling jurors that Thomis was brought in later as a kind of relief pitcher to rescue his faulty first draft, giving the impression that Thomis took it from there. "The lead story was written, as I say, by Mr. Thomis," Johnston told jurors. "I started to pick out the ships. He came back to help me with these. He was waiting on me. We hurried these things through. They disappeared out into the editorial, local room." By "they" Johnston must have meant Thomis and Maloney; the editorial room was the newsroom where, in Johnston's very murky account, the story presumably got rewritten again. It was at this time, he wanted jurors to believe, that two unfortunate elements were added to his article: it acquired a Washington dateline and the information in it was attributed to naval intelligence in Washington.[97]

"The story I published, part of my contribution to this story was the section that deals with the probable force that the Japanese had there," Johnston told jurors. "That is all I had to do with the story at any time. I think that the editor of the paper has told I had nothing to do with giving it to the Naval Intelligence or anybody else." Actually, neither the paper's managing editor, Pat Maloney, nor its aviation editor and rewrite man, Wayne Thomis, did any such thing. They may have taken responsibility for the naval intelligence reference and the Washington dateline (which Johnston also disavowed), but their versions put Johnston at the scene of these two breaches of ethics and acceptable journalistic practice. They did not clear Johnston.[98]

The Maloney-Thomis accounts clearly showed that Johnston had not been altogether truthful about his role in writing the Midway story, but on one crucial point Maloney supported his correspondent: he said that Johnston had no way of knowing that his managing editor had not submitted this hastily contrived article to Navy censorship, or any censorship at all. That was indeed out of his hands. After their story left their little office—handed off to a copyboy—Thomis and Johnston ceased being factors in the production of that article. Maloney did his rewrite, made a call to the paper's Washington bureau chief, then sent the story to the composing room, then went home. Thomis and Johnston remained in their office and resumed their joint effort on the Coral Sea series. "I went on with my work that night," Johnston told jurors. "I knew no more about it." The two pulled an all-nighter. They left the building together around 5 a.m., when Johnston noticed the morning edition in the lobby. He thought the story had been cleared by the Navy. "They must work all night down there in Washington," he mused to Thomis.[99]

Johnston professed his fidelity to Navy censorship. He said that as a civilian accredited to the Navy and, later, as a war correspondent assigned to the Pacific Fleet, he understood his copy was subject to Navy censorship. He said he never had any doubts that he was required to submit whatever he wrote to the senior officer of the unit to which he happened to be assigned. He said he faithfully observed that rule. While traveling with the fleet to and from the Coral Sea, he said he always arranged—one way or another—to have his copy transported back to the Navy censor at Pearl Harbor, in this case Nimitz's chief PR officer, Waldo Drake.[100] Drake, for his part, confirmed Johnston's claim; he gave Johnston a "thumbs up" on the censorship question. Up until the Midway article, the Navy had never complained that the correspondent had ever failed to clear his copy—a point that may or may not have reached the grand jury.[101]

Whatever the jury knew or did not know about his record with the Navy, Johnston let it be known he felt misunderstood, perhaps even somewhat victimized. He certainly seemed to feel unappreciated. He waxed lyrical about his belief in the United States. He informed jurors that he had become a U.S. citizen on 15 December 1941. "I elected to become a citizen of the United States here because this was the country that suited my ideas, where everybody here has a chance," he said, "regardless of what school he went to, and regardless of who his father was, and I knew my responsibilities at the time I took it up." He walked jurors through his personal history, rising up from "a small newspaperman" to a point where he had gained stature and recognition among his colleagues for his journalistic prowess. He had arrived.[102]

"I want to ask you a question," he said to jurors: "do you think that, in that situation—and that was my situation the night this story was written—that I would have written anything or published anything that would break my neck, after I had just got up the ladder?" Johnston then asked, "And do you think I am a fool?" He said he would be a fool to give information to the enemy; this is something he would not do. "In the time that I was with the Navy, I got very fond of it." Johnston paused. "And I felt that I was—excuse me. I felt that I was part of the Navy."[103]

Did Johnston gulp? Did he hold back a tear? The transcript of the grand jury proceeding said only that he paused, but it seemed to be a pause at a crucial moment. He was making this case personal—he felt his personal honor was at stake. "I have a son twenty years of age," he told jurors. "The last word I had from my mother was that he had gone with the Australian army to the war front. He is probably somewhere up there now where they are fighting. If you think I would do anything that would hurt the men in the United States Navy, or my son, there is nothing I can do about it." Johnston at this point sounded a shrewd note by raising the question of intent. "If I am indicted in this case here, I know I haven't done anything—there has been no intent, and they tell me there has to be intent."[104]

Johnston ended his oration with a heartfelt plea. "And if there is anything I have done, and I am indicted on this, it will wreck me forever," he said. "I know in court it will be found out, it must; but that doesn't help me. Meanwhile, my son will hear it, everybody else will hear it. It is not only myself, it is the boys of the Navy themselves, that I have been with. If I have done anything wrong, I should be penalized for it, but I think there is such a thing as intent. That's all I want to say. Thank you."[105]

Thus ended Johnston's grand jury appearance. He was politely asked to leave the jury room and wait outside. He had talked virtually nonstop for forty-five minutes. Jurors sat impassively through the entire discourse. Not one had asked a question, not one ventured a question now. Not one betrayed a leaning one way or the other. Jurors might have been interested in what Johnston had to say about intent. Bringing it up as he did was probably clever; people always seem inclined to consider intentions, whether people have good intentions or bad. Johnston said that for jurors to indict, they would have to find that he had intended to commit a crime. Actually he was wrong about this. Under the provision of the Espionage Act on which he based his case, Mitchell did not have to prove intent. He told jurors on 14 August, "This Espionage Act says that anyone who has access to certain documents, mentioning them, who communicates the contents to someone unauthorized to see them, violates the law."[106] That minimal requirement presumably would make Mitchell's task a little easier, but the issue was not discussed by jurors this day.

Jury foreman Holmes proved himself a wise leader. He advised that jury members not let themselves be moved "away from or toward" any opinion. "Suppose we allow ourselves to be governed by our own common sense and judgment," he said, "and from the evidence as presented on both sides, considering, of course, the statement by Mr. Johnston." If there had been any tendency for jurors to rush to judgment, Holmes's remarks would have dampened that. Assistant U.S. District Attorney Miller also had something to say. "All of the evidence has not been presented in as great detail as it might in a trial," he reminded jurors. "You are not sitting here in judgment. The purpose of the grand jury is to determine whether or not there has been a violation of the statute." As Miller essentially conceded, jurors did not yet know enough to make that determination. The decision would not hinge on intent, as Mitchell had recognized from the outset; it would rest on whether the *Tribune*'s 7 June article had impaired national security. The only people who could answer that were the codebreakers who served in the Navy Department in Washington under Admiral King. They supposedly were on their way. In the meantime, the issue of intent, and the problem of Johnston's truthfulness, would not go away.

～

By Wednesday, 19 August, *Lexington* dive-bomber pilot Robert Dixon had arrived in San Francisco, en route to Chicago, where he was to testify before a grand jury in the *Chicago Tribune* case. Lieutenant Commander Dixon was already something of a legend among Pacific War pilots; his role in the sinking of the Japanese carrier *Shoho* during the Battle of the Coral Sea had earned him wide attention. As did Seligman, Johnston, and hundreds of other survivors, Dixon returned to San Diego on 2 June. Three weeks later, while he was still on leave, he was contacted by the FBI.

That was the first he heard of the *Chicago Tribune*'s controversial 7 June story. Investigators at that time asked him if he knew of Nimitz's secret dispatch, circulated on *Barnett* on 31 May. Dixon said he did; he said he was present when the message arrived in Seligman's stateroom, where *Lexington*'s executive officer sat at a big table surrounded by fellow officers. The pilot said he saw Seligman make a pencil notation containing the names of ships in the Japanese task force; he recalled further they were divided up into a striking force, a support force, and an occupation force. He said he saw the memorandum sitting in front of Seligman; he said he skimmed the memo as it was passed around the table. He remembered vividly that the memo triggered a lively conversation about the makeup of the Japanese armada nearing Midway.[107]

As for Stanley Johnston, Dixon said the correspondent was in Seligman's stateroom when the message folder was brought in. He remembered seeing Johnston walking around, not sitting at the table. If Seligman showed the dispatch to Johnston, Dixon did not see it. Dixon remained in the room about thirty minutes, during which time he lost track of the memo. He had no idea who else saw it or what became of it. Dixon's FBI interview did not answer the big question: How did Johnston obtain that list of Japanese ships?[108]

Dixon's story did not end with this interview. Years later, long after the war, Dixon revisited the Johnston episode while conversing with a close friend, Robert Mason, the editor of the *Virginian-Pilot*, Norfolk's morning newspaper. The version he imparted to Mason differed substantially from the story he told the FBI. According to Dixon's revised report, Seligman regularly showed classified messages to Johnston. "It's obvious now that the transport people had no business decoding flag officer traffic," Dixon told Mason. "I was damn well disturbed when Johnston took notes on the Midway plan— you would have thought he was writing a book, the way he scribbled on and on—and worried what I ought to do." He wondered if he should protest to

Seligman. "In the end I decided what the hell, Seligman was senior to me and I'd keep my nose out of it."[109]

Dixon gave his friend permission to publish the story but only after his death. Dixon died 21 October 1981 (six years after he talked with Mason); Mason's account of their conversation ran in the June 1982 issue of the U.S. Naval Institute *Proceedings* under the title, "Eyewitness." Mason's article may have answered one lingering question surrounding the *Chicago Tribune* affair, but it raised another puzzle: Why did Dixon tell one story to the FBI and another to Mason? There can only be conjecture: officers hated to tell tales that would throw a bad light on another officer. There was great camaraderie among *Lexington* officers, especially after their ordeal during the Coral Sea shoot-out. He may have wanted to protect Seligman. No one will ever know.

By mid-August 1942, Dixon had returned to duty. He was ordered to take command of the air group attached to the carrier *Saratoga*, soon to arrive at Pearl Harbor. Dixon flew from San Diego to the harbor in a flying boat to await the carrier, but when he reached Pearl Harbor, he was handed new orders from Admiral King. He was to proceed to San Francisco and then go to Chicago. He should be prepared to testify before a grand jury about the *Tribune*'s 7 June story.[110]

~

Jurors never heard the testimony of dive-bomber pilot Dixon. Had he testified, he presumably would have passed on at least one of his two versions of events. Would he have restated the account he gave the FBI? Or, instead, would he have told jurors what might have been the "real" story—the variant he conveyed to Robert Mason. What he might or might not have said in Chicago would remain a matter of speculation. Dixon never got past San Francisco. When he arrived there he received another piece of disconcerting news: the Navy had dropped its case against Stanley Johnston and the *Chicago Tribune*. Dixon went back to Pearl Harbor.[111]

Mitchell got a phone call from Biddle halfway through the grand jury proceeding, certainly no later than Tuesday, 18 August. Attorney General Biddle passed on to Mitchell a lightning bolt from Knox: the Navy would not, after all, make available any of its cryptanalysts to serve as expert witnesses in Chicago. The admirals had decided against it; the uniformed part of the department was adamant, and he, Knox, had come around to their point of view, albeit reluctantly. Knox was sorry, but that was that. Biddle was angry. Mitchell was stunned; he admitted later that he actually thought Knox would provide the witnesses. He could not believe that a Secretary of the Navy would make a solemn pledge to an attorney general, as he did in his 29 July letter to Biddle, and then renege, as he clearly had just done. Mitchell thought there was nothing else to do but inform the grand jury.

Just when Mitchell did so is by no means clear, but in all likelihood it was first thing Wednesday morning, 19 August, the day the Navy's special witnesses were expected to show up. Mitchell figured he did not have a case without them. Under prior agreement with Biddle and Knox, Mitchell was not to tell the grand jury why Nimitz's dispatch was so sensitive—that it was a product of the U.S. Navy's highly secret effort to crack the Imperial Navy's code. Giving jurors that background was the job of the Navy's cryptanalysts. Their assigned role was to spell out the dire effects of the *Tribune*'s 7 June article—the very strong possibility that it had tipped off the Japanese that their naval code had been compromised. But those experts would not appear in Chicago. They would not testify. Thus, as Mitchell told Biddle later, the jurors were being asked to indict two people without knowing what crime they had committed or why it mattered. Jurors were in a bind. They could agree only that there had been a technical violation of Navy censorship rules; they did not see a breach of the Espionage Act. Jurors took a vote: they held that no indictment be returned against Johnston, Maloney, or the *Tribune* itself. They decided to drop the case.[112]

Late Wednesday Mitchell caught the next plane back to New York. Before departing he had handed out the following a statement to the press:

> The Grand Jury considering the matter of the publication on June 7, 1942 in the Chicago Tribune and in other newspapers of an article relating to the Japanese Fleet in the Midway Battle, have decided that no indictment should be returned. I was asked by the Attorney General to come here and conduct the inquiry and in so doing to see that the Grand Jury had before them all the facts. I have conducted the inquiry as fully and as fairly as I know how. Those under investigation were given the unusual privilege of appearing before the Grand Jury and explained their connection with the incident. The Jury has considered the case fully and its conclusion that no violation of the law was disclosed settles the matter.[113]

The *Tribune* was on deadline late Wednesday afternoon when the paper's reporter at the Federal Building phoned in the "no indictment" flash. Acting managing editor Maxwell put Pat Maloney on the line as the reporter read Mitchell's statement. Maxwell and Maloney had just hung up when Stanley Johnston ambled into the *Tribune*'s big newsroom. Every staffer in the room rose to greet him. Then Maloney, still on-the-job despite McCormick's order, strolled out of his office. All activity in the cavernous room ceased. Copyboys halted. Typewriters went silent. Copy editors laid aside the headlines they were writing. The editorial department roared a welcome to its chief, mixing applause with cheers.[114]

Maloney thanked the staff for its loyalty, reminded everyone they had a newspaper to put out, and returned to his office. He did not stay there long. He heard loud sounds a short time later when Robert McCormick made one of his rare appearances in the newsroom. Reporters and editors gave their publisher an enthusiastic reception. Once again all work stopped as staffers gathered around their gray-haired, sixty-two-year-old boss. McCormick beamed. "There never has been a bunch like the *Tribune* bunch," he said. "As I have told you before, every member of the *Tribune* is a member of my family."[115]

Then McCormick read a short statement (printed in the *Tribune* the next day with the paper's distinct abbreviations): "I never had the slightest fear of an indictment. I have known Maloney for nearly 25 years, and when I confided the Tribune's honor to him it was with a thoro knowledge of his character. Johnston I have only seen a few times, but his record of heroism and the impression he made upon all who came in contact with him furnished a complete guarantee of his integrity." He concluded, "The attitude of the Tribune is today what it was before the grand jury investigation was launched and as it was the day after Pearl Harbor. Our whole effort is to win the war and we will not indulge in any factionalism excepting insofar as we are persecuted and have to defend ourselves."[116]

Visibly moved by his encounter with *Tribune* staffers, McCormick returned to his office on the twenty-fourth floor, where congratulatory telegrams and phone messages were stacking up. *Tribune* executive Howard Wood happened by his office. "You know, Howard," the publisher said, "I had an amazing experience. I went down to the local room and they all stood up and cheered."[117]

⁓

For a few short days, McCormick was America's favorite publisher. Many of his harshest critics praised the grand jury's decision and slammed Biddle's investigation. "Doubtless the *Tribune* will cry persecution," opined the *Washington Post*, as the *Tribune* in fact did. That caveat aside, the *Post* faulted the government for convening a grand jury without having first established a clear-cut case. The *Post* commented that the probe was especially regrettable in view of the fact that the Secretary of the Navy is a rival publisher. Making Justice's grand jury action even more questionable was the historic editorial animus of the *Tribune* toward the administration. "For these reasons," the *Post* concluded, "we cannot forbear the thought that in allowing the Navy to go ahead with its complaint the administration was guilty of an unfortunate blunder."[118]

The *Kansas City Star* agreed. "The *Star* holds no brief for the *Chicago Tribune*," the paper admitted up front, but it said it could not avoid the conclusion that the government picked out what was at most merely a borderline case in order to attack three newspapers that had been critics of the administration. Thus "[the *Star*] welcomes the decision of the grand jury in blocking what has seemed an attack on the freedom of the press." The *Cincinnati Enquirer, Cincinnati Times Star, Ohio State Journal* in Columbus, the Duluth (Minn.) *News Tribune*, and the *Sacramento Bee* chimed in with similar opinions.[119]

The newspaper industry's trade organ, *Editor & Publisher*, noted that not every call made by the *Tribune* had been defensible. It expressly singled out Maloney's decision to attribute information gathered by Johnston to "naval intelligence" in Washington. Such "stunts" do not constitute standard or accepted newspaper practice, in Chicago or anywhere else, *E&P* lectured. "Bad judgment and bad newspaper practice there may have been," it surmised. "Treachery there was not, and it is inconceivable that the Department of Justice would have seriously expected a jury to find in its presentation of facts a case that would have branded the *Tribune* and its people as enemies of the country. The obvious facts to the contrary were overwhelming."[120]

Of course, the nation did not hear all the facts. That was the way Admiral King and his admirals wanted it. They were undoubtedly relieved that with the exception of Walter Winchell, *PM*, and a handful of other outlets, so few in the media explicitly linked the grand jury case with the Navy's success cracking the Imperial Navy's code.[121] Quite sensibly, from its point of view, the Navy moved to conceal the facts that would have made the government's case comprehensible. The only question was why it took Knox and his colleagues so long to reach an unavoidable conclusion: that they had more to lose by exposure of a crucial secret than they had to gain by punishment of the *Tribune*. Not everyone in the administration appreciated the Navy's logic.

~

Roosevelt exploded when Biddle reported what had happened in Chicago. He could not believe what his attorney general just told him. "I felt like a fool," Biddle said later. He then did what many government officials would do in a similar spot: he blamed someone else. He singled out Knox. Biddle was supported by his assistant attorney general, James Rowe. "I do think the idiocy of the Navy should be pointed out to the President," Rowe told Biddle in a 29 August memo. "It seems that everyone in the United States except the grand jury knows the facts."[122]

Mitchell also faulted Knox. In a letter to Biddle in which he explained the grand jury's action and his own efforts in Chicago, Mitchell targeted for censure Knox's on-again, off-again approach to the case. First, the Navy secretary wanted a strong action against the *Tribune*. Then, after grasping the implications—public disclosure of the Navy's codebreaking success against Japan's code—he cooled down, extending the matter little more than "half-hearted" consent. But when Mitchell proposed the case be dropped, Knox came roaring back, vowing on 29 July to supply the Navy cryptographers who would confirm the damage inflicted by the *Tribune* story. "I feel that they ought to have made a final decision then and there and stuck to it," Mitchell wrote, "and in letting me go to Chicago under the circumstances and then stopping the disclosure at that stage, they sort of sold me down the river and the Department of Justice as well."[123]

In recapping what the grand jury did and why they did it, Mitchell stated his views bluntly. "The case broke down before the Grand Jury because the Grand Jury demanded to know what harm the article had done," he wrote, "and having been forbidden over the telephone to make any disclosures to them about the Navy intelligence methods and the inference the Japs could draw from the *Tribune*'s publication, the jury were left in the air and refused to take the case seriously." According to Mitchell, jury members said to him that without such divulgence, they considered the charge against Johnston,

Maloney, and the *Tribune* to be a purely technical one, that is, a bureaucratic dispute over the paper's failure to strictly observe censorship rules.[124]

Mitchell told Biddle he did his best to put out fires and various flare-ups from grand jury members. Throughout the proceeding, he noted, the jury people read papers and news magazines, some of which raised questions as to whether McCormick and the *Tribune* were being persecuted. Jury members "murmured something" about Knox, a personal enemy of the *Tribune*, instigating the case. "I called their attention to the fact that Secretary Knox had granted the *Tribune*, his supposed enemy, the privilege of having a special correspondent with the fleet," Mitchell recalled. "That did not look like mistreatment to the *Tribune*, and the jury all nodded their heads and appeared satisfied that Secretary Knox was in the clear."[125]

Jury members were also "somewhat aroused" about the actions of officers on board *Barnett* who, from what they could tell, were careless in letting a copy of the secret dispatch lie around. "They brought that up," Mitchell said, "and they asked me why they should be asked to indict Maloney and Johnston for what they said was a technical offense without damage to the national safety, when the officers on the ship were guilty of equal carelessness and nothing was being done to them." Mitchell tried to assure jury people they would get answers to all their questions. Then the unexpected happened. "I received your telephone communication that the Navy had concluded that these disclosures ought not to be made even to a Grand Jury in secret session," Mitchell wrote. "From that time on the case was hopeless, as it soon developed in the Grand Jury Room that they would not indict unless these disclosures were made."[126]

Mitchell said he agreed with the jury. "The Grand Jury were rather flabbergasted at being asked to consider an indictment when the Government refused to disclose to them that any damage did or could have resulted from publication," he stated, "and I am frank to say I would have done the same thing if I had been a juryman myself."[127] Responding to Mitchell's letter (which Biddle had passed on to Knox), the Navy secretary tried to explain his actions. "You are completely correct in your statement that twice the Navy expressed its readiness to have the entire case placed before the Grand Jury for the purpose of securing an indictment," the Navy secretary admitted. Then, about the time the grand jury convened on 13 August, a "change of attitude" occurred on the part of the Navy. What caused the change?[128]

"The truth was that we had just again successfully broken the Japanese code and this fact was of immense value to us in operations then in progress," Knox wrote. "Naturally, this made the military and the Navy extremely apprehensive lest any talk of code-breaking in the newspapers in the United States lead the enemy to take action to cut off this highly valuable source of information." In light of the very great value of this material, "Even I was compelled to admit that the decision must be negative, even though it cost us a chance of bringing the offenders in the *Tribune* case to book," Knox added.[129]

The implications of Knox's letter were sobering. He was saying, in effect, that the Japanese had not changed their naval code. No damage to national security had resulted—or at least had not resulted *yet*—from the *Chicago Tribune* story. Mitchell, of course, had no way of knowing this. He proceeded on a totally different assumption. He continued to present witnesses to the grand jury and wait for new witnesses to confirm a finding that, apparently, had been invalidated at the last minute. Those intel experts—steeped in the extraordinarily secret Ultra program—stayed home. The grand jury, in the meantime, spent four very arduous days trying to make sense out of the sometimes conflicting stories of twelve very different witnesses.[130]

∾

Knox lost some of his standing in the White House. Roosevelt was not pleased by how the Navy secretary had handled his end of the case. Knox remained in the cabinet until his death in April 1944, but with diminished stature. Many in Washington agreed with Texas senator Tom Connally's assessment of him as "a two-cylinder engine in a four-cylinder job."[131] Knox was not the only loser. The Justice Department's prestige took a hit. Biddle never forgave his colleague for his flip-flop in the case. As one Justice Department official summed up the debacle, "Knox pushed Biddle out on a limb, followed him there, then sawed them both off."[132]

Back in Chicago, life returned to normal in the *Tribune* newsroom. McCormick resumed governing the *Tribune* from his spacious twenty-fourth-floor office. Maloney reclaimed his old job; the publisher put him back in as managing editor—a slot he would hold for another eight years. Johnston took a desk in that bustling environment. *Tribune* editors in the months ahead would ask Navy officials frequently about Johnston's commendation. Would he get it? They inquired gently but persistently into the status of his Navy press credentials. Would they be reactivated? No one in authority ever had an answer. McCormick did not seem to mind; he took a fancy to his flamboyant correspondent, now both a martyr and a bona fide hero. He found a place for him in the *Tribune* community. Johnston had a job for life.

EPILOGUE
Fortunes of War

As for Seligman, King cast about for an appropriate punishment.
—*Thomas B. Buell*

Ever since the disturbing phone call he got from Russell Willson, King's chief of staff, on 10 June, the severely battered Seligman had feared his Navy career was over. His sense of foreboding deepened in the weeks ahead. He was grilled several times by Navy and FBI investigators. His low point may have come in late June, while he was still a patient at U.S. Naval Hospital in San Diego. He was visited there by *Lexington* dive-bomber pilot Robert Dixon. After being quizzed by the FBI, Dixon went straight to the hospital where Seligman was a patient and reported to him. "Commander," Dixon said, "the FBI asked me about a certain message on the transport and I gave him all the information I had. The Midway plans message; I'm sure you know what I mean." Seligman did.[1]

By mid-July, Seligman was not only worried, he was on the verge of panic. Feeling harassed by the FBI and abandoned by the Navy, he did something drastic. Even though he had been told by his superiors not to contact civilian participants in the case, he called Stanley Johnston at the *Chicago Tribune*, as noted. When City Editor Don Maxwell picked up the phone close to midnight on 15 July, he encountered an almost hysterical Seligman. Hearing that Johnston was out of the city, Seligman let Maxwell know why he was calling. He wanted the *Tribune* people to understand what he had been going through (see chapter 9). He wondered if the paper was behind him. He blurted out questions. *Are you going to run out on me?* No, Maxwell reassured him. *All Stan talks about is your heroism. You're one of his favorite heroes.*[2]

"Well," the officer replied, "I'm not one of Admiral King's favorites."[3]

Seligman was right about that. From reports submitted by Navy sleuths on the West Coast, COMINCH had pieced together a plausible account of what had happened on *Barnett*. True, some parts of the story were murky. Precisely how Nimitz's message—Dispatch No. 311221—passed from Seligman's hands into Johnston's remained unclear. Did Seligman deliberately show it to the correspondent, as Dixon said in one of his two versions of events? Or had Seligman simply been sloppy in his oversight of this dispatch, thereby letting it slip into Johnston's possession unintentionally? However it happened, and this mystery would never be fully resolved, King knew Seligman to be the senior *Lexington* officer on *Barnett* and, as such, responsible for securing that document. He had failed to do so. "King had put the blame on Seligman," Admiral Louis Denfeld, chief of naval operations, 1947–49, said later.[4]

Horrified by the leak, King took corrective steps. He admonished Nimitz for the slack way his dispatch had been communicated, and he put in place measures to reduce the likelihood of such a leak happening again (see chapter 6). As for those implicated in the miscue, King initially wanted strong action taken against the *Chicago Tribune*. For a time, he went along with the Roosevelt administration's aim to prosecute the paper for violating the Espionage Act. He changed his mind once he grasped the consequences of a public trial. To avoid that danger he was willing to let the *Tribune* slide off the hook, but he was less inclined to be lenient toward the officer he deemed most responsible for the transgression. "As for Seligman, King cast about for an appropriate punishment," King's biographer, Thomas B. Buell, stated.[5]

COMINCH early on did not know exactly what form his judgment might take, although in truth, there were not all that many possibilities to choose from. King raised the matter with Nimitz on 4 July 1942, when the two met in San Francisco for one of their regular conferences. "Cominch stated that Seligman and others involved in the affair were in 'escrow,'" a stenographer recorded in the minutes of the King-Nimitz meeting.[6] King did not say what he had in mind, but whatever it was, in all likelihood it wouldn't be good for Seligman's career.

For an officer supposedly awaiting punishment, Seligman was in surprisingly high spirits in the late summer of 1942. Or so he seemed to Stanley Johnston when the two conversed by phone on 14 September. Seligman had just gotten some good news. He had received in the mail notice that he had been awarded the Navy Cross recommended in May by his superiors, Admiral Fitch and Captain Sherman. The citation said he was being honored for the "extraordinary heroism" he displayed on board *Lexington* during the Battle of the Coral Sea on 8 May. He could now wear a gold star on the Navy Cross ribbon he had earned years earlier during the final stages of the First World War. Seligman asked Johnston if he had gotten *his* citation. "Hadn't heard a thing," Johnston said. "You'll get it," Seligman said. "I heard it was coming through."[7]

If Seligman harbored any resentment toward Johnston for his controversial *Tribune* article, he didn't show it. The two remained friends. When Seligman found out during their conversation that Johnston would soon be in Hollywood on some kind of movie project, he invited the correspondent to see him in San Diego. "I want to tell you some of the amusing things that happened while I was in Chicago," said the suddenly ebullient Seligman. (He had obeyed the Navy's orders to stay away from Johnston during the grand jury proceedings.)[8] Seligman was in a good mood for another reason. His doctors on 31 August recorded that his back symptoms had "practically disappeared"; they judged him "physically qualified" to perform all the duties of his rank. He was cleared for return to active duty.[9]

Awaiting his orders Seligman was uncharacteristically upbeat, but his enthusiasm probably ebbed when he got his new assignment. On 15 September he was directed to Peru, Indiana, to take command of the U.S. Naval Reserve Aviation Base nearby, in the little hamlet of Bunker Hill.[10] With the Wabash River the only significant nearby waterway, this naval base was hardly a nautical hub. It was far removed from the action of the Pacific War. The question, in many minds, and conceivably in Seligman's, was whether Peru happened to be Admiral King's idea of payback for the commander's lapses on *Barnett*. To some people, Peru looked like the American equivalent of Siberia. Seligman seemingly had been banished, ordered to a billet where he was unlikely to ever be heard from again; his career obviously had stalled.

Peru may have seemed unpromising. With a population of little more than twelve thousand, the town was small. Aside from the fact that it was the birthplace of Cole Porter and the home of several famous circuses, it offered few distinctions. But Peru may not have been the backwater it at first appeared. The naval station there had importance. It was new; it had just opened on 1 July. It was established to train Navy, Coast Guard, and Marine pilots, badly needed for the air campaigns that loomed ahead in the Pacific. (Baseball player Ted Williams would be ordered to this site for flight training.) Seligman would run this base; he would direct the training of future Navy pilots. He would have flying duties. In this role he was like many veteran fliers who had been rotated back to shore duty in the states to prepare future pilots for combat.

How Seligman viewed this duty isn't known. He may have regarded it as a poor launch site for an officer with his ambitions to command his own carrier. He undoubtedly expressed himself, but whatever he said doesn't show up in Navy records. He may have liked the place or resented it, but he clearly adjusted well to his leadership role. In May 1943, he became something of a local hero when he ordered base personnel to assist citizens in several nearby towns threatened by rampaging floodwaters. For this effort he won praise from the Red Cross; the governor of Indiana, Henry Schricker; and a mayor or two. "[Seligman] came to our rescue with one hundred of his boys, who without hesitation, volunteered to share the dangers and long hours required to save the lives of many women and children," the mayor of Kokomo, Indiana, Charles V. Orr, wrote Frank Knox. "Our whole citizenship is indeed grateful of the high quality of the Navy," Orr continued, "and especially do we recognize the superb leadership and ability of Commander Seligman."[11]

Orr's words were undoubtedly music to Seligman's ears, but they had come too late to have any bearing on his future. Early in January 1943, Seligman had fallen on an icy sidewalk. He was out of action for days. X-rays showed arthritis in his back, aggravation of an old fracture of one of his vertebra, and spinal problems. His spine was starting to assume an "S" type curvature. He was fitted for a back brace but gave it up after two months because it interfered with his walking. Even with this ailment, he was able to direct rescue efforts in the flooded towns around Peru. His back pain remained.[12] He may have had other difficulties. Rumors circulated that he sometimes drank excessively.[13] The reports may have been unfair, or exaggerated, but there was no question that his physical condition was worsening. For reasons never spelled out in Navy papers, Seligman was relieved of his post in July 1943 and ordered to the U.S. Naval Station at Alameda, California, to assume duties as executive officer.[14]

Seligman's medical problems continued at Alameda. In December 1943, he was admitted to the sick list for seven days with acute gastritis. In March 1944, he was diagnosed with severe gastrointestinal problems along with a worsening back condition. These and other ailments rendered Seligman unable to perform his duties for long stretches. In May, Alameda's doctors recommended that he be retired. Two months later, the Navy's Bureau of Medicine and Surgery concurred, deciding that Seligman was permanently incapacitated because of his back problems, stemming primarily, it said, from injuries sustained during the Battle of the Coral Sea. On 11 July, Navy authorities ordered Seligman retired effective 1 November 1944.[15]

With a firm date set for Seligman's exit, the only issue remaining was the rank he would carry into retirement. Admiral King was thought to have settled the matter. His biographer, Thomas Buell, believed that COMINCH had sealed Seligman's fate during the contentious months of 1942. "With the concurrence of Roosevelt and Knox," Buell wrote, "King arranged that Seligman would never be promoted to captain, and be retired from active duty in 1944."[16] Seligman was certainly being retired in 1944, although his exit may have had nothing to do with King. As for the promotion, the chief of naval personnel on 11 August told Seligman he would be placed on the retired list with the rank of captain, in accordance with Navy regulations (Title 34, Section 404[1]), "having been especially commended for performance of duty in actual combat by the head of the executive department."[17]

Seligman had his promotion. It was approved by Secretary of the Navy James Forrestal (Knox had died in April). Some things were beyond even King's control. As one writer has pointed out, Seligman benefitted from a practice the Navy followed until 1959—upgrading the rank of officers about to retire in what Navy people called Tombstone promotions.[18] His Navy Cross was undoubtedly a factor. However it happened, Seligman retired a captain on 1 November 1944, leaving the service with a 50 percent disability. He settled in Coronado, California, with his wife, Adelia. He surfaced in 1945 to serve as an advisor to the Hollywood movie, *A Bell for Adano*, but he was little heard from after that. If Stanley Johnston stayed in touch with Seligman during his retirement, there is no indication of it in Johnston's files.

‿

Seligman wasn't the only *Lexington* alumnus with whom Johnston remained on good terms. Another was former captain, now rear admiral, Frederick Sherman. Sherman had liked Johnston from almost their first meeting on board *Lexington*. He had recommended Johnston for a citation for the valor he displayed rescuing *Lexington* crew members during the critical moments after their carrier was destroyed in the Battle of the Coral Sea. He stood by Johnston during the darkest days of June and July when FBI investigators, at Hoover's orders, were interviewing naval officers who had had some contact with the reporter. It seemed to Sherman that the FBI was trying to fabricate a case against the journalist; he wouldn't stand for it. He told his interrogators that Johnston was "a very high type of man" who would not steal an official message. He reiterated his support for the *Tribune* reporter in August during his grand jury appearance.

Sherman and Johnston hadn't chatted since late June, when he and Barbara joined the admiral for dinner in Chicago. Now they were about to meet again. En route to the West Coast, where he was to assume command of a carrier task force, Sherman passed through Chicago. On 13 October 1942, he dropped by the Tribune Tower to pay Johnston a courtesy call. Fresh from the Navy Department, where he had served briefly as assistant chief of staff to King, Sherman was full of news. First, he wanted to let the correspondent know how much he appreciated his Coral Sea coverage, and that he particularly prized Johnston's profile of him in the *Tribune* ("Top Man of the Flat-Tops," 9 August 1942). From what Sherman had to say, the publicity had done him some good.[19]

Especially interesting to Johnston was Sherman's characterization of Navy Department sentiment with regard to the government's grand jury investigation of the *Tribune*. According to Sherman, the officers in King's department, after learning of Johnston's 13 July 1942 interview with William Mitchell, were satisfied there was "nothing in the matter." These officers, Sherman informed Johnston, were strongly against the administration. "All action was taken by express order of FDR," Johnston told Pat Maloney, quoting Sherman. Sherman gave the impression the Navy, or at least the uniformed part of it, did as little as it could to support FDR in this case.[20]

∽

By October 1942 Seligman's and Sherman's naval careers had diverged. In twenty-four months, Seligman would be out of the Navy. Sherman, by contrast, was taking a big step toward what would turn out to be a career rich in naval action, achievement, and honors. Before the war ended in August 1945, he would command carrier task forces and task groups that would see combat against Japanese forces in the Marshall and Gilbert Islands, Leyte Gulf, Okinawa, and other combat areas. He would be controversial; his fellow admirals would think him opportunistic, and pilots serving under him would find him abrasive and intolerant. But he would also win the Navy Cross three times and be promoted to vice admiral in 1945. He would retire in 1947.[21]

October 1942 also turned out to be a pivotal month for Stanley Johnston. On 8 October, E. P. Dutton & Co. published his book on *Lexington* and the

Coral Sea, *Queen of the Flat-Tops*, which he had worked on all summer with help from Wayne Thomis. Johnston did run into one obstacle with the book: he was unable to persuade Sherman, or anyone else from the Navy, to write a foreword to it. Sherman received Johnston's request in early August. Sherman had just seen Roosevelt's memo to Knox vetoing a proposal from Dutton that King write the foreword. Sherman initialed the memo, then added a few words of his own: "I have just received a letter [from Johnston] asking this but under the circumstances shall decline."[22]

Writing *Queen*, Johnston took no chances with government censors, printing on the title page the following disclaimer: "The information herein has been inspected by the Office of Censorship, which found no objection." The book turned out to be a tremendous hit. Reviews were overwhelmingly favorable. The *New York Times Book Review* ran its notice on the *Review*'s front page with a dramatic drawing of Coral Sea combat. The newspaper's critic called *Queen* "the most coherent eyewitness story of any sea battle that this reviewer has read." The *New York Herald Tribune Books* section conferred even greater praise on *Queen*, describing it as "one of the most significant and dramatic books the war has yet produced." "The human story told in [Johnston's book]," enthused the *Herald Tribune* writer, "is a story to make the heart of America proud."[23]

Queen became a best seller. It first showed up on the *New York Times* best seller list on 22 November 1942, in thirteenth place; the book reached its apogee on 6 December, when it ascended to the eighth spot. *Queen* remained on the list throughout the rest of 1942. It continued to sell well into 1943; by March 1943, six months after first appearing in bookstores, the book had gone through six printings.[24] Johnston even got some fan mail from admirals. Admiral William V. Pratt (retired), former chief of naval operations (1930–33), lauded the book as "excellent." Admiral Sherman passed on praise from Rear Admiral Charles M. "Savvy" Cooke Jr., principal planning officer for King and the officer who, on 7 June, wanted to hang *Tribune* publisher McCormick "higher than Haman." According to Sherman, Cooke thought *Queen* was the finest Navy book yet written.[25]

～

The success of *Queen* emboldened *Tribune* editors to try again to regain the Navy credentials that would let Johnston cover the war from the front lines. Johnston was hopeful. He radiated optimism in a September letter to his old friend in Pearl Harbor, Waldo Drake, still serving as head of Pacific Fleet public relations.[26] "The little bother that shook the country recently has ended and thank goodness all is well," Johnston mused. He told Drake he was convinced the Navy "never wanted to do anything to me," adding, rather naively, that it was his belief the incident wouldn't affect him adversely. "I am happy there is no kick back [sic] because I am anxiously waiting to get out to sea again with the fleet and hope to be away again soon." He even confided to Drake where he expected to go: "I anticipate being sent Atlanticwards [sic] this time."[27]

Johnston remained upbeat even as his colleagues in Washington heard nothing but doubletalk at the Navy Department. *Tribune* editors couldn't get a straight answer about Johnston's papers. "These bootlickers down here get the jitters anytime Johnston's name is mentioned," Washington bureau chief Henning, told Maloney. "Everybody is afraid to look into his status and it appears they will prefer to leave him suspended indefinitely." Henning advised waiting for a better time before raising the issue again.[28]

Months passed. The hopelessness of Johnston's cause was not fully grasped until March 1943, when Bob Casey, the *Chicago Daily News*'s ace foreign correspondent, asked his boss about it. Meeting Frank Knox in Knox's Washington office, Casey inquired whether the ban on Johnston's papers was permanent. Casey got more doubletalk, but it was doubletalk that left no doubts about where matters stood. Knox told Dixon that the correspondent's credentials were in the hands of those Navy Department officials charged with accrediting journalists. He wasn't going to interfere in their deliberations, or as Casey understood him to say, he "wasn't going to risk being included in future discussions." That was the end of it. Johnston didn't get his papers; he would never again cover any part of the war from a combat zone.[29]

Nor did get Johnston get his medal. Suspicions that the White House had intervened to squelch the citation were confirmed in 1949 when the *Tribune*'s Walter Trohan raised the matter with Secretary of the Navy John L. Sullivan, with whom he was well acquainted. Sullivan had deep roots in the Roosevelt administration. He had served as assistant secretary of the Treasury during the war; he knew FDR. Sullivan one day let Trohan know that highly prized tickets for the 1949 Army-Navy football game were being held for him; Trohan was only half-kidding when he said he'd rather be picking up Johnston's medal. "[Sullivan] told me there is a letter in the file from Knox saying that the President had specifically ordered no medal should be awarded," Trohan informed Maloney. "Looks as though that's sealed."[30]

~

Blocked from covering the war from either the Pacific or European fronts, Johnston still found a way to write war stories. Drawing on published sources, wide-ranging personal contacts, and interviews with Pacific Fleet flyers home on leave, Johnston started work on a sequel to *Queen of the Flat-Tops*. This result was *The Grim Reapers*, a short book that told the story of Fighting Squadron Ten (VF-10), nicknamed the Grim Reapers. The book focused primarily on the naval adventures of its squadron leader, Lieutenant Commander James H. Flatley, whom Johnston had met during the Coral Sea campaign. Uninviting as the book's title may have been, it nevertheless offered readers a lively account of life with a fighter squadron on board the carrier *Enterprise* as it engaged Japanese forces in the Solomon Islands in 1943. Published by Dutton later that year, *Reapers* didn't fare as well as *Queen* in the marketplace, but it did go at least into a second printing.

Johnston also found a way to travel, much to the consternation of the FBI and the Navy Department. On 11 February 1944, FBI agent E. A. Tamm, who had been actively involved in the bureau's 1942 investigation of Johnston, received a confidential query from Captain B. F. Perry of the Office of Naval Intelligence. The subject of Perry's memo: Stanley Johnston. Perry informed Tamm: "Subject transited Balboa, Canal Zone on 10 February 1944 enroute [*sic*] to Lima, Peru." Perry's question: "The Office of Naval Intelligence would be interested in learning of the reasons for Subject's travel to South America, and through what means he was provided with the necessary documents requisite to this travel."[31]

The FBI did some checking. Hoover answered Perry on 4 March, letting him know that Johnston had obtained a passport from the State Department as a correspondent of the *Chicago Tribune*. Rather amazingly, given the cancellation of his Navy credentials, the correspondent ran into no obstacles getting the passport; he obtained it through a routine request. From the State Department, Hoover learned—and so informed ONI—that Johnston intended to visit "practically all countries in Central and South America." His trip was expected to last three months.[32]

Without the Navy's or, for that matter, the FBI's, official blessing, Johnston proceeded to travel to the major cities of Central and South America. His arrival in those places was routinely preceded by an "alert" transmitted by the FBI to "All FBI Legal Attaches" in U.S. government consular offices. The alert made for worrisome reading; it noted tersely that the correspondent had once been suspected by the British of communicating with the enemy. "Desired you be most discreet in event you come in contact with him," Hoover instructed his men. The FBI's attachés were certainly discreet as they monitored the reporter as he moved from city to city. When his plane landed in Asuncion, Paraguay, on 19 March, FBI agent W. R. Hulbert Jr. was at the airport, quietly observing. "[Johnston] talked to few people [at the] airport and departed for Rio de Janeiro same plane," Hulbert informed Washington in a confidential FBI radiogram.[33]

When the FBI finally lost interest in Johnston isn't known, but the correspondent probably kept the bureau's attachés busy for many months, possibly years. He stayed in the region longer than the projected three months. He ended up serving as the *Tribune's* correspondent for Latin America for two years; he was constantly flying in and out of the region. In the late 1940s, he returned to the Chicago office for good. There was a place for him there.

The *Tribune's* old fourth-floor newsroom remained much the same, still headed by its irascible managing editor, Pat Maloney. Maloney continued to be a magnet for trouble. Having emerged somehow unscathed from the Johnston affair in 1942, he found himself in the middle of another jam at the end of the 1948 presidential election. On Election Day, he approved the 3 November headline that stands as one of journalism's iconic bloopers: "Dewey Defeats Truman." The headline was based on the reporting of Arthur Henning, long considered the dean of the Washington press corps. The voting indicated a different result but Henning stood by his story, and Maloney stood by Henning, accepting, as he often did, Henning's judgment. This time it turned out to be wrong, leading to a moment of historic embarrassment for the paper. Maloney survived even this fiasco, but his days were numbered. Beset by health problems, he retired as managing editor in 1950, although he did return to the paper for a time to serve as McCormick's special assistant. Henning wasn't so fortunate. McCormick relieved the seventy-one-year-old Henning of his post; the Washington bureau chief was pensioned off at full salary.[34]

∿

Johnston's *Tribune* career took another turn in 1949. His role in the newsroom had always been awkward. (Maloney said he was a good reporter but a poor writer.) Now he left the newswriting realm for good and joined the

Tribune's promotion department as an editorial assistant. Again his duties seemed murky. It didn't really matter because his responsibilities were about to change one more time. As Robert McCormick's vigor declined in the early 1950s he desired, and in fact required, more and more attention, much of which was provided by *Tribune* personnel. (McCormick, who was childless, often said his only real family was the *Tribune* staff.) When he repaired to Florida for rest and relaxation, he needed company. "There was no couple that I could think of that the Colonel liked better than the Johnstons," recalled former city editor Maxwell. The couple joined him on his Florida jaunts. "[Johnston] took care of the Colonel like a son would take care of his father," Maxwell said.[35]

With McCormick's health less than robust, Stanley and Barbara acceded to the publisher's wishes and that of his closest associates that they move into his mansion at Cantigny Park, his five-hundred-acre estate thirty miles west of Chicago. They helped him as best they could. McCormick could still be a demanding master. One day he handed down an order that trees should be planted on Michigan Avenue. The order came after a McCormick subordinate had already established there couldn't be trees on Michigan Avenue because the car fumes would kill them. McCormick then gave the assignment to Johnston. "I remember Johnston set out and talked with the tree people and now we have trees on Michigan Avenue," Barbara said years later.[36]

McCormick's health failed markedly after an attack of pneumonia in April 1953. Over the next two years, he battled heart disease and cirrhosis of the liver. By March 1955 he was still clinging to life, but just barely. He would awaken at night and, finding himself alone, cry for help. Johnston and other members of the *Tribune* community formed a group they called Watchmen of the Night; they stayed in the old gentleman's room as his life slipped away. On 1 April 1955, at age seventy-four, McCormick died, with Johnston at his side.[37]

⁓

After McCormick's death, Johnston was made general manager of the Cantigny estate, which was left in trust and opened to the public. Johnston's duties were primarily administrative, but he did find time to indulge in an unsuspected hobby: flowers. In 1960 he discovered a mutation on the Peace rose, a well-known garden rose developed by a French horticulturist in the 1930s and given its popular name after World War II by British Field Marshal Alan Brooke. Johnston brought the mutation to the attention of a commercial rose grower; he developed it and called it Chicago Peace. The rose was awarded the Portland (Oregon) Gold Medal in August 1962.[38]

Johnston exercised regularly. He followed a daily routine of jogging around the grounds of the War Memorial Museum of the First Division at the Cantigny estate. His health at age sixty-two seemed strong. But on 13 September 1962 he suffered a heart attack at Cantigny Park. He died shortly afterward. Only Barbara was present at the time of his death. The next day the *Tribune* ran a lengthy obituary celebrating its onetime war correspondent, beginning it above the fold on the front page and continuing it through three columns inside the paper. The obituary was written, fittingly enough, by aviation editor Wayne Thomis, the same writer whom Pat Maloney had assigned during the evening of 6 June 1942 to rewrite Johnson's ill-starred Midway story. "Stanley Johnston led a fabulous life," Thomis wrote. "Few men have combined so much adventure, travel, and danger in their lives and yet retained his zest for living."[39] The *New York Times* also ran an obituary of Johnston.

Johnston was survived, of course, by Barbara. She later remarried. Barbara's new husband was a *Tribune* executive (J. Howard Wood); she lived to be 100. (Barbara died on 18 November 2009 in Lake Forest, Illinois.) Johnston was also survived by the Navy officer whose name will always be ingloriously associated with his: Morton Seligman. After retiring on 1 November 1944, Seligman, joined by his wife, Adelia, lived for twenty-three years in retirement in Coronado, California. He lived almost invisibly. He seems to have gone largely unnoticed during this time; a check of Navy records and various databases turned up no entries under his name.

Seligman died of a stroke on 9 July 1967 at age seventy-two at Balboa Naval Hospital in San Diego. His death attracted only modest attention. His hometown paper, the *Santa Fe New Mexican*, carried a thoughtful obituary, with his picture, on page 7. Also, a two-paragraph wire-service story reporting his passing appeared in *Pacific Stars & Stripes*. The officer probably would have been pleased that his higher rank was used in this obit, which also gave him an extra medal. The article described him as "Capt. Morton T. Seligman, holder of three Navy Crosses and a hero of the battle of the Coral Sea in 1942."[40]

CODA
Did the Japanese Know?

Many of those at liberty . . . had access to any newspaper
which they might desire to purchase.
—*J. Edgar Hoover*

he Imperial Japanese Navy amended its main operational code, the
famed JN-25, twice during the spring and summer months of 1942—
first on 28 May, six days before the Battle of Midway, then again on 14
August, nine weeks after the *Chicago Tribune* published Stanley Johnston's
notorious 7 June article under the headline, "Navy Had Word of Jap Plan to
Strike at Sea."

Navy and Roosevelt administration players in the Stanley Johnston
drama had bickered among themselves about many issues during the
seventy-day span of this Washington-centered fracas. But on one critical
matter most agreed: the Japanese learned from Johnston's story that their
naval code had been broken and, as a result, changed it. Many ended their
days holding the same view that Attorney General Francis Biddle expressed
in his 1962 memoirs, that with the publication of Johnston's reckless and
shortsighted article in the *Tribune*, "we had lost an important advantage in
the campaign for control of the Pacific Ocean."[1]

For Admiral King, commander in chief, U.S. Fleet, Johnston's article
was a national security disaster. Addressing Washington correspondents in
an impromptu, off-the-record press conference, held in his office late in the
afternoon on Sunday, 7 June—the same day Johnston's story appeared in the
Tribune—a highly incensed King let loose a blistering attack on the papers
that carried the article (see chapter 5). He was unequivocal in his assessment
of the harm inflicted by the story: "It compromises a vital and secret source
of information, which will henceforth be closed to us."[2] A few days later, in a

short, bluntly worded note to a skeptical Robert McCormick, King reiterated his view that the Japanese had acquired priceless information: "Obviously, the gaining of such knowledge by the enemy—through the publication of the article—could only lead to his drying up the source."[3]

King later softened his judgment. His change of heart occurred in early August, when Biddle's grand jury was waiting to hear testimony from Navy cryptologists on the dire consequences of the *Tribune* story. But COMINCH and his staff now urged Navy Secretary Knox to withhold those witnesses. Knox did so; he would later tell Biddle that, against all expectations, the Navy had once again cracked the IJN code. That development had come as a pleasant surprise. U.S. Navy cryptanalysts had been stymied since 28 May, when the IJN modified its main code, replacing JN-25(b) with JN-25(c). In the wake of Johnston's story, some Navy officers feared the Japanese might go further. From what King told reporters on 7 June, it appeared he expected the IJN to scrap the JN-25 series and introduce an entirely new cryptosystem. In June he and others thought the Japanese had already done so. If they had, U.S. Navy codebreakers would have had to start from scratch and unravel an altogether different code structure.

But in August, King got word that Navy cryptanalysts were reading the IJN's replacement code, JN-25(c). The Japanese had not junked the JN-25 series after all. If they had not, then harm attributable to Johnston's story was negligible, possibly nonexistent. Clearly, under such circumstances, no good would come from pursuing a high-profile case against Johnston and the *Chicago Tribune*. The U.S. Navy seemed to have been lucky; the Japanese appeared to have missed the story. Perhaps the whole affair had been a tempest in a teapot.

If that's what King now thought, many of his top lieutenants continued to believe otherwise. One group of holdouts resided in King's Office of Communication (OC), whose special unit, OP-20-G, retained overall responsibility for cracking IJN codes. In an internal study on the role of communications intelligence in the Pacific War published in September 1943, the OC reached a grim conclusion on the repercussions of Stanley Johnston's article: "[It] should be recorded here that serious damage was done to the progress of U.S. Naval Communication Intelligence operations."[4]

Navy researchers contended that the *Tribune* story, amplified by all the publicity surrounding it, including Walter Winchell's 5 July 1942 broadcast, caused word of the U.S. Navy's codebreaking coup to seep out into the world and ultimately reach the Japanese. OC's top officers believed the Japanese noticed and did something about it. What else could explain the fact that on 14 August, just a few weeks after the flare-up over the Johnston article, the IJN revamped its code once again, suddenly replacing JN-25(c) with JN-25(d)? Apparently, King and his aides had been premature in their optimism; the recent success scored by U.S. Navy codebreakers had been short-lived.[5] OC's leaders thought the Johnston spectacle had been a factor in this change.

In truth, the OC study did not conclusively demonstrate that the *Tribune* article caused the IJN to make the 14 August code change. But that did not prevent the study's principal author, Ensign John V. Connorton, from strongly suggesting such a connection. "There is no Japanese dispatch which positively links a publicity leak to the changes made in Japanese cryptographic systems," Connorton conceded, but he quickly added, "It is surely more than a mere coincidence that within a few weeks after the Midway expose, drastic changes were made in all Japanese codes and ciphers." Whether it was Johnston's story by itself or the furor it generated "which caused Japan to hear of the decipherment of its codes, there is no way of telling," Connorton wrote.[6]

But hear of it Japan did, he asserted. The confirming evidence, in his view, was the fact that during August and September 1942, the IJN halted or substantially altered practically every one of its codes and ciphers. Some shifts were expected. The IJN revised its cryptologic systems periodically, as did the U.S. Navy, realizing that prolonged use of any one system would invite its compromise. When the Japanese Merchant Ship-Naval Liaison code changed on 1 September 1942, Connorton figured this was probably a normal revision. (It had been in place for a year.) Other changes were more suspicious. The IJN's submarine cipher, instituted on 10 April 1942, closed down after 31 August 1942. Another system, IJN's operational and communication intelligence code, was scrapped on 15 August after just ten months of use. But it was major adjustments to IJN's general purpose system—the well-established JN-25—that was the telltale clue, Connorton believed. "This was immediately after the *Chicago Tribune*'s and Walter Winchell's publicity," he noted.[7]

Forty years later, the Connorton report gained backhanded support from a seemingly impeccable source: the onetime chief intelligence officer of the Pacific Fleet, Rear Admiral Edwin T. Layton. In his 1985 memoirs, Layton agreed with the OC's general finding that the *Tribune* scandal alerted the Japanese to the compromise of their code. But his critique differed from

Connorton's in one critical respect: he did not blame Stanley Johnston or even Walter Winchell for this ruinous leak. Layton thought Johnston's article would have gone unnoticed had the Navy and the Roosevelt administration simply ignored it. For making sure that the Navy did not ignore it, Layton singled out two OC officers he deemed overzealous in their pursuit of the leakers. They were OC's director, Captain Joseph Redman, who guided Connorton's study, and Joseph Redman's younger brother, Commander John Redman, heading OP-20-G. According to Layton, "They were determined to run the culprits to the ground." In so doing, they got King and Knox "stirred up," causing them, in Layton's telling, to favor action against the *Tribune*. The result was the calamitous, and heavily covered, grand jury proceeding. It was this event, Layton argued, that tipped off the Japanese.[8]

"Barrages of publicity surrounded the case," Layton and his co-authors, Pacific war historian John Costello and Captain Roger Pineau, USNR (Ret.), wrote in *And I Was There* (1985). "They could not possibly have escaped the watchful eyes and ears of Tokyo." Less than a week after Biddle announced the grand jury investigation, on 7 August, "the Japanese adopted a brand-new version of the JN-25 code," Layton noted. "All the progress we had made in breaking into the C version of the operational cipher was made worthless when the new D books came into use on 14 August." Many weeks of "grueling intellectual effort" would be required for Navy codebreakers to again break the IJN's main code, Layton stated. His contention that the Redman brothers were responsible for this unfortunate development did not hold water. (Rather, it primarily reflected a deep-rooted feud between Layton and the Redmans.) But there was no question that much time passed before Navy cryptanalysts mastered JN-25(d).[9]

~

Neither Layton nor Connorton claimed that the Imperial Navy had simply dumped the JN-25 series. They knew that could not be done quickly. Building a totally new code and cipher structure would have taken the Japanese many months. And, once developed, putting it in place at Japan's dozens of sending and receiving stations, scattered across more than four thousand miles of ocean, would have taken even more time. The Japanese could not have done anything like that on 14 August. What they did—and both officers agreed on this—was introduce a new version of JN-25—a new codebook and a new cipher to protect the values in that book. Even this rather modest change was no easy task. The up-to-date JN-25(d) codebook, like its pre-decessor, consisted of fifty thousand five-digit groups, each representing a phrase, place, letter, or word: the code group 26556, for example, denoted "dive-bomber." To make things more difficult, each code group was disguised by a yet another five-digit group of a possible fifty thousand random num-bers, called additives, contained in a three-hundred-page volume. The two sets of books could not have been hurriedly slapped together.

In fact, it is around the issue of *time*—the time required to get all this done—where the theories advanced by Connorton and Layton run into trouble. Layton contended that Biddle's 7 August announcement—and the media circus surrounding the whole grand jury episode—somehow reached Tokyo and led the IJN to promptly revise JN-25(c), to go from C to D. Highly improbable, answered at least one Pearl Harbor cryptanalyst familiar with Layton's notion. Layton's scenario simply is not credible, declared Captain Tommy Dyer, the lead cryptanalyst at Pearl Harbor's decrypt unit during 1941–43. He pointed out that breathtaking speed would have been required by IJN cryptologists to revamp this complex, multilayered code in just seven days—the period between 7 and 14 August. "I am relatively convinced that the change in code and cipher that took place shortly after Midway had noth-ing to do with the leak," Dyer said. "To distribute the new material and place it in effect requires a little bit more time. . . . In other words, the changes fol-lowed too closely upon the *Tribune* story to be occasioned by it."[10]

Another problem weakened the Connorton-Layton storyline. Japan's means of following events inside the United States—and thereby detect-ing the *Tribune* scandal—had been curtailed by the war. Powerful receivers in Australia could tune in to Radio Tokyo and pick up useful news about life in Japan.[11] But there was no equivalent of Radio Tokyo in the United States. Radio broadcasting in the United States was highly diversified. For-eign listeners hoping to get clues about happenings in America would have to choose among a profusion of program options available on no fewer than four major broadcasting networks: the Columbia Broadcasting System, the Mutual Broadcasting System, and NBC's Red and Blue networks. Unless an eavesdropper happened to be listening to the Blue Network at 9 p.m. on Sun-day, 5 July, he would not have heard Walter Winchell say "that twice the fate of the civilized world was changed by intercepted and decoded messages." That was all Winchell said; his comment consumed no more than three or four seconds of airtime. Assuming a would-be spy caught that ill-advised fragment, would he have made sense of it? Would he have connected it with Midway?[12] Highly improbable (see chapter 10).

Even before the war, Japan's ability to get accurate news about the United States had been limited. To gaze inside American life and culture, Japanese military leaders relied heavily on material collected and translated by the Domei press agency. Domei, in turn, depended on Reuters, the Associated Press, the United Press, *Life*, *Time*, the *New York Times*, the *New York Herald Tribune*, and military magazines overseas. During the war these sources dwindled, although the military was still able to obtain some news from neutral countries, such as Sweden and Argentina. The German and Japanese navies exchanged some U.S.-related information in 1942, but this source yielded little of value, historians say. In any case the *Chicago Tribune* did not show up on any of the IJN lists of sought-after knowledge sources.[13] Admiral King's biographer, Thomas Buell, concluded that "the Japanese apparently did not read American newspapers."[14]

~

Buell was wrong. The Japanese did read American newspapers when they could get them. They knew about the *Tribune* and they sought copies of it. They wanted to read it, as one student of the Pacific War has convincingly demonstrated. Writing in 1987, intel analyst B. Nelson MacPherson called attention to an intriguing and long overlooked source: an American summary of MAGIC intelligence (i.e., intelligence based on the interception and decryption of Japanese diplomatic signals) of 11 September 1942. Under Section D, "Psychological and Subversive," the summary notes:

1. *Tokyo*: A lengthy Japanese message to Lisbon requests the following:
   a. "Newspapers, particularly the anti-government 'Chicago Tribune' with as many back numbers as possible,"
   b. "'Time' and 'Life' and other magazines."[15]

MacPherson raised a perplexing question: Why did Tokyo, in the middle of a war, ask its Lisbon consulate to seek back issues of the *Chicago Tribune*? As noted, that newspaper was not on any of Japan's "watch" lists. In MacPherson's view, Layton was correct: Tokyo's interest was a direct result of the grand jury extravaganza. He reached this conclusion by a circuitous route. He noted that the Tokyo-Lisbon communication was one of many Japanese messages included in the 11 September summary, some of which had been intercepted weeks earlier. He calculated that the Tokyo-Lisbon message probably originated sometime in early August. "The MAGIC summary of 11 September thus substantiates Layton's chronology," MacPherson reasoned, adding, "This means the *Tribune* dispatch, and the resultant prosecution and publicity, was the most likely source of the compromise of America's cryptanalysis secret."[16]

With the surfacing of the MAGIC summary, all the pieces fell into place, at least as far as MacPherson was concerned. While conceding that the Japanese may have missed the *Tribune*'s original story, as historian David Kahn and others have suggested, "it is hard to see how they could have missed the later publicity of the affair," he argued. "Copies of the *Tribune* would then have been desired in order to provide solid, undeniable evidence that the IJN's ciphers were penetrated, and sufficient reason to change from JN25c to JN25d much sooner than normal."[17]

~

MacPherson got one thing right: The Japanese decision to go after the *Tribune* in September 1942 was indeed a mystery. But his explanation for Japan's sudden interest in this newspaper runs afoul of the same complication that invalidates the Connorton-Layton thesis: IJN cryptologists would not have had enough time between 7 August and 14 August, or even between 7 June and 14 August, to develop a "dictionary" with fifty thousand new code groups and a three-hundred-page book with fifty thousand new additives. Or, for that matter, would the IJN be able to rapidly distribute the two volumes to Japanese outposts dispersed across four thousand miles of ocean, all by 14 August. As Tommy Dyer made clear, the change could not have been made that quickly.

There remained a nagging question: If the media frenzy surrounding the Biddle grand jury had not aroused Tokyo's curiosity about the *Chicago Tribune*, what did? After all, Tokyo did ask its Lisbon representatives to dig up back issues of that newspaper. What was behind that request? Some motivations can be ruled out. The Japanese in all likelihood did not hear Walter Winchell. They probably did not read Stanley Johnston's article in "real time"—when it first appeared. They may have learned of it in a more roundabout way—through a back issue of the *New York Times* or *New York Herald Tribune* reaching Japan through Sweden or Argentina. But those papers carried little news about the Johnston affair, so that channel seems doubtful.

～

Not yet explored is a dizzyingly obvious pathway by which the Imperial Navy could have heard about Johnston's front-page scoop. The FBI worried about it at the time. This story begins in plain sight on 18 June 1942 in what, at first glance, would seem to be an unpromising locale: the New York City waterfront. Berthed along the row of ocean liners was the Swedish chartered vessel *Gripsholm*. The sleek, black-hulled luxury liner was packed with 1,063 Japanese diplomats and nationals. Eleven days after Johnston's article appeared in the *Chicago Tribune*, the *Gripsholm* was gearing up for the first stage of a journey that would take these people home.[18]

The Japanese on board were an intriguing group; they included students, businessmen, and embassy personnel of all kinds, from diplomats and military attachés to miscellaneous aides and clerks (among this ensemble was the now-unseated Japanese ambassador to the U.S., Kichisaburo Nomura). They had been through a trying time, as the great majority had been detained by federal agents in the days immediately following Japan's 7 December 1941 surprise attack on Pearl Harbor. Nearly all had been held under tight security at three secret locations. Closely watched as they were, as well as restricted in their activities and movements, these Japanese citizens nevertheless happened to be in the United States when Johnston's story—an article Harold Ickes said aided the enemy—ran in the *Tribune*. This eleven-day overlap raised questions about what some of these individuals might have seen or heard.

For example, did any of *Gripsholm*'s passengers, during their final days in the United States, read or learn of the *Chicago Tribune*'s 7 June 1942 article that told its readers, "Navy Had Word of Jap Plan to Strike at Sea"? If so, did any of them conclude, or suspect, that the U.S. Navy had broken the Imperial Navy's main code? If they did get that far, did they pass this conclusion, or suspicion, on to military authorities in Japan upon their return?

This may be sheer conjecture, but it certainly is not impossible. Familiarity with the *Tribune* article would have been inconceivable for most detainees; they lived for months under virtual house arrest. The twenty-three Japanese diplomats who had served in the Hawaiian Islands—held for months at a secure site in Dragoon, Arizona—were closely watched all the time. When this group arrived by train in New York City on 10 June, they were rushed immediately to the Pennsylvania Hotel and held there

The *Chicago Tribune*'s 7 June 1942 article

U. S. Navy Knew In Advance All About Jap Fleet

Guessed There Would Be Feint at One Base, Real Attack at Another

The strength of the Japanese with which the American Navy is battling somewhere west of Midway Island in what is believed to be the greatest naval battle of the war was well known in American naval circles, reliable sources in the Naval Intelligence disclosed here tonight.

The Navy learned of the gathering of the powerful Japanese units soon after they put forth from their bases, it was said. Although their purpose was not specifically known at that time, the information in the hands of the Navy Department was so definite that a feint at some American base, to be accompanied by a serious effort to invade and occupy another base, was predicted. Guesses were even made that Dutch Harbor in the Aleutians and Midway Island in the Hawaiian group might be targets.

In Three Sections

It was known that the Japanese fleet—the most powerful yet used in this war—was broken into three sections—first, a striking force; next a support force, and finally an occupation fleet.

It was apparent to Admiral Chester W. Nimitz's strategists in Hawaii that the feint would probably be made by the supporting force, the real blow struck by the striking fleet, with the occupation force standing by, ready to land troops as soon as defenses were broken down.

Had the attack on Midway been successful, Pearl Harbor and the Hawaiian Islands would have been the next point of attack.

The advance information enabled the American Navy to make full use of air attacks on the approaching Japanese ships, turning the struggle into an air battle along the modern lines of naval warfare.

Exactly how the Japanese disposed their units as between Dutch Harbor and the Midway Islands is not known here.

How Forces Were Divided

However, before the fleet was divided for attacks on the Aleutians and Midway, the various forces were made up approximately as follows according to Navy information here.

The striking force: Four aircraft carriers, the Akaga and Kaga of 26,900 tons each, and the Hiryu and Soryu, of 10,000 tons each.

Two battleships of the Kirishima class—29,300 tons, with 14-inch guns.

Two cruisers of the Tone class—new 8,500-ton 6.1-inch gun ships.

Twelve destroyers.

Support Force

The support force is described by the same source as comprising:

One aircraft carrier of the Ryuzyo class, 7,100 tons.

Two Kirishima class battleships.

Four new 8,500-ton cruisers of the Mogami class—including the Mogami, the Mikuma, Suzuya, Kumano with 15 guns of 6.1-inch calibers.

One light cruiser.

Ten destroyers.

Occupation Force

The occupation force included:

Four cruisers—the Chakas, Myoko, Chitore and Choda, all believed of 8,500 tons with main batteries of 6-inch guns.

Two armored transports of the Kunikisma Maru class—converted liners.

Four to six troopships.

Eight to 12 supply vessels.

Twelve destroyers.

Ten submarines.

Well informed as it was the Navy was on the alert for the first movements of this force. When it turned eastward into the Pacific from the vicinity on the Chisima or Kurile Island chain all American outposts were warned.

Real Goal Concealed

American naval dispositions were made in preparation for the various possible attacks the Japs were believed to be planning. Up to this time the Japanese had not committed themselves to any action. They were still in position to turn their real threat against either Dutch Harbor or Midway. By last Tuesday the Americans were able to conclude that a feint was to be made at Dutch Harbor.

Meanwhile, preparations among all available American forces in the vicinity of Midway were being rushed in the hope of striking a telling blow against the Japs. The wisdom of this course became apparent on Wednesday when the feint was made in the form of air raids on Dutch Harbor. The same day the fleets in the Midway area commenced their now historic battle.

(reprinted in *Washington Times-Herald*, in the holdings of the Franklin Roosevelt Library) incommunicado for days. "They were not allowed to see any newspapers whatsoever during the time they were in Arizona and while they were en route to New York City," J. Edgar Hoover wrote. Nor were they allowed access to any newspapers in New York City.[19]

Some detainees were granted somewhat more latitude. Japanese envoys stationed in South America—who had been rounded up and located at Grove Park Inn, in Asheville, North Carolina—were permitted to read the *New York Times*. So were the many Japanese diplomats who had served in Washington, and at consulates around the United States, held since April at White Sulphur Springs, West Virginia. Both sets of detainees were placed on board trains that reached New York City on 11 June. Upon their arrival they were immediately placed on board the *Gripsholm*. "While in West Virginia and while en route to New York City this group was allowed to read the *New York Times* only," Hoover wrote. The *Times* must have sold a lot of papers in June, but from a security point of view, one fact stands out: the *Times* did not subscribe to the *Chicago Tribune*'s news service. It did not run Stanley Johnston's article. The *Times* would not begin its reporting of the *Tribune* scandal until early August—by which time these Japanese travelers would have been long gone and far removed from the offerings of America's media behemoths.[20]

In all likelihood, none of those groups stumbled on the *Tribune* article. They had been too carefully guarded. But they were not the only detainees. There existed a fourth group of about five hundred Japanese citizens—also homebound—which had not been kept as isolated as those sheltered in Arizona, North Carolina, and West Virginia. Arriving from different parts of the country, they started assembling at the Pennsylvania Hotel on 7 June and continued to show up through 11 June. Some had been held for a while on Ellis Island. Others had been detained at various Army camps. Still others had been at liberty for months, learning very late that if they wanted transport back to Japan, they should proceed to New York City. "Many of those who were at liberty," Hoover told Biddle, "had access . . . to any newspaper which they might desire to purchase."[21]

FBI agents wondered what these people might have read. Upon arriving at the Pennsylvania Hotel, they were questioned and searched. Before boarding the *Gripsholm* they were searched again. Their baggage was checked. They were not allowed to take with them any printed matter. They endured a far more rigorous scrutiny than did the diplomats, who surprisingly enough

Admiral Nimitz's 31 May 1942 dispatch, as sent from CINCPAC

U.S. NAVAL COMMUNICATION SERVICE
COMMANDER-IN-CHIEF
U.S. PACIFIC FLEET

CLASSIFIED OUTGOING

Date 31 MAY 42

From: CINCPAC

To: ALL TF COMDRS PACFLT

Info. To: COMINCH

Classification	Originator	C.W.O.
SECRET	25	ECW

Release OP) 00, 01.

System RDO — Show to 11,16,17 1338

CINC PACIFIC FLEET ESTIMATE MIDWAY FORCE ORGANIZATION X STRIKING FORCE 4 CARRIERS (AKAGI KAGA HIRYU SORYU) 2 KIRISHIMAS 2 TONE CLASS CRUISERS 12 DESTROYERS SCREEN AND PLANE GUARD X SUPPORT FORCE 1 DW OR XCV 2 KIRISHIMAS 4 MOGAMIS 1 ATAGO 10 DD SCREEN XX OCCUPATION FORCE 1 TAKAO 1-2 MYOKOS (QUESTION) 1 CHITOSE 1 CHI-YODA 2-4 KAMIKAWA MARU 4-6 AK 8-12 AP 12 DESTROYERS X APPROXIMATE-- LY 16 SS ON RECONNAISANCE AND SCOUTING MISSION MID PACIFIC-HAWAI-IAN ISLANDS AREA.

311221

ORIGINATOR

Admiral Nimitz's 31 May 1942 dispatch, as decrypted on *Barnett*

NAVAL MESSAGE   NAVY DEPARTMENT

DRAFTER	EXTENSION NUMBER		ADDRESSEES	PRECEDENCE
FROM _CINCPAC (NERK)_ RELEASED BY ____ DATE _(2 June)_ _1 JUNE 1942_ TOR CODEROOM _0122/ 0024_ DECODED BY _NEWHOUSE/NEWHOUSE_ PARAPHRASED BY		FOR ACTION	ALL TASK COMMANDERS PAC	PRIORITY ROUTINE DEFERRED
		INFORMATION	COMINCH	PRIORITY ROUTINE DEFERRED

INDICATE BY ASTERISK ADDRESSEES FOR WHICH MAIL DELIVERY IS SATISFACTORY.

may 311221 OCR 1713 J

UNLESS OTHERWISE INDICATED THIS DISPATCH WILL BE TRANSMITTED WITH DEFERRED PRECEDENCE.

ORIGINATOR FILL IN DATE AND TIME	DATE	TIME	GCT

TEXT

FROM CINCPAC INFO TO COMINCH

CINC PACIFIC FLEET ESTIMATE MIDWAY FORCE ORGANIZATION X
STRIKING FORCE FOUR CARRIERS (AKAGI KAGA HIRYU SORYU)
TWO KIRISHIMAL TWO TONE CLASS CRUISERS 12 DESTROYERS SCREEN
AND PLANE GUARD X SUPPORT FORCE ONE UNIT VICTOR OR XRAY
CAST VICTOR 2 KIRISHIMAS 4 MOGAMIS (1 ATAGO) 10 DD SCREEN X
OCCUPATION FORCE (1 TAKAO) ONE DASSWI TWO MYOKOS (QUESTION)
ONE CHITOMS ONE CHIYODA TWO DASH FOUR (KAUIKAWA MARU) JOIN
DASH SIX (AFIRM KING) EIGHT SLANT TWELVE (AFIRM PREP) TWELVE
DESTROYERS X APPROXIMATELY (SIXTEEN) SAIL SAIL ON
RECONNAISANCE AND SCOUTING MISSION MID PACIFIC DASH
HAWAIIAN ISLANDS AREA

COPY DELIVERED TO 20G..   F 35

SECRET

The Foreman

Jury foreman John O. Holmes may have played a larger role in the grand jury's decision to throw out the case against Stanley Johnston, J. Loy "Pat" Maloney, and the *Chicago Tribune* than the jury's transcripts would lead a reader of those documents to believe. By the time jurors convened to hear the *Tribune* case, they had been in session nearly a month; its members were getting impatient and wanted to go home.[1] From Holmes's account of jury deliberations, confided years later in a letter to Robert McCormick, the decision not to indict was a cliffhanger. According to Holmes, most jury members wanted to absolve Johnston and Maloney but indict the *Tribune* as a corporation. Holmes said he argued that "both employer and employee should be treated as one," a view that jury members accepted. He believed this shift in perspective influenced the jury's final decision.[2] No transcript was made for the jury's final day in session, 19 August 1942, when the jurors voted to return no indictment against the *Tribune* personnel. Holmes's letter is the only record of that day's proceedings besides Special Prosecutor William Mitchell's correspondence with Attorney General Francis Biddle.[3]

Holmes undoubtedly acted out of conviction. But another factor might also have been at work: his sister had died during the grand jury proceeding. The *Tribune*'s circulation manager, Louis Rose, learned that the dead woman had an insurance policy that had been offered by the *Tribune* to its subscribers. He cashed the policy; then he detailed one of his staff members to deliver the $2,000 personally to the family of the deceased. Rose later claimed some of the credit for the ensuing grand jury action.[4]

Notes

Introduction

Epigraph. Memoir, Book III, Section 2, p. 323, Box 5, Papers of Byron Price, 1908–1944, Wisconsin Historical Society, Madison, Wis.

1. On 4 June 1942, warplanes from three Pacific Fleet carriers—*Hornet, Enterprise,* and *Yorktown*—bombed and demolished four Imperial Japanese Navy carriers: *Kaga, Akagi, Soryu,* and *Hiryu.* On 7 June, the already-damaged *Yorktown* was lost when it was torpedoed by the Japanese submarine *I-168.*

2. Quoted in "Eyewitness," by Robert Mason, U.S. Naval *Proceedings* 108 (June 1982): 43.

3. *Chicago Tribune,* 7 June 1942. The headline atop the *Times-Herald* story was slightly different: "U.S. Navy Knew In Advance All about Jap Fleet."

4. ULTRA, *Oxford Companion to World War II,* gen. ed. I. C. B. Dear (Oxford: Oxford University Press, 1995), 1165–71.

5. USA ULTRA, by Waldo Heinrichs, in *Oxford Companion to World War II,* gen. ed. I. C. B. Dear (Oxford University Press, 1995), 1171–74.

6. Marshall letter to Dewey, 27 September 1944, *For Mr. Dewey's eyes only,* reproduced in *The American Magic,* by Ronald Lewin (Penguin Books, 1982), 9–12.

7. Joe Rochefort oral history, U.S. Naval Institute, Annapolis, Md., 218–33; see also *Joe Rochefort's War,* by Elliot Carlson (Annapolis, Md.: Naval Institute Press, 2011), 273–74, 348–61.

8. *Newsweek,* 17 August 1942, 64–65.

9. Twenty-five years would pass before Americans learned of the ULTRA secret, primarily through three books: *The Codebreakers,* by David Kahn (New York: Scribner, 1967); *Incredible Victory,* by Walter Lord (New York: Harper & Row, 1967); and *The Broken Seal,* by Ladislas Farago (London: Arthur Barker, 1967).

10. This version of events was erroneously attributed to Lieutenant Commander Edwin T. Layton in an article by Grant Sanger, M.D., titled "Freedom of the Press or Treason?" in U.S. Naval Institute *Proceedings* 103 (September 1977): 96–97. Sanger cited Layton's U.S. Naval Institute "oral history," wherein Johnston was alleged to have discovered the dispatch posted on a *Saratoga* bulletin board and copied it. The main thing wrong with Sanger's story is that no such anecdote can be found in Layton's oral history; Layton did not

write what was attributed to him. Where Sanger got the story about Johnston and *Saratoga*, and why he attributed it to Layton, is unknown.

11. Grant Sanger said he heard this story in a 1959 conversation with
Stevenson. According to Sanger, Stevenson purported to be familiar with
Johnston's grand jury testimony. In this version, the correspondent was rescued from the Coral Sea by a whaleboat from the cruiser *New Orleans*. The
cruiser allegedly transported Johnston to Noumea, New Caledonia. There
it disembarked *Lexington* survivors, turned around, and headed back to
Pearl Harbor, with Johnston said to be still on board. During the return
trip to Pearl Harbor, Johnston supposedly wandered through the captain's
cabin and noticed an open message on his desk; he looked at it and mem-
orized its content. When *New Orleans* docked at Pearl Harbor on 26 May,
Johnston—writing from Honolulu—reputedly filed the story that caused
all the trouble. Unfortunately for Stevenson's theory, if Sanger remembered
it correctly, records show that Johnston was never on board *New Orleans*.
Stevenson's story was recounted by Sanger in his *Proceedings* article cited
above. It is retold in "Spilling the Secret," by Captain Lawrence B. Brennan,
USN (Ret.), printed in the *Universal Ship Cancellation Society*, and available
on the Naval Historical Foundation website at http://www.navyhistory.org.

12. Many excellent books cover the problem of press freedom during wartime. Four particularly good ones are *Perilous Times: Free Speech in Wartime: From the Sedition Act of 1798 to the War on Terrorism*, by Geoffrey R.
Stone (New York: W. W. Norton, 2005); *War and Press Freedom: The Problem of Prerogative Power*, by Jeffery A. Smith (New York: Oxford University
Press, 1999); *Necessary Secrets: National Security, The Media, and the Rule
of Law*, by Gabriel Schoenfeld (New York: W. W. Norton, 2010); and *The
Military and the Press*, by Michael S. Sweeney (Evanston, Ill.: Northwestern
University Press, 2006).

Chapter 1. A Date with Lady Lex

1. Stanley Johnston, interview by William Mitchell, 13 July 1942 (hereafter Johnston-Mitchell 13 July interview), Washington, D.C., *Chicago Tribune* files, XI-175, Box 2, Folder 13, McCormick Research Center (hereafter
MRC), Cantigny Park, Ill.

2. Confidential letter from commander in chief, U.S. Pacific Fleet, C. W.
Nimitz, to commanding officer, *Lexington*, 14 April 1942, included in FBI
investigation into Stanley Johnston and *Chicago Tribune*, FBI records, File
100-HQ-22351-156, Box 1562, Record Group 65, National Archives and

Records Administration II, College Park, Md. (hereafter NARAII), obtained by the writer through the Freedom of Information Act (hereafter FOIA).

3. Stanley Johnston, *Queen of the Flat-Tops* (New York: E. P. Dutton, 1942), 62.

4. Johnston-Mitchell 13 July interview.

5. Ibid.

6. Seligman testimony, 13 August 1942, Department of Justice (hereafter DOJ) file, 146-7-23-25, RG 60, Grand Jury testimony, vols. 1 and 2, pp. 79–80, NARAII.

7. This portrait of Drake is drawn from four sources: Brayton Harris, *Admiral Nimitz* (New York: Palgrave Macmillan, 2011), 145; Robert B. Davies, *Baldwin of the Times* (Annapolis, Md.: Naval Institute Press, 2011), 137; George W. Healy Jr., *A Lifetime on Deadline* (Gretna, La.: Pelican Publishing, 1976), 141–42. Reporters' complaints also show up in Drake's correspondence with his Washington superiors. See letter from Drake to Captain W. A. Kitts III, USN, 20 February 1942, Navy Department, Washington, D.C., and letter from Drake to Captain Leland P. Lovette, USN, Office of Public Relations, Navy Department, Washington, D.C., 1 April 1942, Records Relating to Public Relations, 1940–46, RG 313, Container 4, NARAII.

8. *Memorandum for War Correspondents*, 9 January 1942, Flag Files 1942–1943, RG 313, Box 12, NARAII.

9. Statement of Lt. Cmdr. Waldo Drake, witnessed in Honolulu by FBI Agent Wayne S. Murphy, included in confidential FBI memorandum, 23 June 1942, File 100-22351-156, NARAII. See also radiogram from FBI Agent Ladd to FBI Director Hoover, from Honolulu, 21 June 1942, FBI records, File 100-22351-103, RG 65, NARAII.

10. *Agreement for War Correspondents*, 7 April 1942, Pacific Fleet Public Relations, RG 313, Box 13, Folder for War Correspondents, NARAII.

11. Johnston denied that he was briefed by Drake before he boarded the carrier, although he agreed he had discussed censorship issues with the officer earlier. See Johnston-Mitchell 13 July interview, 13. Drake told two stories. He and his assistant, Lt. James E. Bassett Jr., USNR, in separate statements, 23 June 1942, told FBI investigators they did brief Johnston before he embarked the ship; see FBI records, File 100-HQ-22351-156, RG 65, NARAII. Earlier, however, on 17 June 1942, Drake admitted in a telephone conversation with his Washington superior, Cmdr. R. W. Berry, that he had given Johnston "no specific verbal instructions" on 15 April, the day of the *Lexington*'s departure. See Hoover memo to FBI communications section,

18 June 1942, FBI records, File 100-HQ-22351-55, RG 65, NARAII. Drake's 17 June story appears to be the more credible one.

12. Johnston, *Queen of the Flat-Tops*, 85.

13. This portrait of Johnston is based on two sources. First, see Army G-2 investigation of Johnston conducted in June 1942 by Sixth Corps Area Headquarters, Chicago, Illinois, cited in FBI memorandum submitted by Agent J. R. Yore, 18 June 1942, FBI records, File 100-22351-97, RG 65, NARAII; see also FBI interview with Lt. Cmdr. E. J. O'Donnell, 13 June 1942, Grand Jury records, RG 60, Section 7, File 146-7-23-25, obtained by author via FOIA, NARAII.

14. W. D. "Don" Maxwell, interview by Harold E. Hutchings, 18 September 1974, Tribune Oral History Project, Tribune Company Archives, MRC.

15. "The Stanley Johnston Story," *Chicago Tribune* Promotion Department sketch, 26 March 1942, Kirkland-Ellis Files, XI-175, Box 1, Folder 3, MRC (hereafter "The Stanley Johnston Story," MRC).

16. An article in the 28 July 1957 *Chicago Tribune,* written by aviation editor Wayne Thomis, described Johnston's father as a civil engineer. But FBI agent George E. Lipe noted that Johnston's father was described in the journalist's birth certificate as a fisherman, living in Lismore, New South Wales, Australia. Lipe report, 19 June 1942, FBI case 100-22351-111, RG 65, NARAII.

17. "The Stanley Johnston Story," MRC. See also the *Chicago Tribune* story about Johnston, 28 July 1957, and the *Tribune* obituary of Johnston, 14 September 1962.

18. The charge that Johnston had misrepresented himself as an officer in the Australian army appears in a letter to Johnston in London from the president of Press Wireless, Inc., Joseph Pierson, in Chicago, 16 April 1940. McCormick Papers, XI-175, Box 1, Folder 3, MRC. Press Wireless discontinued its employment of Johnston when it learned of the falsification.

19. This finding reflects the research of Canberra-based historian Joe Straczek. At the request of historian John Lundstrom, Straczek located Johnston's war records at the National Archives of Australia (NAA) in Sydney. The NAA documents confirm Johnston's enlistment in the Royal Australian Naval Reserves as well as the dates of that service and the various units with which he served during his years with the RANR. The author is indebted to both Straczek and Lundstrom for their efforts on his behalf.

20. For workings of the Brigade, see "The Royal Australian Naval Brigade," chapter 12, in *Official History of the Australian War of 1914–18,* vol. 9, 9th ed. (Sydney, Australia: Angus and Robertson, 1941), by Arthur Wilberforce Jose.

21. Muster list showing Johnston assigned to *Cerberus, The Royal Australian Naval Brigade 1914–1920, A Brief History and Nominal Roll,* comp. Sergeant P. I. Blackwell (Canberra: Australian Defence Force Academy, 1994). This document was provided to the author by Joe Straczek.

22. HMS Suffolk logbook, June 1917 to October 1919, China Station (Part 2 of 2), http://www.naval-history.net/OWShips-WWI-05-HMS.

23. Johnston's service record is contained in RAN form, Application for War Gratuity, 27 August 1920, NAA; document provided author by Joe Straczek.

24. Medal Card for Johnstone [*sic*], S.C.S., shows Johnston entitled only to War Medal, issued by District Naval Officer Edgecliff, 11 November 1922, NAA; document provided author by Joe Straczek.

25. Larry J. Frank, "The United States v. The Chicago Tribune," *The Historian* 42 (February 1980): 285–86.

26. "The Stanley Johnston Story," MRC.

27. An FBI report identified her as a dancer at the Paradise Cabaret, Broadway at 49th Street, New York, Grand Jury records, Section 4, File 146-7-23-25, RG 60, NARAII.

28. Stanley Claude Johnston Espionage-J, FBI Memorandum for E. A. Tamm, 16 June 1942, FBI records, File 100-HQ-22351-67, RG 65, NARAII.

29. SPECIAL REPORT, from: Immigration and Naturalization Service, DOJ, to: FBI, 17 June 1942, FBI records, File 100-HQ-22351-53X4, RG 65, NARAII. See also FBI memo by Agent J. R. Yore, 18 June 1942, File 100-22351-97, RG 65, NARAII.

30. "Background of Stanley Claude Samuel Johnston," FBI Summary Memorandum, undated, FBI records, File 100-HQ-22351-181, RG 65, NARAII (hereafter "Background of Stanley Claude Samuel Johnston," FBI). See also Richard Norton Smith's biography of Robert M. McCormick, *The Colonel* (New York: Houghton Mifflin Company, 1997), 434.

31. FBI Memo from Agent C. C. Kimball to Hoover, 17 June 1942, FBI records, File 100-HQ-22351-55X2, RG 65, NARAII.

32. Stanley Claude Johnston, Mrs. Stanley Claude Johnston, née Barbara Beck or Incagnoli, FBI report, 18 June 1942, Grand Jury records, File 146-7-23-25, Section 4, Boxes 771–72, RG 60, NARAII obtained by writer through FOIA.

33. Confidential FBI report, from: Agent J. R. Yore, To: Hoover, 18 June 1942, FBI records, File 100-HQ-22351-97, RG 65, NARAII.

34. Ibid. See also U.S. Naval Intelligence Service report on Johnston, Third Naval District, interviews with Donald K. Neuf and J. B. Pierson of Press Wireless, 17 July 1941, File 100-22351-4, NARAII.

35. "Background of Stanley Claude Samuel Johnston," FBI.

36. Larry Rue letter to *Tribune* headquarters, Chicago, 28 August 1940, "The Stanley Johnston Story," MRC.

37. Smith, *The Colonel*, 434.

38. Stanley Johnston letter to Joseph Pierson, 31 July 1940, Tribune Company Archives, XI-175, Box 1, Folder 3, MRC.

39. Stanley Johnston letter to Joseph Pierson, 12 November 1940, Tribune Company Archives, XI-175, Box 1, Folder 3, MRC.

40. Joseph Pierson letter to Stanley Johnston, 22 January 1941, Tribune Company Archives, XI-175, Box 1, Folder 3, MRC.

41. Louis Huot letter to Joseph Pierson, 15 April 1941, Tribune Company Archives, XI-175, Box 1, Folder 3, MRC.

42. Even though Barbara was in German-occupied France, she and Stanley managed to communicate, although investigators were not sure how. One FBI report suggested they wrote letters passed back and forth by the Vichy regime; another report noted they may have exchanged letters through Switzerland. However they did it, they stayed in touch.

43. Stanley Johnston letter to Joseph Pierson, 11 March 1941, Tribune Company Archives, MRC.

44. Stanley Johnston letter to Joseph Pierson, 17 March 1941, Tribune Company Archives, MRC. Johnston's claim that he contacted Lord Mountbatten early in 1941 must be taken with a grain of salt. As historian John Lundstrom informed the author, Mountbatten was on board the destroyer HMS *Kelly* in the Mediterranean at that time; Mountbatten gained fame when the destroyer was sunk in May 1941 off Crete.

45. Larry Rue cable to *Tribune* headquarters, Chicago, 23 May 1941, Tribune Company Archives, MRC.

46. Maxwell Oral History, MRC.

47. Jerome E. Edwards, *The Foreign Policy of Col. McCormick's* Tribune (Reno: University of Nevada Press, 1971), 12–13, 21–39.

48. How did Johnston obtain his citizenship papers so quickly? Johnston told the *Lexington*'s captain, Frederick Sherman, that the fast action stemmed from his intelligence work for the State Department. He told Sherman the State Department specifically requested that he be quickly naturalized because the type of work he was doing could be better handled if he were an American citizen. (See FBI interview with Sherman by D. A. Fish, 16 June 1942, San Diego, Grand Jury Records, 146-7-23-25, Section 2, RG 60, Boxes 771–72, NARAII.) This was a tall tale. No evidence ever turned

what any other man would have one, Sherman said he had no doubts. "His work was sufficiently outstanding and above what the ordinary man would have done, for me to feel justified in making that recommendation."[10]

Not all the Navy witnesses who followed Sherman into the jury room shared his enthusiasm for Johnston. But they, too, had important stories to tell. Lieutenant Daniel Bonteou was the chief communications officer on board the transport *Barnett*, the ship on which Johnston and several hundred officers and men had returned to the United States after the sinking of *Lexington*. Bonteou had been one of Johnston's harshest critics on the transport. His testimony turned out to be dry, but it was significant. He was asked only to describe how decrypted messages were handled on board the vessel. He restated what he had told the FBI weeks earlier: messages intercepted in the communications center (closed off to all but authorized personnel) were delivered to a decoding room (accessible only through the communications center), where *Barnett* and *Lexington* specialists decrypted the messages and stamped them according to their level of classification: secret, confidential, or restricted. Decrypt officers could tell which was which by the particular code used in the dispatch; the code was determined by the originating officer, an officer like Admiral Nimitz.[11]

Because he was authorized to do so by Navy Secretary Knox, Bonteou presented to the grand jury a copy of Admiral Nimitz's ill-starred 31 May 1942 dispatch. It showed the admiral's estimate of the Japanese force descending on Midway. The exhibit was a reproduction of that dispatch—Message 31121—as it had been decoded on board *Barnett*. It was the centerpiece of the government's case against Johnston. All the crossed out words, misspellings, and rough edges were there. Jurors could see how the ships named in the *Tribune* article matched up with those in Nimitz's dispatch. As did the *Tribune* article, the message divided Japanese forces into three parts: a striking force with four carriers (*Akaga, Kaga, Hiryu, Soryu*) and, among others, two *Kirishimas* (spelled differently from *Jane's Fighting Ships*); a support force, with two *Kirishimas*, along with other ships; and an occupation force, which included strange ship types: one *Chakao*, two *Myokos*, one *Chitosk*, one *Chiyoda*, and to complete the picture, sixteen submarines. "I would like to have the Grand Jury see this message," Mitchell said.[12]

Ordinarily, Bonteou said, this message would be placed in a folder and delivered first to *Barnett*'s commanding officer, Captain William B. Phillips. Then, if the captain had no objections, the folder would be handed to

Lexington's senior coding officer, Lieutenant F. C. Brewer, who would pass it to the *Lexington's* five authorized recipients: the carrier's executive officer, Commander Morton Seligman, and four *Lexington* department heads, Lieutenant Commander Edward J. O'Donnell and three commanders, Herbert S. Duckworth, Winthrop C. Terry, and A. F. Junker. But there were limitations as to what this officer could truthfully tell jurors. Asked whether a copy of this message might have been shown to someone not authorized to see it, Bontecou said he did not know, that he had no way of knowing. *Lexington's* Brewer had circulated it, not him. Brewer was not in Chicago; he had not been lined up to testify on 13 August.[13]

Bontecou did get one pertinent question from a juror. Did Johnston at any time appear near *Barnett's* coding room? "No, sir, not to my knowledge," he said. "I questioned all the men on the ship, and they had never seen him around there." He added that to get to the coding room, an individual would have had to go through the "radio shack," or communications center, an area off limits to all but a few.[14] Bontecou was never asked his appraisal of Johnston, nor did he volunteer it. Jurors never heard his suspicions about Johnston—the concerns about the reporter's trustworthiness he had shared with Captain Phillips and later divulged to the FBI.

Bontecou could not solve one of the nagging puzzles in the Johnston case: What happened to Message 311221 after it left the radio shack? That task fell to the two *Lexington* lieutenant commanders, Edward J. O'Donnell and Edward H. Eldredge. With Mitchell asking the questions, O'Donnell sketched a description of life on board *Barnett* that by now was familiar to grand jurors: Navy officers liked to drink coffee and socialize in the evening. On the evening of 31 May, he and Eldredge wandered over to Seligman's quarters for a cup of coffee. Entering the suite, he encountered Lieutenant Commander Robert Dixon, the commander of a dive-bomber squadron. "[He] mentioned to me there was hot news, or words to that effect, and he indicated a piece of paper that somebody was reading at the table," O'Donnell said. "I can't remember who was reading it."[15]

Asked what sort of paper it was, O'Donnell portrayed it as "a piece of standard Navy scratch paper, white paper with blue lines on it." Horizontal blue lines? "Horizontal blue lines."[16]

Did O'Donnell happen to see what was on this piece of paper? Mitchell asked. "Yes, I saw it," the officer said. "It was a list of Japanese men of war, arranged, as I subsequently found, very much as the dispatchers arranged it, it was secret or not," he snapped. He said the jurors would soon be presented with additional evidence.[26]

∼

Jurors then received an eyewitness account that could have aroused doubts about the *Tribune* correspondent. The story came from two *Lexington* communications watch officers who had been assigned to *Barnett*'s code room: Lieutenant (jg) James B. Johnson and Lieutenant (jg) George Y. McKinnon. The two joined three other *Lexington* communications officers on what Johnson called a Coding Board—an ad hoc group set up on *Barnett* to decode messages transmitted by the Pacific Fleet and other originators.[27] Johnson remembered seeing Message 31 1221 on 31 May; McKinnon remembered decoding it, but he could not recall whether he circulated it to those *Lexington* officers or whether Brewer had. Most witnesses agreed it had been Brewer.[28]

Regardless of who circulated the Nimitz dispatch that night, both Johnson and McKinnon had seen it, and they had seen other secret messages decrypted in *Barnett*'s decoding room. Along with Brewer, they had taken turns circulating them to *Lexington* officers authorized to see them. They knew what was in these messages. They did not like the idea that Stanley Johnston was anywhere near them. "I think the only reason I am here," Johnson told jurors, "is because Lieutenant McKinnon and myself noticed [Stanley] Johnston was in the quarters, where he would be able to obtain things by possibly overhearing, or any way you can pick them up, and newspapermen know how to do it. We had a little trouble with [him] there."[29]

Johnson and McKinnon took their concerns to their immediate superior, Lieutenant I. E. Davis, also on board *Barnett*. "I went with McKinnon to Davis," Johnson said, "and warned him that [Stanley] Johnston was in such a position that he could secure possible information by overhearing or possibly reading over somebody's shoulder at one time or another." The officer admitted he did not actually see the correspondent doing any such thing, but he quickly added that "Johnston impressed me as the kind of fellow who would go pretty far to gain his ends."[30]

After hearing Johnson and McKinnon lay out their concerns, Davis proceeded to give the two younger men a lecture on Navy politics. As Johnson recounted Davis's words, there was a higher-ranking officer involved in the matter: Commander Seligman. "[In] the Navy a higher ranking officer over

you is a higher ranking officer, and there is nothing we can tell him about it,"
Davis told the two junior officers, adding, "There is nothing I can do about
it, or nothing you can do about it, because he is your superior officer." When
Johnson started to protest, Davis cut him off: "[Davis said] that it wasn't up
to him, that it was none of his business."[31]

～

Seligman would seem to have a lot of explaining to do. The officer certainly
did a lot of talking, but he was not in good shape. Still reeling from the
wounds he sustained during the Imperial Navy's 8 May attack on his carrier,
he looked tired, seemed disoriented at times, and still walked with a limp.
His testimony was disjointed; he rambled and veered off on tangents. He had
a hard time remembering things that seemed important to Mitchell. "[My]
memory has been pretty well shattered because I got blown up," Seligman
told jurors, "and I can't remember little details, but I am trying to paste it
together." Among things he could not recall was Nimitz's Message 311221,
received and decrypted on board the transport on 31 May, "I don't remember
that message," Seligman said.[32]

Mitchell informed him that two witnesses—both officers on his staff—
reported that during the evening of 31 May, they saw officers sitting around
the table in his suite looking at a document that was on Navy paper, with
blue lines, and it had written on it, in pencil, an estimate of the Japanese
striking force, support force, and occupation force, with a number of ships
listed under each force. Mitchell asked whether he could remember seeing
anything like that. "I don't remember it specifically," Seligman said, "but it
certainly may have been there." He provided some context, indicating why
this message might have eluded him. "I was in a terrific mental state," he said.
"I had a tremendous amount of work to do. We had 2,400-odd men that
we had to get rehabilitated. We had discussions constantly. There were any
number of messages that came in, and naturally, if you are out there, you are
going to discuss the war."[33]

Would he, or any other officer, have made notes from this or any other
message circulated on *Barnett*? He would, and they would, Seligman said.
"[We] might have a stack this thick," he said, indicating the thickness with his
hands, "maybe twenty, forty or fifty of them, and we would run through them
this way, and put our initials on." He added, "On some, we might stop and
make some notes, because that is a very common practice in the Navy. You

that is, a breakdown into basic groups: occupation force, support force," and he added upon questioning, "an attack force." Mitchell showed O'Donnell a photostat of Message 311221. Had the officer seen this message—the original 311221—that night? "Not that night, no, sir," O'Donnell said. Was it shown to you the next day? "Yes, sir, the next afternoon." Who showed it to you? "One of the young communications watch officers," O'Donnell said, "I don't remember which one."[17]

A slightly astonished Mitchell summed up: "Then, as a matter of fact, you saw in Seligman's quarters there was a piece of paper on which was written the substance of this dispatch, before you saw the original, is that so?"[18]

"Yes, sir,"[19] was the response.

An incredulous Mitchell asked to hear that again. After all, as he understood the routine from Bontecou and other communications officers, decrypted messages were supposed to be circulated just once, then returned to the radio shack and locked in a safe. Mitchell did not say so, but he must have thought, and any juror paying attention would have justifiably concluded, that there had been a fundamental breakdown in *Barnett's*—and Seligman's—protocol for handling secret documents. Now a juror had a question: Did O'Donnell have any idea how the contents of the Nimitz message ended up on a piece of scratch paper? Did he know who made a copy of it? O'Donnell said he did not know. "The original dispatch was not there when I got there," the officer said. "I merely saw this memorandum on the big table there, and I don't even recall in whose possession it was at the time I saw it. I recall reading it over somebody's shoulder."[20]

Mitchell asked about Johnston. Was he in the room? If so, did he see Johnston looking at that piece of paper? "I didn't see Johnston read that memorandum," O'Donnell said, "no, I didn't." But, yes, Johnston was in the room. He repeated what he had earlier told the FBI. "I was first aware of Johnston's presence when, sometime, probably after I read this paper, I can't be sure of the exact time, Johnston came to me and said—the thing I remember most distinctly is, that he came to me and said, 'That will be the hell-of-a-fight, Mac [O'Donnell's nickname]. How would you like to be in it?'—something like that."[21] Johnston's question, of course, indicated that he was familiar with the contents of the scratch paper.

But O'Donnell could take the story no further. He could not explain how Johnston obtained that information. He had no idea why Message 311221 remained accessible a day after the evening session in Seligman's stateroom, when it should have been locked away. He noted that, hypothetically, an officer with appropriate authority could have signed out for it if he needed it for research he was doing. If an officer did so, considering all the detail in the original and to save time, would this officer ever make a memorandum from it—that is, a copy? "He wouldn't make a memorandum, sir, because, in general, that is pretty expressly forbidden," O'Donnell said. He said he could not remember who showed him the original or under what circumstances. He did not know what happened to the piece of scratch paper. New puzzles had surfaced.[22]

~

After hearing the troubling testimony of O'Donnell and Eldredge (Eldredge's account essentially paralleled O'Donnell's), grand jurors found themselves with more questions than answers. Mitchell now began to experience some pushback from jurors. During a pause between witnesses, conversing alone with the jurors in the U.S. attorney's meeting room, Mitchell now heard some jurors take a more benign view of Johnston than he might have liked. The jury's foreman, John Holmes, asked the prosecutor, "How do you account for the fact that a message of so great importance should be left lying on the table in this manner?"[23]

Mitchell said he could not be certain. "One way of accounting for it, possibly, is that some naval officer did make a copy," he told Holmes. "There doesn't seem to be any doubt of that." Holmes remained curious: "Was there on that piece of scratch paper anything that would indicate it was taken from a secret message, or was it just a list of ships?" Mitchell had to admit there was probably no such marking on the piece of paper. "There was merely a list of ships, with the titles," he said, "but I wouldn't want to say that for sure."[24]

Holmes would not let the matter drop. He repeated his question: was Mitchell intending to tell the grand jury that the list of ships presumably seen by Johnston, and presumably shaped by him into a newspaper article, carried no warning that it was drawn from a secret dispatch? "No mark on it," answered Mitchell. "But may I suggest that the article published in the Tribune, that came from that paper on the desk, [it] parallels the original secret message?"[25]

"Then if Mr. Johnston saw that list on the table," Holmes went on, "he had no way of knowing whether it was a secret message of any kind?" Mitchell was now getting impatient. "It is not of vital importance whether he knew up that Johnston did intelligence for the State Department. Other explanations are more plausible. On 13 November 1941, Johnston filed for citizenship under a section of the 1941 immigration law providing for expeditious naturalization of an alien spouse of a U.S. citizen employed abroad by the American government or by a firm engaged in foreign commerce. Barbara Beck's work in Paris in 1941 (for the *New York Times* and the U.S. Consulate) may have enabled Johnston to qualify. (See 2 July 1942 Department of Justice memo, FBI records, file 100-22-351-193, RG 65, Box 1562, NARAII.) An FBI report stated, "It is understood that [Johnston's] acquisition of citizenship was expedited on the grounds that Johnston was married to an American citizen."

49. "The Stanley Johnston Story," MRC.

50. "Accrediting and Instructing of Stanley Johnston as a Correspondent," 9 August 1942, FBI Summary Memorandum, FBI records, File 100-HQ-22351-181, RG 65, NARAII.

51. "The Stanley Johnston Story," MRC.

52. Edwards, *The Foreign Policy of Col. McCormick's Tribune*, 29.

53. On 21 April 1942, Lt. Edward Henry "Butch" O'Hare was awarded the Medal of Honor. A few years later, the *Chicago Tribune* publisher Robert R. McCormick suggested that the name of Chicago's Orchard Depot Airport be renamed in O'Hare's honor. On 19 September 1949, the airport was officially named O'Hare International Airport.

54. "The Stanley Johnston Story," MRC.

55. Ibid.

56. *Directive for War Correspondents*, 28 April 1942, Navy Department, RG 313, Container 10, NARAII.

57. John B. Lundstrom, *The First Team* (Annapolis, Md.: Naval Institute Press, 1984), 165–66.

58. Johnston, *Queen of the Flat-Tops*, 20–24.

59. Ibid.

60. Lundstrom, *The First Team*, 166

61. Johnston, *Queen of the Flat-Tops*, 23–24.

62. Lundstrom, *The First Team*, 47–48, 146, 163.

63. Mark Stille, *The Coral Sea 1942* (Oxford: Osprey Publishing, 2009), 15.

64. "Spilling the Secret," by Lawrence B. Brennan, 2, Naval Historical Foundation, Washington, D.C.

65. Seligman service record, National Personnel Records Center, NARA, St. Louis, Mo.

66. FBI interview with Commander Morton T. Seligman, reported in memo from Agent D. M. Ladd to Quinn Tamm, 13 June 1942, FBI records, File 100-HQ-22351-23, NARAII.

67. Elliot Carlson, *Joe Rochefort's War* (Annapolis, Md.: Naval Institute Press, 2011), 270.

68. The idea that there might be four Japanese carriers was the result of a translation error made by U.S. Navy linguists; in fact, there were only three: escort carrier *Shoho* and fleet carriers *Zuikaku* and *Shokaku*.

Chapter 2. Guts and Glory

1. Johnston, *Queen of the Flat-Tops*, 62.

2. Ibid.

3. Ibid, 214–15.

4. Ibid.

5. Lundstrom, *The First Team*, 126–32.

6. Johnston, *Queen of the Flat-Tops*, 138, 154–55.

7. Ibid.

8. Ibid.

9. Historian John Lundstrom has informed the author that "gangster near fleet" and "It's a Kawanishi snooper" were terms made up by Johnston. Radar picked up those sightings, not a scout plane. Johnston probably used those terms because of censorship, since any mention of radar at that time was strictly forbidden.

10. Johnston's timing was off in this instance. Lundstrom points out that the Mavis did not show up until later in the morning, by which time Fitch and Fletcher had already guessed they had been spotted.

11. Johnston, *Queen of the Flat-Tops*, 170.

12. Lundstrom, *The First Team*, 191, 197–206.

13. Ibid.

14. The widely quoted phrase "Scratch one flat top! Dixon to carrier, scratch one flat top!" was originally quoted in Johnston's *Queen of the Flat-Tops*. Pacific War historian John Lundstrom reports that this quote is in error. For the correct Dixon quote, he refers readers to ComDesRon One (CTU 17 2.4) to CominCh, "Engagement with Japanese Forces 7–8 May 1942" (22 May 1942). See Lundstrom, *The First Team*, 510.

15. Johnston, *Queen of the Flat-Tops*, 193–94.

16. *Lexington* was fortunate to have on board Lieutenant Commander Ranson Fullinwider, a cryptolinguist on loan from Station Hypo, the Navy's

decrypt unit at Pearl Harbor. With his language and crypto skills, he would have been invaluable translating Japanese message traffic picked up by the carrier's radio.

17. Frederick C. "Ted" Sherman, Report of Action—The Battle of the Coral Sea, 7 and 8 May 1942, submitted to commander in chief, U.S. Pacific Fleet, 15 May 1942, http://www.ibiblio.org/hyperwar/USN/ships/logs/CV/CV2-Coral.html (hereafter Sherman, After Action Report).

18. Lundstrom, *The First Team*, 225–26.

19. Johnston, *Queen of the Flat-Tops*, 214.

20. Sherman, After Action Report.

21. Ibid.

22. Ibid.

23. Ibid.

24. Frederick C. Sherman, *Combat Command* (1950; New York: E. P. Dutton, Bantam edition, 1982), 90.

25. Johnston, *Queen of the Flat-Tops*, 250–51.

26. "Writer on Lexington Was Hero in Battle," 25 June 1942, *New York Times*, 8. Thanks to historian Richard Frank for providing this article.

27. Morton T. Seligman, Action in the Coral Sea, May 8, 1942, report submitted to Commanding Officer, Lexington, 14 May 1942, http://www.ibiblio.org/hyperwar/USN/ships/logs/CV/CV2-Coral.html (hereafter Seligman, After Action Report).

28. Sherman, *Combat Command*, 90–91. See also Sherman, After Action Report.

29. Sherman, *Combat Command*, 90–91. See also Sherman, After Action Report.

30. Sherman, *Combat Command*, 90–91. See also Sherman, After Action Report.

31. Ted Sherman's private diary, entry for 21 May 1942; excerpts from Sherman's Pacific War diary were provided by historian John Lundstrom from his own files, a contribution for which the author is extremely grateful. According to Sherman's diary, the captain and his dog were reunited several days later in Tongatabu on the cruiser *Chester*. Upon returning to the U.S. mainland, Sherman and Wags appeared together at several press conferences as he and the dog became a minor celebrities. (Hereafter, entries from this source will be referred to as Sherman diary, Lundstrom Papers.)

32. *New York Times*, 25 June 1942, p. 8.

33. Johnston, *Queen of the Flat-Tops*, 261–63.

34. Sherman, After Action Report.

35. Ibid.

36. Sherman, *Combat Command*, 93

37. Sherman, After Action Report.

38. Johnston, *Queen of the Flat-Tops*, 268–72.

39. Ibid.

40. Lundstrom, *The First Team*, 283–84.

41. Johnston-Mitchell 13 July 1942 interview by William Mitchell, MRC.

42. FBI Memorandum, Re: Stanley Claude Samuel Johnston Espionage-J, 20 June 1942, FBI records, File 100-HQ-22351-92, RG 65, NARAII.

43. USN Deck Logs, *Lexington*, 30 April–2 June 1942, RG 24, Box 5510, NARAII. *Lexington*'s log book was preserved during the Battle of the Coral Sea and augmented later to reflect the movements of the carrier's personnel.

44. The Kingdom of Tonga is the only monarchy in the Pacific. The United States owed its base there to Britain, which earlier in the century had agreed to serve as Tonga's protector. (Tonga terminated its agreement with Britain in 1970.)

45. Johnston, *Queen of the Flat-Tops*, 277.

46. Seligman, After Action Report.

Chapter 3. A Room with a View

Epigraph. FBI Report, "Interviews with Other Than U.S.S. *Barnett* Personnel," Undated, interview with Lt. Cmdr. Edward J. O'Donnell, by Agent T. B. Estep, Carmel, Calif., Grand Jury records (hereafter GJR), Section 7, File 146-7-23-25, Boxes 771–72, RG 60, NARAII obtained by author via FOIA.

1. FBI interview of Ensign O. T. Olson, *Barnett* billeting officer, by Special Agent G. A. Busch, FBI report titled "Interviews with U.S.S. *Barnett* Personnel," 13 June 1942, GJR, Section 7, File 14, RG 60, NARAII.

2. Ibid.

3. *Lexington* survivors were scattered all over the Pacific. Fifty-one survivors remained hospitalized in Noumea; another 14 were taken to the hospital ship *Solace*. The destroyer *Dobbin* transported 182 to Pearl Harbor, while *Yorktown* carried 9 back to Hawaii. Others were accommodated in unnamed locations. See *Lexington* deck logs, RG 19, Box 5510, NARAII.

4. *Yorktown* returned to Pearl Harbor on 27 May. After three days of emergency repairs, the carrier departed Pearl Harbor on 29 May and deployed

to waters northeast of Midway, where it joined sister carriers *Hornet* and *Enterprise* for the Battle of Midway on 4 June 1942.

5. Testimony of Cmdr. H. S. Duckworth, 11 June 1942. Duckworth commented that the Midway situation was a topic of conversation early on board *Barnett*, Greenslade conference, Navy Board of Inquiry, RG 457, Container 1397, NARAII (hereafter Greenslade conference, Navy Board of Inquiry).

6. Testimony of Cmdr. Morton Seligman, 11 June 1942, Greenslade conference, Navy Board of Inquiry (hereafter Seligman testimony, Navy Board of Inquiry).

7. FBI interviews with Capt. William B. Phillips, by Special Agent G. A. Busch, 13–15 June 1942, GJR, Section 7, File 146-7-23-25, RG 60, NARAII.

8. Ibid. See also testimony of Capt. Phillips, Lt. (jg) Fred Brewer, and Lt. (jg) Daniel Bontecou, Greenslade conference, Navy Board of Inquiry.

9. Testimony of Capt. Phillips, 11 June 1942, Greenslade conference, Navy Board of Inquiry.

10. One copy was not returned; it was found 5 June 1942 in a San Diego taxicab, the result of an oversight by a forgetful *Lexington* enlisted man who left it there by mistake. The document was turned over to U.S. Naval Intelligence, Eleventh Naval District, San Diego.

11. Testimony of Lt. (jg) Daniel Bontecou, 11 June 1942, Greenslade conference, Navy Board of Inquiry.

12. FBI interview with Bontecou, by FBI Special Agent G. A. Busch, FBI memorandum, 15 June 1942, GJR, Section 7, File 146-7-23-25, RG 60, NARAII.

13. Seligman testimony, Navy Board of Inquiry.

14. FBI interview with Ensign W. D. Stroud, by Special Agent G. A. Busch, FBI memorandum, 15 June 1942, File 146-23-25, Section 7, GJR.

15. Johnston-Mitchell 13 July interview.

16. FBI Memorandum, 24 June 1942, summary of 23 June 1942 FBI interview with Cmdr. Seligman, at Naval Hospital, San Diego, by Special Agents L. Alex Gilliam Jr. and D. A. Fish, in which he did not deny observations of officers who stated they saw a pencil memorandum containing names of Japanese ships on a table in the dining room of Seligman's suite. Seligman admitted that in the past he had made rough notes of various messages but not secret messages. Still, he said he was willing to accept the word of those officers who stated they saw such a memorandum near him during the evening of 31 May 1942. He accepted responsibility. GJR, Section 7, File 146-7-23-25, RG 60, NARAII.

17. FBI interview with Cmdr. Robert Dixon by Special Agent Harold Nathan, undated, San Diego, included in FBI report, 25 June 1942, prepared by agent William Robinson Jr., GJR, Section 7, File 146-7-23-25, RG 60, NARAII (hereafter Dixon FBI interview).

18. Testimony of Lt. F. C. Brewer, 11 June 1942, Greenslade conference, Navy Board of Inquiry.

19. Dixon FBI interview.

20. FBI interview with Lt. Irving W. Davis, 20 June 1942, conducted by Agent John Anthony Jr., GJR, Section 7, File 146-7-23-25, RG 60, NARAII.

21. FBI interview with Cmdr. A. F. Junker, 14 June 1942, by Special Agent G. A. Busch and Naval Intelligence agent R. M. Brown, GJR, Section 7, File 146-7-23-25, RG 60, NARAII.

22. FBI interview with Cmdr. Morton Seligman, 17 June 1942, by Agents L. Alex Gilliam Jr. and D. A. Fish, summary of their interview covered in a report, 25 June 1942, prepared by Agent William Robinson Jr., San Diego, GJR, Section 7, File 146-7-23-25, RG 60, NARAII.

23. Testimony of Cmdr. Seligman and Cmdr. H. S. Duckworth, 11 June 1942, Greenslade conference, Navy Board of Inquiry.

24. See two FBI interviews with Lt. Cmdr. O'Donnell, the first, by Special Agent T. B. Estep, undated, Carmel, Calif., Estep; the second recorded in FBI report by Agent William J. Robinson Jr., 25 June 1942, GJR, Section 7, File 146-7-23-25, RG 60, NARAII.

25. Nimitz's original dispatch is attached to letter from FBI agent N. J. L. Pieper, San Francisco, to FBI director, 16 June 1942, FBI records, File 100-HQ-22351-44, RG 65, NARAII. (311221 was a date-time group indicating date of the message, the 31st day of the month, and time of its sending, 12:21 p.m.)

26. Navy Department memorandum, prepared by Office of Chief of Naval Operations, to FBI director, 13 June 1942, GJR, Section 7, File 146-7-23-25, RG 60, NARAII (hereafter CNO memorandum).

27. Navy Department memorandum, interview with Lt. Irving E. Davis, by FBI agent John Anthony Jr., 20 June 1942, GJR, Section 7, File 146-23-25, RG 60, NARAII.

28. CNO memorandum.

29. FBI interview with Lt. (jg) F. C. Brewer, 18 June 1942, conducted by Agent J. S. Johnson in Loveland, Colo., GJR, Section 7, File 146-7-23-25, RG 60, NARAII (hereafter Brewer FBI interview).

30. Seligman testimony, Navy Board of Inquiry.

31. Confidential letter from Ensign George Y. McKinnon Jr. to Director, FBI, 18 June 1942, GJR, Section 7, case 146-7-23-25, RG 60, NARAII.

32. FBI Memorandum, summary of 23 June 1942 FBI interview with Cmdr. Seligman, at Naval Hospital, by Special Agents L. Alex Gilliam Jr. and D. A. Fish, San Diego, GJR, Section 7, case 146-7-23-25, RG 60, NARAII.

33. Testimony of Lt. (jg) Brewer, 11 June 1942, Greenslade conference, Navy Board of Inquiry.

34. Ibid.

35. FBI Report, 25 June 1942, prepared by Agent William Robinson Jr., includes 19 June interview with Lt. Cmdr. Edward H. Eldredge, by Agents L. Alex Gilliam Jr. and D. A. Fish, San Diego, GJR, Section 7, File 146-7-23-25, RG 60, NARAII.

36. O'Donnell 25 June 1942 FBI interview.

37. Dixon FBI interview.

38. See "Eyewitness," by Robert Mason, in U.S. Naval Institute *Proceedings*, June 1982, 40–45.

39. FBI Memorandum, 15 June 1942, Re: Newspaper Story Carried in Chicago Tribune and Other Papers Concerning Midway, synopsis of interview with Lt. Cmdr. B. M. Coleman, by Special Agent G. A. Busch, GJR, Section 7, File 146-7-23-25, NARAII.

40. O'Donnell 25 June 1942 FBI interview.

41. Ibid. See also Dixon 25 June 1942 FBI interview.

42. Stanley Johnston's report to *Chicago Tribune* editors, submitted 9 June 1942, recounting his testimony before Navy investigation committee, Navy Department, Washington, D.C., on 8 June 1942, McCormick Papers, Kirkland-Ellis Files, XI-175, Box 1, Folder 2, MRC (hereafter Stanley Johnston's 9 June report).

43. Ibid.

44. Testimony of Capt. Phillips, 11 June 1942, Greenslade conference, Navy Board of Inquiry.

45. FBI interview with Lt. Harold P. Requa, by Agent Harold Nathan, 26 June 1942, San Diego, GJR, Section 7, File 146-7-23-25, RG 60, NARAII.

46. Ibid.

Chapter 4. Hold the Presses!

1. Maloney interview by William Mitchell, 9 July 1942, Washington, D.C., Papers of Robert R. McCormick, Kirkland-Ellis Files, XI-175, Box 2, Folder 13, MRC (hereafter Maloney-Mitchell 9 July interview).

2. Johnston interview by William Mitchell 13 July 1942 interview, Washington, D.C., Papers of Robert R. McCormick, Kirkland-Ellis Files, XI-175, Box 2, Folder 13, MRC (hereafter Johnston-Mitchell 13 July interview).

3. Investigation Report, "Interviews and Check of Records to Determine [Stanley Johnston's] Movements," U.S. Naval Intelligence Service, Eleventh Naval District, San Diego, CA, 12 June 1942, FBI Records, File 100-HQ-22351-21, RG 65, NARAII (hereafter Navy Investigation Report).

4. Johnston's 9 June statement, submitted to Navy officials in Washington and his editors in Chicago, describes the correspondent on *Barnett* finding a piece of scratch paper with names of Japanese ships, copying some or all names onto a separate piece of paper, taking it back to his hotel room, and typing it onto yet another sheet of paper. See also Johnston-Mitchell 13 July interview.

5. Maloney-Mitchell 9 July interview.

6. Undated FBI interview with Lt. Cmdr. Waldo Drake, Pacific Fleet public relations, conducted by agent Wayne S. Murphy, Honolulu Field Division. Drake stated he received two articles from Stanley Johnston while the correspondent was at sea 15 April 1942–2 June 1942; Drake said the articles were censored by a Pacific Fleet representative at Pearl Harbor and sent to commander in chief, U.S. Fleet, Washington, D.C., for disposition; there is no evidence those stories ever reached the *Chicago Tribune*. For how Fleet PR handled Johnston's copy received from the Coral Sea and the South Pacific, see FBI memorandum, unsigned, 20 June 1942, Titled, Stanley Claude Samuel Johnston, Espionage-J, FBI file 100-22351-92, RG 65, NARAII.

7. Most of the early news about the Coral Sea engagement emanated from the headquarters of General MacArthur in Australia. A communique issued by the general on 9 May reported that the battle had "temporarily ceased" and "the enemy has been repulsed." American losses were said to be "comparatively light." The Navy Department in Washington announced a "magnificent victory" in that action but provided no details. The Navy denied Japanese claims that Imperial Navy forces had sunk a U.S. battleship and two aircraft carriers. Navy officials tacitly admitted U.S. forces had suffered some damage, but they added the Navy would release no information concerning that damage while it could be of use to the enemy. No information about the action originated from Pacific Fleet headquarters at Pearl Harbor. See *New York Times* front-page articles for 8–10 May 1942.

8. Johnston-Mitchell 13 July interview.

9. Maloney-Mitchell 9 July interview.

10. Ibid.

11. Ibid.

12. Ibid.

13. On board *Astoria*, "Admiral Sherman informed [Johnston] that inasmuch as he was returning to the mainland, he should clear all publications through the commander-in-chief of the Fleet, Washington, D.C." See Sherman interview by FBI Special Agent E. J. Gebben, 27 June 1942 at Sherman's suite in Wardman Park Hotel, San Diego, contained in FBI memorandum titled Re: Stanley Claude Samuel Johnston Espionage-J, 29 June 1942, San Diego Field Division, FBI, GJR, Section 7, File 146-7-23-25, RG 60, NARAII.

14. Sherman diary, 25 June 1942, Lundstrom Papers. Sherman in the same entry reported that in mid-June he met with Johnston, who assured the captain, by then promoted to rear admiral, that he had destroyed the copy in question before leaving San Diego.

15. Maloney-Mitchell 9 July interview.

16. Johnston-Mitchell 13 July interview.

17. Maloney-Mitchell 9 July interview.

18. Navy Investigation Report.

19. Ibid.

20. Ibid.

21. Maloney-Mitchell 9 July interview.

22. Ibid.

23. Johnston-Mitchell 13 July interview.

24. Maloney-Mitchell 9 July interview.

25. FBI file, File case 100-HQ-22351, Box 1562, RG 65, NARAII.

26. Ibid.

27. Johnston-Mitchell 13 July interview.

28. Ibid.

29. Maloney-Mitchell 9 July interview.

30. Ibid.

31. Ibid.

32. Ibid.

33. Ibid.

34. Ibid.

35. Wayne Thomis, oral interview by Harold Hutchings and Lloyd Wendt, 11 February 1975, Tribune Oral History Project, Tribune Company Archives, MRC.

36. Maloney-Mitchell 9 July interview.

37. Johnston-Mitchell 13 July interview.

38. See Navy interviews with Duckworth and Phillips, 11 June 1942, Greenslade conference, RG 457, Navy Board of Inquiry. Duckworth and Phillips were questioned about Stanley Johnston during a fact-finding conference, held 11 June 1942, in San Francisco, convened by Vice Admiral J. W. Greenslade, commandant, Twelfth Naval District, on orders from Admiral Ernest J. King, commander in chief, U.S. Navy. Besides Greenslade, interviewers were Admiral R. P. McCullough, district intelligence officer; and Captain W. K. Kilpatrick, chief of staff, Western Sea Frontier. RG 457, Navy Board of Inquiry (hereafter Greenslade conference).

39. Smith, *The Colonel*, 355.

40. Johnston-Mitchell 13 July interview.

41. Michael S. Sweeney, *Secrets of Victory: The Office of Censorship and the American Press and Radio in World War II* (Chapel Hill: University of North Carolina Press, 2001), 9.

42. Maloney-Mitchell 9 July interview.

43. Reprinted from the *New York Times*, 15 January 1942.

44. Maloney-Mitchell 9 July interview.

45. Michael Sweeney writes in *Secrets of Victory*, 5, that "American censorship rules in World War II had no built-in legal penalties for journalists who violated the censorship code. If a newspaper or magazine broke the rules, the censor could do little more than publicize the offense and subject the offender to ridicule and competitors' wrath."

46. Maloney-Mitchell 9 July interview.

47. Ibid.

48. As noted, unlike other correspondents who had shipped out with the U.S. Fleet, Johnston was not asked to sign an agreement to obey the Navy's program of mandatory censorship. But he had been briefed on the program, and he readily admitted he had earlier pledged orally to abide by the Navy policy of mandatory censorship as a condition for covering Pacific Fleet news at Pearl Harbor.

49. Sweeney, *Secrets of Victory*, 51–52.

50. Maloney-Mitchell 9 July interview.

51. *Chicago Tribune*, 7 June 1942. The story ran with different headlines in different papers. The *Times-Herald* headline was "U.S. Navy Knew in Advance All about Jap Fleet"; the *Chronicle*'s headline read "A Washington Report: Navy Knew Jap Task Force Was Coming—And Were Ready"; the *New York Daily News*' headline was "Naval Chiefs Knew Strength of Enemy."

52. Johnston-Mitchell 13 July interview.

53. Maloney-Mitchell 9 July interview.

Chapter 5. Aid and Comfort to the Enemy

1. For FDR's morning routine, see Doris Kearns Goodwin, *No Ordinary Time* (New York: Simon & Schuster, 1994), 17; and Robert E. Sherwood, *Roosevelt and Hopkins* (New York: Harper Universal Library, 1948), 206.

2. "They might hate it, but they felt they had to read it," wrote Walter Trohan, referring to the reading habits of Roosevelt and his associates. See Trohan's memoir, *Political Animals: Thirty-Eight Years of Washington-Watching by the Chicago Tribune's Veteran Observer* (New York: Doubleday, 1975), 20, 157.

3. Smith, *The Colonel*, 320–21.

4. Dina Goren, "Communication Intelligence and Freedom of the Press, the *Chicago Tribune*'s Battle of Midway Dispatch and the Breaking of the Japanese Naval Code," *Journal of Contemporary History* 16 (October 1981): 679.

5. Edwards, *The Foreign Policy of Col. McCormick's Tribune*, 90, 132–57.

6. Ibid.

7. Knox, too, liked being addressed as colonel. In Chicago, McCormick was known as the "morning colonel," Knox the "afternoon colonel." See Smith, *The Colonel*, 343.

8. The rivalry between the two publishers is well covered in Richard Norton Smith's biography of McCormick, *The Colonel*. See 356, 394, 421, 428.

9. Lynne Olson, *Those Angry Days* (New York: Random House, 2013), 416–17.

10. Ibid., 411–12.

11. Edwards, *The Foreign Policy of Col. McCormick's Tribune*, 176–78.

12. Ibid.

13. Ibid.

14. Olson, *Those Angry Days*, 416–18.

15. David M. Kennedy, *Freedom from Fear* (New York: Oxford University Press, 1999), 487.

16. Olson, *Those Angry Days*, 418.

17. Ibid.

18. The FBI concluded its investigation in May 1942 without publicly identifying a leaker. The issue remained unresolved until 1962, when isolationist senator Burton K. Wheeler, Democrat of Montana, published his

autobiography. Wheeler disclosed he had been the intermediary between Manly and the leaker of the Victory Program report. According to Wheeler, the document was delivered to him by an Army Air Corps captain. The captain apparently did so at the direction of Army Air Corps General Henry "Hap" Arnold. In 1963 Frank Waldrop, managing editor of the *Times-Herald* in 1942, said a top FBI official told him that Arnold was the guilty party. Arnold reportedly hoped to block the Victory Program because it emphasized land forces at the expense of air forces. See Smith, *The Colonel*, 415–19; Olson, *Those Angry Days*, 418–22; Thomas Fleming, "The Big Leak," 38, no. 8 (December 1987), *American Heritage*.

19. When Hitler appeared before the Reichstag on 11 December 1941 to declare war against the United States, he justified this decision in part as a defensive measure to forestall the huge invasion force described by the *Tribune* and *Times-Herald*. Historian Martin Gilbert suggests, therefore, that Manly's story helped bring about the very thing it was written to head off: America's entry into World War II. See Smith, *The Colonel*, 419.

20. Smith, *The Colonel*, 421.

21. Ibid., 421–24.

22. The evidence for FDR sending in the Marines is weak. In his biography of McCormick, *The Colonel*, Smith writes, "Shortly before his death, King made a hospital room confession to Walter Trohan. According to the admiral, Roosevelt's initial reaction to the Midway story had been to send Marines to occupy Tribune Tower," 432–33. Smith based this story on a memo from Trohan to J. Loy Maloney dated 27 January 1948. King lived eight more years; he died on 25 June 1956. Whatever King said to Trohan, it certainly was not "shortly before his death," nor was it a deathbed confession, as implied.

23. Roosevelt's central role in the action against the *Chicago Tribune* is supported by a Walter Trohan conversation with James Forrestal, undersecretary of the Navy in 1942 and later secretary of defense. "[Forrestal] quite frankly told me Roosevelt was behind the persecution of the *Tribune* and Knox was only too happy to go along," Trohan memo to Pat Maloney, 7 February 1947, McCormick Papers, Correspondence and Memoranda, XI-175, Box 1, Folder 1, MRC.

24. In answer to a 15 May 1964 query from *Times-Herald* editor Frank Waldrop, asking who alerted Navy brass to the 7 June 1942 article, Lt. Cmdr. D. K. Dagle, U.S. Navy, replied that a Navy staff intelligence officer brought the article to the personal attention of Admiral King. Department of Justice case 146-7-23-25, Box 224, Grand Jury records, RG 60, NARAII.

25. Thomas B. Buell, *Master of Sea Power: A Biography of Fleet Admiral Ernest J. King* (Annapolis, Md.: Naval Institute Press, 1980), 203.

26. W. J. "Jasper" Holmes, *Double-Edged Secrets* (Annapolis, Md.: Naval Institute Press, 1979), 108.

27. Arthur H. McCollum, *Reminiscences of Rear Admiral Arthur H. McCollum*, U.S. Navy (Ret.), vol. 2 (Annapolis, Md.: Naval Institute Press, 1973), 472–77.

28. Ibid.

29. Ibid.

30. Ibid.

31. Ibid. Cooke was referring to a biblical character from the Book of Esther who, according to the Old Testament, was a fifth century BC noble of the Persian Empire under King Xerxes. After his plotting against Persia's Jews was exposed by Esther, Xerxes ordered him hung on a gallows fifty feet high.

32. Trohan, *Political Animals*, 178–79.

33. "The Stanley Johnston–Chicago Tribune Case," *A History of the Office of Censorship, 1941–1945*, Box 4, RG 216, NARAII (hereafter "The Stanley Johnston–Chicago Tribune Case," OC).

34. Ibid.

35. Ibid.

36. Memo by N. R. Howard, 7 June 1942, Office of Censorship, Box 1397, RG 216, NARAII (hereafter Howard memo, OC).

37. U.S. Government Office of Censorship, *Code of Wartime Practices for the American Press* (Washington, D.C.: Government Printing Office, January 15, 1942).

38. Ibid.

39. Howard memo, OC.

40. Ibid.

41. Maloney-Mitchell 9 July interview.

42. A 1942 study conducted by the Office of Censorship found that during April, May, and June of that year, 1,882 stories had been submitted to the office before publication and that censors' advice was followed in every instance. "Submissions came from 497 sources. Atop the list was the Associated Press, with 276 inquiries, followed by the United Press and International News Service. Among individual newspapers, the *Chicago Tribune* . . . had the most submissions with fifty-six. The *New York Herald Tribune* was second with 45." See Sweeney, *Secrets of Victory*, 62–63.

43. Maloney-Mitchell 9 July interview.

44. Reached midday by the Office of Censorship, Will Sunday, telegraph editor of the *New York Daily News*, said the article was received via the Chicago Tribune Press Service and hurried into print "by a less than responsible staff on the late trick." He said the story should have been checked with Washington and undoubtedly should not have been published. The OC appears not to have contacted the *San Francisco Chronicle*. See Howard memo, OC.

45. "The Stanley Johnston–Chicago Tribune Case," OC.

46. Howard memo, OC.

47. Ibid.

48. "The Stanley Johnston–Chicago Tribune Case," OC.

49. Buel, *Master of Sea Power*, 250.

50. Walter R. Borneman, *The Admirals* (New York: Little, Brown, 2012), 280–81.

51. Papers of Ernest J. King, 7 June 1942 Press Conference transcript, Press and Press Releases Folder, Container 23, Library of Congress, Washington, D.C.

52. Ibid.

53. Ibid.

54. The Henning-Maloney letter reads as follows:

Mr. N .R. Howard, Office of Censorship, Washington, D.C., June 7, 1942

Dr. Mr. Howard:

In the story in question the Tribune believes it conformed to the censorship code of Jan. 15 last in every respect, for these reasons:

The location of the enemy ships given in the story was no more precise than that contained in Admiral Nimitz's communique. The story located the Japanese warships in the vicinity of Dutch Harbor and Midway Island where they had previously been located by navy communiques. The story identifies the warships making up the Japanese attacking forces. There is nothing in the censorship code forbidding the publication of the identity of enemy ships wherever engaged.

The story contains no statement of the location, movements and identity of U.S. ships not contained in previously published navy communiques. Sincerely yours,

Arthur S. Henning

See Grand Jury records, Section 2, File 146-7-23-25, Boxes 771–72, RG 60, NARAII.

55. Howard memo, OC.

56. Papers of Byron Price, *Memoir*, Book 3, 325, Section 2, Box 5, Wisconsin Historical Society, Madison, Wis.

57. Howard memo, OC.

58. Howard told FBI investigator D. M. Ladd that "it is very doubtful if the story did actually violate the letter of the Code, but it undoubtedly did violate the spirit of the Code." See Ladd's "Memorandum for the Director," 13 June 1942, FBI records, File 100-HQ-22351-24, RG 65, NARAII.

59. Maloney-Mitchell 9 July interview.

60. Papers of Robert R. McCormick, XI-175, Box 2, Folder 1, MRC.

61. Papers of Robert R. McCormick, XI-175, Box 1, Folder 3, MRC.

Chapter 6. Moments of Truth

1. Johnston's 9 June Washington statement, MRC.

2. Present with Admiral Hepburn were Captain Leland Lovette, Captain Frank E. Beatty, and Lieutenant Commander Paul C. Smith.

3. Memorandum from Admiral Wilkinson to FBI Director Hoover, 13 June 1942, regarding conversation of Mr. Stanley Johnston with respect to newspaper article, File 146-7-23-25, RG 60, Boxes 771–72, GJR, obtained via FOIA, NARAII (hereafter Wilkinson memorandum).

4. Wilkinson memorandum.

5. Ibid.

6. Ibid. See also Johnston's 9 June Washington statement, MRC.

7. Ibid.

8. Ibid.

9. The spelling of Japanese ships did not always remain the same. *Jane's Fighting Ships 1941* spelled this ship *Kirisma* in 1941, but later on *Jane's*, along with many Pacific War historians, would use *Kirishima*. What is important is that Johnston used Nimitz's *Kirishima* rather *Jane's Kirisima*, the accepted spelling in 1941.

10. Wilkinson memorandum.

11. Ibid.

12. Johnston-Mitchell interview.

13. FBI Memorandum for the Director, from agent D. M. Ladd, 13 June 1942, FBI records, File 100-HQ-22351-24, RG 65, NARAII.

14. See Johnston's 9 June Washington statement, MRC.

15. Ibid.

16. Ibid.

17. Willson's memo to King and King's staff has not survived, but in a separate memo, on 11 June 1942, to Attorney General Francis Biddle, Willson

wrote, "Johnston when first questioned insisted that he had put together the substance of his article from general conversation on board *Barnett*. He later stated that he had found the text as written by him in his article on a sheet of plain paper on a desk which he used jointly with some of the senior officers with whom he was quartered." GJR, Section 1, File 146-7-23-25, RG 60, NARAII.

18. Johnston's 9 June Washington statement, MRC.

19. Memo from Fleet Communications Officer to COMINCH Chief of Staff, 8 June 1942, Naval Board of Inquiry, RG 457, NARAII.

20. COMINCH to CINCPAC, 8 June 1942, Naval Board of Inquiry.

21. Basegram, COMINCH to U.S. Fleet, 9 June 1942, Papers of Franklin Roosevelt, Map Room Collection, Box 46, Publicity and Press Folder, Roosevelt Library, Hyde Park, N.Y.

22. Memorandum, From: COMINCH, To: Commanders, U.S. Atlantic and Pacific Fleets, Commander, Southwest Pacific Fleet, 20 June 1942, RG 38, CNSG (Crane Naval Security Group) Library, Box 54, File 5750/37, NARAII. The author is indebted to Richard Frank for bringing this document to his attention.

23. Ibid.

24. McCormick quote from article in *Chicago Herald-American*, August 1942, McCormick Papers, I-63, MRC.

25. John F. Floberg letter to Howard Ellis, 9 September 1954, Papers of Robert R. McCormick, XI-175, Correspondence and Memoranda, Box 1, Folder 1, MRC.

26. E. B. Potter, *Nimitz* (Annapolis, Md.: Naval Institute Press, 1976), 36–37.

27. Mary S. Mander, *Pen and Sword* (Urbana: University of Illinois Press, 2010), 62–63, 163. See also "Press vs. the Navy," *Newsweek*, 23 February 1942, 56.

28. Robert J. Casey, *Torpedo Junction* (New York: Bobbs-Merrill, 1942), 324.

29. Mander, *Pen and Sword*, 62.

30. FBI radiogram, Honolulu to Director, 14 June 1942, FBI Records, File 100-HQ-22351-98, RG 65, NARAII.

31. Office of Censorship memorandum, Wm. Mylander to Mr. Howard, 9 June 1942, Subject: Chi Trib Correspondent Didn't Sign Commitment, Office of Censorship Records, RG 216, Box 1397, NARAII.

32. Technically, Drake had a point. The requirement that reporters assigned to warships sign a written censorship agreement was contained in "Regulations for Correspondents Accredited to the Pacific Fleet," effective 12 April

1942. Drake said this document did not reach Pearl Harbor until after Johnston had sailed. See FBI Summary Memorandum, FBI records, File 100-HQ-22351-181, RG 65, NARAII (hereafter FBI Summary Memorandum).

33. Among correspondents and photographers signing censorship contracts *before* Johnston's 15 April departure on *Lexington* were Richard Tregaskis of International News Service, Joseph Harsch of the *Christian Science Monitor*, H. E. Hawkins of Reuters, Wendell Webb of the Associated Press, John Field of *Time*, Ralph Morse of *Life*, Keith Wheeler of the *Chicago Times*, Harry Lang of the *Chicago Sun*, Robert J. Casey of the *Chicago Daily News*, Frank Tremaine of the United Press, and Foster Hailey of the *New York Times*. See CINCPAC Records Relating to Public Relations, 1940–46; War Correspondents Agreements Folder, RG 313, Box 13, NARAII.

34. FBI Summary Memorandum.

35. Nat Howard interview conducted by FBI agent D. M. Ladd, 16 June 1942, FBI records, File HQ-22351-64, RG 65, NARAII.

36. "Statement of Lt. Cmdr. Waldo Drake," witnessed by Special Agent Wayne S. Murphy, 13 June 1942, FBI records, File 100-HQ-22351-156, RG 65, NARAII.

37. Memorandum, Greenslade to COMINCH, Subject: "Investigation regarding potential sources of secret information obtained by Mr. Stanley Johnston," 9 June 1942, Naval Board of Inquiry.

38. Orders to Seligman from Chief of the Bureau of Aeronautics, 9 April 1935, National Personnel Records Center, Military Personnel Records, St. Louis, Mo.

39. Present at the Greenslade conference were Captain W. B. Phillips, commanding officer, *Barnett*; Lt. (jg) Daniel Bontecou, communications officer, *Barnett*; and Cmdr. M. T. Seligman, executive officer; Cmdr. H. S. Duckworth, air officer; and Lt. (jg) Fred C. Brewer, communications watch officer, from *Lexington*.

40. Transcript, Greenslade Conference, San Francisco, 11 June 1942, RG 457, Container 1397, Naval Board of Inquiry, RG 457, NARAII.

41. Ibid.

42. Franklin D. Roosevelt Day by Day, 9 June 1942, FDR Presidential Library, Hyde Park, N.Y.

43. Department of the Navy letter, Knox to Biddle, 9 June 1942, Papers of Franklin D. Roosevelt, President's Secretary's File, 1933–1945, Container 4, FDR Presidential Library, Hyde Park, N.Y.

44. Ibid.

45. Ibid.

46. Francis Biddle, *In Brief Authority* (New York: Doubleday, 1962), 249.

Chapter 7. The Gathering Storm

1. McCormick wire to Henning, 7 June 1942, Papers of Robert R. McCormick, XI-175, Box 1, Folder 2, MRC.

2. McCormick wire to Henning, 9 June 1942, MRC.

3. Memo, Maloney to McCormick, 10 June 1942, Papers of Robert McCormick, XI-175, Correspondence and Memoranda-II, Box 1, Folder 1, MRC.

4. Letter, King to McCormick, 12 June 1942, King Papers, Container 13, Robert McCormick Folder, LOC.

5. Ibid.

6. Kirkland, Fleming, Green, Martin & Ellis.

7. Letter, McCormick to King, 15 June 1942, Papers of Robert McCormick, XI-175, Kirkland-Ellis Files, Box 1, Folder 3, MRC.

8. Letter, Ellis to Maloney, 13 June 1942, Papers of Robert R. McCormick, XI-175, Box 1, Folder 1, MRC (hereafter Ellis letter).

9. Affidavit of Stanley C. Johnston, Papers of Robert R. McCormick, XI-175, Box 1, Folder 2, MRC (hereafter Johnston Affidavit).

10. A small discrepancy is worth noting: in his 9 June statement, Johnston wrote that he left the scratch paper on his desk on *Barnett*. Now, in his 11 June affidavit, he stated that he threw it in the wastebasket.

11. Johnston Affidavit.

12. Ibid.

13. Ibid.

14. Ibid.

15. Ibid.

16. The Navy Department in the 1930s and 1940s was known as Main Navy.

17. For an excellent inventory and description of the IJN circa 1942, see the online site prepared by Jon Parshall and Andrew Tully, The Imperial Japanese Navy Page, http://www.combinedfleet.com/kaigun.htm.

18. To give just one example, the battleship *Hiei* sailed with the striking force that raided Pearl Harbor in December, missed the Coral Sea engagement altogether, then turned up with the occupation force approaching Midway in June.

19. *Jane's Fighting Ships 1942* was not circulated until 1943, so it would have been of no help to Johnston in 1942.

20. *Jane's Fighting Ships 1941*, 280–326.

21. See Appendix C, this volume, for Message 311221 as it was sent from Pearl Harbor, and Appendix D for how it was decrypted on *Barnett*. See Appendix A for *Tribune* article.

22. Jon Parshall and Andrew Tully, *Shattered Sword* (Washington, D.C.: Potomac Books, 2005); see that book's Appendix 2, 455.

23. Email to author from Jon Parshall, 23 April 2014. When Navy pilots sunk a light carrier at the Battle of the Coral Sea, they mistakenly reported it as *Ryukaku*; it was actually *Shoho*.

24. No ships with those names have appeared on any list of IJN ships for 1942. *Jane's Fighting Ships 1942* did list the heavy cruiser *Chokas*, but the 1942 edition of *Jane's* was not issued until 1943 and would not have helped Johnston in 1942. The cruiser *Chokai* sailed with the occupation force, but no ship with that spelling appeared in Nimitz's dispatch. The names *Chakas, Chitore,* and *Choda* were written between the lines of Message 311221 and Johnston went with them. They supply further evidence that Johnston relied almost exclusively on the Nimitz list, because they appear nowhere else on Japanese ship lists. The cruiser *Myoko*, on the other hand, turned up with the Midway occupation force. It is listed in *Jane's 1941*, and it is odd that Johnston said he did not see it there.

25. Johnston followed Nimitz not only in making errors of commission, but also in errors of omission. In a rare but significant lapse, Nimitz's code-breakers at Pearl Harbor, the famed Station Hypo team, failed to pick up any radio intelligence pointing to the IJN's so-called main body trailing some six hundred miles behind the striking force. With the combined fleet's commander in chief, Admiral Isoroku Yamamoto, on board the giant battleship *Yamato*, the main body was a powerful force, consisting of three battleships (including *Yamato*), a carrier group, three destroyer squadrons, and numerous support ships. This force did not show up in Message 311221. Hypo missed it; so did Johnston.

26. *Chicago Tribune*, 13 June 1942.

27. Letter, Maloney to Chesly Manly, 1 August 1942, Papers of Robert McCormick, XI-175, Box 1, Folder 1, MRC.

28. "No newspaper published a line of the [*Lexington*] story until it was officially released on June 12," Byron Price told the Southern Newspaper Publisher Association. Papers of Byron Price, Notebooks VII, Part 2, Box 1, Wisconsin Historical Society, Madison, Wis.

29. McCormick to Henning, 9 June 1942, Papers of Robert McCormick, XI-175, Box 1, Folder 2, MRC.

30. *Chicago Tribune*, 13 June 1942.

31. Letter from Lieutenant R. C. McKee (USNR) to Captain Leland P. Lovette, Office of Public Relations, Department of the Navy, 27 June 1942, Papers of Robert McCormick, XI-175, Box 1, Folder 1, MRC.

32. Maloney-Mitchell interview by William Mitchell, 9 July 1942, 17–18, Papers of Robert McCormick, XI-175, Box 2, Folder 13, MRC.

33. Memorandum for Mr. Early, White House, 11 June 1942, Papers of Franklin Roosevelt, Collection OF-197-A, Box 3, Presidential Library, Hyde Park, N.Y.

34. FBI Memorandum for [Agents], from D. M. Ladd, 12 June 1942, FBI records, File 100-HQ-22351-17, RG 65, NARAII (hereafter Ladd memorandum).

35. Ibid.

36. Ladd memorandum.

37. *Time*, 27 January 1930.

38. Smith, *The Colonel*, 436–37.

39. Henning memorandum to Don Maxwell, 10 July 1942, Papers of Robert McCormick, XI-175, Box 1, Folder 2, MRC (hereafter Henning memorandum).

40. Ibid.

41. The *Tribune* editorialized that responsibility for the incident "lies chiefly at the door of men in public life who have encouraged the making of unreasonable demands by ex-servicemen and inflamed their mistaken sense of judgment." See article written by Wyatt Kingseed, published in the June 2004 issue of *American History Magazine*.

42. In December 1917, Congress approved the Eighteenth Amendment prohibiting the manufacture, sale, or transportation of alcoholic beverages. The amendment took effect on 16 January 1920.

43. Henning memorandum.

44. Smith, *The Colonel*, 278.

45. Henning memorandum.

46. Smith, *The Colonel*, 106, 170.

47. Henning memorandum.

48. Edwards, *The Foreign Policy of Col. McCormick's Tribune, 1929–1941*, 166.

49. Henning memorandum.

50. Biddle, *In Brief Authority*, 245–51.

51. Ibid.

52. Roosevelt's message to Biddle is quoted in a confidential memo from Biddle to Archibald MacLeish, Library of Congress, 15 June 1942, GJR, Section 2, File 146-7-23-25, RG 60, NARAII.

53. Sweeney, *Secrets of Victory*, 76–78.

54. Ibid.; Biddle, *In Brief Authority*, 245–51.

55. Introduction to Justice Department Study, undated, GJR, Section 1, File 146-7-23-25, RG 60, NARAII.

56. Ibid.

57. Ibid.

58. Memorandum to Mr. Lawrence M. C. Smith, Chief, Special Defense Unit, Justice Department, GJR, Section 1, File 146-7-23-25, RG 60, NARAII.

59. Memorandum for the Attorney General, Re: Collection of Newspaper Excerpts, from Lawrence M. C. Smith, 21 May 1942, GJR, Section 1, File 146-7-23-25, RG 60, NARAII.

Chapter 8. A Beautiful Mess

1. *Time*, 27 January 1930. Mitchell was the subject of a *Time* cover story on this date.

2. Hoover memorandum for Mr. Tolson, Mr. Tamm, Mr. Ladd, 15 June 1942, FBI records, case 100-HQ-22351-16, RG 65, NARAII.

3. Ibid.

4. Ibid., Hoover memorandum for Mr. Tolson, Mr. Tamm, Mr. Ladd, 17 June 1942, FBI records, case 100-HQ-22351-13, RG 65, NARAII.

5. Memorandum to the Attorney General from William D. Mitchell, 18 June 1942, GJR, section 2, case 146-7-23-25, RG 60, NARAII (hereafter Mitchell-Biddle memorandum).

6. Memorandum to the Attorney General, from Oscar Cox, 16 June 1942, GJR, section 4, case 146-7-23-25, RG 60, NARAII (hereafter Cox-Biddle memorandum).

7. Cox-Biddle memorandum.

8. Mitchell-Biddle memorandum.

9. Ibid.

10. Ibid. The Espionage Act of 1917 was amended by Congress in 1940 to increase the maximum term of imprisonment from two years to ten years, leaving the maximum fine at $10,000.

11. Ibid.

12. Ibid.

13. Memorandum for Mr. Hoover, from W. D. Mitchell, 18 June 1942, GJR, case 146-7-23-25, RG 60, NARAII (hereafter Mitchell-Hoover memorandum).
14. Mitchell-Hoover memorandum.
15. Mitchell-Biddle memorandum.
16. Biddle-Price correspondence, 19 and 20 June 1942, Office of Censorship, RG 216, Box 1167, NARAII.
17. Memorandum for the FBI Director from D. M. Ladd, 17 June 1942, FBI records, case 100-22351-61, RG 65, NARAII.
18. Ibid.
19. Ibid.
20. Mitchell-Hoover memorandum.
21. Ibid.
22. Maloney-Mitchell 9 July 1942 interview.
23. Ibid.
24. Ibid.
25. Ibid.
26. Ibid.
27. Ibid.
28. Ibid.
29. Ibid.
30. Ibid.
31. Ibid.
32. Ibid.
33. Johnston-Mitchell 13 July interview, MRC.
34. Ibid.
35. Ibid.
36. Ibid.
37. Ibid.
38. Ibid.
39. Ibid.
40. Ibid.
41. Ibid.
42. Ibid.
43. Ibid.
44. Ibid.

Chapter 9. Johnston and Seligman

Epigraph. Don Maxwell memo to Howard Ellis, 15 July 1942, describing phone conversation with Morton Seligman, Papers of Robert R. McCormick, XI-175, Box 1, Folder 2, MRC (hereafter Maxwell memo to Ellis).

1. Hoover memo to Major General Edwin M Watson, 18 June 1942, Papers of Franklin D. Roosevelt, Collection OF, 10B, Box 16, Roosevelt Library, Hyde Park, N.Y. (hereafter Hoover-Watson memo).

2. Ibid.

3. Barbara Incagnoli vs. Albert Incagnoli, divorce papers, State of Illinois, County of Cook, 28 August 1941, FBI records, File 100-HQ2351, RG 65, NARAII.

4. Hoover-Watson memo.

5. FBI memorandum, Subject: Stanley Johnston, To: Directorate-General, British Consulate, Chicago, 13 June 1942, FBI records, File 100-HQ-22351, RG 65, NARAII.

6. Hoover-Watson memo.

7. Confidential letter from Jungmann to Capt. Elmer M. Walsh, Chief, Investigation Division, U.S. Army Intelligence, New York, 3 June 1942, FBI records, File 100-22351 127, RG 65, NARAII (hereafter Jungmann-Walsh letter).

8. Ibid.

9. Ibid.

10. P. E. Foxworth letter to Hoover, 29 June 1942, FBI records, File 100-22351-127, RG 65 NARAII.

11. Investigation Report, Ninth Naval District, U.S. Naval Intelligence Service, 22 August 1941, FBI records, File 100-HQ-22351-55X3, RG 65 NARAII.

12. FBI report by Agent J. R. Yore, 18 June 1942, FBI records, File 100-HQ-22351-97, RG 65 NARAII.

13. McCormick memo to Maloney, 28 August 1941, cited in "The Stanley Johnston Story," *Tribune* sketch of the correspondent, March 1942, MRC.

14. J. H. Brebner letter to Joe Pierson, 10 March 1941, cited in "The Stanley Johnston Story," MRC.

15. Memo by John Hayes, *Chicago Tribune* reporter for Chicago North Shore, 26 August 1941, cited in "The Stanley Johnston Story," MRC.

16. Henning messages to McCormick, 30 August 1941 and 9 September 1941, "The Stanley Johnston Story," MRC.

17. Stimson diary entry for 17 June 1942, Henry Lewis Stimson Diaries in the Yale University Library, located at McKeldin Library, University of Maryland, Call number: Microfilm E748.S883A32, reel 7, vol. 39.

18. Ted Sherman's diary, entry for 25 June 1942, Lundstrom Papers.

19. Mitchell notes, attached to Memorandum for Mr. William D. Mitchell, from J. Edgar Hoover, 18 June 1942, GJR, section 2, File 146-7-23-25, RG 60, NARAII.

20. Report of Medical Survey, U.S. Naval Hospital, San Diego, Calif., 31 August 1942, Military Personnel Records, St. Louis, Mo.

21. FBI Memorandum, Re; Stanley Claude Samuel Johnston, 24 June 1942, GJR, Section 7, File 146-7-23-25, RG 60, NARAII.

22. Maxwell memo to Ellis.

23. Ibid.

24. Maloney memo to Howard Ellis, describing Johnston conversation with Seligman, 16 July 1942, Papers of Robert R. McCormick, XI-175, Box 1, Folder 2, MRC (hereafter Maloney memo to Ellis).

25. Ibid.

26. Ibid.

27. Ibid.

28. Ibid.

29. Maloney-Seligman conversation, Papers of RRM, Box 1, Folder 2, MRC.

30. Ibid.

31. Ibid.

32. Ibid.

33. Ibid.

34. Berry letter to Waldo Drake, 17 June 1942, Fleet Public Relations, CINCPAC file, Container 4, RG 313, NARAII.

35. Letter, F. J. Mead, Royal Canadian Mounted Police, Ottawa, to J. Edgar Hoover, 24 September 1942, FBI records, File 100-HQ-22351-204, RG 65, NARAII.

Chapter 10. Full Speed Ahead

1. William D. Mitchell, Report on the Chicago Tribune Case, For the Attorney General and the Secretary of the Navy, 14 July 1942, GJR, Section 6, File 146-7-23-25, EC RG 60 NARAII (hereafter Mitchell Report to Biddle and Knox).

2. Ibid.

3. Ibid.

4. Ibid.

5. Ibid.

6. Ibid.

7. Ibid.

8. Ibid.

9. Ibid.

10. Memorandum written by *Tribune* staff member E. Ken, undated, based on interview with U.S. attorney Albert J. Woll, Chicago office, DOJ (hereafter Ken-Woll conversation). See also to memo from Walter Trohan to Pat Maloney, 1 September 1942, based on interview with Attorney General Biddle (hereafter Trohan-Biddle interview); both documents in Papers of Robert R. McCormick, XI-175, File 1, Box 2, Folder 5, MRC.

11. This portrait of Biddle emerges from several sources. Among them is Kenneth S. Davis, *FDR: The War President, 1940–1943* (New York: Random House, 2000), 425; see also James MacGregor Burns, *Roosevelt: The Soldier of Freedom* (New York: Harcourt Brace Jovanovich, 1970), 215.

12. Ken-Woll conversation; see also Trohan-Biddle interview.

13. Memorandum for the Attorney General, from Wendell Berge, 27 July 1942, GJR, Section 6, RG 60, NARAII.

14. Memorandum for the Attorney General, from Oscar Cox, subject: The Tribune-Midway Case, 17 July 1942, GJR, Section 6, RG 60, NARAII.

15. Handwritten memo, Cox to Biddle, undated, GJR, Section 6, NARAII. Cox need not have worried. While other *Tribune* reporters would not be punished for Johnston's various infractions, his Navy Department press credentials had already been pulled. Nobody at Main Navy could say when, or whether, he would ever get them back. As of July 1942, his career covering U.S. naval operations appeared very much in doubt.

16. *PM* article, 23 June 1942, from the Stanley Johnston file of Pacific War historian Robert Hanyok, made available to the author.

17. Ibid.

18. Ibid.

19. Papers of Byron Price, Memoir, Book III (Section 2), 1908–1944, Box 5, Wisconsin Historical Society, Madison, Wis. (hereafter Byron Price Memoir).

20. Walter Winchell Papers 1920–1967, transcript of 5 July 1942 broadcast, Billy Rose Theatre Division, Library of the Performing Arts, New York Public Library, Lincoln Center, New York, N.Y. Army Chief of Staff George Marshall tried unsuccessfully to get NBC to remove Winchell from the air on

grounds the broadcaster was revealing sensitive military information. See Neal Gabler, *Winchell: Gossip, Power and the Culture of Celebrity* (New York: Vintage Books, 1994), 322.

21. *On Broadway*, 7 July 1942. Hanyok file; also available on microfilm, Walter Winchell Papers, Billy Rose Theatre Division, Library for the Performing Arts, Lincoln Center, New York, N.Y.

22. Byron Price Memoir.

23. Ibid.

24. Winchell broadcast transcript, 12 July 1942, Billy Rose Theatre Division, Library of the Performing Arts, New York Public Library, Lincoln Center, New York, N.Y.

25. Byron Price Memoir.

26. Union resolutions submitted to Francis Biddle, GJR, Sections 9 and 10, RG 60, NARAII.

27. Byron Price Memoir.

28. Ibid.

29. Frank Knox letter to the Attorney General, 29 July 1942, GJR, Section 6, File 146-7-23-25, RG 60, NARAII.

30. Ibid.

31. Memorandum for the FBI director, from D. M. Ladd, 17 June 1942, FBI records, File 100-HQ-22351-61, RG 65, NARAII.

32. Ken-Woll conversation; see also Trohan-Biddle interview.

33. Townsend Hoopes and Douglas Brinkley, *Driven Patriot: The Life and Times of James Forrestal* (New York: Alfred A. Knopf, 1992), 129.

34. John Gunther, *Roosevelt in Retrospect* (New York: Harper & Row, 1950), 35.

35. Papers of Byron Price, Notebooks IV, August 3, 1942, Box 3, Wisconsin Historical Society, Madison, Wis.

36. *Editor & Publisher*, article by George A. Brandenburg, 15 August 1942; see also *Washington Post*, 8 August 1942.

37. Patrick S. Washburn, *A Question of Sedition* (New York: Oxford University Press, 1986), 95.

38. Ibid. See also *Chicago Tribune*, 8 August 1942. Other papers that carried the Johnston article on 7 June 1942, including the *San Francisco Chronicle*, were not targeted in the Justice Department case.

Chapter 11. McCormick and Knox

Epigraph. Chicago Tribune editorial, 9 August 1942.

1. Recollections of R. R. McCormick, by W. D. "Don" Maxwell, 14–15 February 1975, Tribune Company Archives, Oral History Project, MRC (hereafter Maxwell oral history). See also Smith, *The Colonel*, 437.

2. Maxwell oral history.

3. Ibid.

4. *Tribune* front-page article, 9 August 1942. The FBI men showed up as part of a Justice Department antitrust case against the Associated Press, a cooperative, which had denied membership to McCormick's rival morning newspaper, the *Chicago Sun*. See Smith, *The Colonel*, 423–27.

5. *Chicago Tribune* series, 8–11 August 1942.

6. Ibid.

7. Ibid.

8. Mander, *Pen and Sword*, 62.

9. *Chicago Tribune* series, 8–11 August 1942.

10. Ibid.

11. Ibid.

12. Ibid.

13. Ibid.

14. Ibid.

15. *Washington Post*, 11 August 1942. See also *Washington Times-Herald*, 11 August 1942.

16. *Washington Post*, 11 August 1942. See also *Washington Times-Herald*, 11 August 1942.

17. *Washington Post*, 11 August 1942. See also *Washington Times-Herald*, 11 August 1942.

18. *Washington Post*, 11 August 1942. See also *Washington Times-Herald*, 11 August 1942.

19. *Washington Times-Herald*, 14 August 1942. See also Smith, *The Colonel*, 437.

20. *Chicago Tribune*, 16 August 1942.

21. *Washington Star*, 1 September 1942.

22. Harold Ickes, *Lords of the Press* (New York: Harcourt, Brace, 1939), 54–84; Memo to the President, 17 October 1942, Papers of Franklin D. Roosevelt, Departmental Files, container 59, Roosevelt Library, Hyde Park, N.Y.; *Washington Times-Herald*, 14 August 1942.

23. *Chicago Tribune*, 15 August 1942.

24. Wayne Thomis, *Tribune* oral history, 11 February 1977, MRC.

25. Weymouth Kirkland letter to William D. Mitchell, 13 August 1942, Papers of Robert R. McCormick, Kirkland-Ellis Files, Box 2, Folder 10, MRC.

26. Mitchell's quotes from Albert Woll interview with *Tribune*'s Holt, Memo from Holt to Pat Maloney, 11 September 1942, Papers of Robert R. McCormick, XI-175, memos regarding the grand jury, Box 2, Folder 5, MRC.

27. Maxwell oral history.

28. FBI interview with Lt. Cmdr. Edwin T. Layton, by Special Age Wayne S. Murphy, 13–21 June 1942, Personal and confidential memorandum to Attorney General, from J. Edgar Hoover, Re: Stanley Claude Samuel Johnston, 2 July 1942, GJR, File 146-7-23-25, Section 6, RG 60, NARAII.

29. Ibid.

30. Ibid.

31. Hastings' role in providing this information to Admiral John Godfrey is disclosed in Godfrey's 8 July 1942 memo to British Foreign Office officials; it is contained in the file of historian Ralph Erskine. The author is indebted to Erskine for sharing this and other documents.

32. Bradley F. Smith, *The Ultra-Magic Deals* (London: Airlife Publishing, 1993), 72.

33. Memo written by Admiral John Godfrey, 8 July 1942, Erskine file.

34. Ibid.

35. Memo by Brigadier Walter Cawthorne to Y Board, Joint Intelligence Committee, London, 13 July 1942, Erskine file.

36. See "Censorship a Real Problem in Australia," *Editor & Publisher*, 20 June 1942. Contrary to the contentions of some writers, Lardner did not repeat this story in his *Newsweek* column. A search of *Newsweek*'s May–June issues for 1942 turns up no references to U.S. naval codebreaking either in Lardner's columns or in the news columns.

37. *New York Times*, 9 June 1942. Baldwin probably revealed more about the Navy's secret program than the Navy would have liked. He wrote that one reason the U.S. Navy was prepared to meet the Japanese attack at Midway was due to radio intelligence just as that source had played a role in the Battle of Jutland. As Pacific War historian Richard Frank told the author, "The Jutland reference is key since it clearly implies codebreaking as well as direction finding and traffic analysis."

38. F. W. Winterbotham, *The Ultra Secret* (London: Harper & Row, 1974), 176.

39. Andrew Cunningham "most secret" note to Admiral King, 15 August 1942, U.S. Naval Board of Inquiry, Re: Compromise of Radio Intelligence, RG 457, container 1397, NARAII.

40. Admiral King "most secret" note to Admiral Sir Andrew Cunningham, 17 August 1942, U.S. Naval Board of Inquiry, RG 457, container 1397, NARAII.

Chapter 12. The Grand Jury Decides

1. United Press, "Tribune Men Try in Vain to Testify at Probe," *Washington Times-Herald*, 18 August 1942.

2. Ibid.

3. Mitchell-Woll correspondence, referenced in chapter 11, showed that, to get an indictment, Mitchell would need to win the votes of at least twelve of the eighteen grand jurors assembled for this proceeding.

4. The other papers carrying the story in question were the *Washington Times-Herald*, the *New York Daily News*, and the *San Francisco Chronicle*.

5. Mitchell-Grand Jury colloquy, 14 August 1942, Grand Jury testimony, 181, RG 60, NARAII (hereafter Grand Jury testimony).

6. FBI interview with RADM Frederick C. Sherman, by Special Agent D. A. Fish, 16 June 1942, San Diego, contained in report prepared by FBI agent William Robinson, FBI case 65-1143, GJR, Section 2, File 146-47-23-25, RG 60, NARAII.

7. Ibid.

8. Sherman testimony, 13 August 1942, Grand Jury testimony, 11–23.

9. Ibid.

10. Ibid.

11. Bontecou testimony, 13 August 1942, Grand Jury testimony, 23–52.

12. Ibid.

13. Ibid.

14. Ibid.

15. O'Donnell testimony, 13 August 1942, Grand Jury testimony, 53–70.

16. Ibid.

17. Ibid.

18. Ibid.

19. Ibid.

20. Ibid.

21. Ibid.

22. Ibid.

23. Mitchell-Jury colloquy, 13 August 1942, Grand Jury testimony, 66–69.

24. Ibid.

25. Ibid.

26. Ibid.

27. The other three *Lexington* communications officers on the Coding Board were Lieutenant F. C. Brewer and Ensigns E. H. Railsback and Robert Hebbler.

28. Johnson-McKinnon testimony, 13 August 1942, Grand Jury testimony, 103–21.

29. Ibid.

30. Ibid.

31. Ibid.

32. Seligman testimony, 13 August 1942, Grand Jury testimony, 77–103.

33. Ibid.

34. Ibid.

35. Ibid.

36. Ibid.

37. Ibid.

38. Ibid.

39. Ibid.

40. Ibid.

41. Ibid.

42. Ibid.

43. Ibid.

44. Johnston statement, interview with William Mitchell, 13 July 1942, 47–48 (hereafter Johnston statement).

45. Thomis testimony, 14 August 1942, Grand Jury testimony, 204–23.

46. Ibid.

47. Ibid.

48. Ibid.

49. Ibid.

50. Johnston's statement, 49–50.

51. Thomis testimony.

52. Ibid.

53. Mitchell-Grand Jury colloquy, 14 August 1942, Grand Jury testimony, 146–202.

54. The *San Francisco Chronicle* also ran Johnston's article on 7 July 1942, but its editors were never called to Washington.

55. Waldrop-Sharp testimony, 17 August 1942, Grand Jury testimony, 225–67.

56. Waldrop-Sharp testimony.

57. Ibid.

58. Ibid.

59. Ibid.

60. Ibid.

61. Ibid.

62. Ibid.

63. Ibid.

64. Ibid.

65. Ibid.

66. Ibid.

67. Ibid.

68. Ibid.

69. Ibid.

70. Ibid.

71. Ibid.

72. Mitchell-Grand Jury colloquy, 17 August 1942, Grand Jury testimony, 267–75.

73. Ibid.

74. Mitchell summary letter to Biddle, 25 August 1942, Frank Knox Papers, June–September 1942, Operational Archives, Naval History and Heritage Command (NHHC), Washington Navy Yard (hereafter Mitchell summary letter).

75. Ibid.

76. Mitchell-Jury colloquy, 13 August 1942, Grand Jury testimony, 274.

77. See Mitchell note to Weymouth Kirkland, 17 August 1942, Papers of Robert R. McCormick, XI-175, Box 1, Folder 2, MRC.

78. *Editor & Publisher*, 22 August 1942.

79. Maloney testimony, 18 August 1942, Grand Jury testimony, 329–68.

80. Ibid.

81. Ibid.

82. Ibid.

83. Ibid.

84. Ibid.

85. Ibid.

86. Ibid.

87. Ibid.

88. Johnston statement, 13 July 1942, 54.

89. Johnston testimony, 18 August 1942, Grand Jury testimony, 278–329.

90. Ibid.

91. Ibid.

92. Johnston statement, 13 July 1942, 53–54.

93. Johnston testimony, 18 August 1942.

94. Ibid.

95. Ibid.

96. Ibid.

97. Ibid.

98. Ibid.

99. Ibid.

100. Ibid.

101. "The Stanley Johnston–Chicago Tribune case," Office of Censorship.

102. Ibid.

103. Ibid.

104. Ibid.

105. Ibid.

106. Mitchell-Grand Jury colloquy, 14 August 1942, 174–75.

107. FBI Interview with Lt. Cmdr. Robert E. Dixon, 24 June 1942, GJR, Section 7, File 146-47-23-25, RG 60, NARAII.

108. Ibid.

109. Robert Mason, "Witness," U.S. Naval Institute *Proceedings*, June 1982, 40–45.

110. Ibid.

111. Ibid.

112. Mitchell summary letter.

113. *Chicago Tribune*, 20 August 1942.

114. Ibid.

115. "Tribune Defeats the Navy," *Newsweek*, 31 August 1942.

116. *Chicago Tribune*, 20 August 1942.

117. Howard Wood Oral History, Papers of Robert R. McCormick, MRC.

118. *Washington Post*, 21 August 1942.

119. Editorial excerpts from these newspapers appeared in the 22 August 1942 *Washington Times-Herald*.

120. *Editor & Publisher*, 22 August 1942.

121. One publication did connect the dots: the weekly newspaper *Chicago Times*. It speculated that "if anyone in our naval intelligence had disclosed the make-up of the Japanese attacking force, which presumably our profound scholars in Washington cubby-holes had identified by deciphering the secret Japanese code, there would have been a violation of the Espionage Act. . . . Of course the Japs would immediately change their code and that would hinder our war effort and endanger our fighters until we cracked their new code." Reprinted from *Time*, 31 August 1942.

122. Biddle, *In Brief Authority*, 251.

123. Biddle interview with Walter Trohan, 1 September 1942, MRC; Biddle, *In Brief Authority*, 250; Mitchell summary letter.

124. Mitchell summary letter.

125. Ibid.

126. Ibid.

127. Ibid.

128. Knox letter to William Mitchell, 2 September 1942, Frank Knox Papers, June–September 1942, Operational Archives, NHHC, Washington Navy Yard.

129. Ibid.

130. After the grand jury dismissed the case, Knox asked Sherman, who had just testified, for insights into why the jury had failed to indict. "I explained I couldn't talk too much about what went on in the jury room but explained . . . that they seemed more interested in Johnston as a hero than as a violator of censorship." Sherman put in a good word for Johnston's Coral Sea articles. "Much to my surprise he [Knox] said he hadn't read the articles." Sherman diary, entry for 20 August 1942, Lundstrom Papers.

131. Smith, *The Colonel*, 440–41.

132. "Tribune Defeats the Navy," *Newsweek*, 31 August 1942.

Epilogue

1. Mason, "Eyewitness," U.S. Naval Institute *Proceedings*, June 1982, 40–45. Lieutenant Commander Dixon had concerns of his own. He feared Admiral King would punish him for failing to report Seligman's breach of security when *Barnett* docked in San Diego; "I figured King would be taking my measurements [for a coffin]," he told Mason. His worries proved unfounded; he went on to serve as operations officer under Rear Admiral Frederick Sherman, who later headed carrier task groups on board *Enterprise*, *Saratoga*, and *Bunker Hill*. Dixon retired a rear admiral.

2. Don Maxwell memo to Howard Ellis, 16 November 1948, McCormick Papers, XI-175, Kirkland-Ellis Files, Box 1, Folder 2, MRC.

3. Ibid.

4. Walter Trohan memo to Pat Maloney, 16 November 1948, based on Trohan interview with Denfeld, McCormick Papers, XI-175, Kirkland-Ellis Files, Box 1, Folder 1, MRC.

5. Buell, *Master of Sea Power*, 204.

6. The author is indebted to historian John Lundstrom for contributing this excerpt from Conversations between COMINCH and CINCPAC, 4 July 1942, from his files. The excerpt is from USN microfilm NRS-1972-22, Operational Archives, NHHC, Washington Navy Yard.

7. Johnston to Maloney memo, 14 September 1942, McCormick Papers, XI-175, Kirkland-Ellis Files, Box 2, Folder 5, MRC.

8. Ibid.

9. Recommendation of Ross T. McIntire, Chief of Bureau, Bureau of Medicine and Surgery, 10 September 1942, National Personnel Records Center, Military Personnel Records, St. Louis, Missouri (hereafter MPR).

10. Orders were issued 11 September 1942 by the Navy's Bureau of Personnel and received by Seligman on 15 September 1942; see Report of Compliance with Orders, MPR.

11. Letter from Charles V. Orr, Mayor, City of Kokomo, Indiana, to Col. Frank Knox, 2 June 1943, MPR.

12. Report of Medical Survey, U.S. Naval Hospital, Oakland, California, 27 May 1944, MPR.

13. The report of Seligman's alleged drinking problem appears in "Statement of J. Loy Maloney," an affidavit signed by Maloney on 9 September 1954, attested and approved by Stanley Johnston, MRC.

14. Change of Duty, from Chief of Naval Personnel, 20 July 1943, directs Seligman to Naval Air Station, Alameda, California, for duty involving flying as executive officer, MPR.

15. Letter to Seligman from Secretary of the Navy, Re: Examination by Navy Retiring Board, 11 July 1944, MPR.

16. Buell, *Master of Sea Power*, 204.

17. Letter to Seligman from Cmdr. C. L. Hansen, Officer Performance Division, Office of Naval Personnel, 11 August 1944, MPR.

18. Capt. Lawrence B. Brennan, USN (Ret.), "Spilling the Secret—Captain Morton T. Seligman, U.S. Navy (Retired), U.S. Naval Academy Class of 1919," available on website of Naval Historical Foundation, http://www.navyhistory.org. A version of this article first appeared in the January 2013 issue of *Universal Ship Cancellation Society*.

19. Johnston memo to Maloney, 13 October 1942, McCormick Papers, Kirkland-Ellis Files, XI-175, Box 2, File 1, MRC.

20. Ibid.

21. For Rear Admiral John Towers' appraisal of Sherman, see Edwin P. Hoyt's *How They Won in the Pacific* (New York: Lyons Press, 2000), 319–20.

22. Sherman diary, entry for 17 August 1942, Lundstrom Papers.

23. "The Battle of the Coral Sea," review by R. L. Duffus, *New York Times Book Review*, 18 October 1942; "The Life and Death of an Aircraft Carrier," review by Lincoln Colcord, *New York Herald Tribune Books*, 18 October 1942.

24. Johnston enjoyed a modest windfall from *Queen* in 1944 when he sold the title of his book to 20th Century Fox for $20,000; see Among the Authors, by Frederi Babcock, *Chicago Tribune*, 23 April 1944. (Johnston retained the film rights to the story itself; whether *Queen* was ever made into movie does not show up in *Tribune* records.) The book also found a strong international market. It was published by Jarret in England and eventually was translated into Spanish, Portuguese, and Swedish. This information was unearthed by Arlene S. Balkansky of the Library of Congress from the ProQuest Historical Newspapers database.

25. Johnston memo to Maloney, 13 October 1942, McCormick Papers, Kirkland-Ellis Files, Box 2, File 1, MRC.

26. Drake retained the trust and confidence of Admiral Nimitz despite his failure to require Johnston to sign a censorship pledge on 15 April 1942. Drake's luck ran out in the spring of 1944, when the new Secretary of the Navy, James Forrestal, thought he was not doing enough to generate favorable publicity for the Navy. He was reassigned to Elmer Davis' Office of War Information in Washington. See *Driven Patriot: The Life and Times of James Forrestal*, by Townsend Hoopes and Douglas Brinkley (New York: Alfred A. Knopf, 1992), 192–93.

27. Stanley Johnston letter to Waldo Drake, 14 September 1942, Pacific Fleet Public Relations File, RG 313, Box 13, NARAII.

28. Henning memo to Maloney, 23 September 1942, McCormick Papers, Kirkland-Ellis Files, XI-175, Box 2, Folder 5, MRC.

29. Johnston memo to Maloney, 24 March 1943, McCormick Papers, Kirkland-Ellis Files, XI-175, Box 2, Folder 5, MRC.

30. Trohan memo to Maloney, 25 November 1949, McCormick Papers, Kirkland-Ellis Files, XI-175, Box 1, Folder 1, MRC.

31. Memorandum for E. A. Tamm, FBI, from Captain B. F. Perry, USN, 11 February 194, FBI Records, File 22351-209, NARAII.

32. Confidential Message, Hoover to Captain B. F. Perry, 4 March 1944, FBI records, case 22351-209, NARAII.

33. FBI Communication, 21 March 1944, "All FBI Legal Attaches"; FBI Radiogram, From Asuncion, 23 March 1944, FBI Records, File 22351-209, RG 65, NARAII.

34. Smith, *The Colonel*, 482–85. Don Maxwell succeeded Maloney as managing editor; Walter Trohan replaced Henning as the *Tribune*'s Washington bureau chief.

35. Don Maxwell oral history, McCormick Papers, MRC.

36. J. Howard Wood oral history, McCormick Papers, MRC.

37. Smith, *The Colonel*, 521–23.

38. "Johnston, *Tribune* War Writer, Dies," by Wayne Thomis, *Chicago Tribune*, 14 September 1962, 4.

39. Ibid.

40. "Ex-SF Graduate Dies Sunday in Coronado, Calif.," *Santa Fe New Mexican*, 16 July 1967, 7; "Capt. Morton Seligman," *Pacific Stars & Stripes*, 14 July 1967, 4.

Coda

1. Biddle, *In Brief Authority*, 249.

2. Papers of Ernest J. King, 7 June 1942 Press Conference transcript, Press and Press Releases folder, Container 23, Library of Congress, Washington, D.C.

3. King letter to Robert McCormick, 12 June 1942, McCormick Papers, Kirkland-Ellis Files, XI-175, Box 1, Folder 2, MRC.

4. "The Role of Communication Intelligence in the American-Japanese Naval War," 154, vol. 2, 5 April 1943, prepared by Ensign John V. Connorton, SRH 012, RG 457, Boxes 6–9, NARAII (hereafter Connorton report).

5. Ibid.

6. Ibid.

7. Ibid.

8. RADM Edwin T. Layton, USN (Ret.), Captain Roger Pineau, USNR (Ret.), and John Costello, *And I Was There* (New York: William Morrow, 1985), 453–56.

9. Ibid. In his memoir, Layton floated the idea that the Redman brothers thought that Layton himself, and possibly his friend Joe Rochefort, commanding the Navy's codebreakers at Pearl Harbor, might have been the "culprits" who leaked Nimitz's secret dispatch to Stanley Johnston. Layton's notion was based, in part, on the mistaken belief that Johnston had returned to Pearl Harbor after the Battle of the Coral Sea and somehow had come into contact with Rochefort. However, Johnston did not return to Pearl Harbor; there was no way he could have met Rochefort. There is no way to know what the Redmans believed or did not believe, but Layton's theory is baseless.

10. Capt. Thomas H. Dyer, U.S. Naval Institute oral history, 270.

11. Connorton report, 257–58.

12. Transcript of Walter Winchell broadcast, 5 July 1942, Billy Rose Theatre Division, Library for the Performing Arts, Lincoln Center, New York, N.Y.

13. Ken Kotani, *Japanese Intelligence in World War II*, trans. Chiharu Kotani (Oxford: Osprey, 2009), 11.

14. Buell, *Master of Sea Power*, p. 204.

15. *The "Magic" Documents: Summaries and Transcripts of the Top Secret Diplomatic Communications of Japan, 1938–1945*, SRS 711, RG 457, Box 3, p. 14, Entry 9001-A, NARAII.

16. B. Nelson MacPherson, "The Compromise of US Navy Cryptanalysis After the Battle of Midway," *Intelligence and National Security* 2, no. 2 (1897): 320–23.

17. Ibid. See also David Kahn, *The Codebreakers*, 603–4.

18. Memorandum for the Attorney General, from: J. Edgar Hoover, Re: Stanley Claude Samuel Johnston, 9 July 1942, GJR, File 146-47-23-25, Section 6, RG 60, NARAII.

19. Ibid.

20. Ibid.

21. Ibid.

22. Ibid.

23. In his highly regarded study, *Japanese Intelligence in World War II* (Osprey, 2009), Ken Kotani stated "The Allies had obtained the code books from the *I-go* 124 submarine sunk to the north of Australia in January 1942" (see p. 87). Kotani is not alone in this view. U.S. historians Dorr Carpenter and Norman Polmar in their *Submarines of the Imperial Japanese Navy* (Naval Institute Press, 1986) wrote that since *I-124* sank in water only forty feet deep, U.S. divers were able to enter the sub and remove its codebooks (see p. 19). Edward J. Drea in *MacArthur's Ultra: Codebreaking and the War against Japan, 1942–1945* (University of Kansas Press, 1992), reached a similar conclusion (see p. 74). However, dives to *I-124* made during the 1970s showed no signs that the submarine had been penetrated or could have been entered. One problem: *I-124* sank in water 160 feet deep, not 40 feet as previously thought. Also no evidence has surfaced in U.S. Navy records to substantiate claims that the sub was entered. See Tom Lewis' *Darwin's Submarine:* I-124 (Avonmore Books, 2010), pages 87–98 and Mike McCarthy's *Report: Japanese Submarine* I-124, Maritime Archeology Department, Western Australia Maritime Division. The author is indebted to Richard Frank for bringing this monograph to his attention.

24. Ibid.

25. Ken Kotani, emails to author, 15–16 October 2014.

26. JN-25(d) contained substantial changes over its predecessor: three sets of additive tables, an increase from fifty thousand to one hundred thousand text additives, among other alterations.

27. Information from Pacific War historian Robert Hanyok, 30 October 2014 email to author. See also Geoffrey Sinclair, *JN-25: Operational Code of the Imperial Japanese Navy World War II* (2004).

Appendix E. The Foreman

1. The jurors were John O. Holmes, age thirty-seven, decorator and paper-hanger, Joliet; Mrs. Florence H. Baum, secretary, La Salle; Arthur L. Anderson, age thirty-eight, stockkeeper, De Kalb; Mrs. Caroline O. Bouchard, Chicago; Mrs. Elsie Doe, Chicago; Mrs. Gertrude L. Frisbie, Joliet; Mrs. Ella Henry, Cary; J. Iacopett, age forty, janitor, Chicago; Mrs. Marie Kiehn, Elmhurst; Albert E. Kinson, age thirty-seven, salesman-office appliances, Joliet; Ernest E. Koerner, age sixty-one, plumbing and heating, Frankfort; Mrs. Esther Larson, Lombard; Nels Nelson, age forty-nine, electrical contractor, Woodstock; Arthur Papke, treasurer and accountant, Can Corporation of America, New Lenox; Roscoe R. Rau, executive of Retail Furniture Association, Glen Ellyn; Miss Fay Robinson, Aurora; Mrs. Florence G. Rudiger, Des Plaines; Arthur Sippel, age forty-eight, farmer, Monee; Mrs. Marie H. Suthers, Chicago; Clyde Reynolds, age forty-nine, electrician, Cary. Source: Grand Jury testimony, 13–19 August 1942, RG 60, Enclosures to DOJ File 146-47-23-25, NARAII.

2. Michael Sweeney and Patrick S. Washburn, *"Aint Justice Wonderful": The Chicago Tribune's Battle of Midway Story and the Government's Attempt at an Espionage Act Indictment in 1942*, Journalism & Communication Monographs (2014) 16:1, 7–97, originally published online 5 December 2013. Published on behalf of the Association for Education in Journalism and Mass Communication in partnership with SAGE Publications, Thousand Oaks, CA. Sweeney and Washburn found the Holmes letter among the McCormick Papers at the McCormick Research Center, Wheaton, Ill.

3. Mitchell summary letter to Biddle, 25 August 1942, Frank Knox Papers, June–September 1942, Operational Archives, NHHC, Washington Navy Yard, Washington, D.C.

4. Richard Norton Smith, *The Colonel*, 439. See also Papers of Byron Price, General Writings, Notebooks IV, Box 3, 161–62, September 1943, Wisconsin Historical Society, Madison, Wis.

Bibliography

National Archives and Records Administration (NARA)

NARAII (College Park, Md.) Contains U.S. Naval Records Covering World War II

Record Group (RG) 60: Two major elements. First, Grand Jury Testimony found in Department of Justice case file 146-47-23-25 stemming from August 1942 grand jury investigation of Stanley Johnston, J. Loy Maloney, and unnamed others associated with the *Chicago Tribune*, under the Espionage Act of 1917. Witnesses included seven Navy officers and five journalists. The testimony was unsealed and released to the author by order of Chief Judge Ruben Castillo of the U.S. District Court for the Northern District of Illinois, Eastern Division, on June 10, 2015. The District Court's order was affirmed by the U.S. Court of Appeals for the Seventh Circuit on September 15, 2016.

    Second, Grand Jury Records (GJR) included in DOJ case file 146-47-23-25 released to author under the Freedom of Information Act (FOIA). This file consists of twelve sections and covers approximately 2,500 pages. Material in this case file includes FBI and Navy interviews of witnesses, memoranda, and correspondence related to the August 1942 grand jury investigation of Johnston, Maloney, and unnamed others associated with the *Chicago Tribune*.

RG 65: FBI records in FBI headquarters case file 100-HQ-22351 released to author under FOIA. This file, consisting of approximately one thousand pages, supplements material in grand jury records in RG 60. It includes pertinent FBI documents related to the FBI's investigation of Stanley Johnston, J. Loy Maloney, and unnamed others at the *Chicago Tribune*, leading up to the grand jury proceeding of August 1942.

RG 38: U.S. naval records from the Office of Chief of Naval Operations.

RG 80: Department of Navy records.

RG 216: Records of the civilian Office of Censorship.

RG 313: Records of Pacific Fleet public relations.

RG 457: Radio intelligence files released by National Security Agency; Naval Board of Inquiry.

Collections in Associations, Libraries, Museums, Universities

Colonel Robert R. McCormick Research Center of the First Division Museum at Cantigny Park (Wheaton, Illinois)

Material includes Tribune Company files, business and personal correspondence of *Tribune* personnel related to Johnston-Maloney case, relevant files of Kirkland-Ellis law firm, transcripts of Navy interviews with Johnston and Maloney, oral histories with *Tribune* staffers: Don Maxwell, Howard Wood, J. Loy Maloney, William Fulton, Kermit Holt, and Wayne Thomis (*Tribune* Oral History Project).

Franklin D. Roosevelt Library (Hyde Park, New York)

Papers of the President; the Official File, the Map Room File, and the President's Secretary's File; also, papers of Francis Biddle, Stephan T. Early, Lowell Mellett, William H. McReynolds, John Boettiger, Oscar Cox, Henry Morgenthau Jr., and John Fahey.

Georgetown University Library, Special Collections Research Center (Washington, D.C.)

Francis Biddle Papers. Collection includes J. Edgar Hoover memoranda concerning *Chicago Tribune*'s 4 December 1941 "leak" of Roosevelt Administration's Victory Program.

Library of Congress (Washington, D.C.)

Manuscript Division: Papers of Ernest J. King, including a transcript of his press conference 7 June 1942.

Naval History and Heritage Command (Washington, D.C., Navy Yard)

Operational Archives: Papers of Ernest J. King and Frank Knox.

New York Public Library, Library for the Performing Arts, Billy Rose Theatre Division (Lincoln Center, New York)

Walter Winchell Papers. Material includes Winchell's 1942 columns in the *New York Mirror* and transcripts of his NBC "blue network" radio broadcasts, June–August 1942.

University of Maryland (College Park)

McKeldin Library: Henry L. Stimson Diary (on microfilm).

Wisconsin Historical Society (Madison, Wisconsin)

Byron Price Papers. Collection consists of correspondence; a lengthy, unpublished memoir; and several notebooks compiled while Price was director of the Office of Censorship.

Published Sources

Books

Biddle, Francis. *In Brief Authority*. Garden City, N.Y.: Doubleday, 1962.

Borneman, Walter R. *The Admirals: Nimitz, Halsey, Leahy and King—The Five-Star Admirals Who Won the War at Sea*. New York: Little, Brown, 2012.

Budiansky, Stephen. *Battle of Wits: The Complete Story of Codebreaking in World War II*. New York: Free Press, 2000.

Buel, Thomas B. *Master of Sea Power: A Biography of Fleet Admiral Ernest J. King*. Annapolis, Md.: Naval Institute Press, 1980.

Casey, Robert J. *Torpedo Junction: With the Pacific Fleet from Pearl Harbor to Midway*. Indianapolis, Ind.: Bobbs-Merrill, 1942.

Clark, Delbert. *Washington Dateline: The Press Covers the Capital*. New York: Frederick A. Stokes, 1941.

Collier, Richard. *Fighting Words: The War Correspondent of World War Two*. New York: St. Martin's Press, 1989.

Cooke, John Byrne. *Reporting the War: Freedom of the Press from the American Revolution to the War on Terrorism*. New York: Palgrave Macmillan, 2007.

Davies, Robert B. *Baldwin of the Times: Hanson W. Baldwin, A Journalist's Life, 1903–1991*. Annapolis, Md.: Naval Institute Press, 2011.

Donovan, Peter, and John Mack. *Code Breaking in the Pacific*. London: Springer, 2014.

Dorwart, Jeffrey M. *Conflict of Duty: The U.S. Navy's Intelligence Dilemma*. Annapolis, Md.: Naval Institute Press, 1983.

Edwards, Jerome E. *The Foreign Policy of Col. McCormick's Tribune*. Reno: University of Nevada Press, 1971.

Gies, Joseph. *The Colonel of Chicago*. New York: E. P. Dutton, 1979.

Gunther, John. *Roosevelt in Retrospect*. New York: Harper & Brothers, 1950.

Hailey, Foster. *Pacific Battle Line*. New York: Macmillan, 1944.

Halperin, Morton H., and Daniel Hoffman. *Freedom vs. National Security: Secrecy and Surveillance*. New York: Chelsea House, 1977.

Harris, Brayton. *Admiral Nimitz: The Commander of the Pacific Ocean Theater*. New York: Palgrave Macmillan, 2011.

Healy Jr., George W. *A Lifetime on Deadline: Self-Portrait of a Southern Journalist.* Gretna, La.: Pelican Publishing, 1976.

Hohenberg, John. *Foreign Correspondence: The Great Reporters and Their Times.* New York: Columbia University Press, 1964.

Holmes, Wilber Jasper. *Double-Edged Secrets: U.S. Naval Intelligence Operations in the Pacific during World War II.* Annapolis, Md.: Naval Institute Press, 1979.

Hone, Thomas C., ed. *The Battle of Midway: The Naval Institute Guide to the U.S. Navy's Greatest Victory.* Annapolis, Md.: Naval Institute Press, 2013.

Hoopes, Townsend, and Douglas Brinkley. *Driven Patriot: The Life and Times of James Forrestal.* New York: Alfred A. Knopf, 1992.

Hoyt, Edwin P. *How They Won the War in the Pacific: Nimitz and His Admirals.* New York: Lyons Press, 2000.

Johnston, Stanley. *The Grim Reapers.* New York: E. P. Dutton, 1943.

———. *Queen of the Flat-Tops.* New York: E. P. Dutton, 1942.

Kahn, David. *The Codebreakers: The Story of Secret Writing.* New York: Scribner, 1967.

Kennett, Lee. *For the Duration: The United States Goes to War, Pearl Harbor— 1942.* New York: Charles Scribner's Sons, 1985.

Kinsley, Philip. *Liberty and the Press: A History of the* Chicago Tribune*'s Fight to Preserve a Free Press for the American People.* Chicago: Chicago Tribune, 1944.

Knightley, Phillip. *The First Casualty, From the Crimea to Vietnam: The War Correspondent as Hero, Propagandist, and Myth Maker.* New York: Harcourt Brace Jovanovich, 1975.

Koop, Theodore F. *Weapon of Silence.* Chicago: University of Chicago Press, 1946.

Kotani, Ken. *Japanese Intelligence in World War II.* Translated by Chiharu Kotani. Oxford: Osprey, 2009.

Layton, Edwin T., with John Costello and Roger Pineau. *"And I Was There": Pearl Harbor and Midway—Breaking the Secrets.* New York: William Morrow, 1985.

Lewin, Ronald. *The American Magic: Codes and Ciphers, and the Defeat of Japan.* New York: Penguin Books, 1982.

Lundstrom, John B. *Black Shoe Carrier Admiral: Frank Jack Fletcher at Coral Sea, Midway, and Guadalcanal.* Annapolis, Md.: Naval Institute Press, 2006.

———. *The First Team: Pacific Naval Air Combat from Pearl Harbor to Midway.* Annapolis, Md: Naval Institute Press, 1984.

Mander, Mary. *Pen and Sword: American War Correspondents, 1898–1975.* Urbana: University of Illinois Press, 2010.

Mathews, Joseph J. *Reporting the Wars.* Minneapolis: University of Minnesota Press, 1957.

McMurtrie, Francis E., ed. *Jane's Fighting Ships 1941.* New York: Macmillan, 1942.

McPhaul, John J. *Deadlines and Monkeyshines: The Fabled World of Chicago Journalism.* Englewood Cliffs, N.J.: Prentice-Hall, 1962.

Parshall, Jonathan, and Anthony Tully. *Shattered Sword: The Untold Story of the Battle of Midway.* Washington, D.C.: Potomac Books, 2005.

Potter, E. B. *Nimitz.* Annapolis, Md.: Naval Institute Press, 1976.

Prados, John. *Combined Fleet Decoded: The Secret History of American Intelligence and the Japanese Navy in World War II.* New York: Random House, 1995.

Reis, Curt, ed. *They Were There: The Story of World War II and How It Came About.* Garden City, N.Y.: Garden City Publishing, 1945.

Russell, Ronald W. *No Right to Win: A Continuing Dialogue with Veterans of the Battle of Midway.* New York: iUniverse, 2006.

Schoenfeld, Gabriel. *Necessary Secrets: National Security, the Media, and the Rule of Law.* New York: W. W. Norton, 2010.

Sherman, Frederick C. *Combat Command: The American Aircraft Carriers in the Pacific War.* New York: Bantam, 1982.

Smith, Jeffery A. *War and Press Freedom: The Problem of Prerogative of Power.* New York: Oxford University Press, 1999.

Smith, Michael. *The Emperor's Codes: The Breaking of Japan's Secret Ciphers.* New York: Penguin Books, 2000.

Smith, Richard Norton. *The Colonel: The Life and Legend of Robert R. McCormick.* Boston: Houghton Mifflin, 1997.

Stone, Geoffrey R. *Perilous Times: Free Speech in Wartime, From the Sedition Act of 1798 to the War on Terrorism.* New York: W. W. Norton, 2004.

Summers, Robert E., ed. *Wartime Censorship of Press and Radio.* New York: H .W. Wilson, 1942.

Sweeney, Michael S. *The Military and the Press: An Uneasy Truce.* Evanston, Ill.: Northwestern University Press, 2006.

———. *Secrets of Victory: The Office of Censorship and the American Press and Radio in World War II.* Chapel Hill: University of North Carolina Press, 2001.

Trohan, Walter. *Political Animals: Memoirs of a Sentimental Cynic.* Garden City, N.Y.: Doubleday, 1975.

Waldrop, Frank C. *McCormick of Chicago: An Unconventional Portrait of a Controversial Figure.* Englewood Cliffs, N.J.: Prentice-Hall, 1966.

Washburn, Patrick S. *A Question of Sedition: The Federal Government's Investigation of the Black Press during World War II*. New York: Oxford University Press, 1986.

Articles, Monographs, and Special Studies

Allen, Thomas B. "Midway: The Story That Never Ends." *U.S. Naval Institute Proceedings* 133 (June 2007): 1252

Brennan, Lawrence B. "Spilling the Secret." *Universal Ship Cancellation Society Log* (January 2013), http://www.navyhistory.org/2013/02/spilling-the-secret-captain-morton-seligman/.

Clough, Frank C. "Operations of the Press Division of the Office of Censorship." *Journalism Quarterly* 20 (September 1943): 220–24.

Doan, Edward N. "Organization and Operation of the Office of Censorship." *Journalism Quarterly* 21 (September 1944): 200–216.

Fleming, Thomas. "The Big Leak." *American Heritage* 38, no. 8 (December 1987).

Frank, Larry J. "The United States Navy v. the *Chicago Tribune*." *The Historian* 42, no. 2 (February 1980): 284–303.

Goren, Dina. "Communication Intelligence and the Freedom of the Press: The *Chicago Tribune*'s Battle of Midway Dispatch and the Breaking of the Japanese Naval Code." *Journal of Contemporary History* 16 (1981): 663–60.

MacPherson, B. Nelson. "The Compromise of US Navy Cryptanalysis after the Battle of Midway." *Intelligence & National Security* 2, no. 2 (1987): 320–23.

Mason, Robert. "Eyewitness." *U.S. Naval Institute Proceedings* 108 (June 1982): 40–45.

McCollam, Douglas. "The End of Ambiguity." *Columbia Journalism Review* (July–August 2006): 21–27.

Parker, Frederick D. *A Priceless Advantage: U.S. Navy Communications Intelligence and the Battles of Coral Sea, Midway, and the Aleutians*. CH-E32-93-01, Center for Cryptologic History, National Security Agency, Fort Meade, Md., 1993.

Sanger, Grant. "Freedom of the Press or Treason?" *U.S. Naval Institute Proceedings* 103 (September 1977): 96–97.

Sweeney, Michael S., and Patrick S. Washburn. "'Ain't Justice Wonderful'—The *Chicago Tribune*'s Battle of Midway Story and the Government's Attempt at an Espionage Act Indictment in 1942." *Journalism & Communication Monographs* 16, no. 1 (2014), http://jmo.sagepub.com/content/16/1/7.

Index

About the Author

Elliot Carlson is a longtime journalist who has worked for such newspapers as the *Honolulu Advertiser*, the *Wall Street Journal*, and the *AARP Bulletin*. Carlson is the author of the Chief of Naval Operation's reading list title *Joe Rochefort's War: The Odyssey of the Codebreaker Who Outwitted Yamamoto at Midway*.